THE GREATEST
TENNIS MATCHES
OF THE TWENTIETH CENTURY

THE GREATEST
TENNIS MATCHES
OF THE TWENTIETH CENTURY

Steve Flink

Foreword by Chris Evert

Rutledge Books, Inc.   Danbury, CT

Rutledge Books, Inc.
107 Mill Plain Road, Danbury, CT 06811
1-800-278-8533
www.rutledgebooks.com

Front cover artwork by Victoria Vebell
Interior design and layout by John Laub

Manufactured in the United States of America

Cataloging in Publication Data
Flink, Steve

   The Greatest Tennis Matches of the Twentieth Century

   ISBN: 1-58244-076-X

   1. Tennis -- History. 2. Tennis players -- Biography.

796.34 / 2 / 0922

Library of Congress Card Number: 99-068127

DEDICATION

For my father, Stanley Flink, who inspired me to write about tennis for a living, and was an invaluable ally/editor/mentor in this project; and for my son, Jonathan, who has probably had no choice but to love the game called tennis.

CONTENTS

ACKNOWLEDGMENTS

Many people, both directly and indirectly, have been enormously helpful to me throughout my career as a tennis journalist since the early 1970s. I am grateful to *World Tennis Magazine* founder Gladys M. Heldman and the late Ron Bookman, who was my editor, for giving me the opportunity to write for *World Tennis* from 1974-91. *Tennis Week* editor/publisher Gene Scott has given me the forum to write in since 1992. Bud Collins long ago allowed me to work behind the scenes with him on telecasts and establish a foothold in the electronic world. John Barrett of the BBC and Herbert Warren Wind of the New Yorker have always been helpful advisors. John Roberts of the Independent, S.L. Price of *Sports Illustrated* and Joel Drucker have been the kind of colleagues you always want in your career.

Everyone at the International Tennis Hall of Fame has been supportive. A bow to Jane Brown, Mark Stenning, Melissa Mulrooney, Marilyn Fernberger, Peggy Woolard, Mark Young and Debbie Teixeira.

Alan Little at the Wimbledon Lawn Tennis Museum offered assistance whenever I needed it. Russ Adams supplied much of the photography seen on these pages, and his professionalism is deeply appreciated. Artist Victoria Vebell did a magnificent job with her cover illustration, and teaching professionals Mike Salmon and Mark Drons were kind enough to model on the court. Chuck Kelly encouraged me in this venture and gave me valuable counsel as the project evolved. For saving me every time I was beset by another computer glitch, a salute to Evan Levey. I am indebted to all of the people mentioned above, as I am to the remarkable players I have watched and interviewed.

Last, but not least, I am deeply thankful to my wife, Frances, and my daughter, Amanda, who could not have been more patient on the many days and nights I devoted to researching and writing this manuscript.

Steve Flink
Mount Kisco, New York
October 1999

FOREWORD by Chris Evert

When you look back at the big moments in the history of tennis—at least as I see them—time seems to stand still. When you read this book, time will stand still for you. You will return to special moments in the lives of great players, to times and matches that defined these champions. You will have the chance to relive wonderful points, remarkable shotmaking, and moments that mattered. Some of you will rekindle old memories, while others will learn about great matches you haven't heard of.

In these pages there are a lot of familiar names. Many of them played so long ago, however, that they have become remote figures. In this book, the history-making players will come to life. You will discover not only their styles of play, but also gain insight into their personalities and characters. They will no longer be one-dimensional people.

For me, it is a great compliment to be included in this big picture of tennis in the twentieth century. Tennis is such a wonderful sport, with so many colorful characters, that to be recognized for some of my matches gives me a nice feeling. My rivalry with Martina Navratilova was very special for both of us and, I hope, for the public. Any of us who played in the great matches of this century tried to add something to the history of the game and to bring it to where it is today—an exciting international sport.

Steve Flink is the right person to take on the task of selecting the best matches of the twentieth century. He knows the game of tennis as well as anybody. He is a good journalist, but he also has a tennis player's mind. Steve knew my results and matches better than I did. All through my career in the 1970s and 1980s, it caused much laughter between us when I would be asked a question about my record at a press conference. I would always look over to Steve and he would have the answers. In many cases, I would inaccurately recall an important detail about a match and Steve would have to interrupt me to set the record straight.

I have always admired Steve's style of writing for its fairness and accuracy. We have seen big matches in our lives the same way. He has never written an article about the U.S. Open, or other major tournaments, that failed to capture the essence of a match. We have always been on the same page about tennis.

His fairness is a real strength in his reporting. I have been drawn to that over the years and have admired the fact that he was fair to both players in his reports. It seems to me that many writers do not describe what really happens on the court. Steve characteristically gets deep inside the matches and reports them as well as anyone in the field. I think the readers of this book will agree with me.

Boca Raton, Florida
1999

INTRODUCTION

Although tennis was invented in 1874 by an Englishman, Major Walter Clopton Wingfield, it was not until the following century that the game proliferated and developed a worldwide following. While tennis had many admirable male and female champions in the formative stages, the first towering figures and fascinating match-ups among top players emerged in the 1920's. That was a particularly dynamic decade for tennis and the sports world at large. Tennis, as a viable spectator sport, made strong advances behind such powerful players as Tilden, Lenglen, Wills, and the renowned French "Four Musketeers"—René Lacoste, Henri Cochet, Jean Borotra and Jacques Brugnon.

Now that the first full century of international tennis competition is winding down, I am taking on the considerable challenge in this book of selecting the 30 best matches played during these years. Tennis has expanded dramatically from a sport played and observed almost exclusively by the wealthy, to a much wider and more diversified cast of participants and fans around the world. Most of the major changes in the game have occured in the latter stages of this century. Open Tennis commenced in 1968, when for the first time amateurs and professionals were allowed to compete against each other. The public was given the opportunity at last to see all the leading players confronting the best competition wherever it came from. Two years later the tiebreaker was introduced officially at major tournaments, shortening matches between the big servers and heightening the drama for the spectators.

By putting the great players and climactic matches into historical perspective, a larger story is told about the game and its evolution. The contests stand alone as pieces of a mosaic, but when they are placed in sequence they illustrate how the game has evolved, and signal the champions who have made the most dramatic contributions to that process. By visiting, or perhaps for some readers revisiting, these great moments involving legendary players, we gain a better view of how certain matches shaped tennis history, and why the personalities at their center left such enduring memories.

This journey takes us from Bill Tilden to Pete Sampras, and Suzanne Lenglen to Martina Hingis. Looking in some depth at the most celebrated confrontations, we are reminded of the individual men and women who were pitted against each other in a struggle that tested not only their skills, but their stamina—and, at the end of the day, their imaginations.

In the early days of tennis, the field of competition was limited and the leading players focused their attention on only a few rivals. In fact, defending champions at Wimbledon were given the luxury of an automatic ticket to the final round, which left them waiting for the winner of an "All-Comers" event to find out who they would face in the championship match. That system lasted from 1877 to 1922. Ever since, the title holders have had to endure the arduous progression of six and eventually seven matches to reach their ultimate destination. Over the same span, the array of promising young players clearly multiplied in both the men's and women's tournaments.

Some of the matches I selected for this book are picked from landmark occasions. Other events are less obvious, but nonetheless meaningful to the growth and distinction of tennis competition at the highest level. Most of the matches included are from the major championships—the Grand Slam events. Three are Davis Cup encounters, in deference to that incomparable international team competition. A few were lifted from less glamorous settings, because they transcended the occasion and brought lustre to a particular era. For example, consider the many years leading up to "Open Tennis" in 1968. From the 1930's until that pivotal year, the pros were relegated to near obscurity in the media. They could not play at Wimbledon or Forest Hills or other major championships. But, with few exceptions, they were playing the best tennis in the world. With that fact in mind, I picked three professional matches—one each from the '30s, '40s and '50s—in an attempt to do justice to Vines, Perry, Kramer, Budge, Hoad and Gonzales. The battles waged by these stalwart competitors had to be represented in this collection. In any case, all of the selections are showdowns between distinctive, accomplished players, duels which captured the admiration of the public, and flourished in the recollections of those who reported them.

Let me elaborate briefly on the criteria for the matches I have chosen as the top 30 of the 20th Century. There were a number of important considerations. In my mind, most of the meetings needed to be finals, because so much was riding on the outcomes. Furthermore, it was important to do justice to all of the eras of tennis, to the dominant players who emerged in every decade from the 1920s through the 1990s. Therefore, included in this book are at least two matches from each of those decades. Some readers may question the inclusion of six matches from the '70s, and five each from the '80s and 90's. Why should more than half of the recorded battles be from the last three decades?

The answer is that tennis competition at the highest level had grown profoundly over that period, with a cavalcade of players emerging to capture the public imagination. Included in this segment of the book are Billie Jean King, Jimmy Connors, Bjorn Borg, John McEnroe, Monica Seles, Steffi Graf, Pete Sampras, and Andre Agassi. And it is here that two Martina Navratilova-Chrissie Evert contests—taken from the most memorable rivalry of the century—are described. This is not to suggest that the recent champions were any more compelling than their predessors at the top. Rather, it is my judgment that the public was treated to more widely anticipated matches from the seventies on than ever before.

Another factor must be mentioned. I write about 17 men's and 13 women's matches in the pages ahead. Why not equal treatment? It is my view that the women have irrefutably contributed every bit as much to the game's history as the men. Over the years, however, female champions have lasted longer at the top than their male counterparts, and that distinction somewhat limited the selection process. I decided that no more than two matches should be chosen from the career of any one one player. I did not want this book to be too heavily weighted toward a single champion of either gender. Drawing the line at two matches was the sensible solution. The men, therefore, appear marginally more than the women because of the more frequent turnover at the top.

I have been an avid follower of the game since I was 12, when my father took me out to Wimbledon for the first time. Since that memorable introduction in 1965, I have had the good fortune to be present for 32 of the last 35 editions of the world's premier tournament. I have been an observer at 21 French Opens, and have missed only one United States Championship since 1965. All in all, I have seen an extraordinary amount of top notch tennis across the years. I have made my living writing about tennis since 1974.

Nevertheless, many of the greatest matches of the century were played before I was born. As a historian, I was able to draw on a vast library of material on these matches, relying on books and newspaper accounts about those legendary battles. I interviewed many of the players to get their recollections. In the case of modern matches, I looked at videotapes of some matches and drew on my own experiences of watching these performances in person.

Tennis equipment changed radically over the course of the century. While the dimensions of the court have remained unaltered since the game's inception—78 feet long and 27 feet wide for singles, and nine feet wider for doubles—-racket technology has advanced dramatically. With few exceptions, wood rackets were used by all competitors—recreational and tournament class—until the 1960's. At that time, many highly-rated competitors began switching to steel and aluminum rackets which gave them added power, arguably without much loss of control. In the mid to late 1960s, Billie Jean King, Butch Buchholz, and Clark Graebner were among the ranking players who made the move to steel, and Pancho Gonzales traded in his old and trusted wood model for aluminum. Jimmy Connors followed on the heels of those players with his Wilson T2000, a trademark for nearly all of his career.

Over time, graphite frames were introduced to the marketplace. By the early 1980's, wood was nearly extinct in the upper levels of tennis. John McEnroe went to graphite in 1983, as did Chrissie Evert the following year. As for Connors, he stuck with his T2000 long after it was readily available in the marketplace. Once, in the mid-1980s, he made a public plea to fans watching on television during the U.S. Open. He was running out of rackets. Would someone be kind enough to send him any spare T2000's they might have in their homes? A number of fans obliged, enabling Connors to stick with an antiquated frame to which he was wedded from his youth.

Pete Sampras started playing with a graphite racket as a junior and stuck with it to the end of the century. Wilson at one time took the racket off the shelves, but decided to re-release it because Sampras and other top players kept it so visible on the public stage. Sampras earned a well deserved reputation as a complete player who placed a premium on power—not only on serve, but off the ground. However, when Sampras played an exhibition in Madison Square Garden at the end of 1996 against John McEnroe, both men used wood rackets. Sampras's serve was clocked at over 120 miles an hour, about the same velocity he achieves with a graphite racket. Rackets have undoubtedly contributed to a faster, more explosive modern game of tennis—from the top levels of the professionals down to the club players. And yet, few would have believed that Sampras could exceed 120 mph with a wood racket.

How much have the rackets altered the way top flight tennis is played? Surely, they have made a significant difference. Despite the demonstration by Sampras—a player of rare technical gifts with an effortless service motion—the modern materials have made it easier for leading players to generate pace in all facets of the game. Some players have probably developed heavy and deceptive topspin in ways that might have been impossible with wood. Conversely, the two-handed backhand was made popular in the 1970's primarily by three players: Bjorn Borg, Jimmy Connors and Chrissie Evert. Two of the three (Borg and Evert) played at that time with wood.

A more substantial change in the quality of tennis over the decades has been measured by athleticism. Today's breed of tennis player is better conditioned than ever before, faster off the mark, more prepared to play a strenuous sport to the hilt for hours at a time.

It can still be persuasively argued that if Bill Tilden, Don Budge or Jack Kramer were given modern equipment and today's training techniques, they would have remained at the head of the class.

Remembering the players who stirred our emotions with their talents—provides the narrative of this book. To be sure, this is not a scholarly history of the game—an enterprise which has been taken up by a number of distinguished writers over the years. The view here is more narrowly focused in scope, but made ambitious by the very nature of the material. Closely examining epochal matches illustrates changes in style and strategy, and invariably finds the real drama in the clash of personality and character.

All of the matches included here are between two individuals who have pursued the same lofty goals, but have come to the court with different psychological and athletic resources. The essential excitement of tennis has always been the one-on-one, mano a mano. They are out there on their own, isolated in a space surrounded by spectators, cameras, and capricious weather. The pressure speaks in an inner voice and is fueled by sometimes supportive and occasionally hostile audiences. The best players have been able to summon their finest tennis when it has mattered the most; to perform magnificently in the face of intensely contested exchanges; to rise above and beyond themselves on the big points.

This book is, finally, not merely a compilation of outstanding matches in the 20th Century. I have set out to make it much more than that by examining not only the matches but the atmospherics, the preparation, and the publicity surrounding these events. My purpose has been to provide a reflective picture of how tennis evolved among those inspired players who uniquely gave the game color and suspense. Great tennis requires an almost ineffable excellence on court. It emerges from both the observable and the mysterious. Progression from one tournament to another, training, coaching and equipment are visible details, easily chronicled. The mystery is in the mind and heart of a player who determines that he or she will not be defeated. Finding the words to reveal some of that chemistry is the aspiration of the pages which follow.

As the new millennium dawns, much is being said about the flowering of young talent in all fields of sport. Whether tennis will produce a greater number of transcendent players in the next century than it did in the one now ending is difficult to predict. It is sufficient to observe that there are already many waiting in the wings.

SUZANNE LENGLEN VS. HELEN WILLS

CANNES, FRANCE, FINAL, FEBRUARY 16, 1926

A mythic Frenchwoman plays a young American in what was to be their only meeting. It would never be forgotten.

PROLOGUE

No tennis match played between two women in this century has been more eagerly anticipated than the extraordinary meeting between Helen Wills of California against the Frenchwoman, Suzanne Lenglen, at Cannes on February 16, 1926. They were the two leading players of their era, and they also would be recognized by the cognoscenti as the best in the first half of the century. When they clashed for the only time in their distinguished careers that morning in Cannes, Lenglen was fast approaching twenty-seven and had suffered only a single defeat in the decade. She was a tightly-strung woman, entirely conscious of her fame and popularity, ruled by her deep emotions, as theatrical and graceful as any tennis player has ever been. As the renowned dress designer and historian Ted Tinling observed, "Suzanne was treated like Cleopatra in those days."

Wills was hardly less celebrated, but decidedly more understated as a personality. She was twenty and still a student at the University of California when she took a semester off to travel to France for appearances in a series of tournaments leading up dramatically to a showdown with Lenglen. Wills had already secured three consecutive U.S. Championships at Forest Hills (1923-25) and had established herself unequivocally as the lone authentic threat to Lenglen's enduring supremacy. While Lenglen was known to display her emotions vividly and unrestrainedly, Wills was stoic and stern, unwilling to reveal much about her feelings. She was classified by sportswriters as "Little Miss Poker Face."

The two protagonists were brought up on opposite sides of the ocean by parents with contrasting plans and priorities. Lenglen's father Charles was a wealthy pharmacist who drove his daughter forcefully in the direction of technical and tactical excellence. From the outset, he demanded that Suzanne demonstrate unerring accuracy with her ground strokes. She was admonished that hitting any stroke into the net was an unforgivable mistake, an automatic loss of a point, a self-inflicted wound. Charles Lenglen insisted it was much less a risk to hit within inches of the baseline because you might get the benefit of a good call on a shot that was possibly out.

Charles Lenglen was a perfectionist, placing handkerchiefs at specific locations just inside the baseline and sidelines, testing Suzanne's patience and precision, making her strive for difficult targets. She was unmistakably groomed for success, trained to be a champion by a parent who believed unabashedly that she should settle for nothing less than the best. She responded favorably to his large goals and made them her own.

Wills was guided by parents who were pleased by the prospect of her playing tennis, but she developed an interest in the competitive game largely on her own. Her father, Dr. Clarence Wills, practiced medicine in Berkeley, California. The family lived modestly and did

Suzanne Lenglen

not want to stand in the way of her immense talent once she blossomed on the court as a teenager. But they did not anticipate her worldwide fame and prestige in that arena, not by a longshot. Helen Wills recalled in 1986, when she was eighty, that it was a considerable struggle to get her parents' consent to make the journey to France for the Lenglen confrontation sixty years earlier. "My father didn't see much point in it," she reflected. "And my mother did not want me to go. I don't know why they thought it was the end of the world to leave college for a term and go to the south of France. I almost cried I wanted to go so much. I begged and begged until my parents gave in, and looking back all that fuss doesn't make any sense at all."

Those strong sentiments were released six decades after the shining occasion, when perhaps some of the luster had been lost. But when Wills left California in January 1926 on a one week journey by boat to face a formidable world-class adversary for the first time, she knew she was on a mission, and recognized the need to follow her instincts and widen the range of her tennis aspirations. Neither Wills nor Lenglen could possibly predict how long their imminent contest would live in the public imagination, nor could they know that this would be a solitary experience, a one-time battle for supremacy that would not be repeated.

As the reigning queen of

international tennis, Lenglen was prepared for her collision with Wills, and determined to stage this crucial event in her own country, on the slow red clay courts that she preferred. It was no accident that Wills was required to confront Lenglen in France rather than in the United States, or in a neutral place. Wills was forced to

---

Rain adds suspense to an almost theatrical event.

---

endure the long week of travel and then gradually adjust to her foreign surroundings while practicing for the Cannes tournament. Lenglen was right where she wanted to be, in her homeland, on her favorite slow courts, bolstered by the notion of appearing in front of an audience who would bathe her in the warm fountain of sustained applause.

The dramatic buildup in the several weeks preceding Cannes was palpable. Here was Lenglen, a ferocious yet fragile competitor, a woman with a strong need to control her environment, to set the agenda in every sense. She had appeared only once at the U.S. Championships, coming to Forest Hills in 1921, leaving the courts in tears and turmoil after losing the first set of her match with Molla Mallory, defaulting the match as a severe cold weakened her stamina. Lenglen was so shattered by that experience that she never returned to Forest Hills despite the undeniable significance of that championship.

Wills, meanwhile, had played the vast majority of her tournaments in the United States, competing at Wimbledon only once, in 1924. She had yet to make her mark at that fabled place where Lenglen had succeeded so handsomely over the years. The stylish Frenchwoman moved about the court like a ballerina, and had been victorious on the Wimbledon grass courts during six of the previous seven years.

Both women had performed brilliantly on different continents, but their paths had not yet crossed anywhere in the world. Now, in the winter of 1926, at a time when the game of tennis was clearly on the ascendancy, the imperious Lenglen and the quietly imposing Wills had made an appointment to share a court at last.

Neither woman would experience anything quite like this confrontation again.

THE MATCH

The stage was set at the Carlton Club tournament on the well-kept red clay courts in Cannes. The players were ready. But, as if by design, raising the level of the drama surrounding the proceedings to nearly impossible heights, nature intervened. After Lenglen and Wills easily recorded semifinal victories to reach the final without the loss of a set, rain fell steadily for two days and postponed the alluring matchup. By then, the battle and its significance had reached almost mythical proportions in the worldwide press, and with the football season finished and baseball not yet underway, America attached immense curiosity and passion to the match. It was a story that virtually wrote itself in the sports sections of newspapers all across the United States.

The small facility in Cannes could only accommodate about one-thousand spectators, but others looked down from trees surrounding the facility and still more crowded near the fence behind the court to get at least a partial view of the play. With a scarcity of tickets available for afficionados, an Englishwoman bought up a bundle of them and sold them for as much as $50 a piece—an exorbitant sum in those days.

Ultimately, the weather cleared and the sun was shining as Lenglen and Wills walked on the court at 11 A.M. on a Saturday morning in February of 1926, for their historic showdown. The officials for this important contest were chosen carefully with the full consent of both participants, and the linesmen included Lord Charles Hope and Cyril Tolley, a revered golf champion from Great Britain. Commander George Hillyard—a distinguished veteran who had called many Wimbledon finals—was given the great honor of presiding as umpire. The presence of these Englishmen gave the occasion an air of essential integrity, providing at the very least the appearance of impartiality in the decision making.

Briefly, at the outset, Wills gave Lenglen cause for consternation. The American broke serve for a 2-1 lead by exploiting her superior strength and power off the ground, but then Lenglen retaliated, displaying better ball control than her adversary. With a concentrated run of backcourt craft and superb shot selection, Lenglen moved to a 4-2 lead. Wills stood her ground stubbornly and took the seventh game to close the gap. At that critical stage Lenglen asserted herself, conceding only two more points in the next two games to seal the set, 6-3. But playing this remarkable brand of tennis against such an accomplished rival was already taking its toll on Lenglen, who sipped brandy at the changeovers to calm her nerves.

In the second set, the pattern of play shifted in this engrossing spectacle. Wills began to rule the rallies with her potent strokes off both wings, forcing her foe into mistakes and coming

up with the winner when she had the opening. The American grew visibly more confident and became much bolder in the process as she built a 3-1 lead, but then temporized and lost her edge. With Wills drifting dangerously into cau-

Worldwide attention preceded a contest before a small audience.

tion, Lenglen reestablished her authority and drew level at 3-3, seemingly within striking distance of victory. But the strain was increasingly evident in her demeanor and she walked to her chair at the side of the court to take sips of brandy after psychologically strenuous points, no longer waiting for the changeovers.

Wills was well aware that she was still very much in the match, and recognized that a third set could prove fatal for her fragile foe. The American moved ahead 4-3, then held her penetrating and skillfully placed serve again to reach 5-4. Lenglen was in an agitated state during this stretch, admonishing a boisterous audience to keep quiet, advertising her instability with her actions. But remarkably Lenglen lifted her game once more to take a 6-5, 40-15, double match point lead. Not afraid to lose and still believing she could prevail, the imperturbable Wills walloped a forehand crosscourt for an apparent winner. Both players heard an emphatic cry of "Out!" from the corner of the court. They assumed the ball had gone beyond the line and believed their battle was over.

An exhilarated Lenglen threw a ball in the air in celebration as she came forward to shake Wills's hand, feeling certain she had completed her mission. To her considerable chagrin, she had not. Linesman Hope came forward, pushing

Helen Wills

his way through the flocking fans, urgently trying to get the attention of Commander Hillyard. When he finally reached the chair umpire, Hope explained that he had not made that call on the sideline, that in fact it had been an overly excited spectator who had screamed "Out." Hope confirmed that Wills's scorching shot had been just inside the sideline for a winner.

Hillyard clarified the situation for the players and bewildered fans, and after a brief uproar play resumed with a shaken Lenglen now at 40-30, still at match point. Wills was neither euphoric nor distracted by her second chance to succeed; she simply got on with her task, calm and resolute. She produced a crack-

ling forehand that Lenglen could not return, and moments later was back in business at 6-6.

Lenglen's legion of supporters, and indeed the champion herself, were apprehensive as a revived Wills served. The American sensed the possibility of bringing about a third set. In a long and extraordinarily hard-fought game, Wills had a point for 7-6. She seemed to have gained the upper hand. She believed she was heading toward a sparkling triumph.

But Lenglen was not willing to let go. She fought valiantly to hold Wills back, and broke serve for 7-6. With that burst of effective shotmaking, Lenglen successfully negotiated a second chance to serve for the match. She thoughtfully probed the Wills arsenal, breaking down the American's backhand, arriving at 40-30 and a third match point. Then a first-serve fault. Lenglen paused before hitting her second serve, then tossed. It was a double fault.

Had she squandered too many pivotal chances? Was the game's greatest match player losing her renowned ability to play her best under pressure? She answered those questions without hesitation, moving back to match point for the fourth time, then opening up the court with a deep forehand crosscourt, following with a clean winner into a wide open space.

Contrast in personality and style heightened the tension.

That last perfect placement gave Lenglen a 6-3, 8-6 triumph—in precisely one hour.

This time Lenglen knew her victory was official as she ran up to the net to greet Wills. The Frenchwoman seemed to float on the sounds of an ovation, surrounded by friends and admirers, clutching flowers like a ballerina. Wills—so gallant and poised in defeat, able to detach herself and witness the wild jubilation around Lenglen with fascination rather than frustration—picked up her belongings a few minutes later and departed, almost unnoticed by the swarming Lenglen fans. Wills understood this was France, where Lenglen was larger than life. The American was not feeling sorry for herself, and she unreluctantly admired the persistence and artistry her opponent had exhibited.

"It had to be the most dramatic match I've ever seen," said Tinling, who was fifteen when he witnessed this clash, and subsequently saw more great matches in this century (before his death in 1990) than any other authority. "There will never be anything quite like it again with the whole tra-la-la of the buildup. Suzanne and Helen was the first big show business match in the history of tennis, a sort of precursor for Billie Jean King and Bobby Riggs in 1973. If there was one match I could go back and see again, Lenglen-Wills would be it."

EPILOGUE

The consensus among the experts of the time was that Lenglen and Wills would renew their rivalry frequently, and perhaps rekindle some of the magic evident in their Cannes showdown. But the two superb performers never faced each other again. Wills remained in Europe that winter and spring of 1926, and it seemed inevitable that she would confront Lenglen in the final of the French Championships in June. That would have been another tense encounter on red clay, but this time the stakes would have been even higher with a major championship on the line. As fortune would have it, in the middle of the tournament Wills was stricken with severe stomach pain and sent to the hospital, where she had an emergency appendectomy.

That setback kept Wills out of action for the rest of the major tournaments that season, and removed her from the circuit altogether. Lenglen, meanwhile, went through a crisis of her own. After winning that French Championship easily, with Wills not in her path, she went to Wimbledon in search of a seventh singles title. She was scheduled for an early-round match with Queen Mary in attendance, but a major misunderstanding occurred and

Lenglen did not turn up at the scheduled hour. When she was informed later that afternoon that she had kept the queen waiting, a disconsolate Lenglen could not bear the pain of her mistake, and fainted. She pulled out of the tournament, humiliated by what had happened, unable to get over the embarrassment. That summer, Lenglen signed a contract to play on the first professional tennis tour in the United States, winning all thirty-eight of her head-to-head contests with Mary K. Browne of the United States. But with Wills remaining an amateur and still competing for the great traditional prizes, it was no longer possible for the two superstars to meet each other in official competition.

Wills arrived at the peak of her powers in the years ahead. Between 1927 and 1938, she won eight Wimbledon singles titles—a record until Martina Navratilova broke it in 1990—and collected fifty match victories in a row. That mark has never been equaled in men's or women's play on the fabled lawns of the All England Club.

Returning to Paris with high aspirations, Wills took the French Championships four times from 1928 to 1932 and secured four more of her U.S. Championships at Forest Hills to lift her total to seven. She triumphed in that tournament in 1927, 1928, 1929, and 1931. Wills concluded her career with nineteen Grand Slam tournament titles, a record surpassed only by Margaret Court and Steffi Graf. Wills was beaten a mere three times across the years in twenty-two major events, a standard of excellence no other player has ever achieved.

As Wills's tennis career ended in the late-1930s, an ailing Lenglen passed away. Having struggled with her health for much of the decade, the charismatic woman from France died on July 4, 1938, of pernicious anemia. She was thirty-nine. The tragic departure of Lenglen occurred within days of Wills's final championship run at Wimbledon. But while Wills had thrived on the court into her early thirties, she was sorting through some problems in her personal life.

Suzanne Lenglen and Helen Wills

On her trip to the French Riviera to confront Lenglen, she had met an American stockbroker named Freddie Moody and they soon became inseparable. They were married in 1929, but the union ended in divorce eight years later. In 1939, two years after her breakup with Moody, Helen was married for the second time, to film writer Aidan Roark. They were divorced in the early 1970s.

For twenty-five years thereafter, Helen Wills Moody Roark led a reclusive life in California, although her interest in tennis never waned. She was unfailingly gracious in her remarks about modern champions like Chris Evert and Martina Navratilova. In January 1998, at the age of ninety-two, she passed away.

The death of Wills seemed to stir the embers of debate, among those experts who had observed her career, as to where she stood when measured against Lenglen on the historical tennis ladder. Many have speculated on what might have transpired had they been able to play more matches against each other. The experts have concluded that Wills would surely have surpassed Lenglen within a year of their Cannes encounter, and would have controlled their rivalry in the late 1920s and beyond. Wills was then beginning to reach her absolute prime, while Lenglen was arguably declining.

And yet, many knowledgeable tennis reporters take the firm position that Lenglen at her peak, in the early- to mid-1920s, would have been too cunning and capable even for Wills, and would have dominated during that stretch.

Lenglen's record on paper is far less impressive than that of Wills. She had to settle for eight official major championships, eleven fewer than Wills. But that is a somewhat misleading fact because Lenglen in her time of true triumph was every bit as invincible as Wills became, perhaps even more so.

For tennis historians the Cannes duel achieved an incandescence beyond any other women's match of that time. Both ladies came

What might have been a sparkling series is left to speculation.

away from that contest having gained respect for each other, and having learned something substantial about themselves. Even after the decades passed and a cavalcade of champions succeeded them, Wills remembered her meeting with Lenglen in very lucid terms, and had no regrets that they did not test each other again.

As Wills recalled in 1986, "Suzanne was a great player and had more generalship on the court than I did. She had the game down to a pattern in her mind which was the best according to her ability. I had more power and endurance. But I was not disappointed not to play her again. I remember we all went out to dinner that night after the tennis match, everybody all dressed up in dinner clothes, and I didn't feel sad. I was very young for my age then and I just thought I would win the next time I played Lenglen."   •

BILL TILDEN VS. HENRI COCHET

WIMBLEDON, SEMIFINAL, JUNE 30, 1927

No player had more theatrical flair and tactical acuity than Tilden. Cochet was a gifted shotmaker and a tireless competitor. The two champions staged a classic confrontation.

PROLOGUE

Only one year after the much heralded clash between Wills and Lenglen at Cannes—a battle between a legendary Frenchwoman and a young American of immense promise—Henri Cochet of France and "Big Bill" Tilden of the United States collided in the semifinals at Wimbledon in 1927. As one of the famed "Four Musketeers" from the celebrated Davis Cup team (René Lacoste, Jean Borotra, and Jacques Brugnon were the others) Cochet was a player of remarkable originality and imagination, a competitor of rising fortunes. But in Tilden he was confronting the master of his craft, and the man who had sweepingly dominated tennis all through that decade. Cochet came from a very modest background, but because his father was the secretary of a tennis club in Lyons, young Henri had the opportunity to learn tennis. He had natural gifts, practiced little, and was largely self-taught.

Tilden, on the other hand, enjoyed his childhood in a very comfortable family. He lived a short walk away from the Germantown Cricket Club in Philadelphia, and was considered to be a "mother's boy." His mother kept him out of school until he was fifteen, insisting that he be tutored at home, where he also spent hours listening to his mother play the piano. Tilden once said if he was asked to give up tennis or music, it would be tennis. Nonetheless, he began playing tennis at the age of five. In 1915, during his last year at the University of Pennsylvania, both his father and brother died. Tilden had not been good enough to make the varsity tennis team at Penn. But he would coach the team at the Germantown Academy. Almost inevitably, this led him into competitive tennis at a much higher level.

So towering a figure in his field was Tilden that he became the champion of his country no fewer than six consecutive times between 1920 and 1925 at Forest Hills. At age twenty-six, he had been beaten by his countryman, "Little Bill" Johnston, in the 1919 Forest Hills final. Having suffered that setback, he realized that it was a single stroke in his repertoire that was holding him back. It was time to strengthen his backhand, rather than continue muddling through with his barely adequate defensively designed shot off that side. So he spent the winter of 1920 attending to that task, remodeling his stroke, learning to drive through the ball aggressively. Tilden turned his backhand into a versatile and effective weapon more closely aligned with his classic forehand. His glaring weakness was gone, and his game was decidedly enhanced by the new component, lifting him to another level.

Tilden established himself not only as a supreme ground stroker with nearly impeccable mechanics, but a superb server who could deliver the "cannonball" with regular success, and volley with conviction when he made his infrequent visits to the net. And yet, beyond the wide range of his technical capabilities, Tilden was the first great tactician the game had known. He had an astonishing and intuitive sense of how to play points, what would bother his opponents most, and when he would need to alter his patterns and shift his strategic focus. He relished opportunities to exploit the vulnerabilities of his rivals, picking them apart with sharp and purposeful execution. He was a maestro on the tennis court, a showman, but above all a keen student of the game. As he wrote perceptively in *Match Play and the Spin of the Ball*, "I may sound unsporting when I say that the primary object of tennis is to break up your oppponent's game, but it is my honest belief that no man is defeated until his game is crushed, or at least weakened. Nothing so upsets mental and physical poise as to be continually led into error."

Cochet was just coming into his own as he approached this meeting with the world champion. The previous year at Forest Hills, he had ended Tilden's bid for a seventh straight championship with an impressive victory in the quarterfinals. Earlier in 1926, he had won his own French Championships for the first time on the red clay courts at Roland Garros in Paris. With his fellow "Four Musketeers" he would play a pivotal role in leading France to victory in the Davis Cup for six consecutive years—1927 to 1932. In many ways, he was the ideal opponent for Tilden. He mixed his ground strokes adroitly by varying not only the pace but the length of his shots. His serve lacked Tilden's power and punch but he could place it precisely, and he was deceptive. He could conclude points with uncommon skill on the volley, and no one before his arrival had exhibited such consistent control and effectiveness on the half volley. His flair and flexibility on that shot were striking, and his handling of low balls by making quick, aggressive pickups was something that separated him from the rest of the opposition in that era. He was the best half-volleyer of his time.

Both competitors knew this would be a match of lasting consequences, but neither could have been prepared for the full extent of the drama they would produce in this duel.

THE MATCH

Despite being the dominant player of the decade, Tilden was placed at No. 2 behind LaCoste in this groundbreaking year of seeded players on the grass courts at Wimbledon. The primary reason he was not given the top spot was that he had not been back to the All England Club since winning in 1920 and 1921. In any case, Cochet was seeded fourth. Tilden had moved into the penultimate round with few obstacles and the loss of only one set-to Brugnon in the quarterfinals. In that same round, Cochet had conceded the first two sets to Tilden's capable doubles partner Frank Hunter, but the Frenchman struck back boldly to win in five sets.

With Tilden playing the more confident

Bill Tilden

brand of tennis, the American was the firm favorite to win as they faced each other on a cloudy afternoon. At the outset, Tilden performed with both power and panache. He served thunderbolts that even the quick-handed Cochet could not return. He found the corners with his heavy ground strokes, and dictated the pace for nearly three sets. Tilden took a commanding 6-2, 6-4, 5-1 lead and was on the verge of an unmistakable rout.

As Englishman Stanley Doust wrote in the *Daily Mirror*, "How could anyone have lived against such wonderful lawn tennis as Tilden played? Was there anyone who could beat him?"

Cochet had the answers to those questions. From 1-5, 15-15 in the third set, seemingly caught in a hopeless corner, Cochet proceeded to collect seventeen points in a row on his way to a six game sweep for the set. It was a combination of Cochet's courage and determination and an uncharacteristic lapse from Tilden that altered the complexion of the match, but the American's mastery was over. Despite some resistance from Tilden, Cochet closed out the set.

He was maneuvering Tilden in a manner few had thought possible. Cochet took the fourth set after Tilden recovered from 4-2 down to reach 4-4. Then a resurgent Tilden rediscovered his early match form to break for a 3-2, fifth-set lead.

It seemed that Tilden would regain the initiative and run out the match, but that was not the case. Cochet channeled his energy and emotions into one last four-game burst, and Tilden collapsed down the stretch. At 3-2, he served a pair of double faults and at 3-4 he served two more. An electrifying reversal of fortunes was over, much to the dismay of the proud American who bowed 2-6, 4-6, 7-5, 6-4, 6-3. "Seldom has there been such enthusiasm at a lawn tennis victory," wrote Doust. "Enthusiasm not because Tilden was beaten but because of Cochet's marvelous recovery from what looked like certain defeat to a glorious victory."

Revered American journalist Al Laney of the *New York Herald Tribune* wrote revealingly about it in his book, *Covering the Court*. He conceded, "I could not explain what happened to Tilden then, and I can not now. I think now the explanation might be found in a remark Tilden addressed to me immediately after the match, or as quickly as I could reach the dressing room. 'Maybe you were right,' he said, and he said it with what I thought was scorn, but in a voice that carried a certain hatred, too. He was referring to the statement that he had now passed his best years and could no longer call on his matchless stamina."

EPILOGUE

Not content with one of the most riveting comebacks in the history of big-time tennis, Cochet managed in the final to produce another masterpiece of turnaround. Once again, he trailed two sets to love, this time against the stubborn Borotra. Borotra had won Wimbledon twice—including the year before—and could not have come closer to retaining his title against a coolly defiant Cochet. In this pendulum-swinging battle of the Frenchmen, Borotra—less talented but every bit as resilient a competitor—sealed the first two sets with relative ease, but then lost the next two as Cochet sank his teeth more deeply into the contest.

The fifth set, however, became a forum for Borotra to return almost effortlessly to the top of his game. He moved swiftly to a 5-2 lead

---

Craftiness and stamina were central to a dramatic struggle.

---

and had a match point on Cochet's serve in the eighth game. When Cochet gamely saved himself and held serve, the odds still seemed heavily stacked against him with Borotra serving for the championship at 5-3. Here Borotra had five more match points, but his tenacious adversary was not about to surrender. Taking full advantage of an errant volley from Borotra on the last of the match points, Cochet proceeded to finish off this clash with elan, winning 4-6, 4-6, 6-3, 6-4, 7-5. By virtue of this stunning feat, Cochet achieved a unique record among Wimbledon champions by completing his mission with three straight victories from two sets to love down.

In the ensuing years, Cochet distinguished himself with steady conviction. He won three more French Championships (1928, 1930, and 1932) to lift his total to four. He won Wimbledon again for the second time in 1929, and was the winner of the United States Championsips at

Henri Cochet

Forest Hills in 1928, garnering that championship with another hard-fought, five-set triumph in the final over Frank Hunter. To be sure, his extraordinary exploits at Wimbledon in 1927 set the stage for a very productive period in the years ahead. Overcoming Tilden despite the darkest of circumstances, and then toppling Borotra with similar grit, had propelled Cochet to a stature he had never found before. Meanwhile, he contributed mightily to the enduring success of the "Four Musketeers."

Altogether, Cochet, Lacoste, Borotra, and Brugnon amassed fifty-three major titles in singles and doubles. It was irrefutably the golden age of French men's tennis and there could be nothing quite like it again through the rest of the twentieth century.

And what of Tilden? In many ways, he never fully recovered from the bewildering defeat suffered against Cochet. He was clearly not finished as a major force, ruling at Wimbledon for the third and last time in 1930, after a seventh and last U.S. Championships title at Forest Hills the previous season. But the towering man from Philadelphia—at 6' 2" he was unusually tall for his time— was never quite the same player after the devastating failure to vanquish Cochet. Tilden won ten major championships—seven U.S. and three Wimbledon titles—but took only two of those crowns after his 1927 surrender.

In retrospect, there was a certain logic to his diminished fortunes. He was thirty-four when he fell to Cochet. He had lost his capacity for playing the big points with automatic precision. He no longer controlled the agenda of critical matches with the force of his will and the skill of his shot selection. Tilden had moved irrevocably past his prime, and yet he remained a top-notch competitor for many years to come.

He turned professional in 1931 at thirty-eight, and played until he was nearly fifty. But while his court sense remained unimpeachable, his footspeed was dwindling, and his serve was a much lesser weapon. In his pro tour match series with a first-rate Ellsworth Vines, Tilden came out on the wrong end of a 47-26 record. Seven years later, in 1941, he was obliterated 51-7 in his meetings with another prodigious countryman, Don Budge. By then, he was forty-eight and fading steadily, but he was still a magnificent player.

Sadly, his personal life was shaded by his

stepping beyond the boundaries of the law. Forced to conceal his homosexuality—a sports celebrity's reputation could be ruined by such a revelation in his day—Tilden was sent to prison in 1947 and again in 1949 on morals charges. His arrests were kept relatively quiet by the newspapers, but he had to live with the consequences of his actions.

Meanwhile, Tilden had lost most of his money on ill-advised theater ventures. A man who cherished drama on the tennis court—he was fond of digging deficits for himself in matches so that he could climb out of those predicaments and win in heroic fashion—Tilden invested in plays unwisely, and performed on stage in roles he could not master. None of these ventures worked, but Tilden remained convinced he could be an accomplished actor nevertheless.

His genuine love of tennis was evident until the end of his life. He would show up to play casual doubles matches on friends' private courts in California, dressed in ragged clothing, speaking in his familiar high-pitched voice, instructing his admiring partners what to do. He remained largely a reclusive figure, poignantly trying to recover his high standards. And then on June 5, 1953, at sixty, he died of a heart attack in Los Angeles. He had packed his suitcase and was planning to compete in the U.S. Pro Championships at Cleveland.

He left behind an enviable record. As this century ends, only four men have secured more Grand Slam singles championships. They are: Roy Emerson and Pete Sampras with twelve, followed by Rod Laver and Bjorn Borg with eleven each. But it must be recorded that Tilden's rate of success was equally impressive. He never played the Australian Championships, and failed to win the French Championships in three attempts, but triumphed regularly at Wimbledon and Forest Hills, where he was beaten only ten times in twenty combined appearances. From 1920 through 1926, he led the Americans to victory in the Davis Cup. And he celebrated six consecutive years as the top-ranked player in tennis, a feat not replicated until Sampras did it in 1998.

Tilden was a central figure in the evolution of his sport, and until he lost to Cochet there was no better big-match player. Many writers, players, and historians placed Tilden at the top of the list of players who appeared in the first half of the century. For seven years—from 1920-26—he was virtually unstoppable. He understood the game on a sophisticated level, breaking it down systematically in his orderly mind, calculating the right strategic approach to take away his opponents' strengths and exploit his own.

It must be said that Tilden did not attack as persistently as future champions automatically would. A strong case can be made that it was not necessary in his day to conclude many points with decisive volleys or unanswerable smashes. The design of his court craft was a product of his era, of how the game was played at that time, and of his personal preference for plotting longer points which did much more to reveal his virtuosity and supreme talent for playing chess on the tennis court.

This much is certain: Tilden in the twenties was as masterful a player as the men's game had yet witnessed.   •

HELEN WILLS MOODY VS. HELEN JACOBS

WIMBLEDON, FINAL, JULY 6, 1935

These two very talented backcourt players met many times,
but this clash was their epiphany.

PROLOGUE

Nearly thirty years old, Helen Wills Moody was slightly past her prime as she pursued a seventh Wimbledon championship in 1935. Her best seasons followed her once-in-a-lifetime battle with Lenglen in 1926. After her loss to Lenglen, she was not beaten again until 1933. In that span, Mrs. Moody had taken four French Championships, four United States Championships, and six Wimbledon singles titles. She was as dominant during that stretch as Lenglen had been in the first half of the twenties.

The unbeaten streak achieved by Wills Moody was broken by the perseverance of her countrywoman, Helen Hull Jacobs, who was born in Globe, Arizona, in 1908. The family moved to San Francisco just before World War I, and later occupied a home in Berkeley, California, where Helen Wills had lived. Like Wills, Jacobs learned to play at the Berkeley Tennis Club. She attended the University of California. In 1933, she became the first woman to wear shorts at Wimbledon. She was always a favorite of tennis fans because of her friendly, cheerful manner.

Jacobs, three years younger than her rival, was defending her title at Forest Hills in 1933. She took on her old nemesis in the final. They waged a tough battle in the opening set before Jacobs prevailed, 8-6. Moody answered by taking the second set, 6-3. Jacobs established a 3-0 lead in the third and final set. She seemed likely to move from there to the title, exploiting her comfortable lead.

At that point, Mrs. Moody walked up to the net and conceded defeat. She claimed her back was causing her too much pain to continue. She withdrew to the locker room in her customary long coat, and chose to remain silent on the subject of her default. Four years later, in her autobiography titled, *Fifteen Thirty*, Helen Wills Moody explained why she had left the scene and denied Jacobs a legitimate, full-scale triumph.

Her back had been bothering her for weeks, long before Forest Hills had begun. Her husband, Freddie Moody, advised her not to participate in the National Championships. She believed she might never have the chance to play at Forest Hills again. A few weeks before the tournament, the pain was excruciating, running down her back, into her leg, and even into

Helen Jacobs

the toes of her right foot. At times, her right leg felt numb.

Two weeks prior to the Nationals, Mrs. Moody was forced to withdraw from the Wightman Cup (U.S. vs. Great Britain) team competition after being examined by doctors who cited symptoms of instability in her vertebra. She took it easy for a few days, then resumed light practice. In her mind, she had to ignore the injury, or else she would be revealing weakness and apprehension.

Wills Moody reached the final of Forest Hills more on reputation than execution. After her semifinal victory, it rained heavily for an entire week, delaying the final. In that time off, she isolated herself in her room near the courts, but did not do anything physically strenuous. Her body stiffened. When the rain finally ceased, she faced Jacobs, who had consulted with Suzanne Lenglen earlier in the year about how to play Wills Moody. Lenglen urged Jacobs to hit short crosscourt shots to draw her opponent forward.

Wills Moody described that 1933 final with Jacobs in her book. She wrote, "I was trying to meet the competition of the match and at the same time was carrying on another fight within myself—one that was between my brain, which was commanding, and my muscles, which were bound in an iron-clad spasm trying to protect the injured nerves of my back. When I could not break through their grip, I was unable to bend or run, and when I could the pain was blinding. . . . I knew it was the end when the stadium began to swirl in the air, and I saw Miss Jacobs and the court on a slant. If I had fainted on the court, it would have been thought a more conclusive finish to the match in the eyes of many of the onlookers, for then they would have been convinced that I could not continue. However, my choice was instinctive rather than premeditated. Had I been able to think clearly I might have chosen to remain. It was unfortunate that Miss Jacobs could not have had a complete victory, as it would have been had I been able to remain a little longer on the court. But being naturally selfish, I thought only of myself. I could understand her feeling of disappointment, but the match would have ended this way no matter against whom I had been playing."

Mrs. Moody went into the hospital and stayed there for a month. She had a weight placed on her leg, pulling on it to build strength. She feared she would not play the game of tennis again. The following January, she took osteopathic treatments, and that made a substantial difference. She was clearly on the mend, but playing Wimbledon in 1934 was out of the question. She was asked to write about the event by the *London Daily Mail*, and enjoyed the detached experience.

By the spring of 1935, Wills Moody was ready to make another run at Wimbledon, prepared to pursue a seventh title on the grass courts at the All England Club. During her absence, Jacobs had flourished. At Forest Hills in 1934, she took the championship of the United States for the third consecutive year, defeating the rising Sarah Palfrey Fabyan in the final.

Physical problems take their toll as both careers wind down.

Jacobs, however, had never won Wimbledon. To round out her record and place herself irrevocably among the great players of her era, she needed that title. The two Helens had a great deal in common. Both had trained in their formative years at the Berkeley Tennis Club in California, and they shared the experience of attending the University of California.

Despite the common threads that ran through their lives, there were fundamental differences. Jacobs's game contrasted sharply with that of Wills Moody. Jacobs was comfortable anywhere on the court, volleying with confidence and aggression, smashing capably. She had a prodigious doubles record, where she put her attacking skills to good use.

Her singles game did have some holes in it. She had to find ways to disrupt Wills Moody, who was more powerful and precise off the ground. Wills Moody hit through the ball unfailingly and found the corners with regularity, forcing her opponents into defensive positions all the while. Jacobs relied heavily on underspin off both sides, and did not break her adversaries down as easily from the backcourt as Wills Moody could. And yet, Mrs. Moody was often heavy footed and vulnerable against short angles and drop shots. Jacobs was a better athlete, quicker at covering the whole court.

THE MATCH

Jacobs had a distinct advantage over Wills Moody as they advanced through the women's draw at Wimbledon in 1935. She had been competing steadily and knew essentially what to expect from herself. Wills Moody had been out of action since her abrupt departure against Jacobs two years earlier at Forest Hills.

In that time, Wills Moody had slowly reacclimated to the rigors of playing competitive tennis, pursuing points which had once been automatic but no longer were. Mrs. Moody played a couple of minor tournaments in preparation for Wimbledon, but even that plan had its pitfalls as the constant rain in England cut deeply into her schedule and left her considerably short of where she wanted to be in her tuneup.

Having been away from the game for so long, Wills Moody was seeded fourth at Wimbledon, one place behind Jacobs. The Englishwoman Dorothy Round was seeded first and Germany's Hilde Sperling—who had won her first of three straight French Championships that year—was the No. 2 seed.

Round bowed in the quarterfinals and Sperling was routed by Jacobs 6-3, 6-0 in the semifinals. Wills Moody had a frightening round of sixteen meeting with Slecna Cepkova. The Czechoslovakian had Mrs. Moody in disarray for a set-and-a-half. The American trailed by a set and was 4-1 down in the second. She

recovered her poise and her will just in time to salvage a three-set victory. That was the only set she conceded on her way to the final. Miss Jacobs did not lose any sets in her half of the draw. The two Americans had set up a widely anticipated final match, their first since 1933 at Forest Hills.

As Al Laney wrote in the *New York Herald Tribune*, "Receiving the first service, Miss Jacobs brought into play the chop stroke she has made her own and Mrs. Moody swung into the ball and hit for the corner. There was the story of the match given in its very first exchange. For thirty games to follow Mrs. Moody attacked and

---

The appealing quality of discipline and resolve entrances audiences.

Miss Jacobs defended and each player did her part superlatively well."

Mrs. Moody's hard hitting boosted her to an early lead against an opponent who had been beaten in all three of her previous appearances in the Wimbledon final. Moody took a 3-0 lead in the first set before Jacobs found her range. Jacobs struggled back to 3-3 and had Moody at 0-40 in the crucial seventh game.

Mrs. Moody had drifted into a difficult patch at that stage, losing eleven points in a row. Had she lost her serve again to trail 3-4, she conceivably would have surrendered the set. Instead, with her confidence restored, Moody held on for 4-3, broke in the following game, and served out the set, 6-3.

Jacobs was well aware that Moody was not in top tournament shape. She began directing her ground strokes closer to the sidelines, making her opponent move as much as possible, trying to tire her rival in the process. By the middle

Helen Wills Moody

of the second set, that pattern was succeeding. From 3-3 in the second set, Jacobs collected three games in a row to draw level at one set all.

With the capacity Centre Court crowd murmuring, Moody held up her hand and asked for quiet as she started serving the opening game of the third set. It was apparent then that she was weary. After a pair of hard fought games, Jacobs broke for 2-1 as Moody's serve seemed devoid of all pace. Although Mrs. Moody managed to break back for 2-2, she lost her serve again in the following game. At 3-2, Jacobs slipped to 15-40, saved the first break point, and then reached deuce with a solid smash. After a series of deuces, Jacobs held on for 4-2.

Serving in the seventh game, Moody rebounded from 15-40 to deuce, only to miss an easy overhead from short range, well wide of the sideline. Jacobs got the insurance break for 5-2, and served for the match in the eighth game. She reached 30-30, two points from the triumph, but Moody was not obliging. She broke for 3-5.

In the ninth game, Mrs. Moody served to save the match. Both players were bearing down frantically. One long point after another was played. Neither woman wanted to take any unnecessary chances with so much riding on the outcome of this game. A resolute Jacobs arrived at match point. She had the gumption to go into the net. Moody lifted a lob into the air. Jacobs was poised to smash it out of the reach of her adversary. If she could connect solidly, the match would belong to her.

An instant before contact, a burst of wind

blew the ball slightly away from a baffled Jacobs. She sent her overhead tentatively into the net. Mrs. Moody had saved a match point, and she held her serve for 4-5. Jacobs still had

The interplay of agility on one side and strategy on the other.

another chance to close out the account, another opportunity to win it on her serve. At 5-4, she served for the match a second time.

Once more, Jacobs progressed to 30-30, two points from the triumph. Moody added velocity to her shots and played them into safe spaces, several feet from the sidelines. She broke back gamely for 5-5, then held for 6-5. With Jacobs serving to save the match in the twelfth game, the two competitors endured a three deuce game. Moody reached match point. They had one of their longest rallies of the day. Jacobs got the short ball she wanted, approached the net, then had a volley well within her range with the court open ahead of her. She overplayed it. The shot landed long. Mrs. Moody was the victor, 6-3, 3-6, 7-5, coming through for the seventh time at Wimbledon, denying Jacobs the chance to secure a first crown.

Mrs. Moody offered an intriguing analysis of her turnaround in *Fifteen Thirty*. She wrote of her recovery from match point down, "I knew naturally that the set point had been saved, but there was no way to tell that the match had been rescued. During the last couple of games, my 'wind' had returned—why, I don't know. It may have been 'second wind' or it may have been a quieting down of the breathing process induced because of the demands of what seemed to me to be an emergency."

Both Wallis Myers and Al Laney had their notions of why Helen Wills Moody had persevered. Myers wrote in the *Daily Telegraph*, "Courage, as Stevenson has said, respects courage, and both these girls, inspired by the intensity of the other's, revealed more of it on Saturday than I have ever seen on a lawn tennis court. Yet valor, like the other virtues, has its limitations; it was the technique of Mrs. Moody which finally triumphed. In fluent footwork, Miss Jacobs was the superior; without this supreme asset she never could have made those wonderful redemptions in the corner that startled both the crowd and her opponent. But Miss Jacobs, with all her great agility and her unbreakable heart, had not the 'happiness of style' that belonged to her adversary."

Laney wrote in the *Herald Tribune*, "No women's match in the longest memory at Wimbledon ever has been fought with such grimness or presented so many tense situations. It is not likely that Miss Jacobs ever played so well before or that she will ever come so close again and fail. She staked all of her unyielding defense against Mrs. Moody's unremitting attack and, although she defended wonderfully well for an hour and a half—so well, in fact, that she saw her greatest ambition about to be realized—her defenses finally crumbled under pressure of an attack that never let up from the first point to the last."

EPILOGUE

When Moody did not return to Wimbledon in 1936, the gallant Jacobs took her chance at last to win the world's most prestigious tennis tournament. Late in 1935, Jacobs was offered $50,000 by a promoter to play a professional tour series against Moody. Determined to make her breakthrough at Wimbledon, she turned the lucrative offer down. She was well rewarded for her decision.

In the 1936 Centre Court final, Jacobs had her fifth opportunity to win a Wimbledon championship match. She met Hilde Sperling and led by a set and 3-1. Sperling bounced back, took the second set, and fought hard all through the third, but Jacobs triumphed, 6-2, 4-6, 7-5.

Jacobs made it to the final of the U.S. Championships in 1936 for the fifth year in a row, took the first set from the gifted Alice Marble, but bowed in three sets. Top seeded in defense of her Wimbledon title in 1937, Jacobs was beaten in the quarterfinals by Dorothy Round. Mrs. Moody had secluded herself again in her married life in California. When she wrote her autobiography in 1937, she seemed to have put her tennis career behind her, looking forward to other endeavors away from the arena.

But in 1938, she could not resist one more journey back to Wimbledon. She had not lost a match there since 1924, had amassed seven singles titles since, and seemed incapable of playing anything but her best tennis in that preeminent setting. Mrs. Moody and Jacobs met each other in the final for the fourth time. They were engaged in a typically spirited showdown when Jacobs aggravated an ankle she had injured in her quarterfinal. Jacobs was serving at 4-4, 40-30 when she landed painfully on the

Greatness in the triumphs and the defeats.

sore ankle. Thereafter, she could put up only token resistance as Moody glided to a 6-4, 6-0 victory for a record-breaking eighth singles title.

Mrs. Moody was approaching thirty-three. She realized her resources were dwindling, and quit competitive tennis. Jacobs remained a fomidable force for a few more years, reaching two more Forest Hills finals, losing both to the blossoming Alice Marble in 1939 and 1940. She left the game with five major singles championships in her possession, fourteen fewer than the major trophies won by Moody. Jacobs, who passed away in 1997 at 88, was overshadowed by Moody on one side of her career and Marble on the other. But there was no doubt about her standing as one of the finest players of her era. •

FRED PERRY VS. ELLSWORTH VINES

PRO TOUR SERIES OPENING, NEW YORK, JANUARY 7, 1937

A dashing Englishman and his explosive American rival played a magnificent pro tour against each other. This was the first battle of a scintillating series.

PROLOGUE

The 1920s was a crucial decade in the evolution of tennis as a sport worthy of widespread international attention. The impact of Bill Tilden, the "Four Musketeers," Suzanne Lenglen, and Helen Wills gave tennis an immeasurable boost. It was a time of unparalleled glamour and growth for tennis, a period of passionate interest among fans everywhere in the world.

The decade that followed was almost as remarkable in its cavalcade of champions. Late in the 1930s, the Americans, Don Budge and Alice Marble, achieved eminent successes. Their personalities and performances were alluring to all close followers of the game. Two other men made their mark during that period and established themselves as great stars of their era: The versatile Californian, Ellsworth Vines, and the dashing Englishman, Fred Perry. Vines played semi-profesional baseball when he was fifteen, and center for the USC varsity basketball team in his sophomore year. But it was tennis that engaged his deepest commitment.

Perry was born in Stockport, England, a textile town not far from Liverpool. His father

Sam worked as a spinner in the mills but became a union president at twenty-one and a Justice of the Peace before he was thirty. The Perry family moved to London after World War I, where Fred attended the County School, winning honors in cricket and soccer. He also became a champion Ping-Pong player, winning the world championship at Budapest—the first non-Hungarian to do so. He started to play tournament tennis at the age of fifteen, and at twenty he qualified for the 1929 Wimbledon.

The American and the Englishman showcased their talents appealingly. Vines came to the forefront first. He provided a bright series of matches in 1931 and 1932. In the former season, still a few weeks shy of his twentieth birthday, "The California Comet" and the British star clashed for the first time in a match of meaning. Vines—the No. 1 seed among U.S. players—took on Perry, the top-seeded foreign participant, in the semifinals of the U.S. Nationals at Forest Hills. Perry led two sets to love before Vines brushed him aside in five sets. Vines then won the tournament—his first major—over fellow American George Lott (who became one of the all-time great doubles players) in four sets.

In 1932, Vines captured both Wimbledon

Fred Perry

and Forest Hills. A very slender 6′ 2″, he weighed about 140 pounds. Vines, nevertheless, was a power player of remarkable strength. His big first serve was a "cannonball" opponents did not relish trying to return. He could crack the forehand with demonic speed and depth. He set the pace in most of his matches with the sheer velocity of his strokes. As the esteemed critic Lance Tingay of the *Daily Telegraph* wrote in *100 Years at Wimbledon*, " It is to be doubted if

ever a player hit the ball harder than did Vines in his last three rounds at Wimbledon in 1932."

At that 1932 Wimbledon, he defeated the gifted Australian, Jack Crawford, in the semifinals after Crawford had accounted for Perry in the previous round. Vines then handled Englishman Bunny Austin with ease in a straight-set final. He staked his claim as the best amateur player in the world when he safely defended his turf at Forest Hills. Seeded first again among Americans, he made a gallant recovery from two sets to love down in the semifinals and ousted countryman Cliff Sutter. In the final, he beat top foreign seed, Henri Cochet, 6-4, 6-4, 6-4.

After taking those three major tournaments in 1931-32, Vines was in a position to turn professional. He elected to remain in the amateur game for 1933, but was not up to the same standards. At Wimbledon, he did manage to play

---

The allure of an English outsider who wanted to win.

---

inspired tennis for the fortnight. He confronted Crawford in the final. The Australian reversed the result of their 1932 semifinal meeting, prevailing 4-6, 11-9, 6-2, 2-6, 6-4. Perhaps somewhat shaken by that loss in one of the most heralded Wimbledon finals, Vines fell again at Forest Hills, bowing in a straight set, round-of-sixteen match against a scrappy and diminutive compatriot named Bitsy Grant.

Furthermore, Vines lost a major battle with Perry in the U.S.-Great Britain Interzone final of Davis Cup at Paris. Vines led two sets to one before dropping the fourth set 7-5. In the fifth, serving at 6-7, Vines collapsed after hitting a serve. He had twisted an ankle severely earlier, but would not surrender because he did not want to be called a quitter. He fought on despite the pain until that fourteenth game, when he fell on his way to the net. The match was abruptly over. Vines left the court only half conscious.

Despite his failure to hold on to his coveted crowns, Vines had not seriously diminished the reputation he had built for years, and he turned professional after the 1933 season.

Meanwhile, Perry was just coming into his own. The Englishman had not emerged from a privileged background. When Perry decided to try lawn tennis, he was given an ultimatum by his father that he had to make his mark within a year. His father took him out of school and gave him that brief time frame to demonstrate his potential.

Perry met the paternal standard. Before he became twenty-two he was good enough to represent his nation on the Davis Cup team. In 1933, when he was twenty-four, he captured his first major championship at Forest Hills, winning the U.S. Nationals over Crawford, recouping from two sets to one down to take the final in five sets. He would win that tournament two more times.

Perry was progressing rapidly. From 1934-36, he was the best player in the world of amateur tennis. Perry secured the Australian Championship title in 1934, and won the French Championships a year later. He won three consecutive Wimbledon singles titles in that stretch. In the first of those finals, he took apart Crawford in straight sets. In the 1935 and 1936 finals, he routed Germany's Gottfried von Cramm in straight sets. But oddly, Perry was not greeted with enthusiasm by the crowd at Wimbledon.

In *Fred Perry, An Autobiography*, he explained why he believed he was given short shrift by the fans. "I've always been regarded as an upstart who didn't really belong in such exalted company," he wrote. "I was someone who didn't have the right credentials for this noble game. But I don't think the frostiness of the Wimbledon crowds towards my first victory in 1934 was simply a question of snobbery or resentment. There was more to it than that. You

Ellsworth Vines

Perry learned to compete wherever he went, relying on his own convictions to carry him through. His third and last triumph at Forest Hills raised his number of major championship victories to eight. In the process, he demonstrated beyond doubt that he was at his best under intense pressure. After overcoming Crawford in that five set final of 1933, and holding back the American Wilmer Allison 8-6 in the fifth set of the 1934 final, Perry stopped Don Budge, 2-6, 6-2, 8-6, 1-6, 10-8, for the 1936 American Championship title.

The triumph over Budge transcended pride. Perry knew he would be turning professional after the tournament but the offer would be larger if he beat Budge. He led two sets to one and was prepared to start serving the first game of the fourth set when the umpire announced a ten-minute intermission. Perry remembered that the match had already been stopped once, and he did not want to take another break. Incensed, believing—probably erroneously—that the American officials were trying to give an advantage to a tiring Budge, Perry was disconcerted throughout the fourth set.

At 5-3 in the fifth, Budge served for the match (with new balls) but double faulted that critical game away. Perry collected three games in a row and served for the match himself at 6-5. Budge drove four blazing winners past Perry to break back for 6-6. The Englishman went on to another break for 9-8 and served out the match. He was ready to leave his amateur days behind him and he signed a large contract to become a professional. Perry would be touring in 1937 with his old rival from the United States, Ellsworth Vines.

Vines had been playing professional tennis

see, they had never really seen an Englishman of this era who didn't like to lose. I freely admit I wasn't a good loser: I didn't go out there to lose and it hurt me very much if I did. I was confident and I was arrogant, because in one-to-one confrontations like boxing and tennis you have to be."

since the start of the 1934 season. In his rookie year, Vines bested Tilden 47-26 in their seventy-three-match series. He celebrated his twenty-third birthday late in that season. Tilden was forty-one. The younger man was too potent and agile for the aging champion. The following year, Vines won the most matches on a tour with Tilden, Lester Stoefen, Bruce Barnes, and other players. Vines was the winner over Tilden and other rivals again in 1936. He was familiar with the debilitating lifestyle of professional tennis.

So a rivalry which had begun much earlier in the decade was ready to resume in a grueling series of battles fought across the United States. Two of the game's authentic champions—men who had played the game in the best-known settings from Roland Garros to Wimbledon to Forest Hills—were competing again under very different circumstances.

Appropriately, the first Perry-Vines match on their 1937 tour took place in the noisy arena of Madison Square Garden in New York City.

THE MATCH

On a cold evening in January 1937, Vines welcomed Perry to pro tennis before a record crowd of 17,630. The highest priced tickets sold for $9.90 as the fans paid more than $58,000 at the gate, an unsurpassed figure at the time. The American audience was eager to witness the Englishman's transition after he had left behind an enviable record in the amateur game. Since both men would be in direct combat all through a long season, it was an important opportunity to gain a psychological edge with a victory in New York.

The first set was pivotal. With Vines serving his customary cannonballs and blasting away forcefully off the forehand, little separated the two players at the outset. They both wanted to get on the board in the opening set of this best-of-five-set confrontation. Perry was showing his innate capacity to take the ball on the rise,

---

The toughest testing ground was a string of one-nighters.

---

whipping his continental forehand into the corners, neutralizing Vines's power as often as possible.

Vines kept firing away with his powerful shots. They were on level ground until 5-5. Perry proceeded to raise his game a small yet significant notch to take the last two games for the set. He attacked Vines's second serve, moved easily around the court, and played the big points with assurance.

Vines gathered his game admirably in the second set, getting an early break, serving better than he would at any other stage of the match. He was clearly a confident man, going for his points more freely, picking on Perry's backhand with persistence. Vines collected that 6-3 set without much difficulty, and at one set all he looked capable of finishing the job.

Perry was not buying that perception. He was fitter and fresher. The British player found the range off his forehand again, seldom allowed Vines to break down his backhand, and was sound and thoughtful in the forecourt. He took the third set, 6-3, with some superb returning at the end, and effective attacking on serve. Perry had a two sets to one lead. He liked his chances.

At the start of the fourth, Vines tried desperately to even the match. He held serve commandingly and made Perry work harder on his own delivery. Vines played perhaps his highest quality tennis of the match.

It was not enough. Perry was too competitive a player to allow Vines back into the match. Stubbornly, Perry pushed on with his all-court tactics, keeping Vines at bay, maintaining his momentum. With two confident service games at the end, Perry closed it out in style, defeating Vines, 7-5, 3-6, 6-3, 6-4.

Allison Danzig wrote in *The New York Times*, "Perry concentrated throughout on Vines's backhand and it was the vulnerability of the American there that hastened his downfall. Once the weakness was exposed, Perry attacked it incessantly, and in the fourth set Vines' backhand crumpled. The victor

---

A long run that might have gone either way.

---

played a beautiful match in which attack and defense were skillfully blended. He could stay back and trade drives with Vines in magnificent rallies, waiting for an error or the winning opening, or he could go to the net and put away his volley with all the dispatch of Vines. Perry's handling of Vines's service, too, was a vital factor. He not only got the ball in play but scored outright winners with deftly shaded passing shots straight down or across court from the backhand. Those returns had Vines shaking his head in discouragement."

Perry had struck the first telling blow, but there was much in store for both players in their 1937 campaign.

EPILOGUE

In the end, Perry and Vines played a total of sixty-one times that season. Perry had taken a 3-0 lead when he backed up his New York triumph with wins in Cleveland and Chicago. Vines then went into the hospital with nervous exhaustion. Tilden took his place for a while. When the Californian returned, he gained the upper hand and came out on top 32-29. The matches were played mostly in the United States, but they expanded their series into England and Canada to give it international credibility.

As Perry observed in his autobiography, "I quickly discovered the professional life was far different from the one I had been used to. Now I was pitched into a fast and furious way of living. In the winter we travelled everywhere by train and when the weather got better we went by car for greater convenience. There were usually four or five hundred miles between stops, which made the travelling hectic and complicated."

The stress on both players was considerable. They would play a singles match at approximately 7:30 in the evening. In the big cities like New York, Los Angeles, Boston, and San Francisco, they would play best-of-five sets while they settled for best-of-three in smaller settings. They would follow with a doubles match, then race for the train that would take them to the next destination.

The players frequently had no time to shower before they departed, and they had no time to eat or find the refreshments they needed. They would arrive in the next town the following morning, go straight to their hotel, and meet with reporters who would ask the same questions over and over again. They would go back to their rooms to get some sleep, waking at 4 P.M. in time to have a meal. By 6 P.M., they were off to rival radio stations to give their tour crucial publicity. And so it went.

They played on every conceivable kind of surface and setting, indoors and out, on slow and fast courts. Sometimes when they competed in school gymnasiums, the baseline had to be moved in a few inches. Perry remembered standing with his back against the gymnasium wall and pushing off as he maneuvered to make his return of serve. Once, they even appeared in New York's majestic Yankee Stadium, with a court marked out between first and second bases.

An enduring friendship formed on and off the court.

After their 1937 tour was over, Vines and Perry pooled their resources and bought into the Beverly Hills Tennis Club with the money they had made from their series. It was an exclusive club then with only 125 members and six courts, along with a modest clubhouse. Perry and Vines altered the layout, added a swimming pool, and modernized it in many ways.

In that time, as business partners, they socialized with people like Errol Flynn, David Niven, Charlie Chaplin, and the Marx Brothers. After they had finished with their alterations

and were ready to operate, Perry and Vines played a doubles exhibition. Perry and Chaplin faced Vines and Groucho Marx. Chaplin walked on court carrying an enormous number of rackets and a large suitcase. When he opened the suitcase, Groucho Marx emerged. The crowd erupted in uproarious laughter.

Perry and Vines remained business partners in this enterprise until the 1950s, and were friends for life. They also took ownership of the professional tennis tour in 1938. Vines was then following his passion for golf and taking time to qualify for events in that sport. Nevertheless, Vines beat Perry, 48-35, in a 1938 series. In 1939, Budge—the new pro—stopped Vines, 21-18, and handled Perry, 18-11. As late as 1942, when he was thirty-three, Perry competed in professional tennis against a variety of opponents. Vines had withdrawn by then.

Perry passed away in 1995 at eighty-five. Eleven years earlier, Wimbledon had accorded him their highest honor, erecting a Fred Perry statue just inside the grounds of the All England Club. He was deeply touched by the gesture, posing proudly for pictures with friends in front of the statue, accepting the accolade with grace and humility. Vines died at eighty-two in 1994. They were two of the game's trailblazers. They were among the best ever to play the game, and their time on the road together provided a bright and memorable chapter in professional tennis history. •

DON BUDGE VS. BARON GOTTFRIED VON CRAMM

DAVIS CUP, WIMBLEDON, JULY 20, 1937

Perhaps the best of all Davis Cup matches pitted a German nobleman against America's most Promethean shotmaker.

PROLOGUE

When the United States took on the Germans in the Interzone Final of 1937, the Davis Cup was a team competition of mounting prestige all around the world. But the Americans were particularly determined to win that year because they had not triumphed since Bill Tilden's teams had won every year from 1920-26. Now, eleven years later, John Donald Budge considered the return of the Cup as his mission. Budge was twenty-two, nearing his absolute prime, and playing tennis with such uninhibited confidence that only a scant few could stay with him when he was anywhere near the top of his game.

Budge had grown up in Oakland, California, and was a superb athlete who played all the popular team sports, including baseball and basketball. His father had been a professional soccer star in Scotland, but moved to California because of respiratory illnesses. Don preferred baseball as a boy, and paid little attention to tennis until he was thirteen. His brother, Lloyd, was playing on the tennis team at the University of California at that time and

persuaded him to take tennis seriously. Red-haired and fleet of foot, Budge developed a complete game that was built around his magnificent backhand, the best the game had yet seen. Trained by renowned teaching pro Tom Stow, Budge struck his backhand so forcefully that he made the stroke his most formidable weapon. He came over the ball with a shade of topspin, producing a sweeping follow through, spreading apprehension among his opponents with the power and accuracy of his shot. By the end of the century, many students of the game still rated the Budge backhand as the best in history. He also served with velocity and deception, volleyed effectively, and with Stow's help he remodeled his forehand and made it dependable.

Only weeks before this infamous 1937 cup showdown, Budge had won the tournament at Wimbledon with extraordinary ease, capturing the first Grand Slam singles championship of his career. In 1936, still developing his game, Budge had been beaten in a four-set semifinal by Fred Perry on Centre Court. Perry then ousted Cramm by the barely credible scores of 6-1, 6-1, 6-0 to take his third Wimbledon in a row, and his second straight final from the German. Later that summer, Perry narrowly defeated Budge in a five-set U.S. Championship final, and then turned professional.

With Perry out of the picture, Budge had a clear path at Wimbledon in 1937, and he took it. Conceding only a single set on his way to the final, Budge confronted Gottfried von Cramm in the championship match and the top-seeded American halted the No. 2 seed from Germany, 6-3, 6-4, 6-2. Coming off that uplifting victory, Budge was eager to demonstrate his prowess again when he returned to the scene of his triumph to face Cramm in the Davis Cup faceoff. The German had been around the upper crust of tennis much longer than Budge. He was Baron Gottfried von Cramm in Germany, a scion of an aristocratic Prussian family. Cramm was one of seven sons of a Hanover nobleman who introduced him to the game on their own tennis court.

By the time he was twenty-eight, he was a shrewd veteran who had captured the French Championships twice. In the 1934 final, he had beaten Jack Crawford in a hard-fought, five-set final, and in 1936 he stopped Perry 6-0 in the fifth set of their championship match. The Baron had not appeared in three consecutive

---

The motivating power of the Davis Cup was patriotism.

Wimbledon finals without great talent. He excelled off the ground and had a reliable return of serve off both sides, but his record in Paris proved that he preferred slower courts where he could orchestrate points deliberately and more easily exploit his tactical acumen. In any event, he knew he would need to play the

match of his life to beat Budge in this Davis Cup encounter. They were back on the same grass courts where they had met weeks before, and he had posed few serious problems for Budge on that occasion.

THE MATCH

The circumstances surrounding this contest were intriguing on a number of levels. There was no more patriotic endeavor in tennis than representing your nation in the Davis Cup, and yet the contradictions and complexities of the experience were troublesome. The coach of the German team was none other than "Big Bill" Tilden, the same man who had performed so nobly for the United States from 1920-30. Now, only seven years later, Tilden was using his peerless knowledge of the game to help another country defeat his own nation. Surely, although he never acknowledged it, Budge was apprehensive about what Tilden would advise Cramm to do this time.

Meanwhile, on the morning of the match, Budge left tickets at the gate for the popular American comedian Jack Benny and columnist Ed Sullivan, at the request of motion picture star Paul Lukas. When Budge took care of that favor, he had no way of knowing just how important his meeting with Cramm would be. The United States was leading Germany 2-1 in the best-of-five-match series, and Bitsy Grant was opening the final day's program against Henner Henkel. If Grant could prevail—not an unreasonable supposition—Budge's battle with Cramm would be nothing more than a "dead rubber" (having no effect). But Henkel had come through to bring Germany back to 2-2, placing

Don Budge and Baron Gottfried Von Cramm

immense pressure on Budge and Cramm and rewriting the drama's climax.

The elegant German was on his way out of the locker room when he was suddenly summoned back by chief of protocol Ted Tinling, a man best known as the premier women's tennis dress designer of his time. Tinling would make his presence known in many capacities during the century. He umpired for Suzanne Lenglen as a teenager. As a player of modest stature, he competed against both Bill Tilden and Lew Hoad. He designed wedding dresses for Maureen Connolly and Chris Evert. And, late in his life, he worked tirelessly behind the scenes as a voice of reason between players and administrators at all of the major tournaments.

Tinling was aware that someone was on the telephone asking to talk with Cramm, but the Englishman did not want to hold up the proceedings. He admonished the German to hurry. "Come on, you can't keep Queen Mary waiting." The Baron followed his own instincts and told Tinling he had better take the call. "It might be an emergency," said the German.

While Tinling and Budge stood within hearing distance of Cramm's telephone conversation, they did not have a clue who was at the other end. When Cramm concluded the brief conversation and gathered his belongings, he told Tinling and Budge in an understated manner. "It was Hitler," Baron von Cramm, who was known to have no sympathy for the Nazis, said. "He wanted to wish me luck." That was as much information as Cramm wanted to volunteer. But half a century later, Budge speculated, "Hitler was apparently telling Cramm that they had had enough of the Americans winning everything in the Olympics over there. They were hoping—and Hitler was hoping—that Cramm could beat me and bring the Cup back to Germany."

And so the battle began. The American broke the German to establish a 5-4 first set lead and served for the set in the tenth game. Budge connected with four consecutive first serves, directing each one of them deep into the box,

figuring he could force Cramm into either weak responses or errors. The Baron was in no mood to follow that script. He produced four straight dazzling return winners. Having performed that significant feat, Cramm carried on and seized the first set 8-6 with another service break in the fourteenth game.

The pattern of the second set was very similar. Budge went up a break again but could not hold the lead. Later, serving at 5-6, Budge bolted to a 40-0 lead, but that game slipped inexplicably from his grasp. The set went to the German, 7-5, and the American was in a deep deficit, down two sets to love. But rather than dwell on his losing predicament, Budge was fueled by an inner anger he refused to reveal to the Centre Court audience, or to his concentrated opponent. Finding the range off his backhand, serving with more authority, cutting down considerably on his errors, Budge took the third set, 6-4, earning a much appreciated ten-minute rest period in the locker room. After that reprieve, it was apparent that the man from the United States was on his way to a

Hitler loomed in the background for both players.

comeback, while the self-assured ease of his opponent seemed to erode.

The German had served with more penetration and precision than Budge over the first two sets, but no longer. Budge broke at love in the first game of the fourth, broke once more to reach 3-0, and glided through the set 6-2 to reach a fifth set. He would recall later, "Cramm always said that anytime he got anyone into a fifth set, he felt he had a 3 to 1 advantage over them because of his physical condition, and because he had won so many five set matches without any losses."

Balancing that set of facts was this: Budge was gaining confidence as he began the fifth set. The ten-minute break after the third had given him time to rest and reassess his plans. But Cramm was also ready at the start of that final set, and with his piercing service returns doing

A struggle that went beyond skill and stamina.

the damage again, he took a commanding 4-1 lead. At courtside, Tilden was delighted with Cramm's progress, and was confident that the German had the momentum and the shotmaking to close out the contest in style. Tilden— ever the showman—turned around from his seat and flashed a victory sign at Henner Henkel, who was seated just a few rows behind Lukas, Benny, and Sullivan. Incensed by what he considered Tilden's inexcusably poor taste, Sullivan had to be restained by Benny and Lukas from going after Tilden and throwing a punch. Through it all, Tilden smiled smugly, seemingly delighted to arouse the wrath of Sullivan and others. But Budge knew he was not beaten.

"I held my serve for 2-4," he said decades later, "and then when Cramm was serving in the seventh game I said to myself, 'I'm getting a little of the worst of it from the baseline so if he misses his first serve, I'm going to take the second serve and go into the net behind my return.' I played inside the baseline to receive his serve so I had a good head start. Fortunately for me, he missed his four first serves by inches and I was able to take his second serve and make good, deep approach shots

to set up winning volleys. So I broke his serve and now it was 3-4 and I was serving."

Budge had correctly sensed the right game plan. While it was true that he needed some luck as Cramm missed that succession of first serves by the slimmest of margins, Budge had shrewdly calculated that Cramm's high-kicking second serve was vulnerable. The kicker bothered many players with weak backhands, but here Budge had the opportunity to exploit fully his aggressive shot off that side. He took all the returns on the rise—negating the effectiveness of the kick serve—and was on his way back into the match.

Budge held for 4-4, and then twice served to save the match at 4-5 and 5-6. Had he wavered in the least in either of those games, Cramm would surely have had him. But Budge was typically assertive when it counted. At 6-6, he broke Cramm to take a 7-6 lead. In the following game, it was Cramm who made a last, heroic stand. He saved four match points, but Budge came through on the fifth with an astonishing winner. The American raced to his right for a wide forehand on the dead run, cognizant that Cramm was in a strong position at the net. The instant before he made contact with the ball, Budge realized he would be unable to stop himself from toppling to the turf. As he looked up after falling on the grass court, he could not judge where his shot had landed. He was informed by the wild reaction from the crowd. Budge got up, and scrambled to the net to greet a sportsman of the highest standards. "Don," said Cramm, "this was absolutely the finest match I have ever played in my life. I'm very happy that I could have played it against you, whom I like so much." Budge had triumphed, 6-8, 5-7, 6-4, 6-2, 8-6.

That both men played brilliantly is validated by the statistics: Cramm made 105 placements and only sixty-five errors, while Budge had 115 placements and only fifty-five errors. Budge served nineteen aces, Cramm seventeen.

When the long and exhausting confrontation was over, Budge had carried the United States into the Challenge Round to face and eventually defeat the British. Budge was greeted in the locker room by Jack Benny. "He thanked me for the tickets," Budge remembers, "but he did it in a very lukewarm way. He said, 'Thanks a lot Don, I appreciate your getting me the tickets today. It was a nice win.'"

Budge was disconcerted by Benny's indifference. But three months later—when Budge was playing the Pacific Southwest Championships in Los Angeles—Benny approached Budge effusively, congratulating him again for the great Davis Cup triumph over Cramm. Budge was delighted by Benny's belated reaction, but also baffled.

"Jack, you weren't this enthusiastic right after you saw the match. How come you are so much more animated now?" Budge had asked. "He told me that my match with Cramm was the first he had ever seen and that since then he had seen a lot of tennis matches which were terrible by comparison."

Budge places that victory in a category of its own among his most cherished moments. "It was the best and most important match that I ever played," Budge said when he was in his seventies. "Coming right after I had beaten Gottfried at Wimbledon in the final of the tournament in straight sets, we were trying as hard as we could to win the Davis Cup, which the

U.S. had not done for a period of eleven years. So it was not only a personal thing but also a matter of helping my country win the Davis Cup which meant so much to me."

When putting things in perspective, winning is a good place to begin.

Asked in 1987 if he might have suffered some long-term psychological damage if he had not managed to overcome Gottfried von Cramm in their monumental battle, Budge replied, "I don't think so. I still think I would have won the Grand Slam the next year, but who knows? Maybe I wouldn't have. I just don't think the loss of one match—even one as important as this—would have hurt me that much. If you took one point away and gave it to Cramm, he would have been the winner. So one point one way or the other isn't going to kill you. Once a match is over, it shouldn't cloud the rest of your career."

EPILOGUE

The following year, Budge became the first tennis player ever to sweep the four major championships and record a "Grand Slam"—a description used by Allison Danzig, the distinguished tennis analyst.

At the end of 1937, former U.S. champion, (and Tilden rival) "Little Bill" Johnston had invited Budge to lunch in California, hoping to persuade him to turn professional while his earning power was substantial. He had received offers in the range of $50,000 to play pro tennis, and that was an exorbitant sum in those days. Johnston feared that Budge might seriously injure himself and lose financial security by remaining an amateur for the 1938 season.

"It was damned nice of Billy to give me his advice," said Budge in 1998. "But I told him I was going to take a chance and try to become the first to win the four major championships in one year. No one had ever done that so I felt I would be worth more to any promoter if I achieved a Grand Slam."

Budge was rewarded in many ways for his bold thinking. From the outset, his all-consuming quest for a Grand Slam fell neatly into place. Cramm, the player who would surely have been his worthiest adversary, was detained by the Nazis in Germany, and beset by personal problems. Perry and Ellsworth Vines were playing one-night stands on the pro tour, and were ineligible for the four major championships. No one else had the talent or the temerity to test Budge comprehensively. The determined American had good reason to expect success.

Budge did have one serious problem—his health. In 1998 on the sixtieth anniversary of his golden season, he said, "That year my health was at its worst. I lost my voice in the finals of

---

Pulling a tooth cleared the way
for a Grand Slam.

---

the Australian. Then I had diarrhea during the whole French Championships in Paris and had to have sandwiches brought to the court for me during my matches. At Wimbledon, I lost my voice again. So not long before the U.S. Nationals at Forest Hills, I went to a dentist in New York and he discovered that I had an abscessed tooth which had been bugging my whole system. He gave me a shot of penicillin and yanked the tooth and at Forest Hills I was stronger again."

The record shows that Budge was so much better than his peers in amateur tennis that even his struggle to stay well did not hinder him significantly. In the opening Grand Slam event at the Australian Championships, he lost only one set in the entire tournament, dropping the opening set to the Australian Adrian Quist but winning easily from there in four. At the French Championships, he had his only five set Grand Slam match of the year, but he produced his best to take the final set, 6-1, against Franjo Kukuljevic of Yugoslavia. He conceded no more sets in winning that tournament.

On the grass at Wimbledon, back at the same hallowed site where he had won the tournament the year before and where he had overcome Baron von Cramm in their classic encounter, Budge did not drop a set. He then completed his cycle through the majors by winning Forest Hills again at the cost of only a single set—to his doubles partner Gene Mako. Budge had too much versatility and firepower for his friend and he stopped Mako, 6-3, 6-8, 6-2, 6-1.

Reflecting on his 1938 sweep of the majors six decades later, Budge was relieved and appreciative that he had managed his mission so smoothly despite feeling below par for most of the season. "I was lucky as hell to get through that year doing that well, not knowing I needed to get the poison tooth out of my body. It is amazing as I look back because the only final that lasted over an hour was the one with Mako at Forest Hills. I beat John Bromwich in a 57-minute Australian final, defeated Roderich Menzel in 58 minutes in the French final, and although rain delayed my Wimbledon final with Bunny Austin, the playing time was still under an hour. Gene Mako knew my game and was playing very well at the time, so that final was a tougher test for me."

In the fall of 1938, about a month after his Forest Hills triumph gave him the Grand Slam, Budge did turn professional, signing for approximately twice what he had originally been offered a year earlier. He had nothing left to interest him in amateur tennis and had won the last six major championships in a row, dating back to Wimbledon in 1937. In those two years, he had suffered only three defeats.

Budge maintained his momentum when he started his professional career and toppled the best players in admirable fashion. From 1939 through 1942, he was the best in the business, defeating Vines, 21-18, in their 1939 series and handling Perry, 18-11, in their battles contested the same year. In 1941, he crushed an aging Tilden fifty-one matches to seven, and in 1942 he won fifty-four of seventy-two matches in a round-robin tour against the likes of Bobby Riggs, Frank Kovacs, and Fred Perry. Budge was on top of the world. As he said recently, "I was the amateur champion for two years and then the pro champion for many years after that. There was no one who could beat me. Just think of how many more Wimbledons I could have won?" Immodest perhaps, but true.

As for Cramm, he survived his difficulties at home and continued competing on a high level for a long while. He had lost the 1937 U.S. Championship final to Budge two months after their historic Davis Cup duel. Then he reached the final of the Australian Championships in doubles with Henkel early in 1938, but his political problems escalated. Refusing to show sympathy for the Nazi cause, he was sent to

---

Two superb competitors weathered the years with few regrets.

---

prison by the Gestapo that year. After World War II, however, he resumed competition and took the last two of his six German Championship titles in 1948 and 1949. By then, he had turned forty.

Cramm represented Germany in Davis Cup competition as late as 1953 when he was forty-four. He remained formidable in singles and doubles, but was devoting the bulk of his time to being a businessman. He became president of a tennis club in Berlin and earned a good reputation in that role. Not until Boris Becker arrived in the upper echelons of the game as a robust teenager in the 1980s, was there a player of Baron von Cramm's caliber in Germany. He had won fifty-eight of sixty-eight singles matches for Germany in the Davis Cup, had taken two Grand Slam singles titles, won the French and U.S. doubles championships, and reached three consecutive Wimbledon singles finals. He had lived a long and productive life in and around tennis. When he was killed in a 1976 car crash, he was sixty-seven.   •

SARAH PALFREY COOKE VS. PAULINE BETZ

U.S. NATIONAL CHAMPIONSHIPS, FINAL, SEPTEMBER 2, 1945

Four years earlier, these two versatile Americans met on this very court. When World War II finally ended, they once again faced each other for the championship of their country.

PROLOGUE

The first half of the 1940s was a traumatic time in the world at large, and a complicated era in the world of sport. World War II was uppermost in all minds. In tennis, the Australian Championships were not played from 1941-45. The French Championships were canceled from 1940-45. Wimbledon ceased in the same years. It was left to the American Championships to keep international tennis alive. The field consisted predominately of Americans for that stretch, and the players took great satisfaction in reaching the National Championships of the United States. It was the only Grand Slam tournament then, and the ultimate target of every leading player who appeared.

In 1941, the sprightly Sarah Palfrey Cooke came forth to capture her first major singles title with a final-round triumph over countrywoman Pauline Betz. Married then to the renowned American player Elwood Cooke (a Wimbledon doubles titlist), the lady from Boston had been playing in her country's championships since 1928, when she was fifteen. She had been a final-ist in 1934 and 1935, losing both times to Helen Jacobs. Sarah was the fourth of six children. Her socially prominent family lived in Brookline, Massachusetts. All five Palfrey sisters captured at least one national championship.

Seeded second behind Betz in 1941, Sarah toppled the favorite, 7-5, 6-2. A former student of the esteemed Hazel Hotchkiss Wightman, Palfrey Cooke's talent had long been highly visible. In capturing her Forest Hills victory in 1941, she added a newfound boldness to the mix. A well-rounded player with forceful ground strokes and a gift for the volley, she had been beaten by the immensely popular Betz three times earlier in that season before turning the tables in their most significant meeting.

The next three years at Forest Hills belonged exclusively to the self-assured Betz, who grew up in Los Angeles. Her father was a businessman but her mother was a physical education teacher who taught her to play tennis. With Palfrey Cooke competing at Forest Hills only once between 1942 and 1944, Betz was unbeatable at home. Miss Betz was a clutch performer. In 1942, seeded second, she held back third-seeded Margaret Osborne 7-5 in the final

Pauline Betz

ized. Proud of her performance but almost guilty about the verdict, she was conflicted by the experience.

In an article published in *World Tennis*, Betz recalled the remorse she felt. . . "that Helen should lose to a player like me." Gradually, she grew accustomed to competing favorably against the best players in the women's game. She finished second in the United States, behind Palfrey Cooke in 1941, then rose to the top for the next three years. By 1945, Palfrey Cooke was back, and a friendly rivalry resumed.

Sarah had been raised to play top-level tennis. Mrs. Wightman believed unreservedly that Sarah had extraordinary potential. Furthermore, she insisted that Sarah stand up and be counted as a competitor who could prevail under different kinds of pressure. Herbert Warren Wind wrote an entertaining and informative piece about Hazel Wightman in *The New Yorker* magazine. In that account, he told a revealing anecdote about the student and the teacher. Sarah Palfrey—as she was known then—was playing a demanding match on a summer day. Her mother turned to Mrs. Wightman in the stands and told her she was concerned that it was too hot a day for her daughter to be competing.

Hazel Wightman responded, "Sarah can win this match easily if she'll only quash qualms."

Sarah Palfrey did her fair share of quashing,

set, then triumphed against top-seeded Louise Brough, 4-6, 6-1, 6-4, in a fierce final.

The following year, Betz stopped Doris Hart in three tough sets before overcoming Brough again in another three set final. In 1944, collecting her third championship crown in a row, she halted Osborne 6-3, 8-6 in the final. She did not overwhelm the opposition, but found ways instead to wear them down with consistency and concentration.

Betz did not take up tennis until she was fourteen, but made swift and steady advances, reaching the American top ten in 1939 when she was twenty. She moved up to third in the nation the following year when she had her first big win over Helen Jacobs, a player she had idol-

piling up the victories on her own and in partnership with a range of accomplished partners. Between 1930 and 1941, she had won no fewer than nine U.S. National doubles championships with four different partners, including Alice Marble, Helen Jacobs, and Margaret Osborne duPont. She won the U.S. National mixed doubles championships with three of the greatest male players of all time: Fred Perry (1932), Don Budge (1937), and Jack Kramer (1941).

This gracious woman might well have won at least one more time at Forest Hills between 1942 and 1944 if she had appeared. As it was, Betz burst into her own during that time and controlled her country's main tennis event. By 1945, Palfrey Cooke was back to play for the second time since she had beaten Betz in the 1941 final. They would stage an illustrious reunion.

THE MATCH

Palfrey Cooke—seeded second behind Betz—advanced to the final without the loss of a set, defeating fourth-seeded Louis Brough, 6-3, 6-4, in the semifinals. Betz dropped only one set on her way to the title match, ousting No. 8 seed Doris Hart, 6-3, 6-2, in her semifinal.

The gracious women of the tennis court learned to compete.

The final matchup had all the ingredients for suspense and sparkle. Miss Betz had perhaps the best backhand in the women's game, a flowing, flat stroke which rarely let her down. She had greater agility than her opponents, but Palfrey Cooke had a slightly superior forehand and a decidedly better net game. As Betz wrote

in a 1949 book titled, *Wings on My Tennis Shoes,* "I have always found Sarah Palfrey Cooke harder to pass than any of the others, as her anticipation is such that she is usually waiting at the right spot. Although her volley has not the great power of Brough or Hart, her angles and touch-stop volleys have always been equally effective."

Mrs. Cooke started auspiciously, creating a 3-1 lead with her forcing, flat forehand neutralizing Betz's outstanding backhand. The 1941 titlist was setting the agenda. Betz responded by sweeping five games in a row for the set. Palfrey Cooke was broken twice in that span as Betz sprinkled the court with placements delivered effortlessly from her left side. The top seed had pulled in front persuasively.

Palfrey Cooke answered firmly in the second. She reassembled her game creatively to reach 5-2, and served for the set in the ninth game, but Betz halted her again, rallying to 5-5. Palfrey Cooke was not swayed by her opponent's stubborness. She kept advancing to control play from the forecourt. Holding for 6-5 and then 7-6, she sealed the second set with another break in the fourteenth game as the Betz comeback was stymied.

The fluctuating fortunes of both players continued. Betz was grimly resolved to take the title. She needed to avenge her defeat in the 1941 final and subsequent losses at the National Clay Court Championships and on the grass courts of Rye, New York. She wanted a fourth U.S. National Championship in a row. She had believed that nerves had cost her the 1941 final, writing in her memoir, "When I walked out before a packed stadium to face Sarah Cooke, I wished myself anywhere else in the world—or out of it. I mumbled to myself throughout the

Sarah Palfrey Cooke

contact solidly with her volley. It sailed over the baseline. Palfrey Cooke was champion of the United States for the second time, a 3-6, 8-6, 6-4 winner over Betz.

"In a beautifully fought battle that had the 10,000 spectators in a state of breathless excitement," wrote Allison Danzig in *The New York Times*, "with the outcome in doubt to the last stroke, Mrs. Cooke rose to her most shining moments when her fortunes seemed to be ebbing fast, to snatch victory from a valiant rival through the sheer brilliance and enterprise of her attack."

Elaborating later in his report on the reasons why Mrs. Cooke succeeded, Danzig said, "Mrs. Cooke won because she had the better game and because she played it to the hilt when anything short of her best would have been inadequate in the final stages. There was purpose and calculation in her every stroke and she had the weapons to profit by the openings her strategy effected. With all her attributes, Mrs. Cooke had to play the finest tennis she has shown in years to overcome Miss Betz's magnificent resistance. The new champion's performance was almost perfection in the last three games. Her ground strokes were infallible and she hit so deep and at such angles that she had her rival running frantically after the ball."

7-5, 6-2 match about the fiendish wind and the way it blew all my shots out and how it stopped blowing whenever Sarah hit a ball. I had a bad case of centre-court jitters and Sarah wouldn't cooperate to the extent of missing a few shots and letting me gain some confidence."

Four years later, in this absorbing 1945 reprise, Betz was an improved version of herself. The top seed moved ahead by a break in the final set, serving at 4-3. If she could hold twice more from there, the championship would stay within her grasp.

Mrs. Cooke knew as she changed ends for the eighth game of the third set that she would need to break back at once. She did just that, then held for 5-4. The burden had shifted back to Betz, who was serving to save the match in the tenth game. She found herself down 15-40, double match point. Having been the victim of too many punishing volleys from Palfrery Cooke, Betz came forward herself, and made

EPILOGUE

Returning to married life, Palfrey Cooke moved into semiretirement in 1946. With her congenial but toughest opponent stepping aside, Betz had her best year. She lost only four times in twelve tournaments, and won both Wimbledon and Forest Hills. After reaching the final of Wimbledon in her lone visit to the All England Club, she woke up with a head cold and sore throat. A doctor gave her penicillin to fight the infection.

Betz was still bothered by an overwhelming anxiety which had gripped her since the night before her final against Louise Brough. She was picked up by a limousine that morning for the trip to Wimbledon, her tension exacerbated by sharing the ride with her opponent. Betz remembered feeling like "an unhappy goldfish" moments after walking on to Centre Court to play for the championship she coveted above all others.

Gradually, she found her emotional footing. Breaking twice in the first set, controlling the tempo in the second, Betz beat Brough 6-2, 6-4 to win Wimbledon. She later recalled, "It took me a few days to come out of a state of semi-shock and realize that I had won the championship I had dreamed about since I first picked up a racket. Until I had actually won Wimbledon, tennis had been my goal in life and motivating force. But following the championship I had a feeling of completion, and never again was to feel the same eagerness and enthusiasm for tournament tennis."

Despite those sentiments, Betz managed to reach her sixth consecutive U.S. Championship final (setting a female record which she shares with Chris Evert) and won the tournament for the fourth time with an 11-9, 6-3 win over a still-emerging Hart. Betz was twenty-seven, on top of her game, and ahead of the world competition—a woman who had realized her ambitions.

In the winter of 1947, Betz traveled to the Riviera for some tournaments in the sun. Before leaving on that trip, she had spoken with Palfrey Cooke during The National Indoor Championships in New York. They talked about the notion

---

An era when playing for money was unacceptable.

---

of playing on a professional tour against each other. Elwood Cooke said he would survey clubs across the country for a reaction to the idea. He told his wife and Betz that he would send out letters to the clubs to get their responses.

Now, a month or two later, while she was out of the country playing in amateur events, Betz was receiving cablegrams from the United States Lawn Tennis Association. They were up in arms about the mere idea of Betz and Palfrey Cooke playing professional tennis. In essense, the USLTA was claiming Betz was a professional because she was simply exploring the possibility of playing for money.

Betz was besieged by queries from reporters in New York, London, and Paris. They all told her she had been declared a professional. She soon discovered that she and Palfrey Cooke had been suspended by the USLTA from amateur competition. That meant the two leading American players—arguably the two best in the world—would be barred from Wimbledon and Forest Hills. Betz would not be able to defend her cherished Wimbledon crown. Both players were told there would be no hearing on the matter until after Wimbledon and Forest Hills were over.

Betz recalled, "Several New York papers had me bursting into tears as I received the news, but it actually affected me very little, though I did think I had been struck a low blow. I would like to have defended my Wimbledon title, but I didn't think that any future grandchildren would care whether Grandma had won the United States Championships four or five times."

A week or so later, Betz received a phone call from Sarah Palfrey Cooke, who told her that she wanted to proceed with a pro tour. Betz thought it over and ultimately agreed with her friend that they should give it a go. There were, however, snags as they staged their series of matches during 1947. They

Setting the stage for women's professional tennis.

would be slated to play each other somewhere in California, and discover they were supposed to be competing in Texas on the same evening. They had not anticipated the complexities of playing one-night stands after careers filled with week long (or at least weekend) tournaments.

Those problems were confronted and the wrinkles ironed out over time. Sometimes Betz and Palfrey Cooke would play for a guaranteed sum of money. The standard was $350 for a weekday and $500 for a Saturday or Sunday match. In other instances, they would play for a

certain percentage of the gate, often 60 percent. They traveled everywhere by car. They competed frequently at schools and colleges. There was no accurate record kept of their numerous contests, but both women were delighted by the opportunity to be paid for their talent on the tennis court.

Two years later, Betz married sportswriter Bob Addie. She played one more pro tour in 1951 against "Gorgeous Gussie" Moran. That same year, her old rival—long divorced from Elwood Cooke—married New York communications executive Jerome Danzig (not related to the writer Allison Danzig). She lived the rest of her life with him in New York and worked from 1965 until 1991 as an advertising representative for *World Tennis*. She passed away in 1996 at eighty-three.

For much of that time—before a hip operation forced her away from the courts—Sarah Palfrey Danzig arranged a regular Tuesday doubles game in New York with clients from the advertising community. It became known around town as "Sarah's Game," and everybody who was anybody in that world wanted to play. Sarah would regale her friends and business associates with tales of playing "customer tennis" with people who were pleased to share a court with a champion.

When friends would ask her to name the best tennis match she had ever played, she always answered, "My match with Pauline Betz at Forest Hills in 1945. I played as well as I could have played, and Pauline was terrific. It was a great match for both of us."   •

JACK KRAMER VS. DON BUDGE

U.S. PRO CHAMPIONSHIPS, FOREST HILLS, JUNE 19, 1948

A remarkable contest between the dominant player of the 1930s, and the leading competitor of the 1940s. The quality of world tennis had been lifted by both men in different times.

PROLOGUE

As a boy growing up in Las Vegas, Nevada, long before he moved with his family to California during his high school years, Jack Kramer was the quintessential all-American kid. He played baseball, football, and basketball. His father was a senior engineer for the Union Pacific Railroad. As a seven-year-old, Jack had seven mitts, a catcher's mask, and a wide collection of bats and balls. He did not turn to tennis until he was thirteen. He had broken his nose and separated his ribs in accidents suffered on the football field. Kramer's mother decided she would not stand by any longer while Jack came home bruised and battered from contact sports. She purchased a second-hand tennis racket and gave it to her embarrassed son who pleaded with her not to let his friends know what she had done. He had the same mistaken notion that many other young Americans harbored at that time—that tennis was simply a game for sissies. He did not want to be humiliated by his buddies.

But in the fall of 1934, when he was thirteen, Kramer's family moved to San Bernardino, California, and in that community tennis was popular and highly regarded. In the new environment, Kramer came to love the game and started playing it regularly. He devoted himself enthusiastically to junior tournaments, and won the National Boys' 15 Championships in 1936. Two years later, in 1938, he captured the National Interscholastic Championships. He was on his way to the top tier of tennis, and he knew it.

By 1943, Kramer was polished enough as a player to reach the final of the U.S. National Championships at Forest Hills. Kramer lost to Lieutenant Joe Hunt, a fighter pilot who subsequently gave his life in combat during World War II. Kramer had joined the Coast Guard, but by the beginning of 1946 had been discharged and he returned with overwhelming zest and ambition to amateur tennis. From the early stages of 1946 through the 1947 season, he was nearly invincible. The only match of consequence he lost in that stretch was to the Czechoslovakian left-hander Jaroslav Drobny, in the round of sixteen at Wimbledon in 1946, bowing 2-6, 17-15, 6-3, 3-6, 6-3. Blisters contributed to his defeat, but he made no complaints.

Later that year, Kramer was triumphant at

Jack Kramer

Forest Hills, halting countryman Tom Brown in a straight set final to take the United States Championship. The following year, he seized the two most prestigious championships, making the summer of 1947 particularly meaningful. At Wimbledon, he swept through seven matches and lost only thirty-seven games, routing Tom Brown, 6-1, 6-3, 6-2, in the final.

Coming home to defend his title at Forest Hills, he confronted another American, Frank Parker, in a hard-fought final. Kramer was down two sets to love, but he played his way out of near defeat and prevailed in five sets.

That triumph coupled with his Wimbledon victory was crucial for Kramer. It set the stage for him to turn professional. As he said in 1997 on the fiftieth anniversary of his triumph on Centre Court, "I guess I was the first one to win Wimbledon playing in shorts. I enjoyed visiting with the king and queen, and it was a wonderful afternoon for me when I won Wimbledon. I am sorry I never had another chance to have that exhilarating feeling of standing up in the Royal Box in the post-match ceremony. They later moved it down to the Centre Court itself. But it was quite a thrill for me and it was the most important stepping stone towards the professional career I had in mind for myself."

Having said that, Kramer realized that his value to the pro promoters would be that much larger with Forest Hills added to the package. In 1946-47, Kramer had been beaten only three times, but a fourth defeat in an event of the magnitude of Forest Hills would have tarnished his prestige as a world champion moving confidently into the professional arena. Although Kramer did drop his debut pro tour match against Bobby Riggs, at New York's Madison Square Garden on December 26, 1947, in front of more than fifteen thousand fans, he was not to be denied often in those days.

In his overall tour of one-night showdowns against the crafty Riggs, Kramer came out on top 69-20 during 1947-48. He would dominate the pro game for the next five years against other formidable foes. In the middle of this period, he had his only significant career confrontation against the durable Don Budge. Budge had lost much of his sting by then after a shoulder injury robbed him of essential power on his overhead and serve, but as a proud and disciplined competitor he

---

An injury-hampered Budge takes on the top professional.

---

was determined to keep his high ranking while making some hard-earned money as a professional.

He was thirty-three and Kramer was approaching twenty-seven when they clashed at the U.S. Pro Championships in Forest Hills in the summer of 1948. In 1946 and 1947 while Kramer was wrapping up his amateur career so successfully, Budge was struggling. The Budge who had overwhelmed all of his chief rivals in pro tennis from 1939 to 1942 was gone, and his opponents knew what had happened to his shoulder during the war. Riggs was especially adept at exploiting a wounded adversary, and the guileful American stopped Budge in twenty-three of forty-four matches contested in 1946-47. He lobbed Budge ceaselessly, knowing Don could not hit the overheads effectively.

When he joined Kramer, Riggs, and other professionals on the lawns of Forest Hills in 1948, Budge was anxious to return to the top of his game. The U.S. Pro Championships was the tournament that mattered more than any other to the leading professional players, and a "dream match" developed between the best player of the 1930s and the greatest competitor of the 1940s.

THE MATCH

Budge and Kramer ended up on the same side of the draw. Kramer nearly missed his appointment with his revered rival, surviving despite a less-than-top-of-the-line performance against Welby Van Horn. Kramer astutely explained the importance of his battle with Budge in his 1979 book, *The Game, My 40 Years in Tennis* (with Frank DeFord). After clarifying that winning the U.S. Pro was Budge's one and only chance to get back on top after his losing tour against Riggs, Kramer wrote of his meeting with his fellow American, "It was a great match. Although Don and I are only a few years apart, we never played in the amateurs, and the bond-drive exhibitions we played during the war (when they let amateurs and pros share the same court) were only that—exhibitions. We played later several times, but this match in June of 1948 was really the only time we met under tournament conditions with something on the line. All that was lacking was that only one of us, me, was in his prime."

As Kramer recalled, he was sending his best shot right to Budge's strong side. Kramer's inside-out forehand—hit with biting sidespin and allowing him to take control in the forecourt—was a shot he would not give up, even if it meant going up against a stroke as lethal and overpowering as Budge's backhand. Kramer was the man who had galvanized the game with his style of play. He introduced what was known as the "Big Game," wasting no opportunities to conclude points with telling volleys, rushing the net religiously behind his serve, approaching behind his return whenever possible, avoiding long rallies if he had the chance to force his way in. No one had ever built such a commanding and all-out aggressive approach to match play before.

But Budge presented Kramer with problems. He virtually took away Jack's serve-and-volley game because his returns were so penetrating, and made Kramer wait for the appropriate mid-court ball before coming in. Kramer found himself squandering opportunities after taking the opening set. He wanted a two-sets-to-love lead and pressed hard to achieve it, but Budge was counterattacking magnificently on an oppressively humid afternoon. Budge sealed the long second set, 10-8, by finding the narrow openings to drive the ball past Kramer, and

---

A duel between a peerless volleyer and a top groundstroker.

---

when he pinned his opponent to the baseline Budge had the advantage in prolonged points.

Budge's successful bid to take the long second set inevitably carried him straight through the third and now the underdog led two sets to one. Twice, Budge broke Kramer to establish fourth-set leads, but Kramer replied promptly each time to get back on level terms. Kramer managed a remarkable forehand crosscourt placement at full stretch on the run when Budge led 2-1, deuce. Later, Budge served for a 5-3 lead. If he could hold in that vital game and do it once more after that, Budge would gain a win of major dimensions.

Kramer knew he had no alternative but to take risks that might raise his game, and he did. In the next three games, he won twelve of seventeen points to finish off the set. From then on, Kramer was in control, collecting twenty-four of twenty-five points in the fifth set as Budge faded in the heat. Both men recognized the con-

Don Budge

sequences of their confrontation. Kramer's pride and match playing prowess had prevented Budge from making one last push to the top. Budge had shown his gutsiness for three sets and nearly came through in four, but he did not have the stamina to take it in five. Budge had come agonizingly close to a victory that might have given him another year or two of big-time matches, but he was beaten by a better player in the end—6-4, 8-10, 3-6, 6-4, 6-0.

Kramer would defeat Riggs in a four-set final the next day to claim the U.S. Pro title, and from there he would tour in 1949 and 1950 with a brilliant but still budding Pancho Gonzales. Kramer controlled their match series, 96-27. Considering the era, Kramer made good money for his efforts, taking in $85,000 against Riggs and $72,000 against Gonzales.

In a 1950-51 series, Kramer bested a sprightly Pancho Segura, 64-28, despite Segura's searing two-handed forehand drives and returns. Kramer believed Segura's two-hander was one of the best-ever shots in the history of tennis. In 1953, his final complete year as a professional player, Kramer overcame the Australian Frank Sedgman, 54-41. But Budge was no longer a prime-time player. He played on into the fifties but his skills had been sorely diminished and his legs could not carry him around the court with the alacrity they once provided.

EPILOGUE

Following his distinguished playing years, Kramer took on a wide range of roles in the game. For the next ten years, he was the promoter of the pro tour, signing all the leading amateur players to contracts, lining up locations for the matches, and finding a forum for this small legion of the game's greatest players. Kramer carried on in this capacity until the early 1960s, hoping that "Open Tennis" would arrive soon and allow all of the best players "amateur and professional" to compete on the same courts. Among those who signed contracts with Kramer were the Australian "Whiz Kids," Lew Hoad and Ken Rosewall, and the American star Tony Trabert.

Talking about his time as a professional player and promoter, Kramer said not long ago, "I felt insistent that we should always try to follow the more successful way that golf was promoting itself, adding players to their game, getting courses built, and so forth. So I think the

The evolution of big box-office tennis bore Kramer's mark.

idea of me playing the tour with Riggs and Segura and Gonzales and Sedgman and then becoming the promoter, where I tried to get the best amateur player of each year to play in the pros, sold the game tremendously well, especially in America."

After "Open Tennis" was initiated in 1968, Kramer remained an indispensable figure. He came up with the concept for an international "Grand Prix" of tournaments culminating with The Masters for the top eight players in 1970. That structure for men's tennis remained in place right through the century. In 1972, Kramer was named the first executive director for the Association of Tennis Professionals (ATP), the men's players association. The following year, Kramer and his players stood firmly behind Yugoslav player Nikki Pilic, who had been suspended from Wimbledon by the International Tennis Federation.

Renowned players like Rod Laver, John Newcombe, Stan Smith, and Arthur Ashe boycotted the biggest tournament of them all in protest over Pilic's suspension, which they felt was unjustified. The players were treated harshly by large segments of the British press, but no one was hit harder than Kramer, who was criticized vitriolically. A man of firm convictions and unshakable integrity, Kramer would say more than a decade later, "I was proud of what we did with the boycott. I think it showed something about my character and competitiveness."

Meanwhile, Kramer was the game's keenest analyst on television from the 1950s into the 1970s. He covered fourteen Wimbledons in that period for the BBC, and all but two U.S. Championships between 1952 and 1973 for the three major U.S. networks. After his stint as executive director of the ATP, Kramer served ably on the Men's Tennis Council. He was a first-rate tournament director in his hometown of Los Angeles, and a vital voice of reason behind the scenes. Looking at the major figures in the world of tennis across the twentieth century, no one was as multifaceted as Kramer. No one accomplished as much in so many roles. If there was a "Man of the Century" in tennis, it was surely Jack Kramer.

Budge also remained a fine ambassador for the game. After stretching his career as long and as far as it would go, and reaching his last U.S. Pro final in 1953 against Gonzales at the age of thirty-eight, Budge would be seen at all the major championships, observing the emerging champions, sharing his knowledge of the game, and enjoying the surroundings. As he grew older and became more removed from younger generations of players, very few knew much about his vast accomplishments. Hardly anyone sought his counsel. But John McEnroe did in the early 1980s when he was losing consistently to Ivan Lendl, and Budge was delighted to pass along his views.

"John is the only modern player who ever asked me to talk about anything that was wrong in their game," Budge said in 1998. "I was happy to point out to him what I had noticed, which was that he was giving Lendl too many angles to pass him. I told him to approach the net down the middle and cut those angles off. He began beating Lendl regularly after that."

For his part, Budge learned some vital lessons early in his career that he carried with him unfailingly for the rest of his life. Recalling his early matches with Fred Perry, Budge said, "I didn't know what the game was about until I first played Fred Perry. He dominated the play and I wondered why, until I realized he was taking the ball early on the rise and rushing me off the court. That was when I realized I had to change my game. Once I started taking the ball early and hitting

harder, the game became easy for me because I could jump on everyone."

Budge turned eighty-three in 1998, but still attended the French Open, Wimbledon, and the U.S. Open as the ITF's guest. They honored him on the sixtieth anniversary of his Grand Slam. Remembering Budge's triumphs over the years,

---

The afterlife of champions can also serve the game.

Kramer spoke about how highly he regarded Budge as a player. Asked then where he placed Budge on the historical ladder, Kramer responded, "Don was totally equipped with the best all-around game that we have ever had. I still believe that. I don't know what these young players today would be doing against Don, but if they came in against him Don would knock the ball at their feet or pass them. And he would come in himself on good ground strokes. I still believe he is the best player I ever competed against or saw."

Budge admired Kramer every bit as much. He said, "The players who competed against Kramer would pick him over anyone because he was someone who only volleyed once. In other words, you had to pass him the first time because you didn't get too many shots at him when he was up at the net. He would put that first volley away almost every time. I don't know how I would have done if I had come up against Jack in 1938 when I was going for the Grand Slam. I would have had a hard time against him."

Recalling his compelling 1948 match with Kramer at Forest Hills, Budge confessed, "When you are involved in a match like that you don't always know how good it was, but everyone said it was a great match. I had those two service breaks in the fourth set, but I couldn't put it across. I think I controlled play a little better than Jack did in that match, but he still beat me. He was a great player."

Asked if there is anything he would have done differently in his tennis career, Budge ruminated, "I don't have many regrets, but I wish I could have played when the game went open. We wouldn't have needed the pro tours with one-night matches to make our money. We could have made it by winning tournaments where the prizes amounted to a lot more than playing one-nighters, and people would have been paying a lot more attention to what we were doing."

Most authorities rank Budge and Kramer among the top-ten players of all time, and many place them in the top five. Budge has the more glamorous record because he is one of only two men ever to win the Grand Slam, but Kramer, at his best, was surely the better man. Only on clay could Budge have contained Kramer, but it seems safe to say that Kramer would have had the edge on all of the faster surfaces with his ability to set the tempo and apply pressure relentlessly.

In any event, their Forest Hills battle belongs in a treasure chest as one of the rare gems in tennis history. It was a match that received little recognition because professional tennis was played in such obscurity in those days, but the longer view of history will keep it sharply in focus as long as tennis remains in our field of vision.   •

MAUREEN CONNOLLY VS. DORIS HART

WIMBLEDON, FINAL, JULY 4, 1953

No one could challenge the daunting "Little Mo" more convincingly than the well prepared Doris Hart. This was their most compelling confrontation.

PROLOGUE

During the 1920s and 1930s, Suzanne Lenglen and Helen Wills Moody dominated the world of women's tennis in regal fashion. They seldom lost matches, and their contrasting personalities attracted fervent supporters. Other players of great talent emerged in the late 1930s and through the 1940s. The Californian, Alice Marble—winner of four United States singles championships and one at Wimbledon—was the first pure serve-and-volleyer among the women. Pauline Betz and Sarah Palfrey Cooke had days of triumph in the 1940s.

As the curtain opened on the 1950s, another Californian came onstage. Maureen Connolly was relatively short (5' 4") and somewhat stocky. Her father, who became a lieutenant commander in the U.S. Navy, was an accomplished athlete. He divorced his wife when Maureen was four years old, and she did not see him again until her adult years. Maureen was raised by her aunt and her mother. She learned how to play the piano and went to a ballet class when she was five years old. At the age of nine, she was one of two fine young tennis players competing in her hometown of San Diego, and was so transfixed by the game that she resolved to make it her major extracurricular interest.

Connolly built her game entirely around flat, clean, piercing ground strokes. She drove through the ball in exemplary fashion, getting extraordinary depth on her shots, dictating matches with her sound execution and superior concentration. The fate of her clashes with the opposition was almost always in her hands. She hit very hard, missed very infrequently, and made her rivals work for every point.

Connolly was propelled into top-flight tennis by Eleanor "Teach" Tennant, the same exacting woman who had guided the career of Alice Marble in the late 1930s. Tennant pushed Connolly incessantly. They met when Connolly was twelve and she shaped her student's game for a productive period until they parted ways in 1952 when Maureen was nearly eighteen.

In her autobiography, *Forehand Drive*, Connolly wrote revealingly about her strong-minded instructor. "Tennis, to Teach, was never a game, it was a battle, and no field marshal mapped strategy more carefully. She scouted every formidable opponent I faced and spotted

Maureen Connolly

successful. At sixteen, Connolly became the youngest ever to win the championship of her country. Not until 1979 when Tracy Austin won the U.S. Open was that record broken. Connolly triumphed at Forest Hills in 1951, defeating Doris Hart and Shirley Fry, who were seeded first and second in the event.

She made her first journey to Wimbledon in 1952. She had sadly parted with Tennant, who wanted her to withdraw from the tournament because of an injured shoulder. Two points from defeat in the fourth round against Susan Partridge, Connolly came through 6-3, 5-7, 7-5. She took the title with wins over Fry and Louise Brough, another accomplished American. Then at Forest Hills, Connolly defended her title with repeat victories over Fry and Hart.

strength and weakness with absolute accuracy. She was the field officer, I the troops, and we went into action with deadly purpose and total concentration. If Teach knew the enemy, she also knew me, and how close she might drive me to the breaking point in practice before easing the pressure. . . . Her confidence was a living, glowing thing, without limits, and she had the magic power of being able to transfer it. Lose was not a word in her tennis vocabulary. Teach believed everything in my life should be sublimated to tennis."

That all-embracing dictum was highly

There were high expectations for "Little Mo" in 1953. Appearing in the Australian Championships for the first time, she ousted her doubles partner, Julie Sampson, 6-3, 6-2, on the grass in the final. At the French Championships in Paris, she accounted for Hart, 6-2, 6-4, in the final, thus avenging a loss to the same player weeks before at the Italian Championships. She was at the halfway point in her bid for a Grand Slam, a player of growing stature.

As she set her sights on Wimbledon, she had the wise Australian coach Harry Hopman helping her develop strategy. She was not happy with the caliber of her tennis on the way to the final, but it was good enough to get her there. Connolly conceded only eight games in ten sets contested over five matches. She dismissed the third-seeded Fry, 6-1, 6-1, in the semifinals, but attributed that score to Fry's poor play rather than her own inspiration.

Waiting for the top-seeded Connolly in the title match was Doris Hart, the No. 2 seed and a player of the highest caliber. Hart had a misleadingly frail appearance. As a child, she had suffered from a knee infection that threatened to leave her crippled when she was not yet two years old. A false rumor later circulated that she had battled polio. Because of an error in diagnosis, her infection spread until it was feared she might have gangrene. One specialist recommended that she have her leg amputated. Her father consulted the family doctor, who rejected amputation and performed a minor operation on the Hart kitchen table to drain off the infected fluids. Her ailment actually was osteomyelitis, which prevented her from walking properly until she was three. Doctors believed she would always walk with a limp and the family moved from St. Louis to Florida so that she could swim every day in salt water, which seemed to help. At ten, following her older brother Bud, she took up the game of tennis.

In her twenties, Hart progressed rapidly. She took the Australian Championship singles title in 1949, won Wimbledon in 1951 with a 6-1, 6-0 rout of Fry in the final, and captured the French Championships in 1950 and 1952. In 1951, she was the top-ranked player in the world with Connolly residing one place behind her. She was a formidable all-court competitor who excelled on all surfaces, and a top-notch doubles player who would secure twenty-nine of her thirty-five major championships alongside a range of talented partners in women's and mixed competition.

If anyone was going to deny Connolly the Wimbledon singles title of 1953, it was Doris Hart. She had the experience and the guile to get the job done. She was not apprehensive about playing her illustrious compatriot. She welcomed the challenge.

THE MATCH

At 11:45 on the morning of her final-round match with Hart, Connolly went to Queen's Club to practice. She worked out on an indoor varnished wood court which made the grass seem slow by comparison. Hopman lined up the Australian Davis Cupper Mervyn Rose to practice with "Little Mo."

Both Hopman and Rose stood at the net and punched volleys, sending Connolly from side to side to work on her ground strokes. Connolly then moved up to the net while they fired from the baseline. After that, all three players practiced volleys at close range.

The entire session lasted only half an hour, but Connolly had herself primed for the big occasion. She sat in a hot bathtub for five minutes for relaxation, then went out to Wimbledon. At 1:30—half an hour before the final—she hit for fifteen minutes with another Australian Davis Cupper named Ken Rosewall.

Connolly returned to the locker room and waited in the wings with Hart to be summoned to Centre Court. The players made their much applauded entrance, then started a battle each would call her best. The tennis was wonderful from the outset as both players were bold without making careless mistakes. The two Americans held their serves for the first seven games of the match, giving little away, making the most of their openings.

Serving at 3-4, Hart suffered a wounding double fault and that brief lapse was critical. Connolly gained the break for a 5-3 lead. But the Californian delivered two double faults of her own in the ninth game to allow Hart back into the set. Hart held on for 5-5. With the two women locked in a grinding backcourt battle, they held even. But Hart had to serve to save the set at 5-6. She did so ably.

Connolly was backing up her useful, but not extraordinary, serve with a barrage of forehand and backhand drives. She kept Hart at bay with her power and accuracy. Hart served again at 6-7, slipped to 0-40, then saved two set points. At 30-40, she could not contain Connolly who seized the set behind a cluster of beautifully struck backhands.

Hart served at 1-2, 40-0 in the second set but lost the game. Connolly was once again in command with a 3-1 lead. Hart rallied to 3-3 with a concentrated run. They stayed on serve to 4-4. The ninth game was the hardest fought of the match. It reached deuce six times. Hart gallantly pursued the favorite in closely contested baseline exchanges. She rarely approached the net, knowing Connolly could produce extraordinary passing shots off both wings.

At last, after eighteen points and a series of wonderful rallies, Connolly held for 5-4 and was four points away from a second Wimbledon and third consecutive Grand Slam title. Hart was serving to save the match. She played as if she were ahead, moving to 5-5 after a solid game. Connolly forged ahead on serve again to 6-5. This time, Hart could not win a point. She had thrown everything she had at Connolly, including her chop forehand, an array of disguised drop shots, and flat, penetrating drives. In the end, it was to no avail. With Connolly adding velocity to her shots and bearing down visibly on every point, she broke at love to complete an exhausting 8-6, 7-5 triumph.

"I can't stop shaking," Connolly told Alan Hoby of the (London) *Sunday Express*. "That's the toughest match I've ever had and I'm still all keyed up. I certainly never played better."

Hart felt essentially the same way. She told Hoby, "I went out to attack Maureen. I concentrated on hitting the ball down the middle and waiting for the opening. It was the best I've ever played against Little Mo. . . . But it wasn't enough."

The British press concurred with the players about the match. As J. L. Manning wrote in the *Sunday Dispatch*, "There will never be perfection in sport, but I was near to seeing it yesterday at Wimbledon. For an hour Maureen Connolly and Doris Hart showed hardly an error of judgment, a slackening of concentration or a weakening of effort in a never-to-be-forgotten lawn tennis match. At the end of this mag-

---

A paradigm for the rising level of women's tennis.

---

nificent demonstration of what two determined girls can achieve in sport, Little Mo had won. And she had won the hard way. The 26 games were loaded with 187 points, each fought for with ice-cold skill and with unrelieved application of the game's best arts. All those points, but just four surrendered on service faults. What a lesson for our girls!"

Connolly herself would rate her match with Hart at the top of her personal list of best performances. In *Forehand Drive*, she recalled that Hart told her as they came off the court, "Maureen, this is the first time in my life I have lost a match and still felt as though I had won it." Connolly confessed, "For me, it was a

---

Two women at their best in victory and defeat.

---

tremendous win. I had played the finest tennis of my life, my game soared, and to have won against such a great adversary, at the very height of her game. . . it's a thrill beyond description."

EPILOGUE

Only one major tournament stood between Connolly and a Grand Slam. No woman had ever swept the "Big Four" in a single year. The only tennis player who had realized that feat was Don Budge fifteen years earlier. Connolly came to New York for Forest Hills feeling she could handle any opponent after her testing time at Wimbledon.

The Californian was in convincing form all through the tournament. There was no glimmer of apprehension. She was on the edge of an astounding accomplishment, and was playing with a sense of serenity. Connolly knew she was the best player in women's tennis, and was eager to confirm her talent at a place where she had thrived.

In the quarterfinals of Forest Hills, she took on the fast-rising African-American Althea Gibson, a powerful, attacking player who would win both Wimbledon and Forest Hills in

1957 and 1958. Gibson was called frequently for foot faults, but did not correct the flaw in her technique. The crowd began booing as the match was disrupted by repeated infractions. Connolly won, 6-2, 6-3, feeling relieved that the fiasco was over, and baffled by Gibson's continuous footfaulting.

In the semifinals, she repeated her Wimbledon win over Shirley Fry, winning with an identical 6-1, 6-1 score. All that was left to complete her mission was a final round encounter with Hart. Connolly wrote in *Forehand Drive*, "It was not the same Doris who opposed me at Wimbledon for most of the match. In the second set I had her 5-2. Then she had a bold and glorious stand, and a crowd of 12,000 roared encouragement to her as she came up and I led by a scant game, 5-4. The crowd was tense now; the pressure was on as I served. I made it 15-0 when Doris netted a shot. I reached 30-0 on a service ace. Then, on a placement, I made it 40-0. In our next rally, I smashed a forehand cross-court for an outright placement, taking the game, set, and match, 6-2, 6-4. That slashing drive was to be my Forest Hills swan song."

Having secured her Grand Slam, Connolly seemed invincible in the next Grand Slam events. She won the French Championships for the second time in 1954 with relative ease, then won her third-straight Wimbledon with a 6-2, 7-5 triumph over Louise Brough of the United States, erasing a 5-2 deficit to take five consecutive games for the title. She had collected six major championships in a row, and had secured the last nine Grand Slam events she had entered, dating back to the 1951 Forest Hills tournament.

Back home in San Diego after winning the

Doris Hart

U.S. Clay Court Championships, Connolly went horseback riding with two friends. They came around a blind curve and saw a cement-mixer truck heading in their direction. The sight of that truck made the horses uneasy. Connolly and her friends shouted at the truck driver, hoping he would slow down or stop.

The driver didn't seem to notice them. He

stayed in the middle of the road. The horse in front of Connolly reared and the truck driver could not stop in time. Maureen felt the harsh pain in her right leg as she fell off her horse. Her right leg buckled when she tried to get up. It had been "slashed to the bone."

As Connolly sat on the side of the road, she was assisted by a trained nurse who happened to be passing by. An ambulance was called. She soon found out at the hospital that calf muscles had been severed, and the fibula bone broken. She was not yet twenty years old, but her tennis career was over.

Not long after, Little Mo married and had a daughter. She came to terms with her tragedy and conducted tennis clinics whenever possible, working informally with aspiring players. She wrote an entertaining, sharp-edged column for *Tennis Magazine* in the 1960s, and did some

---

A valiant athlete accepts misfortune without despair.

---

television commentary and newspaper reporting at Wimbledon in the 1950s and 1960s. In 1969, at thirty-four, Connolly passed away, a victim of cancer.

Doris Hart, in those years after Little Mo's accident, played a number of fine winning matches. She had lost four finals at Forest Hills, two to Margaret Osborne duPont in 1949 and 1950, and two to Connolly in 1952 and 1953. Later in that summer of 1954, she took her U.S. Championship at last in one of the tightest finals ever—6-8, 6-1, 8-6 over Louise Brough. Hart saved three match points in the final set.

In 1955, she won Forest Hills again, less arduously, defeating Pat Ward, 6-4, 6-2, in the final. By then she was thirty, and decided to ease out of tennis competition, taking an enviable record with her.

Hart was clearly not a Connolly in singles, but she joined her friendly adversary as one of only twelve players (men or women) to capture all four of the major championships.

In the last analysis, Connolly would have surely collected at least half a dozen more major titles. She might well have won another Grand Slam. As British writer Duncan Macaulay wrote in a piece published in *The Fireside Book of Tennis*, "Had Connolly been able to compete for another five or six years, her total of major championships could well have been quite unparalleled. As it was, she deserves to be ranked among the very greatest women's singles players ever to have lived. And her character and temperament remained durable and unruffled in all circumstances." •

LEW HOAD VS. TONY TRABERT

DAVIS CUP CHALLENGE ROUND, MELBOURNE, DECEMBER 30, 1953

On a damp and demanding day "Down Under," the Australian and the American produced a performance of skill and sparkle with both men stretched to their limits.

PROLOGUE

The 1950s were the "Golden Age" of Davis Cup competition. The international men's team competition had grown in stature since its inception at the turn of the century. The pride of playing for country rather than self was an inspiring endeavor for the leading players of that era. Later, after Open Tennis emerged in 1968, the major tournaments took on an unprecedented significance. With the professional calendar more crowded than ever before, Davis Cup gradually was forced to compete for the priorities of the top players.

In 1953, that was not the case. At the time, the rivalry between the United States and Australia was flourishing. The two countries met in the "Challenge Round" (the finals) of the cup for the tenth consecutive time since 1938, including a six-year gap in 1940-45 when World War II forced a postponement of the competition. The Americans and Australians delighted in representing their nations during this highly charged period. They looked to produce great performances in a conflict unlike any other in their game. They hoped and believed they could contribute something larger than the sum of their own achievements.

As the United States and Australia assembled in Melbourne for the 1953 Challenge Round, the Americans came to the Kooyong stadium knowing they had their work cut out for them. Captain Billy Talbert, one of the game's great ambassadors who was a member of the victorious U.S. Davis Cup teams of 1948 and 1949, brought two men who would try to carry their country to triumph. One was Wimbledon champion Vic Seixas, a native of Philadelphia, and a diligent competitor who would win the U.S. Championships the following year. The other was Tony Trabert, who had grown up in Cincinnati. A few months earlier, Trabert had secured his first major singles title at Forest Hills, taking the U.S. Championship with a straight-set victory over Seixas in the final. Trabert, the son of an engineer, had played basketball at the University of Cincinnati, and also won the U.S. Intercollegiate tennis singles title while there in 1951. A year earlier, at the French Championships of 1950, he had taken his first major prize, claiming the doubles crown with

Lew Hoad

Trabert had a well-rounded strategy featuring an extraordinary backhand. Off that side, the rugged, muscular Trabert could release flat, forcing drives, or he could come over the ball to produce slight topspin. His forehand was not as flamboyant, but it was stable and aggressive. He was a first-rate volleyer off both sides, his smash was formidable, and his serve was an underrated strength. Trabert had the tools to compete against anyone, and the versatility to shine on all surfaces.

The Australian captain was the renowned Harry Hopman, a former player who had as his team anchors the "Whiz Kids," Ken Rosewall and Lew Hoad. Rosewall had won two Grand Slam events that season, the Australian and French Championships. Hoad, barely nineteen, had won three Grand Slam doubles championships in 1953 alongside Rosewall, but had not hit his stride yet in singles.

Even so, Hoad was already a frontline player. Blonde and burly, Hoad was one of the most explosive shotmakers of his time. Hoad's father was an Australian tramwayman. Lew quit school early to pursue his tennis career. He could fire winners off both flanks with no hesitation, hitting his ground strokes with immense power, serving with authority, volleying with remarkable assurance. He could hit the ball with blinding speed, but he could hurt his chances with rash mistakes, errors born of impatience and lack of restraint. Be that as it may, Hoad was a player

one of the all-time-great doubles players, Billy Talbert, now the non-playing U.S. captain.

Trabert had spent the first half of 1953 finishing an obligation to the armed services. When Trabert joined Seixas for the Challenge Round a few days after Christmas, he was twenty-three. A good athlete and determined competitor, Trabert was maturing observably as a tennis player. His sound, attacking game was just what his nation needed on the grass courts at Kooyong.

of pure and raw talent who could strike fear into anyone when he was on his game.

As the best-of-five-match battle between the two nations commenced, Trabert and Hoad each gave their teams reason to cheer. Hoad routed Seixas in straight sets to put Australia out in front, then Trabert answered with a 6-3, 6-4, 6-4 win over Rosewall. In the doubles, Hoad and Rex Hartwig were decisively defeated by Trabert and Seixas. The U.S. held a 2-1 lead heading into the last afternoon. The pivotal contest would see Hoad facing Trabert.

THE MATCH

On a damp day with rain falling lightly on the grass courts at Kooyong, Trabert and Hoad walked on court deeply aware of the magnitude of the moment. If Trabert prevailed, he would clinch the world team championship for his country. The Americans had suffered three consecutive defeats against the men from Down Under from 1950-52. They wanted to regain possession of the coveted Davis Cup, and Trabert was in a position to make that happen.

The first set was fought indefatigably by both players. It lasted twenty-four games. Through the first twenty-three, there was not a single service break. Both men were playing grass court tennis of a very high quality, backing up their big serves with solidly struck first volleys. They were returning serve adeptly, but the conditions were slick and negotiating a service break was no simple task.

Trabert, however, was frequently on the verge of sealing the set. Hoad was living precariously, facing break point no fewer than eleven times in a cluster of different service games. Trabert was making more effective returns, forcing Hoad into binds, then narrowly missing his mark. With Trabert serving at 11-12, 30-40, Hoad made a low, chipped return. Trabert had to lift his volley as he approached the net. Hoad had followed his return in and Trabert was required to make a choice. He moved to his backhand side. Hoad cut off his volley and made a volley of his own past Trabert into the open court. Hoad had the set, 13-11. The capacity crowd of 17,500 at Kooyong applauded loudly.

In *The Story of the Davis Cup*, Alan Trengove wrote appealingly, "The crowd's thunderous applause was echoed by groups clustered around radio sets throughout the continent. Outside the stadium, in Glenferrie Road, a tram conductor clambered onto the top of a stationary tram, making sure he avoided the electrified pole. He saw the scoreboard and shouted the news to the passengers."

The grass court was increasingly greasy as the soft rain fell intermittently. In a 1999 interview, Trabert recalled that he told captain Talbert he wanted to wear spikes when he was behind 2-3 in the second set. Trabert said, "You would run up to the net, put the brakes on, and slide 10 or 12 feet. I told Talbert I was going to put on the spikes. Talbert spoke to the referee, Cliff Sproule, who talked to Hopman. Hopman said, 'My boy's okay.' "

Trabert was at a loss to explain why, but Hoad—despite the slippery court—did not want to switch from his tennis shoes to spikes. Trabert reluctantly kept his tennis shoes on as he served at 2-3. He remembers, "When I served that game, I came in twice and just fell making routine moves trying to go right or left. He broke me and held for 5-2. When we changed ends of the court that time, I put on spikes without asking anybody. I wanted to see who was going to take them off of me. By that time I was down a set and a break."

The shift to spikes gave Trabert the firmer footing he sorely needed. Although Hoad served out the second set at 5-3 despite a 15-40 deficit—building a two-sets-to-love lead in the process—the American was encouraged by his improved mobility. Trabert moved swiftly to a 4-1 third-set lead. At the changeover after the fifth game, Hoad finally made the switch to spikes himself.

Even so, he lost his serve again, and with it the set, 6-2. The players took a brief intermission and returned to the locker room. When they resumed the match, Trabert was still confident. As Alan Trengove reported, "Hoad was unable to slide into his shots and his form had become patchy. . . . Trabert now was repeatedly going to the net behind his sliced returns that kept low on the wet turf, and Hoad made errors trying to pass him."

Trabert sustained his fast-paced tactics. He took the fourth set, 6-3. As they moved into the fifth, the rain was falling and the balls were heavier. Trabert was at a distinct disadvantage as he served the entire set from behind, but

he was holding his delivery with ease. On his way to 5-5, he lost a mere eight points in five service games.

Hoad had slipped and tumbled onto the damp grass as he chased a Trabert volley. He was stretched out on the court, not moving for a few long moments. Then, as Trengove recounts, "Hopman jumped up, grabbing the towel from his lap. As Lew looked up, Hopman threw the towel over his player's head and said, 'Come on, Musclebound, you can't lie there forever.' "

Tony Trabert

Hoad grinned, got up, and held. Both players tenaciously protected their service games. Trabert served to save the match at 4-5 and completed the task. Hoad, undismayed, forged ahead, 6-5.

In the twelfth game, Trabert served again to save the contest. Hoad opened with a perfect placement off the return, and struck with great

Rainfall and spiked shoes add to the drama.

power past a charging Trabert. The Australian then used his court sense again to force the American into an errant volley for 0-30. Trabert hit a hard first serve, which missed its mark. He then went for the wide second serve in the deuce court, attempting to avoid the Australian's lethal backhand wing. The serve was out.

The double fault put Trabert at 0-40, but neither he nor Hoad heard the call. They played the point out with Hoad finally hitting an apparent winner. Trengove reported that few in the crowd had heard the linesman cry "fault," and they thought Hoad had won the point with a placement. Trabert, realizing he had double-faulted and was now triple match point down, believed the crowd had cheered his double fault in a breech of traditional tennis civility.

As Trabert said forty-six years later, the incident still alive in his memory, "I thought it was unfair for them to clap my double fault. They say in retrospect that Lew hit a forehand down the line that would have been a winner and that is why they were clapping. That is all history and hindsight."

Either way, Trabert was understandably distressed at the time, placing his hands on his hips for a long moment, looking up disapprovingly at the crowd. At triple match point, his percentage first serve was directed deep to Hoad's backhand. The Australian returned the serve with a sharply angled crosscourt winner. Trabert was beaten by a superb final stroke, broken at love. Hoad triumphed, 13-11, 6-3, 2-6, 3-6, 7-5.

Trabert said recently, "That match stands out for me as I look back at my career, even though it was a losing cause on my part. It was Davis Cup and we could have won the Cup if I had won my match. It was a special match for its importance, its competitiveness and the length of it."

It was left to Seixas to salvage victory for the United States. With the two countries locked at two matches apiece, the American confronted Rosewall the next day. Seixas battled gamely, after losing the opening set, to take the second. His comeback did not last. Rosewall was too consistent, ruling in four sets, keeping the Cup in the capable hands of the Australians.

EPILOGUE

In 1954, Trabert and Seixas returned to a spacious stadium seating 25,578 in White City (Sydney). This time, the Americans toppled Hoad and Rosewall to take back the Cup. When Trabert and Hoad clashed again, the Australian served for a two-sets-to-one lead at 7-6 in the third. Trabert saved a set point in the fourteenth game, and went on to win the set, 12-10. He took the match in four sets. Hoad would tell Trabert years later, "You should have won in 1953 in Melbourne and I should have won the next year in White City."

Trabert mused, "Winning the cup in 1954

was the biggest thrill I ever had in tennis because I was representing my country. Instead of the umpire saying, 'Game Trabert;' he says, 'Game, United States.' And you suddenly realize that you are representing at that stage 185 million people. You are halfway around the world with a chance to do something for your country. In those days, the Davis Cup was huge."

Trabert celebrated what he calls his "banner year" in 1955. After losing to Rosewall in the semifinals of the Australian Championships in the first Grand Slam event of the season, he swept the last three major tournaments at Roland Garros, Wimbledon, and Forest Hills, where he vanquished both Hoad and Rosewall in straight sets. Beaten only five times in twenty-three tournaments that year, he closed out his amateur career in style.

Trabert turned professional in December 1955, lost his series with Pancho Gonzales seventy-four matches to twenty-seven, and played on productively into the early sixties. He became U.S. Davis Cup captain from 1976-80, with two of his teams taking the title. Beginning in the early 1970s and continuing through the 1990s, Trabert was a superb analyst for CBS television at the U.S. Open and elsewhere.

Hoad had his best amateur season after Trabert's departure for the pro ranks. In 1956, he beat Rosewall in a four-set Australian Championship final, came through at Roland Garros to claim the French title, then ousted his doubles partner Rosewall again in the Wimbledon final. Hoad was closing in on a Grand Slam, ready to become the first man since Budge, in 1938, to sweep the four major titles in a single year.

The dynamic Australian with the high velocity game came within one match of his goal, only to lose to a flawless Rosewall in four sets at Forest Hills. Following that superb season—reminiscent in many ways of Trabert's 1955—Hoad turned professional, barnstorming with Gonzales.

Looking back upon his battles with Hoad, Trabert would say generously of his adversary, "If Lew Hoad played his best and I played my best, he would beat me because he was more talented and more gifted than I was. But I had the ability to stay at a pretty high level. That is how I won three of my five Grand Slam singles titles without losing a set. I could get up for a tournament and stay there. So if I caught Lew when he was down a little bit and he was not quite at his best, I could beat him. But when he was playing as well as he could play, he could play as well as anybody."

Trabert—a proud, earnest, and ultimately humble man—is not comfortable placing himself in historical context. And yet, he concludes, "From the time I got out of the service in June of

Enduring qualities of athletic skill inspires mutual esteem.

1953 until the end of 1955 I won five Grand Slam singles and four Grand Slam doubles championships. That was a pretty short time to win all those Grand Slam events. I think I would certainly be somewhere in the top ten of all the American players, but that is up to other people to figure out. All I can say is my mother thought I was the best ever."   •

PANCHO GONZALES VS. LEW HOAD

U.S. PRO CHAMPIONSHIPS, CLEVELAND, FINAL, MAY 4, 1958

This encounter pitted the power of Gonzales against the prodigal talent of Hoad in a stupendous indoor collision.

PROLOGUE

Richard "Pancho" Gonzales was perhaps the most evocative tennis champion of the twentieth century. Standing 6' 2", weighing a muscular 180 pounds, staring down rivals and officials with defiant, gleaming eyes, he strode onto a tennis court like a gladiator and stirred audiences all over the world. Of all the great male players who competed during the second half of the century, only Ken Rosewall and one-time protégé Jimmy Connors remained formidable for as many years as Pancho.

He was driven by powerful private engines—exploding with rage at linesmen who gave him questionable calls and showing disdain for opponents who were disturbed by his antics. Pancho was one of seven children born into a Mexican-American family, who lived on the south side of Los Angeles where tennis was surely not the game of choice. During the depression, the entire family lived in two rooms. His father was a housepainter, and his neighborhood was impoverished. As a young boy, Pancho became fascinated by the game of tennis. When he was thirteen, he started to skip school and hang around various Los Angeles tennis centers. He was almost entirely self-taught and in 1943 became the No. 1 boys player in southern California. He controlled his matches with the coiled force of his personality, turning many of his appearances into dramatic experiences that reached beyond the boundaries of the tennis court.

Even as a junior player, Gonzales was seldom far away from the center of conflict. When he was fifteen, he told the Southern California Tennis Association that he was going to drop out of school to concentrate on his tennis. They told him that dropping out was unacceptable. Gonzales would not obey. He was suspended for a year from all official tournament competition.

By his late teens, Gonzales had put most of the commotion behind him and was moving forward as a world-class player. He won back-to-back United States Championships at Forest Hills in 1948 and 1949, making a fiery comeback from two sets to love down in the latter final against Ted Schroeder. Those twin triumphs gave Gonzales the credentials he needed as the leading amateur to graduate into professional tennis.

The transition was perilous in the early days. Jack Kramer had been competing as a pro for two years and was the better player. He played 123 matches against Gonzales in 1949 and 1950. Kramer won ninety-six of those contests. Kramer made the case in his 1979 book, *The Game*, that Gonzales had been given a false sense of security after recovering so admirably against Schroeder at Forest Hills in 1949. It made Gonzales believe he was better than he actually was.

As Kramer said, "Pancho was just in way over his head. He had no idea how to live or take care of himself. He was a hamburger-and-hot-dog type of guy and had no concept of diet in training. I had learned,

Pancho Gonzales

for example, that if we got a couple of days off in a row I had to stop eating or I couldn't burn it up. He'd eat at the same pace and I always beat him in the next match. On the court, Pancho would gulp Coca-Cola throughout a match. I had learned from Perry and Budge to bring sweetened tea to the court. . . . Also, Gonzales was a pretty heavy cigarette smoker."

Despite the humbling indoctrination, Gonzales worked to establish his position in pro tennis. After being crushed for two years by the match-playing prowess of Kramer, Gonzales gradually ironed out the wrinkles in his game and in his training. By 1953, he had developed winning habits. He took his first U.S. Pro

Championship title that season over Don Budge after losing the previous two finals to Pancho Segura. He repeated as champion of that important event for the next four years, defeating the wily Segura in the finals of 1955-57.

Meanwhile, Gonzales was taking over the pro tour of one-night stands. He beat both Frank Sedgman and Segura in 1954, defeated Trabert, 74-27, in 1955-56, and handled Rosewall 50-26 the following year. A new challenger was needed for Gonzales. With his big first serve and fluent second delivery—both were the best in his trade—he could overpower his opponents across the board. He had a first-rate overhead, a solid and forceful volley off both sides, and ground strokes that did not betray him despite their lack of sparkle.

As the 1958 season approached, it was apparent who was best equipped to tour with Gonzales. It was an Australian who was in many ways a more gifted player. He had much more punch off the ground. He could serve nearly as well. He was a dazzling shot-maker with decidedly more flair than Gonzales, and perhaps a better overhead. His name was Lew Hoad.

Hoad had joined the pro ranks in 1957 following his outstanding 1956 season. At 5' 8", he was about six inches shorter than Gonzales. His series with Gonzales began late in 1957. Hoad had won his second consecutive Wimbledon

---

A rivalry that produced explosively fascinating tennis.

---

singles title in July. He was supremely talented in every facet of the game, but some keen observers believed he did not have the psychology of most champions, the fierce will to win under any circumstances.

In the Hoad-Gonzales 1958 tour, they started in Brisbane, Australia. After thirteen matches, Hoad was in front 8-5. Kramer recalled years later how Gonzales competed courageously with bleeding fingers in Adelaide while Hoad coped with a painful forearm muscle in Sydney. They returned to the United States and Gonzales closed the gap to 9-7. Hoad burst into brilliant form again to take an 18-9 lead. He seemed to have the American measured.

On March 1, 1958, the two toughened competitors played on a cold, crisp evening in Palm Springs. Hoad woke up the next morning with a stiff back. Thereafter, Gonzales ruled the rival-ry. But they had many rigorous duels in front of them during the late fifties, most notably in the historic final of the U.S. Pro Championships in Cleveland.

THE MATCH

Over time, the tournament shifted locations and moved from one arena to another. Even the official name of the event was altered. Ultimately, it would be known as the United States Professional Championships, arguably the most prestigious of all events for those who competed for money. In 1958, however, it was called The World Pro Championships and it took place at The Arena in Cleveland.

Gonzales and Hoad came to town with the cream of the crop in their profession. They were joined by Tony Trabert and Pancho Segura, an aging Fred Perry, and the 1944-45 U.S. champion Frank Parker. Gonzales ousted Segura, 6-4, 6-3, in his semifinal; Hoad accounted for Trabert, 6-2, 13-11. The most important Gonzales-Hoad clash was on course.

Throughout the spring on their tour, the American and the Australian had played an absorbing series of matches. Between March 31 and April 20, they played twenty-one times. They moved in and out of towns like Atlanta and New Haven, Philadelphia and Montreal, Princeton and Bermuda. Gonzales held only a slim 12-9 edge in that span.

In Cleveland, they were to play on a fast canvas court. The conditions were suited to both contestants. They were mean fast-court players. By now, they knew each other's games inside out. The edge in this final would go to the player who executed better on the big points. Since Hoad had suffered his back injury two months earlier in Palm Springs, he began to produce some surprisingly good tennis against his glowering adversary.

With 2,700 fans watching the American and the Australian's climactic match the first weekend in May, it became clear that service breaks were difficult but essential. Hoad got the early break for 2-0 in the opening set and held throughout to prevail, 6-3. Gonzales did not

Lew Hoad

want to fall into a deeper deficit. He served steadily to 4-4 in the second set, but could not gain a break himself. Hoad then broke through with some blazing backhands to take a 5-4 lead. Self-assured and given the chance, Hoad held on comfortably to take the second set, 6-4, for a two-sets-to-love lead.

The third set featured both men at their best. An obstinate Gonzales was willing to pursue any policy to keep himself in the match. He persisted with his firepower on serve, backed up by decisive volleying. Hoad was anxious to finish his job in straight sets, knowing that Gonzales was a warrior who would not surrender. Gonzales had the advantage of serving first in the set, but Hoad was staying with the favorite through every sequence.

The pressure grew on the twenty-three-year-old Australian. Gonzales kept inviting him to concede the set, but Hoad refused. In a battle between the two premier servers in professional tennis, neither man was found wanting. Gonzales kept moving in front, only for Hoad to blast his way back to even territory.

From 4-5 in this pivotal set, Hoad served to save it eight times. Gonzales pressed him, but to no avail. Hoad answered his adversary emphatically every time. He was quick and confident in the forecourt, cutting off the volleys at short range, reading nearly every Gonzales passing shot, giving the American few second chances.

Gonzales remained on course. He held on for 13-12 and finally proceeded to set point on the Australian's serve. Hoad came in behind a penetrating approach. Gonzales responded meekly off the backhand. His passing shot was tentative. But the ball hit the tape, and somehow fell over. Set to Gonzales, 14-12.

Buoyant after that good fortune, Gonzales coasted through the fourth set, 6-1, behind two service breaks. He gained an early fifth set break, and there was no halting him from there. The American, five days shy of his thirtieth birthday, was much fresher and fitter in the end. Hoad was hindered by a leg injury late in the contest. Those facts notwithstanding, it was a superb match that decorated the greatness of both players.

As Chuck Heaton wrote in the *Cleveland Plain Dealer*, "The three hour match—played before an estimated 2,700 fans—was the longest and perhaps most exciting in the nine years the pros have fought it out in Cleveland. The sixth straight World Pro Championship for swarthy Pancho added blonde Lew to a list of final victims which includes Don Budge, Frank Sedgman and Little Pancho Segura."

Tournament promoter Jack March wrote in *World Tennis*, "According to Don Budge, Bobby Riggs and Pancho Segura, it was the greatest match they had ever seen. It was also the single greatest display of shotmaking, with Aussie Lew Hoad making most of the shots but losing

The highest praise came from their professional peers.

the match. . . . It was the first time Gonzales was up against an opponent who surpassed him in stroke equipment, condition, anticipation, speed, and court coverage. But Gonzales won this year on brains, fight, and guts."

March later reflected, "For the first time, distinct weaknesses were revealed in Gonzales' game. These weaknesses were never evident before because Gonzales had never faced a stronger, faster, and better player than himself. It is a credit to the champion that he could beat a player whose stroke equipment was superior."

Gonzales himself recognized one department of his game as instrumental in his triumph. He told Chuck Heaton, "Lew and I both play the same style of tennis that we have used on the tour. My serve worked as well as it ever has. In fact, it was even clicking for me in the sets I lost. Lew was just volleying too well for me in the early part of the match. Then he slowed down and wasn't getting to the net quite as fast. That always makes the other fellow look better."

Gonzales was asked about his shrewd lobbing and semi-lobbing to work his way back into big points. He responded, "That's a trick I learned from 'Little Sneaky' Segura. It's a change of pace that keeps the other guy running. In a long match like this, all of those steps add up."

Was Gonzales fortunate to overcome Hoad in their most celebrated meeting? Perhaps. The fact remains that his tenacity was crucial to his cause. He made his own breaks by competing so fiercely in the latter stages of the third set when he could easily have succumbed. He recognized one fundamental fact: Great matches are taken not only by the better player, they are won by those who want them the most.

EPILOGUE

Gonzales and Hoad finished their 1957-58 tour with the American the winner in fifty-one of eighty-seven matches. In 1959, they met again for the World (U.S.) Pro Championship. The gap between them had widened considerably. Gonzales was the victor, 6-4, 6-2, 6-4. Two years later, Gonzales took that title for the eighth and last time with a straight-set win over Sedgman.

He remained a complicated man, wearing his grievances disdainfully, altering his moods so frequently no one could ever be certain what to expect from him. In any case, he remained a major force in professional tennis through the

---

The style and temperament of Gonzales intrigued both fans and players.

---

sixties. He would play during his thirties in relative obscurity, testing himself against the leading competitors who turned pro after taking major championships.

Hoad struggled in many ways. After that spring of 1958, the record reveals he was never quite the same player. He competed hard and often splendidly, but his level of consistency decreased. He could not play past his pain and be the soaring competitor he had once been. That was a sadness for him, and for tennis. Hoad was not even twenty-four when he produced so many magical moments during his tour with Gonzales in 1958. Thereafter, he was permanently past his peak.

Despite his decline, he was still a strikingly good tennis player. After Rod Laver won his first Grand Slam as an amateur in 1962, he turned professional and was battered by Hoad all through the early stages of 1963. Hoad continued to surprise Gonzales in some pro events in the mid-sixties. *World Tennis* editor Gladys M. Heldman wrote of Hoad in 1964, "Lew is still the most exciting shotmaker in the world."

Historians have had a hard time deciding where Hoad belongs among the all-time great players. His time at and near the top was relatively short. And yet, most experts place him in a category alongside Ellsworth Vines. At their best, both of these big hitters could have held their own with anyone on given afternoons when they were in full form. Hoad was in that zone when he battled against Gonzales in Cleveland during their final of 1958. The Kramer analysis: "When you sum Hoad up, you have to say that he was overrated. He

---

Hoad's abbreviated career was nonetheless vividly remembered.

---

might have been the best, but day-to-day, week-to-week, he was the most inconsistent of all the top players. Overall, he lost to Rosewall, to Gonzales, to Segura, to Trabert. . . . Generally, he is held in higher esteem that he deserves. . . . But when Hoad felt like getting up, boy was he something."

In the sixties, Hoad's back trouble became an inescapable burden. He could no longer play the same dazzling brand of tennis. By the time Open Tennis arrived in 1968, it was entirely too late for Hoad. He did appear in the first open Wimbledon that June, and was seeded seventh, a sentimental gesture by the committee. He reached the third round but fell in five sets to the South African Bob Hewitt. When he competed there for the last time in 1970, John McPhee wrote about him lyrically in *Wimbledon: A Celebration*. "Hoad on Court 5, weathered and leonine, has come from Spain, where he lives on a tennis ranch in the plains of Andalusia. Technically, he is an old hero trying a comeback, but, win or lose, for this crowd it is enough of a comeback that Hoad is here. There is a tempestuous majesty in him."

Gonzales was able to claim a much higher mark for himself in the early history of the Open Era. He, too, was a heroic figure returning to the places that had barred him for decades while he played as a professional. But, unlike Hoad, Gonzales's body had not penalized him. He could still survive tests and produce performances that were reminiscent of his prime. The glint in his eyes, the fluid serving, were adamant.

He was still Richard "Pancho" Gonzales. •

ALTHEA GIBSON VS. DARLENE HARD

U.S. CHAMPIONSHIPS, FOREST HILLS, FINAL, SEPTEMBER 7, 1958

Gibson was seeking a sweep of the Wimbledon and U.S. Championships for the second year in a row, but Hard was an inspired, elusive opponent.

PROLOGUE

If a ranking was established by consensus to grade the finest players in the twentieth century, Althea Gibson would not be placed among the top ten. She peaked for too brief a period, and did not dominate the game in the manner of other champions. She did not have the chance to show her talent during the era of open tennis which began in 1968, and created new incentives.

Nevertheless, Gibson was one of the most significant tennis players of the century. Born in South Carolina, raised primarily on the streets of Harlem in New York, she was the first African-American player to win a major title. Her journey to the game's showcase events was littered with obstacles her adversaries never encountered.

Gibson led a largely impoverished life during her youth in New York. She had a complicated relationship with her father, who worked as a garage attendant. Althea was the oldest of five children, and perhaps the most rebellious. She frequently challenged her father's authority. It was not uncommon for him to whip her.

She freely admitted in her autobiography, *I Always Wanted to be Somebody*, that she often deserved his wrath. Her father hoped that Althea would become a female prizefighter, but that never came to pass.

On occasion, Althea and her father had fist-fights. She did not blame him for these outbursts, but she would go from time to time to the Society for the Prevention of Cruelty to Children to escape the hostility and the heated exchanges. She detested school and avoided attending classes with creative zeal. After finishing junior high school despite her extraordinary string of absences, she did not move on immediately to high school.

Gibson was helped by the welfare department, who put her on an allowance. In her teens, she took up paddle tennis on the streets of New York, not far from her parents' Harlem home. The court was about half as long as a tennis court, the racket much shorter. A New York City employee spotted her on the streets playing paddle tennis, and bought her a couple of secondhand tennis rackets that cost about $5 apiece.

Gibson's introduction to the new game

Althea Gibson

larger role in the development of Arthur Ashe.

By 1949, when Gibson graduated from high school at age twenty-one, the ATA was able to use its influence to convince the United States Lawn Tennis Association (the official governing body) that Gibson should have the opportunity to compete against white players in sanctioned tournaments. She would complete her education on scholarship at Florida A & M when she was twenty-five. By then she understood the importance of playing good tennis.

Her first taste of unsegregated competition was in 1949. (In 1948, President Harry Truman had desegregated the armed forces.) The following year, she appeared in her first U.S. National Championships and nearly toppled Wimbledon titlist Louise Brough in a much-heralded second-round match. After an inauspicious start, Gibson came from behind gamely to take a 7-6 final-set lead. Thunderstorms stopped the match, and experience ruled when play resumed the next afternoon. Not without resistance, Brough swept three games in a row for a 6-1, 3-6, 9-7 triumph. But Gibson had given a glowing account of herself on her first appearance at the championship.

Curiously, she did not progress rapidly

started informally on handball courts, but as she approached her fourteenth birthday, Althea was given the opportunity to take lessons and play at the Cosmopolitan Club in Harlem. A year later, at fifteen, she was playing tournaments under the auspices of the American Tennis Association, an organization devoted to helping African-American players. She became the ATA Junior Girls' champion before she was eighteen in 1944, and again in 1945.

Belatedly, Gibson finished her high school education in North Carolina, assisted in her efforts by the ATA. One of the people who encouraged and supported her tennis aspirations at that time was Dr. Walter Johnson of Lynchburg, Virginia, who would play an even

thereafter. In 1952, she broke into the American top ten at No. 9, rising to No. 7 the following year, then falling to No. 13 in 1954. Her growing pains could be attributed at least in part to the nature of her game. At 5' 11" she was uncommonly tall and powerfully built. She was a confirmed attacking player with a big serve-and-volley game. That style of play almost always takes longer to nurture than that of a baseliner.

In any case, Gibson was becoming discouraged by her stalled status. She did, however, rise to No. 8 in the nation in 1955. At that point,

---

Gibson's belated improvement brought her many rewards.

---

she was weighing other options, including a stint with the Women's Army Corps. That venture was curtailed when she was approached at Forest Hills in 1955 about playing a U.S. State Department Tour of southeast Asia along with three other American tennis players. She accepted the invitation, which set the stage for her most productive years.

After concluding the Asian tour early in 1956, she was nearly unbeatable in the first half of the tournament season, capturing the Italian Championships and her first Grand Slam crown at the French Championships in Paris. The oddsmakers made her an overwhelming favorite to win Wimbledon that year. If she could prevail on the slow red clay of Paris—the surface she liked least—how could she fail on the fast grass courts at the All England Club?

She could, and did. The accomplished Shirley Fry—an immensely capable countrywoman—upended Gibson in the quarterfinals of Wimbledon, the finals of Forest Hills, and again in the title match at the Australian

Championships the following season. Gibson had made large strides and was the second-best player in the world. She would not settle for that level much longer.

In 1957, she made her long-awaited move to the top. At Wimbledon, she was the No. 1 seed, and worthy of that honor. In six matches, she did not drop a set. In the final, she vanquished countrywoman Darlene Hard, 6-3, 6-2. At Forest Hills, she captured the American Championship for the first time with identical ease. Once more, she did not concede a set in six matches, defeating Brough, 6-3, 6-2, in the final.

Gibson had secured the two most important titles in tennis in the space of a few months to demonstrate irrefutably that she was the world's best woman player in 1957. Her high-risk game was supplemented by smarter shot selection and a better grasp of the percentages. She had a strikingly improved capacity to hold her own in backcourt exchanges.

In 1958, Gibson held on safely to her Wimbledon crown, defeating Great Britain's future champion Angela Mortimer, 8-6, 6-2, in the final. She had defended her turf skillfully at the All England Club, and looked to replicate that victory at Forest Hills.

Darlene Hard, meanwhile, had emerged as a credible rival for the towering Gibson. Hard, playing for Pomona College, had captured the U.S. Intercollegiate Championships. She had once wanted to be a pediatrician and earned an impressive scholarship from Pomona, where she completed her premedical requirements, but the attraction of high-level tennis drew her away from further study. As a child, she had delighted in watching the best women in the country play at the Los Angeles Tennis Club.

Over time, her mentors included Hazel Wightman and Sarah Palfrey Danzig.

She was twenty-two when she played at Forest Hills in 1958, nine years younger than Gibson. About six inches shorter than Althea, she played the game with the same elan. She, too, was a strong serve-and-volleyer.

Hard had made her debut in the American top ten in 1954 at No. 7. She was the fourth-best player in her country in 1957, and held that ranking through the 1958 season.

Hard had made a major impression in the women's game. Not only had she reached the 1957 Wimbledon final before losing to Gibson, she had also been a semifinalist at Forest Hills two months later. One match away from another final against Gibson, Hard had lost to Brough. Be that as it may, she was now approaching her prime.

THE MATCH

Both Gibson and Hard proved to be the class of the field at Forest Hills. The top-seeded Gibson did not drop a set and had only one remotely stressful test on her way to the title contest. That was her quarterfinal assignment against the big-hitting British competitor, Christine Truman. The No. 7 seed stayed with the favorite through an arduous opening set, but Althea took over thereafter and won, 11-9, 6-1. She had a much more comfortable, 6-4, 6-2, victory over the ambidextrous Beverly Baker Fleitz (the No. 8 seed), 6-4, 6-2, in the semifinals.

Having concentrated on college tennis during the first half of 1958, Hard was unseeded at the U.S. Nationals. On her path to a final-round meeting with Gibson, she removed two of the seeds. The Californian took a hard-fought 8-6, 10-8 third-round match from the British left-hander Ann Haydon, the No. 3 seed. In the quarterfinals, she surprised sixth-seeded Sally Moore, 6-4, 6-3. Then Hard stopped her compatriot Jeanne Arth, 7-5, 6-2, in the semifinal.

"The final," wrote Mary Hardwick in *World Tennis*, "was a great contrast in personality and temperament. Althea was determined almost to the point of grimness, and Darlene, who last year was bouncy, carefree, and a bundle of fun, appeared older, wiser and much more grown up. The result of this clash of personalities was one of the best women's finals we have had in many years."

There was an unexpected control in the challenger's game.

Hard displayed her versatile volley as she established an early 3-1 lead in the opening set. The Californian kept attacking behind serve, and looking for the openings to work her way forward during Gibson's service games. Gibson counterattacked with authority to get back to 3-3, producing first-rate passing shots off the forehand in her revival.

The underdog was not visibly bothered by Gibson's rally. She collected three consecutive games to close out the set, keeping her returns dipping at Gibson's feet when the favorite followed her serve in, stepping up the pace on her returns, backing up her own serve aggressively. Hard was on top of her game, providing much sterner opposition than had been the case the previous year at Wimbledon. The Californian had made the most demanding of stretch volleys. She had covered the court with surprising speed, retrieving reliably, making

Gibson work inordinately hard to finish off points.

Hard was serving at 1-1, 40-0 in the second set, still controlling the tempo of play with her deliberate tactics, continuing to keep Gibson on guard. The defending champion realized she needed to raise her game creatively and quickly. She did just that. Exploiting errors from Hard, Gibson recouped to break for a 2-1 second set lead. Gibson confidently climbed to 3-1, then ran out the set without the loss of another game as Hard penalized herself by missing too many first serves. In fact, Hard delivered a double fault when she served at 1-5 and set point down to underline her predicament. The complexion of the match changed, but the players were locked at one set all. The battle was still in progress.

In the first two games of the final set, Hard momentarily recovered some of her earlier accuracy and authority, but when Gibson held for 2-1, her opponent could no longer answer the call. The defending champion released the full range of her power on serve, spanking her volleys with an added edge, pelting the corners with her ground strokes, and returning serve with increased efficiency. Hard fought valiantly, but to no avail. Gibson collected four of the last five games for a 3-6, 6-1, 6-2 triumph and a second straight American Championship to back up her two-year unbeaten run on the Centre Court of Wimbledon.

A year earlier, Gibson had been presented with her champion's tro-phy by Vice President Richard M. Nixon. This time, she was accorded that honor by the distinguished Secretary of State John Foster Dulles. As Hardwick wrote in *World Tennis*, "Darlene appeared careless, but it was the variety in Althea's game that created this impression. Althea began to find exquisite touch with her lobs as Darlene advanced to the net. She lobbed repeatedly within inches of the baseline.

"Althea told the gallery that she was retiring from amateur competition for one year to devote herself to a singing career. Her reign has

Darlene Hard

been brief and unique. Her loyal fans at Forest Hills will miss her next year."

EPILOGUE

Gibson did indeed pursue that singing career. She had been given a good reception the previous year when she sang a few standards at the Wimbledon champion's dinner. And yet, that was not the form of entertainment the public wanted from her. Gibson sensibly decided to go back to tennis, exploiting her Wimbledon and Forest Hills triumphs of 1957-58, by turning professional.

In 1960, she played on a tour against her old and friendly amateur rival Karol Fageros, her roommate on the State Department tour of 1955-56. Gibson had defeated Fageros—a former American top-ten player—with ease in her last few years in the amateur game. With money on the line, Althea maintained the psychological and physical edge. She won 114 of their 118 matches.

No one else was available or willing to challenge her on another professional tour, so Gibson left tennis and tried her hand at professional golf. That venture was unsuccessful. She never came close to reaching the level she had attained on the tennis court. When Open Tennis was introduced in 1968, she entered a selected number of tournaments, but did not fare well. She turned forty-one that year, and was too old and too far removed from top flight tennis to make a go of it.

Having settled in New Jersey as a teaching professional, Gibson played mixed doubles at the U.S. Open in 1973 with Arthur Ashe. That was merely a chance to perform again on a major stage, to allow young followers of the game a glimpse of how good she once was. It also permitted people who admired her in the fifties to refresh their memories. Gibson and

---

Gibson confronted racism without rancor or design.

Ashe lost their opening-round match in straight sets, but the verdict did not matter. The symbolism did.

Gibson was never comfortable when asked to represent her race in a role transcending tennis. As she wrote in *I Always Wanted to be Somebody*, "I have never regarded myself as a crusader. I try to do the best I can in every situation I find myself in, and naturally I'm always glad when something I do turns out to be helpful and important to all Negroes—or for that matter, to all Americans, or maybe only to all tennis players. But I don't consciously beat the drums for any special cause, not even the cause of the Negro in the United States, because I feel that our best chance to advance is to prove ourselves as individuals. . . . This doesn't mean I'm opposed to the fight for integration of the schools or other movements like that. It simply means in my own career I steer clear of political involvements and make my way as Althea Gibson, private individual."

Elaborating on that theme, Gibson said, "Someone once wrote that the difference between me and Jackie Robinson is that he thrived in his role as a Negro battling for equality whereas I shy away from it. That man read me correctly. I shy away from it because it would be dishonest of me to pretend to a feeling I don't possess. . . . I'm not insensitive to the great value to our people of what Jackie did. If he hadn't paved the way I probably would never have got my chance. But I have to do it my way. I try not to flaunt my success as a Negro. It's all right for others to make a fuss over my role as a trailblazer, and of course, I realize its importance to others as well as myself, but I can't do it."

That philosophy had carried her far. She was the best woman player in the world for two straight years, the winner of five Grand Slam championships, and a woman who moved well beyond her early struggles in New York to build a more expansive life. Without fully realizing it, or wishing it upon herself, she was a quiet crusader of sorts who opened up a multitude of doors and windows for Ashe and others.

As for Hard, she did her best work in the early 1960s. In 1960, she took the French Championships, withstanding some grueling tests along the way. In the quarterfinals, she stopped the South African Renee Schuurman, 11-9, in the final set. With that task behind her, Hard beat her doubles partner Maria Bueno in the semifinals, and then Yola Ramirez in straight sets to claim the title.

Darlene Hard was never easily dismissed but often underrated.

Three months later, Hard won the United States Championship at Forest Hills, taking that title over Bueno. In all, she won twenty-one major titles, nineteen in women's and mixed doubles. She won the women's doubles at Wimbledon four times, and was victorious at the U.S. Championship six times. The last of those successes was in 1969, when she was thirty-three, and far removed from her best competitive days.

Hard had joined forces with Francoise Durr of France. They lost the first eight games against the strong partnership of Margaret Court and Virginia Wade. But with the Forest Hills gallery cheering their every move, Hard and Durr came through to win in three sets. That victory when she was well past her prime was convincing evidence that Darlene Hard was a supreme doubles player.

In the end, Gibson must be celebrated not simply as a tennis champion, but as a person who moved the game forward through her example and by virtue of her perseverance. She came off the streets of Harlem and took her talent all over the world. At her best, she was an alluring performer, the woman who set the agenda in most matches.

Freelance journalist Stan Hart wrote a book called *Once a Champion* in 1985. When he asked Gibson to recollect her greatest match, she replied. "It was in 1958 when I defended my title at Forest Hills. Darlene Hard, who I had always beaten, was ready for me that day. She came out attacking me, serving, volleying. I mean outwitting me, outplaying me, and everything else. That is, until I threw up five perfect lobs and they landed on the chalk of the baseline. Every time she came to the net. I'd throw up a lob and make her run to retrieve them, and then, of course, after five times in a row, five times to no avail, it was all over."   •

MARIA BUENO VS. MARGARET SMITH

WIMBLEDON, FINAL, JULY 4, 1964

The graceful artist from Brazil took on the tall athlete from Australia. As always, they brought out the best in each other.

PROLOGUE

Over the first half of the 1960s, two women set the agenda and settled more big matches than any other players. They delighted galleries all over the world with their contrasting personalities yet similarly aggressive styles. They attacked each other's games unwaveringly and intelligently, and more often than not brought out the best in each other. Brazil's Maria Bueno and the Australian Margaret Smith were clearly the preeminent players of that era, taking the women's game into another realm, a slower but in many ways more captivating type of serve-and-volley tennis than that of the men. Bueno-Smith matches were not to be missed. They added value to the major championships simply by showing up.

Both players had made their mark by the time they clashed in the 1964 Wimbledon final. Smith, who grew up in New South Wales, Australia, was the daughter of a foreman at a cheese and butter processing plant. Her first tennis racket was given to her by a sympathetic neighbor. She began refining her game on the sly at a private tennis club not far from her home. When she was eight years old, she would creep under the fence of the courts to play against boys who were members of the club. She won her first tournament before she was ten.

Margaret was a natural left-hander when she began playing the game as a young girl. She was persuaded to switch the racket to her right hand by boys in her neighborhood who made fun of her. As she explained in her book, *Court on Court, A Life in Tennis* (with George McGann), "I got so many taunts that I finally switched the racket to my right hand and played that way thereafter. I've always felt that if I had remained a left-hander I would never have experienced so many problems with my serve."

Difficult or not, Smith made the adjustment. By 1964, she had secured five consecutive Australian Championships. Earlier that year in Brisbane, she won with remarkable command of the court in a 6-3, 6-2 final-round triumph over countrywoman Lesley Turner. A month before that she had taken her second singles championship on the red clay of Roland Garros, winning the French Championships in Paris with a come-from-behind, three-set victory over

Bueno. Two years earlier, she had erased a match point against her in a three-set win over Turner on the same court.

In 1962, Margaret had ruled at Forest Hills, taking the U.S. Championship title. On that occasion, Smith stopped the talented American, Darlene Hard—Bueno's accomplished doubles partner—in a hard-fought, 9-7, 6-4 final. In the 1963 Centre Court title match at Wimbledon, she was too good for an American named Billie Jean Moffitt (soon to be Billie Jean King). Smith triumphed, 6-3, 6-4.

She was well on her way to a record-breaking career. Not yet twenty-two, she had nine major singles titles in her possession. She was nearly six feet tall, and despite her large frame (the press constantly referred to her as statuesque), she covered the court swiftly. She was particularly adept at blanketing the net, making the stretch volley with regular and unprecedented success, showing her opponents how tough it was to drive the ball past her. A superb athlete, Smith could count on her strength to carry her through long afternoons of competition.

Bueno's father, Pedro, was a veterinarian who had an interest in tennis. Though demure and trim, she grew tall enough at 5' 7" to make her presence known. She, too, had enjoyed multiple successes in England and elsewhere in the years leading up to a vintage 1964 Wimbledon. While Smith was more of a programmed player who won her matches through self-discipline and careful application of her skills, Bueno was at her core an artist. A fluid shotmaker who often played points spontaneously, she took great pleasure in being inventive and bold. She was

Maria Bueno

something of a ballerina on the tennis court (not unlike Suzanne Lenglen), gracefully gliding through many of her matches, making shots effortlessly. With this deceptively flowing ability, Bueno captured the Wimbledons of 1959-60. The following year, she was almost always in bad health and there was some talk that she might not compete again. But she returned with vigor in 1962, and was soon on her way to the top of her game.

In the 1959 Wimbledon final, Bueno had halted the No. 4 seed Darlene Hard, 6-4, 6-3,

---

Bueno and Smith produced the pleasure of elegant competence.

---

to win her first major crown. She was only nineteen, and seeded sixth in that event. The Brazilian conceded sets in her second and third round matches, but did not drop another in her last four appearances as her game seemed to improve every time she stepped on court. The following year, she returned as the favorite, seeded No. 1. She lost only one set in that tournament—to the No. 4 seed Christine Truman in a 6-0, 5-7, 6-1 semifinal victory—and defeated No. 8 seed Sandra Reynolds of South Africa, 8-6, 6-0, in the final.

Bueno's success was international. She had also captured two U.S. Championships at Forest Hills. In 1959, she had a close call with the American Jeanne Arth before escaping 4-6, 6-3, 7-5 in the third round. She took off confidently from there, not losing another set, defeating Hard and Truman in decisive meetings at the end. Four years later, she got her title back at Forest Hills, coming through with a pair of clutch victories to close out that first-rate tournament.

In the semifinals, Bueno took on the formidable Englishwoman Ann Jones, a left-hander who knew how to use every inch of the court. Six years later, Jones would crown her career by winning Wimbledon, but in this collision she failed to make good on an early lead over an out-of-sorts Bueno. Jones won the first set and was not behind until 6-5 in the final set. Bueno prevailed, 9-7, in the third. In the final, she had another top-notch match against Smith, who had beaten her the previous year in the semifinals. Bueno was dazzling in this duel, and she clipped Smith, 7-5, 6-4.

On that occasion, the Brazilian was down 1-4, 0-30 in the second set, about to be pushed into a final set by the persistent Australian. Bueno simply turned up her intensity, sharpened her familiar shots, and did not lose another game. It was among the most celebrated sets of her career, and it left Smith dazed and disconsolate when it was over. Bueno loved nothing more than big match conditions, delighting in performing with her back to the wall. Bueno's record worldwide was comparable to Smith's; the difference between them was Smith's mastery of her native turf, her complete domination of the Australian Championships.

As they approached this Wimbledon Centre Court clash, their accomplishments elsewhere in the Grand Slam game were similar. Smith had won two French Championships along with one triumph at both Wimbledon and Forest Hills. Bueno had her twin triumphs at Wimbledon and Forest Hills but had not prevailed in Paris. The moment had arrived for them to collide again in a major final, and they both were ready.

Margaret Smith

THE MATCH

Appropriately, Smith was the top seed at Wimbledon in 1964, while Bueno was placed second. On her way to the final, Smith had only one match that gave her cause for consternation. In the third round, she came up against 1962 titlist Karen Susman, who was not playing regularly anymore on the circuit. Susman was still a seasoned grass court player. She gave the Australian a thorough test in the opening set, looking very impressive in the process, but Smith prevailed, 11-9, 6-0. She moved on easily to the semifinals where she met Billie Jean Moffitt. The American had beaten the top-seeded Smith in the second round two years earlier, then reached the final the previous year before losing to Margaret, 6-3, 6-4. This time, Smith won by the identical score.

Bueno played superlatively all through the tournament, until she faced the canny Lesley Turner, the No. 4 seed, in the semifinals. Turner's forceful, flat ground strokes were very effective on the low bouncing grass, troubling Bueno all through the first set. Bueno shrewdly made adjustments, and rebounded, 3-6, 6-4, 6-4.

The final that all close followers of the game had wanted was on the line. Could Bueno summon the inspiration to overcome Smith with her superior, if streakier, shot-making? Would Smith gain the upper hand with her physical advantages, her reach at the net, her greater size and strength? Who would stand up better to the pressure of a Wimbledon final, an experience unlike any other in the sport?

At the outset, Smith was riddled with apprehension, suffering from serious anxiety as she often did before Centre Court matches. In the opening game, Margaret double faulted on break point, her second serve falling feebly into the net. The Australian broke back at love for 1-1, boosted visibly by a backhand half volley pass as she attacked behind her return for 0-40.

The revival was brief. Flashing a superb backhand passing shot with slice down the line for break point, followed by a well-concealed backhand slice lob over Smith's head, Bueno had the break again for 2-1. The Brazilian mixed her game adroitly to hold for 3-1, but serving in the sixth game she wasted three game points and Smith drew level at 3-3.

At 4-4, Smith's emotional fragility surfaced again. At 15-40, she attempted an American twist second serve which landed in the wrong service box, ten feet wide. Bueno was not going to waste her opportunity to serve out the set. At 5-4, 40-30, she stayed back on her second serve, then worked her way in behind a backhand slice approach which clipped the sideline. Smith's running forehand passing shot was wide. Bueno had secured the set, 6-4.

Troubled by her loss of the opening set, Smith fell behind 15-40 in the first game of the second. Here she was helped by an overanxious Bueno, who missed a backhand return and a backhand passing shot. At game point, Smith found her confidence, making a classic forehand volley winner at full stretch. She broke in the next game with three soundly struck passing shots for 2-0, then served a commanding love game for 3-0 as she connected with every first serve.

Sensing the possibilities at that stage, Smith broke again for 4-0 with a backhand return winner past a charging Bueno. Soon

Margaret stood at 4-0, 40-15. Bueno's piercing returns brought her back to deuce. Smith double faulted, saved the first break point, only to double fault again at break point down. Bueno held on from 30-30 for 2-4. Smith sorely needed to reassert herself in the seventh game on serve.

She fell far short of that goal. Off the mark with four out of five first serves, double faulting once more, she was broken again by a tricky chipped backhand return to her feet. At 3-4, Bueno missed seven of eight first serves, but she survived that game by producing some excel-

---

Smith relinquished a big lead and lost momentum.

---

lent play from the backcourt. Bueno had climbed to 4-4. Would she run out the match as Smith dwelled on her lost chances?

The ninth game stretched into nine deuces. Bueno reached break point five times. Yet Smith remained steadfast, connecting on seventeen of twenty-two first serves, and finding other ways to unsettle Bueno. On game point, the Australian stayed back after a first serve, a tactic that worked as the Brazilian drove a forehand return wide. At 5-5, Smith was obstinate on serve again, holding from 15-40, saving two break points. She had fought her way to 6-5.

Smith held at love for 7-6 with deft volleying, then held at love again for 8-7 by scampering in alertly to cover a drop shot before snapping an overhead into the clear. With Bueno serving at 7-8, Smith increased the pressure. She moved in behind her return of Bueno's second serve to put away an emphatic forehand volley. After Bueno netted a backhand volley, Smith drove a stinging forehand passing shot down the line to force Bueno into an errant volley. Despite squandering the 4-0, 40-15 lead, Smith had reached far inside herself to seal the set.

Until the middle of the final set, Smith seemed to be the better player. She lost only two of fourteen points in three dominant service games, connecting on thirteen of fourteen first serves. She was getting better depth on her serve, closing in tighter for the first volley, forcing Bueno into more mistakes. At 1-2, Bueno was break point down. She saved it with a flourish, punching a penetrating first volley, retreating rapidly for a lob from the Australian and smashing it away. Bueno lifted herself to game point with a strong forehand volley placement off a Smith down-the-line passing shot. Bueno held on for 2-2.

Smith served an ace to hold for 3-2. Bueno was not daunted. She held at love for 3-3 with a flat backhand passing shot, then broke Smith for 4-3. Margaret had served-and-volleyed before moving back for an overhead as Bueno lifted a

---

Bueno fashioned a remarkable streak of winning shots.

---

lob high into the air. Smith's smash lacked severity, and Bueno drove a forehand crosscourt that forced Margaret into the backcourt. Bueno came in and Smith missed a backhand pass. The net had been taken away from her. The match seemed to be slipping away as well.

Bueno moved to 5-3 at the cost of only one point. In concluding that game, she was letter perfect. The Brazilian charged into the net behind her serve, made a solid, deep volley, and knew where Margaret was going with the passing shot before Smith did. Bueno was on top of

the net for a scintillating forehand volley winner. Smith served to save the match at 3-5, double-faulted to 0-30, and fell behind 15-40, double match point. Bueno lofted another effective lob, forcing Smith to play a soft overhead. Anticipating that response, Bueno moved in and played a backhand half volley approach from mid-court.

The ball floated high over the net but Smith was too stunned to react. She stood there deep in the court, frozen, realizing she had no chance to reach the ball. Bueno had hit a nearly impossible shot at match point to prevail, 6-4, 7-9, 6-3. In collecting the last four games in a row, Bueno had won sixteen of nineteen points. Her streak to the finish line was reminiscent of her Forest Hills victory over Smith the year before. Bueno was the Wimbledon champion for the third time, and had never been better.

As the eloquent David Gray wrote in *The Guardian,* "Miss Bueno was scoring points with capricious ease. The Brazilian spent points as wastefully as ever, but in the crisis of the match she invariably found it possible to produce luxurious quantities of shots which were rich and imaginative, graceful and deadly. She was the more effective server, she did not miss a smash and, in the recollections of even the oldest members, no woman has hit so many beautiful and piercing forehand volleys. She stirred the Centre Court as she did in the first dazzling days of her royalty."

EPILOGUE

Later that summer, Bueno underscored her status as the best player in the world by winning Forest Hills for the second straight year. In the final, she routed the capable American, Carole

Graebner, 6-1, 6-0. Smith—who was beaten only twice all season—was ousted in three sets by Susman in the round of sixteen. The Australian had captured the Australian and French Championships but Bueno had taken the two most important titles in tennis by coming through at the All England Club and Forest Hills. She had lost a significant meeting to Smith in Paris, but had gathered the two prizes she valued the most. It was her most productive season.

The following year, Smith was leading Bueno, 5-2, in the third set of the Australian Championships final when the Brazilian had to retire with an injury. Smith went on to win Wimbledon by taking Bueno 6-4, 7-5 in a well-played final. She also took the U.S. Championships with a final round win over Billie Jean Moffitt. Her lone Grand Slam defeat was in Paris, where she lost the final to the meticulous backcourt play of Turner. Smith was nearly invincible across that season, winning fifty-eight matches in a row, and capturing eighteen tournaments during the year.

Bueno, hampered severely that year by a knee injury, underwent surgery. She was not the player she had been in 1964, but the following year she was revitalized. In the 1966 Wimbledon, Smith and Bueno were seeded first and second again. Bueno moved as expected to the final but Smith was ousted by Billie Jean Moffitt King, who had married in the autumn of 1965. King beat Bueno for the title.

The Brazilian was in peak form at Forest Hills, winning the U.S. Championship for the fourth and final time, capturing her last Grand Slam championship. In the final, she was down 0-2 in the first set against the determined Texan, Nancy Richey. From that juncture, Bueno's virtuosity was too much for her doubles partner,

with whom she had won at Wimbledon two months earlier. Bueno soared to a 6-3, 6-1 victory. She was not yet twenty-seven when she collected that crown with bright sequences of free-wheeling shotmaking. It seemed entirely possible that Bueno would celebrate another five years in the upper echelons of the game.

In fact, she would no longer play at that level. Beginning in 1967, she was hindered by a wide assortment of injuries. The primary problem for Bueno was her arm. That year, she lost in the round of sixteen at Wimbledon to the rapidly rising American, Rosie Casals. She withdrew from the U.S. National Championships at Forest Hills, where she was seeded sixth. The pain was persistent near her shoulder. Bueno was drifting out of tennis, much to the dismay of her large legion of admirers.

The following year, she did play respectably in the majors. King defeated her in the quarterfinals of the first French Open. Richey beat her in the same round at

---

While Smith rose to new heights, Bueno was beset by injuries.

Wimbledon. At Forest Hills, she performed better than she had for a long while. At that initial U.S. Open, she was seeded fifth. In the quarterfinals, she upset the No. 4 seed Margaret Smith Court, 7-5, 2-6, 6-3—their last meeting of consequence. Maintaining that form in her semifinal session with King, Bueno took the first set before bowing 3-6, 6-4, 6-2. She was ranked in the top five in the world for the year.

The pain in her arm persisted. Bueno's career was essentially over. She did make what amounted to a sentimental comeback in 1976 and 1977, when she was in her late thirties, but the majestic match playing qualities were gone. Her comeback was brief, although it must have been worth her while since fans greeted her appearances with genuine warmth. Bueno remained a powerful presence on the tennis stage, even if her skills and speed had been diminished.

Smith was another story. She continued her complete domination of the Australian Championships, extending her streak to seven consecutive titles in 1966. In 1967, Smith married Barry Court, and she pondered retirement for a while. By 1968, with Open Tennis a reality, Margaret Smith Court was not content to rest on her laurels. She turned twenty-six in the middle of that year. She had not realized all of her ambitions, and was determined to come back to the courts triumphantly, sharing the victories with her husband, who joined her on the road and provided much encouragement. Barry Court wanted his wife to enjoy her tennis, and she did.

The first year of the open game was lukewarm for Margaret. She was shy of her best as she reacquainted herself with the rigors of match play. Not present for the French Open, she was seeded second at Wimbledon behind King, appearing for the first time on the draw as Mrs. B. M. Court. In the quarterfinals, she fell surprisingly to countrywoman Judy Tegart 4-6, 8-6, 6-1. She won the U.S. Nationals over Bueno, but the Brazilian retaliated in the quarterfinals of Forest Hills. Court took her place, however, among the top five in the world despite her lackluster showings in the two foremost tournaments.

In 1969, she had one of her greatest seasons, sweeping three of the four major championships, losing her lone "Big Four" match to the British left-hander Ann Jones in the semifinals of Wimbledon. At the age of twenty-seven, she had already captured a total of sixteen major singles titles.

There was much more in store for this woman of quiet dignity and high ambitions.   •

ROD LAVER VS. TONY ROCHE

AUSTRALIAN OPEN, SEMIFINAL, JANUARY 25, 1969

At the peak of his powers, Laver was confronted by a tenacious countryman. They fought ferociously through a long afternoon in debilitating heat.

PROLOGUE

Very few players in the annals of tennis have earned such universal respect and admiration as the Australian, Rod Laver. A somewhat sickly child, he grew up on his father's cattle ranch in Queensland. Left-handed and low key, he became an explosive competitor who expressed his personality through the inspiration of his inventive shotmaking. A champion capable of winning on any surface, he established himself as only the second man to win the Grand Slam (the other was Don Budge) when, in 1962, he seized the four major championships of Australia, France, Great Britain, and the United States. The press and the players called him "The Rocket."

Laver was twenty-four when he completed that run. He had shown extraordinary determination when the big points of a match were being contested. Laver's pattern of play was appealingly different from most left-handers. He did not rely too heavily on his serve. His game involved mastering all the shots. He could win his share of points with cleverly directed kick and slice serves, pulling his opponents wide in both the deuce and advantage courts, then punching irretrievable volleys into open spaces. But what distinguished Laver from most of the competition was his versatility off the ground. He ushered in heavy topspin long before the arrival of Bjorn Borg, but Laver did more damage, in many ways, with both the forehand and the backhand than the Swede could deliver.

The hallmark of his fully rounded game was the passing shot. A relatively small man at 5' 8", he moved swiftly and surely, with exemplary footwork. Even when he was on the run, he could drive the ball past his opponents with astonishing force and accuracy, demoralizing them with counterattacking instincts. Furthermore, Laver would tantalize his rivals with his cleverly concealed underspin lobs off the backhand. He probed and picked his rivals apart astutely. In short, Laver had the entire package, including an unflappable temperament.

Laver was, however, a habitual risk taker who had his share of off days. He played daringly and almost defiantly, always looking for new ways to win rather than merely avoiding a loss. He took his chances sensibly, seeming to balance his tactics between percentage and

Tony Roche

possibility. In his 1962 Grand Slam season, he moved in and out of precarious positions throughout the four majors. He started his venture smoothly at the Australian Championships, but then was forced into three exacting five-set struggles at the French Championships in Paris.

Down match point in the fourth set against countryman Marty Mulligan, Laver escaped and won, 6-2, in the fifth. Another Australian (and fellow left-hander) Neale Fraser pushed The Rocket to 7-5 in the fifth set of the semifinals. In the final, he trailed two sets to love against future doubles partner Roy Emerson, but salvaged that one, 3-6, 2-6, 6-3, 9-7, 6-2. At Wimbledon, Laver climbed much closer toward the top of his game and lost only one set in seven matches, crushing Mulligan, 6-2, 6-2, 6-1, in the final. And then at Forest Hills, Laver surpassed himself, winning against Emerson in a four set final.

After that historic Slam, Laver turned professional. His rookie season of 1963 was inevitably a rude awakening. He had graduated with honors from the amateur game, but the brigade of seasoned professionals—ranging from Rosewall to Gonzales—sent him back to the classroom. The level of play was higher across the board. By 1964, Laver had made the improvements, and he was unofficially the best player in the world again right up to the emergence of Open Tennis in 1968. The previous year, Laver had returned with the professionals for an all-pro event at Wimbledon, and had won it without much suspense. He had also taken the U.S. Pro Championships three of four years between 1964 and 1967.

When Laver, Rosewall, Gonzales and company were permitted at last to play the major championships, Rod was indisputably the man to beat. He lost to Rosewall in the first open tournament at Bournemouth, England, in April

1968, and fell again to his Australian compatriot in the French Open final. The slow, red clay plainly favored Rosewall's more compact ground strokes. A few weeks later, when everyone assembled at Wimbledon for the return of the professionals, Laver more than lived up to his billing as the best of them all.

The top-seeded Laver worked his way assiduously through the draw, challenged strongly in almost every round. The American, Gene Scott, took a set off him in the first round, as did another solid serve-and-volleyer from the United States, Marty Riessen. Great Britain's left-hander, Mark Cox, a leading amateur who upended the professionals Gonzales and Emerson to reach the Bournemouth semifinals, pushed Laver into a rigorous four set encounter in the round of sixteen. Then 1966 Wimbledon finalist Dennis Ralston took Laver all the way into a fifth set before bowing 6-2. Laver's hardest assignments were behind him as he handled U.S. Davis Cupper Arthur Ashe in a straight set semifinal, followed by a 6-3, 6-4, 6-2 triumph over countryman Tony Roche, the No. 15 seed.

Roche was showing the form that everyone had expected of him since he had captured the French Championships in 1966. He was one of many talented Australians, the son of the town butcher in Tarcutta, New South Wales. He turned professional in 1967 and joined "The Handsome Eight" for the WCT Tour. A stocky left-hander, Roche would become one of the premier doubles players of his time alongside the esteemed John Newcombe. But with his exploits at Wimbledon in 1968—including a straight set upset of the No. 2 seed Rosewall in the round of sixteen—Roche was showing how good he could be on his own.

Like Laver, Roche was not a big server. He relied on an excellent heavy kick in the deuce court and a productive combination of the kicker and the slice in the advantage court. The serves were calculated to allow Roche to close in tight for his first volley, and he was tenacious at the net. His backhand volley—the best in the game then and easily one of the top five of all time—was a devastatingly potent weapon, produced with textbook form. It was his defining shot.

In that Wimbledon final of 1968, Roche had no chance to make his mark as Laver soared from the middle of the first set and swept through the match, 6-3, 6-4, 6-2. Although Laver performed unevenly two months later at Forest Hills in a five set, fourth round loss against the South African, Cliff Drysdale, he was ranked No. 1 in the world for the first year of the open era.

THE MATCH

When the 1969 season started for most of the players in Sydney, Roche had toppled Laver in the final. The twenty-three-year-old Roche was no longer daunted by the prospect of playing against his venerated countryman. He realized that his game matched up better now against Laver's than just about any other leading competitor, primarily because he was another

Roche had proved himself in doubles but wanted to win on his own.

left-hander. In any case, Laver was top seeded at the first Grand Slam event of the year in Brisbane at the Australian Open, while Roche was placed at No. 4. Both men had difficult paths as they progressed to a semifinal meeting.

Rod Laver

Laver was nearly pressed into a fifth set by Emerson, who was serving at 7-6 in the fourth late in the evening. Laver held him off to record a 6-2, 6-4, 3-6, 9-7 round-of-sixteen victory. He then ousted Fred Stolle, 6-4, 18-16, 6-4, in the quarterfinals. Meanwhile, Roche moved through easily into the quarterfinals by over-coming his doubles partner, and No. 5 seed, Newcombe, in five sets after falling behind two sets to one. So it was that Laver would face Roche in the semifinals of the first major championship of the year. Laver hoped for another Grand Slam, but knew he could not afford to look beyond this event. Roche had not won a

RUSS ADAMS

Tony Roche

break serve. The extreme heat made breaking serve a tall order as the ball moved faster through the air. With Roche serving at 5-5 in the first set, Laver made his move, closing out that chapter with a cluster of low returns. Set to Laver, 7-5.

Volleying even more effectively in the second set, Roche stubbornly stood his ground. He did not want to allow his adversary the advantage of a two-sets-to-love lead. He played with intense concentration. Both combatants held on to their serves in that set, knowing that one break would decide it, sensing that whoever broke through would have the momentum to run out the match. With Roche serving in the forty-first game of a very long and straining set, Laver finally achieved the break, then held serve to win, 22-20. The top seed now possessed an almost insurmountable two-sets-to-love lead in debilitating humidity.

Roche was not willing to accept defeat. Having stayed the course for so long he seemed not discouraged about his chances in the third. Roche pursued his points in an unyielding fashion during the third set and finally secured the break when Laver served at 9-10. The players retreated to the haven of the locker room for the traditional ten-minute break at the end of the third set, and took showers. Dressed in fresh tennis clothes, they returned with Laver still holding a safe but slimmer lead, two sets to one.

That edge disappeared rapidly as Roche glided to 5-0 in the fourth, breaking Laver in the

major title since his championship run in Paris three years earlier. And with the other semifinal pitting the Spaniard, Andres Gimeno (an upset winner over No. 2 seed Rosewall), against the Australian Ray Ruffels, it was expected that the winner of Laver-Roche would take the title.

They clashed during a very hot afternoon on a grass court in poor condition, producing one capricious bounce after another. But both men settled quickly into their business, moving in behind their serves, connecting solidly with their approach volleys, playing the grass court game skillfully. With the temperature rising to 105 degrees Fahrenheit, both men had to be conscious about conserving energy, picking their moments carefully as they attempted to

second and fourth games, holding his own delivery with growing assurance. Laver managed to hold serve in the sixth game before Roche closed out the set in the seventh. The only advantage left to Laver was serving first in the final set.

Summoning everything he had in reserve, Laver found depth on serve again, and Roche could not sustain the pace of the previous set. With both players controlling matters on their serves, the fifth set seemed to be scripted much like the first three. With Roche serving at 3-4, Laver wanted to make certain he converted any chances that might come his way. He wrote in his book, *The Education of a Tennis Player*, (with Bud Collins), "You can slam away when your opponent isn't too sound, or clearly dominate him, but I was in with Tony Roche in the decisive set, and it was no time for pride or flamboyance. I was going to scratch and dig and bloop the ball over any way I could."

Laver surmised that with the court producing so many irregular bounces, he needed to be particularly cautious, chip his returns low, and hope for the best. He got to 15-30 in that pivotal eighth game. Roche sent his first serve down the middle in the advantage court, trying to spin it into Laver's body on the backhand side. Laver went with his plan, chipping the ball crosscourt, going for the safe shot. Roche believed the ball was going out, and still thought it was his point when the shot landed. But the linesman made no call.

Roche was livid. Instead of being level at 30-30, he was down 15-40. He served-and-volleyed at 15-40, and Laver launched a fearsome topspin backhand down the line. Roche tried to cover it, but his forehand volley fell in the net. Laver had the break for 5-3, and he did not let a closeout elude him. It was an exhausting 7-5, 22-20, 9-11, 1-6, 6-3 victory. In one fortunate and striking moment, a four-and-a-half hour match that had hung in the balance swung around to Laver. Roche had played possibly the match of his life and still lost. Laver kept his customary composure and made the most of his opportunities; Roche lost his emotional restraint late in the fifth set, and it cost him the match.

Be that as it may, it was a match for the ages. Billie Jean King watched the contest almost in awe, and wrote about it eloquently in an account for *World Tennis*. As King saw it, "Laver and Roche displayed every shot in the book, often in the same point. Tony lobbed over Rod's head; Laver raced back, sliding 15 feet to get to the ball, then hit one of his incredible backhand flick winners which Tony, even more incredibly, managed to reach. We saw drop volleys, spins, fantastic baseline exchanges, great overheads and superb retrieving. Because of the heat at least half of the 2,000 spectators left before the match was over. None of the players who were watching so much as stirred. . . . [At 3-4 in the fifth] mild-mannered Tony, his shirttails floating behind him, turned in surprise to the linesman and queried him as follows: 'Did you actually make that call? Did you really see the ball? Do you think I stood out there for four-and-a-half hours to get a call like that?' "

Acknowledging the breaks that went his way, Laver was buoyed by his win over Roche. In the final, The Rocket coasted against a passive Gimeno and came away a 6-3, 6-4, 7-5 winner to capture the first of the four majors.

EPILOGUE

Four months later, Laver set his sights on Paris and the French Open. He came close to making a second-round exit when he faced his countryman Dick Crealy, a streaky player who took the first two sets of their meeting. But Laver was the beneficiary of some good luck again. After the third set, the match was delayed until the following morning. A new day provided the opportunity to put the finishing touches on a 3-6, 7-9, 6-2, 6-2, 6-4 victory.

Thereafter, Laver was unstoppable on the clay. He dropped the first sets of his quarterfinal and semifinal contests with Gimeno and Okker, but never looked like he would give further ground. In the final, reversing the 1968 result, Laver took Rosewall apart, 6-4, 6-3, 6-4. He would say later of that victory, "From a sustained standpoint, my game was elevated against Kenny to the biggest peak I ever reached on clay. Once in a while you might play five games where you go bang, bang, bang, and all the shots go in and you just can't miss. But

---

Laver continued his quest for another Grand Slam.

---

then you come back to your senses. That day against Kenny, I kept it up for three sets."

Two down, two remaining. Laver was half way to winning a second Grand Slam. He was favored by a larger margin at Wimbledon than he was in Paris. But the second round was again a menacing time for the Australian maestro. He trailed Indian Davis Cupper Premjit Lall, 3-6, 4-6, 3-3, before sweeping fifteen consecutive games for the match. Future titlist Stan Smith drew Laver into another five set test in

the round of sixteen, but it was his semifinal with a scintillating Ashe that everyone would remember.

Ashe was sprinkling the court with one winner after another off his dazzling backhand, employing that stroke with awesome potency, giving Laver little chance to respond. As Laver reflected afterward, "I could only hope Arthur would hit earth at some stage because he was playing unbelievably well. He was thrashing the ball past me. He almost outplayed himself."

Ultimately, Ashe did just that. He found it impossible to maintain his ferocious and relatively error-free brand of play, and Laver calmly kept on track. The ginger-haired Australian got the job done, 2-6, 6-2, 9-7, 6-0, answering Ashe's soaring first set three times.

In the final, Laver was locked at one set all, but down 1-4 in the third, against the best grass court player of them all, John Newcombe. Had Newcombe managed to move on and establish a two-sets-to-one lead, he might well have won. But Laver caught him, took the third, and came away a 6-4, 5-7, 6-4, 6-4 winner.

He was closing in tight on his target now, only one major championship away from the Grand Slam. He would be back on the lawns of Forest Hills, at the U.S. Open, where he had completed the Slam seven years earlier. In the round of sixteen, Laver came upon a player who would beat him one year later on the same court, a man who possessed some of the purest strokes in modern tennis, Dennis Ralston. Ralston took a two-sets-to-one lead into the locker room for the ten-minute intermission. Laver, during the break, listened intently to some words of wisdom from his comrades Stolle and Emerson.

They told him he was tossing the ball too

---

low on his serve, urging him to make an adjustment and raise his first serve percentage. Laver obliged, and ran away from Ralston in the last two sets, coming home with a 6-4, 4-6, 4-6, 6-2, 6-3 victory. In the quarterfinals, Emerson provided stern opposition, but after a slow start Laver gradually gained the upper hand and prevailed, 4-6, 8-6, 13-11, 6-4.

Laver now took on the defending champion Ashe. His versatility was too much for the American. Laver succeeded, 8-6, 6-3, 14-12, propelling himself into the final. He was only a single match away from his goal. His opponent was a rugged serve-and-volleyer who had been his most formidable rival all year long. The No. 3 seed, Tony Roche, had achieved significant wins over the still formidable Pancho Gonzales, and reached the final by ousting Newcombe, 8-6, in the fifth set. He had come this far to reach his first Grand Slam tournament final since losing to Laver at Wimbledon the year before. Roche was eager for revenge this time around.

Roche had every reason to believe in his chances. He held a winning record over The Rocket for the year, defeating the game's greatest player on no fewer than five occasions. He knew he was viewed with high regard by Laver, who was not fond of playing fellow left-handers. Why was Roche such a difficult puzzle for Laver to solve? Newcombe had observed, "One factor was the way Tony served so well into Rod's body. The other factor was that in 1969 Tony Roche was playing bloody good tennis."

Roche took the first set narrowly as both players moved carefully on the wet grass court. They were competing on a Monday afternoon in front of a half-empty stadium at Forest Hills.

At one stage, there were six consecutive service breaks. Roche then served for the first set at 6-5. Laver struck back, only to fall away again. Roche finally took it, deservedly, 9-7.

Roche triumphed over Laver five times that year.

Laver felt that the court was getting increasingly slick, so he asked tournament director Billy Talbert if he could put on spikes. He said afterward, "Billy had told me he wanted me to start the match without the spikes but he had no problem with my switching to them later if I felt I needed them."

Laver changed to the spikes at the start of the second set, and it was clear that his mobility was enhanced. He began making his customary on the run passing shots. He took the second set at the cost of only the sixth game. After the first game of the third, there was a thirty-one minute rain delay, but Laver was not going to be halted by anything or anyone, neither the elements nor his friend Roche. Laver devised a 7-9, 6-1, 6-2, 6-2 victory. His second Grand Slam was a far more impressive feat than his first because he had faced the leading players in his field rather than only the best of the amateurs as he had in 1962.

A self-deprecating Laver said in 1989, "It's not as tough fronting up a second time. I had it all going for me. I just didn't feel I had that huge amount of pressure. I figured all I could do was prepare. When you do that, you are fortunate to play your best tennis. As Tony Trabert says, it's amazing how lucky you get when you prepare. I think there is a lot of truth in that."

Newcombe, one of the game's sharpest analysts as well as an all-time great player, says of Laver's 1969 campaign, "Rocket read the battle plan perfectly that year. He knew when to change and when not to change his game plan. I really admired him for coming up with a slight but important tactical change to keep us off balance."

As Laver summed it up himself, "Winning a second Grand Slam changed my whole life. But I always get brought back to reality when I remember the matches I lost very convincingly. I don't put myself in any category that says I'm the best that ever lived. I really don't. There are so many ups and downs in a career, but it's nice to know I've been put down as one of the top players of all time."

After 1969, Laver slowly receded from his peak. He was thirty-one by the time he won Forest Hills to seal his second Slam, so a decline was expected. He continued as a major force in the sport and was a prolific tournament winner in 1970 and 1971. In fact, he had a superb run indoors during the winter and spring of 1971. By winning thirteen matches in a head-to-head competition called the Tennis Champions Classic against Newcombe, Roche, Ashe, Ralston, and company, Laver earned a total of $160,000, a record sum in those days.

Roche, meanwhile, remained a hard luck fellow. In 1970, he made it back to the final of Forest Hills, but lost in his second straight U.S. Open final to Rosewall, the same man he had halted at Wimbledon two years earlier. He had won the U.S. Pro Championships in Boston earlier that summer with a five set win over Laver, so his failure to come through at Forest Hills was a deep disappointment.

Roche remained an enormous success in doubles alongside Newcombe, with whom he won Wimbledon five times. But in singles he never did collect another Grand Slam title after taking the French Championships as an amateur in 1966. In 1969, despite several victories over Laver, he lost the two that mattered the most in Brisbane and New York. He held the distinction of being a premier rival for the great Laver when the Rocket was at his peak, but did not do himself full justice. By 1971, he started having severe problems with his elbow. He went to visit a faith healer in the Philippines and had a recovery of sorts—reaching the Wimbledon semifinals in 1975 before losing in five sets to Ashe—but this was not the Roche of 1968 to 1970.

Tony Roche will be remembered above all for his showdowns with Laver in 1969, his distinguished final round appearance against his countryman at Forest Hills, and his extraordinary match against Rod at Brisbane. Laver had no tougher test all year in his Grand Slam quest. •

PANCHO GONZALES VS. CHARLIE PASARELL

WIMBLEDON, FIRST ROUND, JUNE 24-25, 1969

In the longest match on record at Wimbleton, the volatile Gonzales and the quietly driven Pasarell put on a heroic display of fast court tennis which took two days to complete.

PROLOGUE

Puerto Rico's Charlie Pasarell was a teaching professional's perfect model of how to play the game of tennis. His strokes were taken straight out of the book. He hit the ball cleanly and precisely off both sides. His forehand was his most penetrating shot, and an opponent served to that side at his own peril. He was authoritative at the net, punching his volleys sharply, moving nimbly back under lobs to employ his flawless overhead.

Pasarell was not merely a flamboyant stylist, which might have been considered a genetic quality because his father and mother were both singles champions of Puerto Rico, and his brother was ranked in the American top forty. Charlie was a competitor who agonized over every point. After big matches in the major tournaments, he would frequently be heard replaying each critical shot in excruciating detail to his colleagues. He was known among the people in his profession as an uncommonly decent man, perhaps too generous of spirit.

In the middle 1960s, he was among a promising cast of gifted Americans expected to perform effectively in the big events. Pasarell was the classic fast-court competitor who played his best tennis on grass. With three of the four Grand Slam events held on that surface during his prime, he was prepared. Critics and fellow competitors were in agreement regarding Pasarell. It was a matter of marrying talent with temperament. He had the former, but seemed to lack the latter on too many occasions.

Be that as it may, Pasarell had moved to the top of the rankings in the United States as an amateur in 1967. His picture appeared on the cover of the U.S.L.T.A. yearbook the following spring. He looked convincingly like a world champion, reaching for a backhand volley with his weight moving forward, his knees bent, his arms extended. Pasarell's 1967 rise to No. 1 in his country featured two essential achievements: He defeated his close friend and revered rival Arthur Ashe to win the U.S. Indoor Championships, and he toppled the defending champion Manuel Santana in the first round of Wimbledon. No one had ever upset the titleholder in an opening round men's match in the history of the tournament.

Pasarell was as dedicated a craftsman as

Pancho Gonzales

anyone in his field. In many ways, he probably cared too much, coming down hard on himself after losses, remembering every missed opportunity with complete clarity. Pasarell was still an amateur when Open Tennis started in the spring of 1968. He was clearly one of the "dangerous floaters" in the draw at Wimbledon that summer. In the second round on Centre Court, he took a two-sets-to-one lead over the No. 2 seed Ken Rosewall, and led, 2-0, in the final set. But he was beaten, 6-3, in the fifth.

As a veteran of the American Davis Cup team, Pasarell—a keen student of the game—had profited from the wisdom of some excellent coaching over the years. One of his mentors was Pancho Gonzales. Gonzales had delighted in sharing his deep knowledge of the game with the younger American players of the 1960s before the advent of the Open Era.

To most of these young men—Arthur Ashe and Cliff Richey were others in that camp—

Gonzales was a hero. They had grown up watching and reading about him. They recognized in Gonzales much of what they aspired to be themselves. He embodied the ineffable characteristics of a champion. Pancho's advice on strategy and tactics was always welcomed.

When Open Tennis was introduced in the spring of 1968, Gonzales's role among his countrymen was altered. After nineteen years away from the major championships, he was permitted at last to compete again in those events. In the twilight of his career, he was rejuvenated by the chance to appear again at Roland Garros, Wimbledon, and Forest Hills.

Gonzales was perhaps the greatest tennis player never to have won Wimbledon. He had last played there when he was twenty-one in 1949. Seeded second, he bowed in the fourth round. After Forest Hills later that summer, he turned professional. In the inaugural open season, he was a surprise semifinalist at the French Open. At Wimbledon, seeded eighth, he fell in an early round to the Russian Alex Metreveli, a future finalist. At the U.S. Open, Gonzales was in strikingly good form, ousting the second-seeded Tony Roche to reach the quarterfinals, then losing an elegant battle with the Dutchman Tom Okker.

As the 1969 Wimbledon approached, Gonzales and the other leading players realized that Rod Laver was the putative favorite. Gonzales wanted to make amends for his disappointing return in 1968. As for Pasarell, he hoped to give the Centre Court audience a demonstration of his grass court skill.

When the draw for the 1969 Wimbledon was released, Pasarell found himself slated to play one of the game's legendary figures, a fellow American sixteen years his senior named Gonzales.

THE MATCH

The two Americans walked onto Centre Court at nearly 6:30 P.M. on Tuesday, June 24, 1969. They looked like a pair of movie stars taking the stage. In the *London Times*, Rex Bellamy described Pasarell deftly. "Splay-footed and broad-shouldered, he has the shambling gait of some Western heroes. He walks with a drawl, arms swinging menacingly at his sides as if itching for a challenge to a fast draw."

Shifting his attention to Gonzales, Bellamy wrote, "Gonzales is one of the few personalities in Wimbledon history who can dominate the Centre Court instead of letting it dominate him. The man smoulders with character. There are dark, brooding depths in his intense concentration. He has the loose-limbed ease of the natural athlete. He has the mannerisms of the well-rehearsed actor treading a familiar stage—the fingers of his left hand flicking away the sweat and hitching his sodden shirt back to his shoulders."

As the combatants waged a service battle in the fading early evening light, it was clear that the opening set would be settled by a single break. Gonzales and Pasarell earnestly went about their business, comfortable on the fast green surface, producing their effortless moves with graceful efficiency. They were searching

for that one opportunity to break. In the forty-sixth game of a marathon set, Pasarell finally broke Gonzales to seal the first set, 24-22. Sets like this one led to the adoption of the tiebreaker the following year.

Gonzales wanted the match postponed at that point because of darkness, but his request for a suspension of play was denied. Infuriated by the rejection, distressed by the loss of the long opening set, the forty-one-year-old seemed distracted in the second set. His concentration completely broken, his rhythm gone on serve, Gonzales collected only a single game. With

Russ Adams

Charlie Pasarell

Pasarell up two sets to love, the match was halted. Gonzales had banged his racket against the back of the umpire's chair when he left the court after two hours and eighteen minutes. He was booed by an audience largely unsympathetic to his actions. It was nearly 9 P.M. as the players departed in the darkness.

They returned on Wednesday afternoon in bright sunlight. The third set had the tone and texture of the first. Both men were unbreakable on serve, and the urgency for Gonzales grew with every point. He was resuming this conflict at two sets to love down, and could afford no lapses. The older American held his delivery fifteen consecutive times in that third set, but Pasarell assiduously tended his own pattern of play.

In the thirtieth game, serving to save the set for the eleventh time, Pasarell missed five straight first services. He opened that game with a double fault, then served another for 15-40. When Gonzales sent a stinging forehand passing shot down the line to force an errant backhand volley from Pasarell, he had the break, and with it the set.

The Centre Court crowd of nearly fifteen thousand showered warm applause upon Gonzales. He was still trailing two sets to one, but the bright light of the new day was giving him cause for optimism. Both players had chances to break early in the fourth. Despite three double faults, Pasarell escaped two break points to hold for 1-1. Gonzales connected with fourteen first serves in a row in the following game, but still needed to cast aside a break point himself.

Pasarell seemed certain of himself and his chances as he served at 3-4. In that critical game, however, he faltered. He missed five of six first serves. At 30-30, Gonzales struck. He dinked a backhand passing shot crosscourt, forcing Pasarell to play an ineffectual backhand volley down the line. Gonzales was in place and rolled a forehand passing shot crosscourt for a winner to reach set point. Surprised and apprehensive, Pasarell double faulted, his second serve hitting the net.

Gonzales easily served out the set, holding in the ninth game without missing a single first serve. Pancho had moved his delivery from corner to corner throughout the set, keeping Pasarell off guard. His depth, placement and variety were awesome. Along the way, he hit his target with twenty-nine of thirty-four first serves, an astonishing percentage in light of his immense power.

With the Centre Court fans applauding him generously, Gonzales had brought himself back to two sets all. He had left his early misfortunes behind him. He seemed fully capable of completing a victory.

Pasarell still had the advantage of youth. Moreover, he would be serving first in the fifth set. Pasarell made the most of it. He moved through the early games of the final set with an air of confidence, perhaps buoyed by the sight

---

Over two days, both players reached new heights.

---

of Gonzales leaning wearily on his racket between points. In the first six games of the fifth set, neither man was close to a break point. In that stretch Gonzales conceded only two points in three service games while Pasarell allowed his adversary only five.

At 3-3, in the seventh game, Gonzales applied pressure with a rush of energy. He reached 15-30 with his favorite tactic, following his backhand chip return into the forecourt to challenge the charging Pasarell. The veteran's return was low and effective. Pasarell volleyed up. Gonzales was perfectly positioned for a backhand volley winner. Pasarell was pushed to deuce in that game, but he held for 4-3 when

A fifth set which no witness will ever forget.

another Gonzales chip-and-charge failed. Pasarell punched a forehand volley calmly past Pancho for 4-3.

At 3-4, Gonzales was debilitated. At 40-30, he produced a weak first serve and then surrendered the point with an off-target backhand first volley wide down the line. Pasarell was two points away from serving for the match. But Gonzales once again summoned hidden strength, serving deep to the Pasarell backhand to elicit a mistake, then cracking an ace to reach 4-4.

Pasarell seemed unperturbed. He held for 5-4 with a safely guided inside-out smash well out of his opponent's reach. Serving in the tenth game, Gonzales was in deep trouble. On the first point, he retreated for a smash as Pasarell lofted a fine lob off his backhand side. Gonzales mishit the overhead off the top of his frame for 0-15. Pasarell made it 0-30 when his forehand passing shot clipped the net cord and provoked an error from Gonzales. Then Pasarell played a solid, chipped backhand return and Gonzales's volley was long.

It was 4-5, 0-40 in the fifth. Gonzales was triple match point down. He moved in behind his first serve, played a percentage volley crosscourt, and Pasarell went once more for the lob with his backhand. The shot was long. Gonzales

added pace to his next first serve deep to the backhand to force Pasarell to return long. It was 30-40. Another first serve from Gonzales was answered by a fine backhand return from Pasarell. Gonzales bent low for the forehand volley, and placed it deep down the line. Pasarell lobbed over Gonzales, and the older man turned and scampered after it.

If the ball had landed inbounds, the match would have been over. It was inches out. Deuce. Gonzales served-and-volleyed, played one cautious overhead, then put the second one away emphatically. He was at game point. Pasarell recovered to deuce, two points away from victory again. Pasarell made another testing return but Gonzales went behind him with a firm backhand volley down the line to lure his foe into another mistake. When Pasarell missed a return on the next point, Gonzales had held almost miraculously for 5-5, saving three match points in the process, earning a sustained ovation from an appreciative audience.

Pasarell may have been troubled by Gonzales's bold stand, but the twenty-five-year-old did not show it. At 5-5, 15-30, he seemed at his rival's mercy. Gonzales stepped around his backhand for a forehand reverse crosscourt passing shot. The shot missed narrowly. Pasarell held for 6-5. An emboldened Pasarell went after Gonzales full force again. He stepped up his pace to coax Gonzales into a backhand volley error for 0-15. He took the net away from the older man with a well-placed lob, then closed in tight for a forehand volley winner, making it 0-30.

When Gonzales popped his forehand volley up meekly on the following point, Pasarell unhesitatingly drove a flat backhand crosscourt passing shot into the clear. Gonzales stood at triple match point against him for the second time. He served deep to the backhand, placed his volley deep, and clipped his overhead confidently for a placement to make it 15-40. He served deep to the backhand again, directing his volley to Pasarell's weaker backhand wing. Pasarell went down the line with a passing shot, keeping the ball tantalizingly low. Gonzales read it early, opened his racket face, and deposited a delicate, angled forehand drop volley winner for 30-40. Swinging with deceptive speed, Gonzales then released a strong first serve to Pasarell's backhand. The return was well out. Deuce.

Gonzales advanced to game point before Pasarell responded with a superbly struck forehand passing shot

RUSS ADAMS

Pancho Gonzales

crosscourt. Deuce for the second time. Pasarell made a first-rate low forehand return off a second serve. Gonzales displayed his considerable courage, executing another extraordinary forehand drop volley for a winner. At game point for the second time, Gonzales came through with a classic serve-and-volley combination, then put away his second volley with cool efficiency. It was 6-6. The crowd gave the older American another rousing round of applause.

The younger man had endured a pair of humbling setbacks. Gonzales had twice held from triple match point down, saving six match points. Pasarell met that stern challenge with

perhaps his best service game of the match. He held at love, did not miss a first serve, and finished off that game with an ace for 7-6.

The players changed ends of the court and took only twenty seconds as they toweled off and sipped their refreshments. The tiebreaker would be introduced to the Grand Slam events the following year at Forest Hills. Wimbledon would begin with the tiebreak in 1971. But as Gonzales and Pasarell came down the stretch in a record-breaking encounter on Centre Court, they did not sit down as they moved from one side of the court to the other. Television had not established that imperative yet.

Gonzales gathered himself for another crisis. He served at 6-7, missed an approach for 0-15, then collected four points in a row with calm authority. He was back to 7-7. His problems were not behind him. Pasarell held at the cost of only a single point for 8-7, concluding that game with an ace wide to Pancho's forehand. Gonzales glided to 40-15, was caught at deuce, then reached game point for the third time. Pasarell connected with a backhand chip return crosscourt for a winner. On the next point, he ran around his backhand for a forehand passing shot.

For the seventh time in three different service games, Gonzales was down match point. On the previous six, he had not missed a first serve. This time around, he did. Nevertheless, he came up with a second serve of remarkable depth. Pasarell could not attack it. Gonzales closed in for an aggressive first volley. Pasarell had no alternative. He went back to his trusted lob off the backhand. His touch was gone. The ball was out by a wide margin.

On the next two points, Gonzales took command at the net again. Pasarell lifted a lob long, then another. It was 8-8. Pasarell must have been dismayed, but he held easily for 9-8. Gonzales served to save the match for the fifth time at 8-9. He found the range with all five of his first serves, coming up with three service winners, making it 9-9 by drawing Pasarell wide to the forehand with the serve, setting up a forehand volley winner. He conceded only a single point in that game.

At 9-9, Pasarell seemed to buckle. He served a double fault for 0-15. Gonzales made him stretch low for a forehand volley, which he punched crosscourt. Pasarell poked the ball wide. It was 0-30. Tearing a page out of Pasarell's playbook, Gonzales lobbed cross-court off the backhand. Pasarell was caught off guard. The shot landed safely in the corner. Now it was 0-40. Gonzales waved his arms in a brief display of animation. He then guided a backhand return down the line. Pasarell could not handle the low forehand volley.

Gonzales had broken at love, and was set to serve for the match. A deep second serve provoked Pasarell into a backhand error for 15-0. Gonzales put away an overhead off a midcourt lob for 30-0. Pasarell charged in behind his return of serve but Gonzales placed a backhand volley that went behind his foe for a winner. He then held at love as Pasarell's last futile lob off the backhand landed long. Gonzales had connected on fifty-seven of sixty-nine first serves in his triumphant fifth set.

With the capacity Centre Court audience now standing to deliver a roar of acclamation, the victor stood for a moment in the sunshine, contemplating an incredible two-day turnaround. When he left the court with an understandably despondent Pasarell, Gonzales had succeeded, 22-24, 1-6, 16-14, 6-3, 11-9, in a record-breaking five hours and twelve minutes. It was the longest match in Wimbledon history.

Pasarell was on the threshold of victory seven times.

Two hours and fifty-four minutes of that monumental effort had taken place on the second day. After saving the seven match points and twice holding from 0-40, triple match point down, Gonzales had collected twelve of the last thirteen points to take the match.

"His was one of the greatest individual achievements in tennis or any other sport," wrote Rex Bellamy in the *London Times*. "This is a man who was born to greatness and did not scorn the gift."

Lance Tingay of the *London Daily Telegraph* put Gonzales lucidly into perspective. He wrote, "Ricardo Gonzales, who has never won the singles at Wimbledon and almost certainly never will, yesterday put himself into the annals of the championships as predominately as any champion ever did. Despite its heroic standards, this was only a first round match. It is one of the tragedies of lawn tennis that Wimbledon never saw Gonzales at his peak."

On the same afternoon that Gonzales celebrated his comeback against Pasarell, Rod Laver found himself down two sets to love against the Indian, Premjit Lall. Laver was destined to win his second Grand Slam. Every match he played was given close scrutiny by the cognoscenti. But even this ultimate champion seemed forgotten in the glow of Pancho's timeless triumph.

Charlie Pasarell

EPILOGUE

Gonzales reached the round of sixteen of that tournament without difficulty, but then he bowed to Ashe in a well-played, four set skirmish. Later in 1969, he strung together four remarkable matches in a row to win the Howard Hughes Open in Las Vegas. He knocked out John Newcombe, 6-1, 6-2, ousted Rosewall, bested Stan Smith, and then routed Ashe, 6-0, 6-2, 6-4, in the final.

In January 1970, as he approached forty-two, the astounding American defeated Laver in a five set match at New York's Madison Square Garden, a victory achieved only four months after Laver had won his Grand Slam. He stopped Laver again that spring. On his best days, he was still good enough to beat anyone in the world. At Wembley, outside London, in November 1970, he stopped Smith again, saving seven match points in another display of grit under pressure. When he was three months away from his forty-fourth birthday, Gonzales became the oldest player in the Open Era to win a singles tournament. He finished the season among the top ten in his country.

Gonzales passed away in 1995 at sixty-seven. He had led a tumultuous life, marrying six times, twice to the same woman. One of his

The inner resolve of Pancho Gonzales defied analysis.

wives was Rita Agassi, the sister of Andre Agassi, with whom he had a son. To the end, he was a man of many moods and inner conflicts.

Asked in the late 1980s how the champions of his time might have fared against the leading players who followed him, Gonzales replied, "If you took the athlete of my time in the 1950s and played him in 1987 under the same circumstances, he would be much stronger, play much harder, and therefore he would play better. If you took the player of 1987 and sent him back

to the middle fifties, he wouldn't play any better than the players who were around then."

No one who observed Gonzales in a major tournament would scoff at his thesis. By performing so skillfully in his early forties and upending so many leading players when he was well past his prime, Gonzales demonstrated that he was certainly among the all-time great champions in his sport. Does he belong up there in a class with Kramer, Budge, or Sampras? There are always those who, perhaps nostalgically, would say yes.

Charlie Pasarell is one player who will testify that Gonzales must be considered to be among the most fearsome competitors of the twentieth century. Pasarell, who became a prominent tournament director, is no doubt still replaying his match with Gonzales, and still wishing he could find a way to alter the result.   •

BILLIE JEAN MOFFITT KING VS. MARGARET SMITH COURT

WIMBLEDON, FINAL, JULY 3, 1970

Both champions were hindered by injuries, but went gamely about their business in the most hard fought of their many struggles with each other.

PROLOGUE

The world of women's tennis was irrevocably changed by the arrival of Billie Jean Moffitt in the early 1960s. Full of bounce and brio, dynamic and demonstrative, she wasted no time in establishing herself not only as a great player, but also as a powerful personality. It was apparent from the outset of her ascendancy that she would leave some lasting impressions in her sport, both on and off the court. Coming out of California, she broke into the top five in the United States in 1960. Billie Jean had been brought up in a religious Bible-reading, middle-class family. As a young girl, she wanted to do missionary work. Her father was a fireman, and her brother Randy became a pitcher for the San Francisco Giants. She was invited to play tennis at a local country club by a friend who told her she had to wear white. Her mother made a pair of white shorts and her friend lent her a racket. When she heard about free tennis lessons at a local park, she saved her allowance until she had $8, with which she bought a tennis racket with violet-colored strings. She later told people that the moment she owned her own racket, she knew what she was going to do with her life.

She achieved worldwide prominence. Visiting Wimbledon for the first time, she took the doubles title alongside Karen Hantze Susman in 1961. They won it again the next year, when Susman also secured the singles title. Billie Jean was surely a player of immense promise then, although for two years (1961-62) she had to settle for a No. 3 American ranking behind the veteran Darlene Hard and Susman.

In those years, the intensely competitive American was establishing her serve-and-volley game, refining it, learning to cope with a multitude of highly competent backcourt players who liked the targets she presented to them with her net-charging style. And yet, she precociously imposed her authority in big matches. At the 1962 Wimbledon, she encountered the top-seeded Margaret Smith in the second round. In that setting, she demonstrated how dangerous a player she would become.

Smith swept through the first set, losing only a single game. Moffitt countered to take the second, but the Australian surged to 5-2 in the third with relative ease. At 5-3, the favorite

Billie Jean Moffitt King

served for the match and reached 30-15, only two points away from the triumph. Moffitt was not intimidated. She broke back, took four games in a row, and created a major upset with a 1-6, 6-3, 7-5 win. The American entered the quarterfinals where Ann Jones ended her run.

In 1963, Billie Jean reached the final of Wimbledon, the first time she had appeared on her own in the title match of a major event. She toppled both Maria Bueno and Jones to get there, but Smith avenged her 1962 defeat with a 6-3, 6-4 victory. Moffitt was clearly a formidable force in singles, capable of controlling many fast court matches with her aggressive style. For the next few years, though, the achievements of Bueno, Smith, Jones, and Nancy Richey were more consistent.

It all changed for Billie Jean in 1966. She had taken on a new last name. With her husband Larry King, she would establish the groundbreaking World Team Tennis in the 1970s. She captured her first of three consecutive Wimbledon singles titles that summer, defeating Bueno in the final. In the semifinals, she beat the top-seeded Smith, 6-3, 6-3. King had moved to the zenith of her world, finishing the year as the universally acknowledged No. 1 female competitor.

Her 1967 season was even better. At Wimbledon, she won the title without the loss of a set, cutting down Jones in the final. At Forest Hills, she took the championship of her country for the first time, defeating Jones again for the title. When Open Tennis commenced in 1968, King set the pace for the third consecutive season, although her status at the top was seriously challenged. In the semifinals of the French Open, her countrywoman and chief domestic rival, Nancy Richey, upset her in a three set semifinal. Richey had made a stirring comeback to eclipse King three months before at New York's Madison Square Garden in a small invitational event. On that occasion—with the two premier Americans meeting for the first time since Richey had taken their last clash at Forest Hills in 1964—Richey trailed, 6-4, 5-1, but captured twelve games in a row for the victory, saving a match point along the way.

King was not easily stripped of her confidence. She won Wimbledon, coming from behind to oust Jones (who served for the match) in a three set semifinal. Then she defeated Judy Tegart in a 9-7, 7-5 final. Despite a final-round defeat at the U.S. Open against the big serving Englishwoman, Virginia Wade, King held her ground at the top.

Not so in 1969. As Margaret Smith Court displayed her match-playing prowess all though the season—losing only once in the four major events—King had by her standards a lackluster campaign. At the Australian Open, she was soundly beaten by Court 6-4, 6-1 in the final. King lost in the French Open quarterfinals to another accomplished baseliner, and two-time former titlist, Lesley Bowrey, in straight sets. She sought a fourth Wimbledon singles championship in a row, but did not find it, falling in the final against an inspired Jones. With one last opportunity to capture a major crown, King met Nancy Richey in a dramatic showdown on the U.S. Open Grandstand court. Richey stopped Billie Jean for the second time at Forest Hills and the third time in a Grand Slam event, winning 6-4, 8-6. Court beat Richey in the final.

After her very productive 1969 season, Court wanted to capture all four major titles in 1970. She made that her mission. Having won nineteen of twenty-four tournaments the previous year, her confidence was at an all-time high. In five matches at the Australian Open, she lost a mere twelve games, defeating Kerry Melville, 6-1, 6-3, in the final.

Mrs. Court figured to have more comprehensive tests in Paris on the slow red clay that blunted her big game to some degree. In the second round, she faced a future finalist, Olga Morozova. Morozova was not a typical clay-court player. She was cut from almost the same

---

The best women in the field meet in a climatic showdown.

---

cloth as Court, attacking whenever possible, seeking the chance to volley. She nearly toppled the favorite before Court came through, 3-6, 8-6, 6-1. The path from there was clear. Not conceding another set the rest of the way, Court beat Germany's elegant Helga Niessen, 6-2, 6-4, in the final.

Halfway to her destination, Court came to Wimbledon. She carried with her many memories of hard defeats against talented rivals, losses she believed she could have prevented. Centre Court had been a burdensome place for her to perform in across the years, making her self-conscious at crucial moments, reducing her at times to tentative, makeshift shots. She knew this would be the hardest hurdle. She also realized that her chief adversary on the lawns of the All England Club would very likely be Billie Jean.

They had confronted each other several times that season. Court had beaten King indoors at Dallas and at the U.S. Pro Indoor in Philadelphia. King stopped Court in Sydney, only to lose to Court the next time on hard courts in South Africa. In Durban, King defeated Court. They were the two finest female players in the game; avoiding each other was a virtual impossibility. The rivalry flourished because so little separated them. Adding to Court's challenge was King's affection for the Centre Court surroundings. She was absolutely enamored of the place. She would often go out to the grounds before the start of the tournament and sit in the ghostly shadows, thinking about how much history had been made in that empty arena, knowing she could play better there than anywhere else.

The stage was set for an exhilarating match. Court was halfway to her goal of the Grand Slam. King was primed for her favorite event. The fans anticipated an unforgettable contest.

THE MATCH

Neither the top-seeded Mrs. Court nor the No. 2 seed Mrs. King was unduly troubled en route to their final round matchup. Court lost a long opening set to No. 8 seed Helga Niessen, but recouped quickly and thoroughly for a 6-8, 6-0, 6-0 quarterfinal victory. In the semifinals, she ousted the diminutive Californian, Rosie Casals, 6-4, 6-1. King, too, was pushed to three sets only once. In her quarterfinal, she trailed the towering Australian Karen Krantzcke. Thereafter, King held the upper hand in a 3-6, 6-3, 6-2 triumph. She followed with a 6-3, 7-5 success against the

---

Once again injuries hobbled

both players.

Frenchwoman, Francoise Durr. The two best players had reached the final, with Court striving to win her third Centre Court crown and King hoping to capture her fourth.

Heightening the drama surrounding this occasion was the physical uncertainty of both combatants. Court had taken four injections in the hours leading up to the match to soothe a sprained ankle. She wore a brace for further protection. King was bothered by a bad knee that had lingered for a long time. The two players were in unmistakable pain throughout their struggle, and yet they did an honorable job of concealing their ailments and got on with their business at full force. As King would contend later, "I can't see where her ankle was hurting her at all. She was trying for everything. In the heat of the battle you forget about injuries like that."

King practiced what she preached, wincing only on occasion, moving surprisingly well under the circumstances. These were two seasoned professionals giving nothing away, willing to extend themselves to their limits and seemingly beyond, knowing that the final of Wimbledon is not a time for offering excuses. That attitude was reflected by the length and scope of a tremendous opening set that witnessed King often on the edge of success. Three times—at 5-4, 7-6, and 8-7—she served for it. Court ably denied her every opportunity.

King revealed unexpected vulnerability on the last of those chances. At 8-7, she served a double fault for 15-30. She missed a low backhand first volley on the following point off a trademark stroke from the Australian—a surgically sliced backhand return. King had missed four consecutive first serves in this critical segment of the match, but she finally connected at 15-40. Court was prepared, made a solid return, then lobbed offensively over King. Billie Jean chased it down but could not get the ball back into play. It went to 8-8.

After a sequence of four straight service

breaks, both women settled into solid holding patterns. Court held at love for 9-8; King responded with a love game of her own for 9-9. Each was successful on three out of four first serves in those games. Both were serving with more sting and better placement now, setting up easier first volleys, taking complete command at the net. They both held to knot the score at 10-10.

The pattern continued. Missing only one first serve again, Court held at love for 11-10. Conceding only one point, King leveled at 11-11 with a magnificent backhand volley winner past a chip-and-charging Court. Serving at 11-12, King found herself down 30-40, one point

away from losing the set. She missed her first serve, but came in behind the second, punched an assertive first volley, and opened up the court for a coolly controlled forehand drop volley. Defiantly, King had reached 12-12.

At this stage, Court would not have surprised veteran observers if she had fallen victim to self-doubt, after rescuing herself so persistently every time King served for the set. But the Australian was remarkably composed, almost serene. She held on safely for 13-12.

With King serving, Court moved to 0-40, triple set point after a series of commanding returns. She managed to take the set at last with a backhand crosscourt return that forced King

Margaret Smith Court

into error. Court had won the set, 14-12. The match, however, was a long way from finished.

After an early exchange of service breaks at the start of the second set, the two supreme serve-and-volleyers launched another prolonged battle. Court exploited her extraordinary reach at the net, and her overhead was a

---

An array of saved serves and near misses deepened the tension.

---

weapon of security. King displayed her superb volleying technique—the best of all the women—and her touch off the backhand was notable as well. Time and again, she exploited the drop shot off that side to lure Court in. King was more creative; Court had the edge as the slightly better percentage player. As King would say many times afterward, "I knew everything Margaret was going to do and could figure out almost every time whether she was going crosscourt or down the line. But that did not mean I could stop her from executing exactly what she wanted."

At 5-6 in the second set, King served for the second time to save the match. She was poised once more under humbling pressure, holding serve with one of her patented backhand drop volleys. Court made it 7-6, exploiting the primary weakness in Billie Jean's game, the forehand return in the deuce court. With King serving at 6-7, 0-30, she was precariously close to making an exit. Court's return was at the American's feet. King managed to make a deep half volley off the backhand. Court tried to come in off her next shot and had King stretching for a forehand volley. King knew she had to spank that volley or the court would be wide open for the Australian. The

volley was firm and Court could not handle the pace.

King had more danger ahead. Court reached match point with a telling backhand volley down the line. King missed her first serve but came in calmly behind a deep second delivery. Court's slice backhand return was unusually high. King's approach volley had too much on it. She held for 7-7.

Although Court marched to 40-0 in the next game, she encountered strong resistance from King. The American collected the next four points to reach break point, but Court hit a high backhand volley winner for deuce. King got to break point for the second time, only to net a routine backhand. Court proceeded to play two solid overheads in succession, holding for 8-7, preventing Billie Jean from serving for the set and altering the pace of the contest.

King—perhaps more worried about her knee—was staying back frequently on first and second serves, but skillfully orchestrating the points and maneuvering Court with precision. Court kept pressing forward, exploiting her reach at the net. She held for 9-8, with five straight first serves finding their mark. King prevailed for 9-9 after coming within two points of defeat.

Court conceded only one point on her way to a 10-9 lead. King served to save the match for the sixth time. Court went briskly to work, reaching 15-40, double match point with one of her teasing slice backhand down the line passing shots. King's response was decisive. She produced a perfect inside-out overhead winner, then released a stinging service winner to Court's backhand side.

King had saved two match points in this game, three altogether. But her woes were not over. On the next point, King played one of her backhand drop shots to force Court in, then lobbed over the Australian. King followed with another drop shot, but this time Court caught her with a scathing forehand down the line. At match point for the fourth time, Court attacked. King replied with a courageous backhand down the line pass, clipping the sideline.

The Centre Court audience was exhausted by the determination and ingenuity of two all-time greats. They showered applause on Billie Jean as she stood once more at deuce. Moving in swiftly for a low ball on her forehand, Court passed King with sidespin. It was match point for the fifth time. King attacked Court's backhand and covered the attempted pass. She delivered a forehand volley winner crosscourt. Deuce for the third time.

Court must have been agonized by her missed opportunities, but she did not reveal even a trace of apprehension. She raced to her right for a forehand passing shot which grazed the net cord, forcing King into a volleying error. Down match point for the sixth time, King stayed back behind her second serve. Court sensibly chipped-and-charged, coming in on the American's backhand side. King drove the ball crosscourt. The shot went tamely into the net. Court was a worthy 14-12, 11-9 winner after two hours and twenty-seven minutes.

It was a record-breaking afternoon on a number of

fronts. The Court-King clash was the longest-ever women's final at Wimbledon with its forty-six games, exceeding by two the record set by Lenglen and Dorothea Lambert Chambers in 1919. Furthermore, the twenty-six-game opening set was the longest ever in any singles final contested by men or women in that event. This protracted battle, superbly fought by the two greatest female players of their era, raised the level of respect for women's tennis enduringly.

Court would confess later, "I have never had a harder match than this and I have never played better at Wimbledon than I have this year."

Lance Tingay wrote in *The Daily Telegraph*, "It is academic whether there have been better finals. Perhaps there have been one or two. This, though, was among those that will be long remembered, and had the American

RUSS ADAMS

Billie Jean Moffitt King

instead of the Australian got the decision, sporting prowess would have been just as well rewarded."

In her fifth consecutive Wimbledon singles final, King had given a great performance in defeat. The fact remained that Court had captured her third straight Grand Slam singles title in the 1970 season. She had taken a 3-2 lead in her Wimbledon career series with King, gaining a 2-0 edge in finals. More importantly, Court stood only one major title away from a Grand Slam.

EPILOGUE

Court came into the U.S. Open at Forest Hills with growing confidence, while King had to step aside and skip the last of the Grand Slam events for the season. The American decided to bypass the championship of her country to have a much needed knee operation. Court thus became an overwhelming favorite. Who else could stop her on the grass courts in New York?

Court was strikingly efficient in her five matches on the way to the final. She was winning so easily that the pressure of her historic quest was vastly reduced. In the semifinal, she met Nancy Richey, her final round victim the year before. In a mere twenty-seven minutes she removed the American baseliner, 6-1, 6-3.

Court was still concerned about her ankle, which raised her incentive to win all of her matches in short order. On her way to the title match, she lost a total of only thirteen games. Richey was the only player to extend Court to 6-3 in any set.

The morning of her final against Casals, Court went to a church. She wanted spiritual calming before she played the most important match of her life. Casals stayed with her until 2-2 in the first set. Then Court collected four games in a row. That 6-2 first set verdict was typical of the entire fortnight. Court was almost there. But she conceded in her book, *Court on Court, A Life in Tennis*, that she lost her concentration at that stage. "Suddenly my mind began to wander as I began anticipating victory," she wrote. "Consequently, I dropped my service, not once but three times in a row as Rosie stormed back to take the second set 6-2 and even the match. The huge crowd of 14,000, quite naturally on the side of their compatriot, cheered wildly as they sensed a major upset. But the roars for Rosie had a quieting effect on me. As we took our places for the final set, I prayed: Dear Lord, please help me. I can't lose now."

Court proceeded to break Casals at love for a 2-0 final set lead, and never looked back, progressing to a 6-2, 2-6, 6-1 victory. She had become only the second woman to win the Grand Slam. Court deserved her triumph. In an extraordinary two-year stretch, she had

---

The diminutive challenger took whatever opportunities there were.

---

won seven of the eight Grand Slam singles championships. At twenty-eight, she had realized her grandest dream with her sweep of the majors.

Four months later, Court ousted a countrywoman of originality and immense talent. In the final of the Australian Open, she took her tenth title in that Grand Slam championship with a closely contested 2-6, 7-6 (0), 7-5 win over Evonne Goolagong. The two Australians clashed again in the final of Wimbledon. Goolagong, nineteen, toppled Court, 6-4, 6-1, after ousting King in the semifinal round.

Court did not return to the U.S. Open because she was expecting her first child. She came back strongly in the summer of 1972. Despite a semifinal loss to King at the U.S. Open, Court knew her game was moving in the right direction. Her 1973 season was reminiscent of 1969 as she took three of the four Grand Slam events, falling only at Wimbledon in a surprise semifinal loss to a rookie professional named Chrissie Evert. Court had beaten Evert in an engrossing French Open final, 6-7, 7-6, 6-4, after Evert served for the match at 5-3 in the second set. It was easily one of Court's top five victories during her career.

Thereafter, Court declined. She had two more children. She staged a few more comebacks in 1975 and 1977. After the latter season, when she was thirty-four, she withdrew from serious competition and returned to a more tranquil life with her family in Australia. She took with her an unparalleled record, which included twenty-four Grand Slam singles championships (eleven Australian Opens, five French Opens, five U.S. Opens and three Wimbledons) and sixty-two majors (including women's and mixed doubles). With her prodigious numbers, Court was considered by tennis writers as the best female tennis player of all time.

King moved on resolutely after her 1970 loss to Court at Wimbledon. Faster and more agile after her knee operation that autumn, she had one of her greatest years in 1971, taking the U.S. Open, becoming the first woman athlete to earn more than $100,000 in a year, winning nineteen tournaments, and playing a pivotal role in the first full year of the Virginia Slims circuit for women. The women had broken out on their own the previous year when *World Tennis* publisher/editor Gladys M. Heldman signed nine leading women, led by King, to professional contracts, and convinced Joe Cullman of Philip Morris to bring Virginia Slims in as the tour sponsor.

Women players were beginning to build commercial events.

Heldman had been the crucial leader behind the bold move to establish a separate identity for women's tennis. King had emerged as a champion on and off the court in advocating the cause. That did not distract her from gaining the No. 1 world ranking among nearly all the authorities. In 1972, King had a remarkable record, winning her first French Open, capturing Wimbledon for the fourth time, and securing a third championship of her country at Forest Hills. Never before had she won three major titles in a year; the pity was that she skipped the Australian Open at the start of that season. Had she made the journey Down Under, she might have replicated the achievement of Court and Connolly (1953) by capturing the Grand Slam.

King's 1973 season was not as successful, but it was a productive time for her. Before she turned thirty in November, she won her fifth Wimbledon with a signature performance against Evert in the final. Two months later, she recorded her most renowned triumph when she ousted Bobby Riggs, 6-4, 6-3, 6-3, in the famed "Battle of the Sexes" at the Houston Astrodome. The match was witnessed by 30,472 spectators that evening in Texas, and an enormous television audience.

King had hoped to avoid such a confrontation, but when Court lost her match with Riggs on Mother's Day, without much resistance, 6-2, 6-1, King felt compelled to accept the challenge. The fifty-five-year-old Riggs was a master hustler who had won Wimbledon in 1939 before moving on to professional tennis nearly a decade later. Court was not prepared for Riggs, but the savvy King fully understood what was at stake.

Margaret Smith Court

Billie Jean King advanced the women's game profoundly with her contribution to the Virginia Slims circuit, and her triumph over Riggs. She had started the 1970s with her narrow and dramatic loss to Court, and had moved into the middle of that decade with untrammeled ambitions. By then, her riveting rivalry with Court was ending, but she would face other fierce challenges in the immediate years ahead. •

ROD LAVER VS. KEN ROSEWALL

WCT FINALS, DALLAS, MAY 14, 1972

Rosewall, at 37, and Laver, at 33, produce a sparkling nationally televised indoor showdown. Their match measurably enhanced the public interest in tennis.

PROLOGUE

His appeal to tennis purists was without bounds. He hit the ball so cleanly and efficiently that his strokes appeared to have been lifted right out of the pages of a manual. His footwork was exemplary. And at 5' 7", weighing in the range of 140 pounds throughout his entire career, Ken Rosewall lasted longer than anyone else in the upper ranks of the men's game in the twentieth century. A master of understatement about himself and his successes, Rosewall let his accomplishments speak for him. They spoke with striking clarity.

Another in the remarkable line of authentic Australian champions, Rosewall came from a family of very modest means. His father bought a grocery store that had three clay tennis courts behind it. It was here that Ken learned to play tennis, using a racket with a sawed-off grip that made it easier for him to play as a small boy. From the courts behind the store, Rosewall progressed steadily over the years toward a world-class game. His style of play enabled him to reach high levels in his teens. His fundamentals were so sound and consistently reliable that he seldom gave a poor performance. Diminutive

and dark haired, Rosewall came of age quickly during his days as an amateur in the 1950s. He won the Australian and French Championships in 1953 when he was only eighteen, and joined his country's esteemed Davis Cup team that same season. He took the Australian final with unexpected ease over countryman, Mervyn Rose, 6-0, 6-3, 6-4. In Paris, he defeated the nimble American, Vic Seixas, in a four-set final.

Most experts placed Rosewall at No. 2 in the world among the amateurs for 1953. He was demoted to No. 3 in 1954, but in 1955 and 1956 he rose to No. 2 again. In that period, Rosewall was the model of precision and purposeful play. He reached his first Wimbledon final in 1954 before losing to the obstinate left-hander from Czechoslovakia, Jaroslav Drobny. He won his second Australian Championship in 1955 with a straight set conquest of his fellow "Whiz Kid" Hoad. And at Forest Hills in 1956, he denied Hoad a Grand Slam by ousting his doubles partner, friend, and rival in a four set final.

That string of successful ventures gave Rosewall the opportunity to sign a fourteen-month, $65,000 professional contract, which he wisely did. As Laver would discover six years later, professional tennis was of a considerably higher quality than the amateur game, and Rosewall rapidly had to come to terms with that reality.

It was in the late 1950s that he devised a new strategy. He learned to get in behind his serve on fast surfaces against the likes of Pancho Gonzales, Tony Trabert, and Pancho Segura as a means of self-protection. Although he did not alter his serve in a substantial way— it remained a deep, safe, tricky slice that was hard to attack—he began backing it up with a superb first volley. Although he lost his 1957 pro series to Gonzales, he was still evolving as a competitor and developing his resources. Despite dropping fifty of seventy-six tour head-to-head meetings with Gonzales that year, Rosewall remained upbeat.

His standing in the professional game was similar to where he stood among the amateurs. He improved steadily in some of the most prestigious tournaments. He won the Roland Garros pro event in 1960 by defeating Hoad, and took Wembley indoors in England over Segura, a brilliant tactician with an incomparable two-handed forehand. In 1961, Rosewall upended Gonzales in Paris and Hoad at Wembley. He toppled Hoad at Wembley again in 1962 while overcoming Gimeno in the same event.

From 1963-67, Rosewall held his ground ably in the obscure world of professional tennis.

Rod Laver

When the professionals started sharing venues all over the world with the amateurs, Rosewall was perhaps the best prepared player at the outset. He won the first "open" tournament in history on the clay courts at Bournemouth, England by defeating Laver in the final. At the French Open, he was victorious over Laver in the final again, 6-3, 6-1, 2-6, 6-2. He had triumphed once more at Roland Garros in the world's premier clay court championship fifteen years after his initial triumph.

Rosewall faltered in 1969 but recovered during 1970.

Rosewall would turn thirty-four late in 1968, but he played like a man much younger. Although he was seeded second at Wimbledon and third at Forest Hills, he did not reach either final round appointment with the top-seeded Laver. Roche cut him down in the round of sixteen at Wimbledon, while Okker stopped him in the semifinals of the U.S. Open. Most experts ranked him third in the world that year behind Laver and U.S. Open titlist Arthur Ashe.

Rosewall had a lackluster 1969 season, although he did reach the French Open final again. That was his only Grand Slam confrontation with Laver. Nevertheless, in 1970, Rosewall came through once more in a major championship. Seeded third, he dismissed No. 2 seed John Newcombe in straight sets, avenging his five set loss to his fellow Australian in the Wimbledon final two months earlier. In the Forest Hills final, he surpassed Roche, 2-6, 6-4, 7-6, 6-3. Fourteen years after he first won Forest Hills, Rosewall had done it again, setting a record for spanning so many years between titles.

An aging Rosewall was on the ascendancy. He won the 1971 Australian Open with an emphatic 6-1, 7-5, 6-3 triumph over Ashe in the final, taking that title eighteen years after his first triumph. At Wimbledon, he was beaten soundly by Newcombe in the semifinals, and he did not defend his U.S. Open title. But at the end of that year, having just turned thirty-seven, he conquered Laver in the first World Championship Tennis Finals championship match at Dallas.

Rosewall won that inaugural event for the top eight participants on the circuit 6-4, 1-6, 7-6, 7-6, and Rex Bellamy of the *London Times* wrote, "This three hour match was so thrilling that the strain of watching it—never mind playing it—became almost unendurable." Rosewall was the recipient of a check for $50,000, the largest tournament cash prize awarded at that time.

Laver at thirty-three was playing superlative tennis himself at that stage, although he was no longer able to make it last for two weeks at a major. That had become apparent the year before when British left-hander Roger Taylor beat him in the round of 16 at Wimbledon, and Dennis Ralston ousted him in the same round at the U.S. Open. In 1971, he lost to Mark Cox in the round of sixteen at the Australian Open and was cut down by Tom Gorman in the quarterfinals at Wimbledon.

Despite his setbacks in the major events, Laver was still dangerous in the one week events. He won four WCT tournaments and was the top ranked player on that tour heading into Dallas. But while he was still regarded by his colleagues as the best, Laver was ranked third in the world for 1971 behind Newcombe and Stan Smith, the U.S. Open champion.

As the leading players shifted back indoors in the winter and spring of 1972 for the now established WCT circuit, Laver wanted to get another crack at Rosewall in Dallas, which had become one of the five top tournaments in tennis. En route to Dallas, Laver beat Rosewall in both Philadelphia (at the U.S. Pro Indoor) and Toronto. Laver won five tournaments in that run-up while Rosewall took only two. It was time to settle the supremacy issue in Dallas.

THE MATCH

Laver and Rosewall took their expected places in the final of the eight man Dallas playoff. Laver downed Newcombe routinely in straight sets, but then needed to make a concerted effort to escape against the solid serve-and-volley game of the American Marty Riessen. Laver came from two sets to love down to win in five. He conceded only three games in the last three sets. Rosewall handled the Americans Bob Lutz and Arthur Ashe with relative ease. And so the rematch was a reality, and despite his difficulty with Riessen, Laver seemed certain to win on this occasion.

Competing on a medium-speed, supreme court carpet, both players sparkled. Laver tried to set the agenda with persistent serve-and-volleying, but Rosewall countered with his own stamp of authority. Most importantly,

RUSS ADAMS

Ken Rosewall

both men produced passing shots of contrasting styles. Rosewall exploited his vintage slice backhand to the hilt, driving the ball past Laver through very small loopholes, making dipping chip returns to Rod's feet, lobbing with touch and disguise. Laver delivered devastating doses of his explosive topspin backhand, whipping them by Rosewall with high velocity, hiding his intentions until the last possible instant.

At the outset, Laver was too sharp and versatile. He surged to 4-0, then 5-1. Rosewall appeared out of luck, but not for long. In winning the next three games, he served two love games, broke Laver once, and almost got another break when Laver served for the set at 5-4. Laver was

twice down break point in the tenth game but he kept pressing forward and his volleying saved him. Laver had the set, 6-4, and the lead.

Rosewall was not dismayed. He was neutralizing Laver's heavier hitting game with his accuracy, and he collected the next two sets, 6-0, 6-3. He was dismantling Laver in every department, making the percentages work for him, forcing Laver to go for improbable winners. When Rosewall seized the early break to move ahead 3-1 in the fourth, his control of the match seemed complete. Laver was well aware that his time to respond was limited. He raised his returning game slightly, and Rosewall wavered to some degree. Laver was back in business at 3-3. They proceeded to a tiebreak.

Ken Rosewall

Once more, Rosewall established an edge. He led 2-0 in the tiebreak before conceding the next four points. A brilliant backhand pass lifted Laver to 5-2, and he took that sequence convincingly, 7-3. Laver was even at two sets all, and anxious to get on with his task in the fifth and final set.

So, too, was the indefatigable Rosewall. With his backhand flowing, his serve carrying sustained depth, and his volley crisp and compact, he built a 4-2 lead. Laver was in yet another bind, wondering how he could dig himself out. He did it with typically robust hitting off both sides, making the break back in the seventh game with a scorching backhand down the line. Laver held at love for 4-4, but then faced a match point at 30-40 in the tenth game. Methodically, he delivered an ace down the middle and held on courageously for 5-5.

Both players held to reach a climactic tiebreaker. In these latter stages of the fifth set, Laver seemed invigorated compared to the lethargic Rosewall. As Richard Evans wrote in *World Tennis*, "Watching Rosewall stand there, forlorn and boyish as ever, waiting for the ball-boy to throw him the ball, one felt there was no way he could win. He was so tired he couldn't even catch the ball; when it fell out of his hand, he watched it roll away as though the effort of bending down with his racket to flip it up was beyond him. But the second he put that ball in play he was a different man."

When Laver hit a forceful return at Rosewall's feet to make it 3-1 in the tiebreak, he was ready to win the only important title of his time to elude him. But Rosewall took his next service point to close the lead to 3-2. Then Laver suffered a double fault for 3-3. As they changed ends, Laver appeared shaken by Rosewall's recovery.

Nevertheless, Laver attacked, Rosewall lobbed long, and it was 4-3 for the favorite. Laver followed with a stinging shot directed at Rosewall's midsection. Volleying off his belly button, Rosewall watched his shot go wide. It was 5-3 for Laver. He was two points away from his goal. This match was his for the taking.

Rosewall would not surrender. He came in, punched his volley crosscourt, and Laver needed one of his dazzling forehand winners on the run. He tried to hook the ball back into the court from a wide position, but he was off the mark. Rosewall now had four points to Laver's five.

Laver produced a fine serve, only to be caught helpless by a surgically struck Rosewall backhand chip return. Laver's half volley was long. Now it was 5-5. Serving to Rosewall's backhand was always a dangerous gambit, but Laver went to that side again. Rosewall sliced

---

Rosewall's apparent fatigue could mislead his opponents.

---

the return with speed and accuracy down Laver's forehand sideline. It was a clean winner. Rosewall led, 6-5. Match point for the underdog.

They had been engaged in this superb encounter for more than three-and-a-half hours, and Laver's temerity had kept him in the match several times when Rosewall seemed certain to win. But this time, there was no answer. Rosewall's first serve went deep to the backhand. The return failed. Rosewall had won, 4-6, 6-0, 6-3, 6-7, 7-6, and the crowd of over eight thousand in Moody Coliseum rose spontaneously to its feet, applauding both players with heartfelt admiration, feeling as much sorrow for Laver as joy for Rosewall.

WCT Executive Director Mike Davies—a professional player himself during the 1960s—said at the presentation ceremony, "Ladies and gentlemen, that is probably the greatest tennis match I have ever seen in my life." Some might have seen Davies's comment as self serving, given that he was a highly paid employee of Lamar Hunt's organization. He was, in fact, Hunt's right-hand man. All the same, the match was worthy of the comment. The standards set by the two Australians that May afternoon were awesomely high.

Five years later, looking back fondly on his triumph over Laver, Rosewall said, "It was just a flip of the coin as to who won that match.

Probably my form was equal in every set while Rod's was rather up and down. That 6-0 set was just not normal against a player like Rod Laver. But it was very rewarding for me because WCT was the first world professional circuit and it really helped make tournament tennis what it is today."

EPILOGUE

Rosewall's assessment of Laver resonated often thereafter. Laver had some productive years. He was ranked No. 8 in the world on the ATP computer for 1973, finished No. 4 for 1974, and ended 1975 at No. 10. In 1975, he took on then world champion Jimmy Connors in a special Las Vegas challenge match shown on CBS television. For two sets, Connors made the thirty-six-year-old Laver look older. The younger man was blasting Laver off the court. It appeared that Laver had made a misjudgment by playing Connors, especially in a best of five set showdown.

Appearances were misleading. Laver's pride was wounded, and he was unwilling to make an embarrassing exit in a match seen by so many viewers across America. He made an exhilarating run through the third set, took it 6-3, and fought honorably through a high tension fourth set. At 4-5, Laver was serving to save the match. Five times he fought off match points before making it to 5-5. The crowd in Las Vegas applauded the dignified Australian not only for that brave stand, but for the breadth of his long and illustrious career.

From 5-5, Laver had little left in his competitive resources. Connors confidently closed it out, 6-4, 6-2, 3-6, 7-5. He was irrefutably the better player on that day. However, what might

have happened had both men been placed in a time warp when they were at peak efficiency? There were few knowledgeable observers who doubted that Laver would have been the master under those circumstances.

After 1974 and 1975—when Laver had some stirring struggles with a budding Bjorn Borg (including a five set loss in Dallas in the latter year)—the Australian left-hander cut down considerably on his schedule. He made a final appearance at Wimbledon in 1977 during the centenary celebration, acquitting himself admirably in a four set, second round loss to the capable American, Dick Stockton, the No. 9 seed, who was at his best. Laver then withdrew from the men's tour and moved on to the seniors, but not before scoring a good win over New Yorker Vitas Gerulaitis in a WCT event. Gerulaitis was ranked No. 4 in the world for that year.

Rosewall, meanwhile, used his Dallas 1972 triumph as a springboard to other substantial achievements. He was ranked sixth in the world for 1973, finishing two places above Laver on the charts. Rosewall turned thirty-

Very few players could match the durability of the two Australians.

nine at the end of that year. It seemed certain that he had left his days as a big time competitor behind him. How could he hold his own against much younger and presumably stronger opposition?

With his sterling showings at the two most prestigious tournaments of 1974, Rosewall answered those questions. At Wimbledon, "The Little Master" was seeded ninth, but he put together a string of feisty matches to reach

Rod Laver (left) and Ken Rosewall

the final. Rosewall removed the big-serving Roscoe Tanner—a future finalist—to set up a quarterfinal meeting with No. 1 seed Newcombe, winning that one, 6-1, 1-6, 6-0, 7-5. In the semifinals, he was down two sets to love and match point in the third set tiebreaker against the 1972 titlist Stan Smith. Rosewall revived to oust the No. 4 seed in five sets. In the final, he met the charismatic Jimmy Connors. The surge was over. He could not contain the American left-hander, bowing 6-1, 6-1, 6-4. But Rosewall had made it to his fourth Wimbledon final twenty years after his first, setting another record with that feat.

At Forest Hills, the leading players knew they had to look out for Rosewall as he took his polished game on to the grass for a last, serious chance of winning a major event. Seeded fifth, Rosewall lasted longer than anyone but Connors. He stopped the second seeded Newcombe, 6-7, 6-4, 7-6, 6-3, in the semifinals to

reach a second consecutive Grand Slam tournament final. His title match with Connors was delayed until Monday afternoon by rain. The sports pages projected a significantly stronger showing from Rosewall against his American adversary this time. Yet Connors—covering the court with great speed, producing a string of winners on the run, serving with more bite than usual—was even better than he had been at Wimbledon, crushing Rosewall, 6-1, 6-0, 6-1.

The devastatingly one-sided result could not alter the fundamental fact that Rosewall had been the runner-up in the two showcase events when he was thirty-nine. No man in the modern era had played as well at that age. Still, the journey was not over, the will was undiminished, his celebrated ball control as artful as ever. Rosewall was No. 6 in the world at the end of 1975 when he was forty-one. In 1977, at forty-three, he won his last tournament in Hong Kong.

"I'm not the biggest guy in the world," reflected Rosewall in 1977, "and I was always told I would probably never have a very long career—that I'd never last physically. But I've been able to prove a lot of people wrong. I still have the desire to play and I'm still happy to train hard and work hard. Tennis has been my life."

Laver could have said essentially the same thing about himself. He, too, always relished the challenge of competition. The difference after Dallas was that Laver's body was not as generous as Rosewall's. He suffered lingering injuries. More importantly, Laver's tactics were not made to last as long as Rosewall's. Be that as it may, both men loom large in the history of the game. Laver is regarded by many astute analysts as the greatest player ever to grace the courts, and Rosewall holds the distinction of playing top-flight tennis for more years than anyone else. Together, they probably contributed more top-of-the-line singles matches than any other duo. Too many of those luminous battles were lost in the wilderness of professional tennis during the 1960s, when accurate records were not kept. In many ways, their 1972 Dallas clash made up for the lost showdowns with timeless vitality.   •

RUSS ADAMS

Ken Rosewall

STAN SMITH VS. ILIE NASTASE

WIMBLEDON, FINAL, JULY 9, 1972

The unflappable Smith and the mercurial Nastase gave the capacity Centre Court crowd a dramatic and entertaining battle.

PROLOGUE

They stood at opposite ends of the field in every conceivable respect. Stan Smith grew up in southern California. He graduated from USC in 1969 and was an all-American tennis player. A tall and uncommonly disciplined man, he played the game in a programmed way. At 6' 4", he was one of the tallest champions of all time. With his size 13 shoes and long legs, Smith was an intimidating figure, but nothing came naturally to him. He worked extraordinarily hard to achieve his successes, building his game largely around one of the most potent and productive first serves of his era, backing it up ably on the volley, developing penetrating but not spectacular ground strokes. Smith was a master of restraint who knew how to exploit every opportunity.

Ilie Nastase, on the other hand, had so much virtuosity that he often did not know quite what to do with it. He spent his childhood in Bucharest, Romania, where his father had become a guard at the Romanian national bank. Ilie was one of the most gifted players ever to step on a court. He was primarily a counterattacker, capable of releasing dazzling passing shots on the dead run from anywhere on the court. He was the first player who could hit topspin lobs off both sides. He could be quick, and when his mind was clear he could be cunning, but too frequently he found himself in quandaries of his own making.

While Smith was a superb sportsman who refused any invitation to lose his composure, Nastase could come unraveled with surprising ease, needlessly quarreling with linesmen and umpires, berating himself in a variety of languages, tormenting his opponents with his tempestuous behavior. He was a boy disguised in a man's body, snapping unreasonably even when barely provoked, turning from laughter to anger inexplicably. His fellow players seldom knew what to expect next from Nastase, and Nastase's mood swings were so extreme that he was usually hard pressed to understand them himself.

As the players prepared for Wimbledon in 1972, the fifth year of Open competition, many of the biggest names in the game were missing. Laver and Rosewall were absent. The 1970-71 titlist, John Newcombe—another of the great Australians—was not there. Arthur Ashe would not be participating. All of these leading players were playing for Lamar Hunt's World Championship Tennis circuit. Hunt and Wimbledon were involved in an unresolved political dispute. As a consequence, too many of the game's finest were not appearing at the premier showcase.

Fortunately for the fans, Smith and Nastase were not linked with WCT and were not forced into that boycott. They were, therefore, seeded first and second at the All England Club. Both men brought strong credentials with them to the grass courts. Smith had progressed significantly over the past five years. In 1968, he had been a member of the victorious U.S. Davis Cup team, joining fellow Californian, Bob Lutz, to take the doubles in the Challenge Round against Australia. The following year, he surpassed Ashe, Clark Graebner, and Charlie Pasarell to become the top-ranked player in America. In 1969, he had also won the U.S. National Championships at the Longwood Cricket Club in Brookline, Massachusetts.

Smith performed solidly in 1970, but that season paled in comparison to 1971 when he collected his first Grand Slam title, toppling Jan Kodes of Czechoslovakia to win the U.S. Open at Forest Hills. He was ranked by nearly all experts in that pre-ATP computer year at No. 2 in the world behind Newcombe, who stopped Smith in five tough sets at the Wimbledon final. Having won Forest Hills the previous September, Smith was moving up. He wanted at least one major title in 1972.

In the 1971 Wimbledon final against the crafty Newcombe, Smith had dropped the first

RUSS ADAMS

Ilie Nastase

set, but then confidently collected the next two. He believed he was going to win. He had Newcombe in a critical bind. In 1999, when asked to analyze his 1971 meeting with Newcombe, Smith said, "After winning those second and third sets in that final, all I was worrying about was what I was going to say in my victory speech. I ended up losing, and I felt I let that one get away."

Smith made a mistake in underestimating Newcombe's resolve, but his Forest Hills triumph two months later had served to elevate his expectations. Furthermore, he had enjoyed a distinguished first half of 1972, which included four tournament wins on the American indoor circuit. In two of those finals—at the National Indoor in Maryland and the Hampton Indoor in Virginia—Smith had toppled Nastase. His exceptional fast court standards were too much on those occasions for the Romanian, who could compete favorably on any surface but preferred the red European clay where he could demonstrate his athleticism to greater effect.

And yet, the questions surrounding Nastase in 1972 were essentially the same as any other year: Could he maintain his emotional stability for two weeks? Would he avoid his usual series of ill-advised altercations? Was he capable of controlling his imagination and signaling to his opponents that he would not surrender to his darker impulses when he faced crucial points?

His answers to these kinds of questions had not been encouraging earlier that year. Facing the American Clark Graebner in the semifinals at the Albert Hall indoor event in London, he fell into his familiar pattern of self-destruction. Graebner was a muscular man. Tall and strong, he switched back and forth between glasses and contact lenses, and he came to be known as "Clark Kent" or "Superman," depending on his appearance. Graebner was also a formidable player who was ranked seventh in the world in 1968 when he reached the semifinals of both Wimbledon and the U.S. Open. That same year he was the No. 2 American behind Arthur Ashe, and they led the United States to victory in the Davis Cup.

At Albert Hall, trailing 3-1 in the first set against Nastase, Graebner chased a short, wide ball near the net on his forehand side. He was prepared to make the shot when he realized he would have hit a ballboy who was crouching dangerously close to the court. The umpire, an elderly man somewhat slow to react, realized soon enough what Graebner had done and he accepted Graebner's request to play the point over.

Nastase should have recognized that Graebner was well within his rights to ask for a "let," but he started muttering, "Why we play let, I don't understand. Why play let?" Graebner won that game to close the gap to 3-2, and at the changeover he earnestly tried to explain to his opponent why he had stopped his swing and, therefore, deserved to have the point played again. Nastase had known Graebner for five years, but now he completely ignored him. As they changed ends of the court, Graebner walked up to the net and made a polite attempt to get Nastase's attention. "Nasty," he called, using his rival's nickname. "Nasty," he repeated. No response.

Finally, frustrated and angry, Graebner climbed over the net, walked up to Nastase at the opposite baseline, and grabbed Nastase's shirt by the collar. Then "Superman" spoke his mind while a quivering Nastase listened apprehensively.

"You got away with this crap against Cliff Richey in Paris with the stuff you pulled on him at The Masters," Graebner warned Nastase, "but you are not going to get away with it against me." He then advised Nastase that he had better stop the gamesmanship or he would take his

---

Graebner's patience was sorely tested by Nastase's antics.

---

steel racket and wrap it around Nastase's neck. Graebner walked back over to his side of the net and swept through the following four games to win the first set, 6-3. Nastase seemed frozen in fright. After the loss of that set, Nastase walked up to the umpire and announced, "I too scared to play anymore. He say he hit me." Nastase then defaulted by walking off the court. Both players retreated to the locker room and held court in opposite corners with reporters. Tension permeated the air. It took Ion Tiriac to break the stalemate. Tiriac walked to the center of the room, raised his hands to command everyone's attention, then said, "Now I know what to do. I climb over net, threaten my opponent, and I will become champion of the world." The room filled with laughter.

But this was only one among many embarrassing incidents involving the mercurial Nastase, and they were no laughing matter. He was giving away too much ground with his outbursts, and encouraging opponents with his self-defeating actions. At his level of the game—at or near the top of professional tennis—mental strength and a disciplined temperament were imperative, and Nastase too often was found wanting in both departments.

The Romanian had reached the final of the French Open the previous year before losing to Kodes, and was seeded second behind his conqueror in 1972. But he had the misfortune to meet future champion Adriano Panatta in the first round and he could not handle that demanding assignment. Smith was seeded third in Paris and he advanced to the quarterfinals, bowing in four sets against eventual titlist Andres Gimeno of Spain. Now, at Wimbledon, both Smith and Nastase had ample time to adjust to the English grass courts after their setbacks in France, and they realized their chances were enhanced significantly by the absence of the marquee names playing on the WCT Tour.

THE MATCH

All through the tournament, Nastase was dazzling on the grass courts of the All England Club, and he was calmer than usual. He boosted his morale in the second round when he stopped Graebner—who had beaten him twice before in this tournament—in four sets. In the round of sixteen, Nastase defeated 1971 semifinalist Tom Gorman, a future American Davis Cup player and captain. In the quarterfinals, Nastase maintained his dominance over his future doubles partner Jimmy Connors, routing the American in straight sets. Becoming more proficient with each match, Nastase cut down third seeded Manuel Orantes of Spain—again in straight sets—to win his semifinal.

Smith, meanwhile, was not playing as skillfully as he could on grass. Compatriot Sandy

A fateful meeting between opposites aroused the spectators.

Mayer pushed him to four rigorous sets in the third round. Journeyman Australian Ian Fletcher took a set off him in the round of sixteen. And, in the semifinals, Smith had to come from behind to win another four set meeting with Kodes in a repeat of the 1971 U.S. Open final. So the top two seeds had reached the title match as expected, and their clash was precisely what the tournament needed.

By all accounts, it had not been a scintillating fortnight for the men. The women had created considerably more intrigue with the first-ever meeting between the defending champion, Evonne Goolagong, and Floridian, Chrissie Evert, the inevitable world champion in the making. The men had been hit hard by the cavalcade of champions forced away by the WCT/Wimbledon impasse. The fans and players sorely missed Laver, Rosewall, Newcombe, and Ashe. Now it was up to Smith and Nastase to make up for it all with a gripping final-round showdown.

They came through handsomely on that count, but not on cue. Until 1982—when Connors and McEnroe lit up a listless, cloudy day with their fierce five set final—the men's singles finals were usually contested on Saturday afternoons after the women decided their title matches on Friday. But a hard and ceaseless rain fell on Saturday, forcing a one day postponement of the Smith-Nastase final. Thus, the pair of twenty-five-year-olds had to wait until Sunday to settle their score.

The delay was disturbing to both competitors, but Smith characteristically handled the matter with equanimity. The traditional champions dinner is held every year on the evening of the men's final, and Smith was not about to be held back by superstition. Asked in 1999 how debilitating it was to have his final with Nastase delayed for a day, Smith said, "It was hard, and it always is. That is the worst part of sport. Nastase and I had both told the master of ceremonies at the Wimbledon Ball that we would not be attending, but I ended up deciding to go. I rented a tuxedo at 3 o'clock on Saturday, the rained out day of the final. . . . So I went to dinner with my wife Margie and my friends, Donald and Carole Dell. Then I went to the Wimbledon Ball and cut in on Billie Jean King, who had

won the women's title and was dancing with her husband Larry. The British people didn't think that was too appropriate for me to have that so-called victory dance with Billie Jean before I had even won the tournament, but it was spontaneous and the photographers came out while everyone oohed and aahed."

Smith was far from overconfident, but he had a talent for behaving in a relaxed manner no matter how stressful the circumstances. He was undaunted as he stepped on court Sunday afternoon to confront Nastase. As for the Romanian, he had contained himself throughout the tournament, but his high strung nerves were apparent from the start of the final.

Nastase pressed his American adversary persuasively in the opening set. At 2-2, Smith needed to fight his way out of three break

Stan Smith

RUSS ADAMS

Stan Smith (at net) and Ilie Nastase

points, but he held on to his serve despite the difficulty. Then at 4-4, the American succumbed. Nastase was making the towering American bend and stretch for almost every first volley, and he was reading his foe's serve exceedingly well. On the fifth break point in the ninth game, Nastase played an effective low, chipped return, and Smith netted the forehand volley. Nastase served out the set in the tenth game, gaining the early one-set lead.

Nastase then became frantic instead of using the first set success as psychological capital. Although Smith double faulted at break point in the first game of the second set to give his opponent the immediate edge, Nastase was a man with a muddled mind. Despite losing his serve another time, Smith still moved to a 4-2 lead. He closed out that chapter, 6-3, and methodically seized the third set by the same score. During this stretch, Nastase seemed a confused and even pathetic figure.

The Romanian stylist was blaming his mounting problems on his rackets. His Italian friend Michele Brunetti was sitting in the first row of the player's section and Nastase frequently called out between points in Italian to Brunetti. At one stage Brunetti and an official from the Romanian Tennis Federation vacated their seats as though Nastase's torment forced them to make some kind of symbolic move. Nastase changed rackets, but no matter what tension he found in the stringing, he was not content.

Smith took little notice of all the fuss and simply pressed on, hoping to finish his business swiftly. He got the early break and served for a 5-3, fourth set lead. But Nastase halted him there with some tantalizing returns. Nastase was no longer coming apart at the seams. He had suddenly left his woes behind him and was in the process of regaining his touch on the grass. He broke Smith easily again and fought his way to two sets all on a startling run of characteristically flamboyant points.

In the fifth game of the final set—with the score locked at 2-2—Smith squandered a 40-0 lead and had to save three break points before advancing to 3-2. Smith played those pressure points thoughtfully and forcefully. "I was conscious of not trying to play to his pace because he took so little time between points," Smith recalled. Smith deliberately took a few extra, but essential seconds longer on the break points to make certain he was ready, and he was. Then at 4-4, Nastase had Smith down 0-30. On that swing point of the match, Smith was as fortunate as he had ever been on any big point in his entire career. He lunged desperately for a forehand volley at full stretch. Making contact off the edge of the racket frame, connecting with

---

Rain delays the Final, and Smith is psychologically stronger.

---

wood as well as gut, Smith somehow made a freakish drop volley that fell over for a winner.

At that moment, Nastase had every reason to be incensed and disconsolate. Had Smith not made that almost miraculous volley, Nastase would have had him at 0-40, triple break point. Winning one of those points, Nastase could then have served for the match. Instead, Smith moved back to the much safer territory of 15-30 and he held on for 5-4. A predictably dismayed Nastase drifted dangerously. He fell behind in the tenth game at 15-40. But he could still be dogged. He forced Smith to come up with sure winners, and the American could not handle the assignment. Nastase earned an enormous ovation as he held on for 5-5 with some gritty play under pressure.

Smith believed that he might be letting it all slip from his grasp, but he served a solid game to hold for 6-5. Then Nastase coasted to 40-0 in the twelfth game, only to find Smith rousing himself. The American struck two winning returns and was also the beneficiary of a double fault from Nastase. It was deuce. Another bruising forehand return from Smith put him at match point for the third time, but Nastase was in tight for a winning volley. Once more, Smith applied the pressure with a clean placement off the forehand, and that gave him match point No. 4. Smith lofted a lob which was much shorter than he would have liked, but it was almost too easy for Nastase. He reached too quickly for the high backhand volley and dumped it into the net. Smith gleefully raised his arms. Nastase stood there too stunned to realize what had happened. With the crowd applauding emotionally, the Romanian with the long dark hair and the lanky American shook hands. Match to Smith, 4-6, 6-3, 6-3, 4-6, 7-5.

It had taken two hours and forty-five minutes for Smith to overcome Nastase in the single biggest match of both men's careers. Shortly after it ended, Jack Kramer summed it up succinctly for the BBC television audience. He said, "The better competitor beat the better tennis player today. Stan won this one with character."

EPILOGUE

Smith and Nastase were both featured prominently during the second half of the 1972 season. At Forest Hills—with all of the big names back in business and a much stronger field than Wimbledon—the top-seeded Smith fell in the quarterfinals against his friend and

Davis Cup teammate, Arthur Ashe (the No. 6 seed) in straight sets. Ashe moved on to the final, where he met none other than Nastase, who was seeded fourth. Ashe and Nastase had a match neither would easily forget.

Ashe seemed well on his way to a second Open title. He was a decidedly better player than he had been in capturing the first U.S. Open of 1968. He was much more certain now of what he wanted to accomplish, and how he wanted to go about getting there. When he took a two-sets-to-one lead and went up a service break early in the fourth against Nastase, Ashe seemed certain to have victory in hand. He was leading 3-1 in the fourth with a break point for 4-1. Nastase had been behaving abysmally, throwing tantrums, spitting, cursing, and abusing the linesmen.

Had Ashe reached 4-1 and gained the insurance break, Nastase would not have recovered. But Ashe missed a backhand return when he had the opening. Nevertheless, he still held on for 4-2. Then Nastase found the range off his graceful topspin backhand, making Ashe miss his suspect low forehand volley. Nastase took four straight games for the set and eventually came through, 3-6, 6-3, 6-7, 6-4, 6-3, for his most important title.

When it was over, Ashe put on a rare display of public emotion. He sat in a courtside chair, his head in his hands, fighting unsuccessfully to hold back the tears. In the presentation ceremony moments later, Ashe congratulated Nastase on winning his first major title, and then without rancor he admonished his conqueror, saying, "Ilie is a great player and someday he will be a better one if he learns to control his temper." While Ashe was delivering his congenial advice, Nastase was standing off to his right waving his winner's check while some in the crowd laughed.

Victory on the grass at Forest Hills was a sweet remedy for Nastase's painful failure at Wimbledon. Ashe's despondency lingered for a very long time. Months later, playing a tournament in London, Ashe was asked about the residual sadness of his loss to the Romanian. He declared, "Sometimes I wake up in the middle of the night thinking about that match. All I needed to do was to hold my serve twice from 4-2 in the fourth and I would have had a second U.S. Open title."

Sound advice from Ashe has little effect on Nastase.

A month later in Bucharest, Nastase and Tiriac had the benefit of meeting the United States in the Davis Cup final on their clay courts at home. Because Nastase had been the runner-up at Wimbledon and the U.S. Open champion, the Romanians were counting heavily on him to carry his team to a first-ever triumph. Tiriac had been a celebrated figure longer than Nastase and was a master politician. At the time, he was Nastase's mentor but he would later become the manager for future champions Guillermo Vilas, Boris Becker, and Goran Ivanisevic.

Smith remembers, "Tiriac was telling everybody that the chances of the U.S. winning were about one out of ten. Unfortunately, most of the guys on our team believed him." Even the implacable Smith—a man who seldom sold himself short—had his doubts, especially about his chances of toppling Nastase on the slow, red clay. While Nastase thrived on the slow courts where he could exploit his backcourt versatility, Smith often found himself in untenable positions. The surface forced him to make major compromises with his aggressive game. He had to do too much scrambling from the baseline. His powerful presence was unmistakable on any fast surface, but on clay he was a less effective player.

In the opening match of the best of five series between Romania and the United States, Smith sensed that Nastase was overwrought. The burden of being the central figure in the proceedings was beyond Nastase. He served for the first set against Smith at 9-8, but played that game poorly. Smith broke him for 9-9 and never looked back. Playing with poise and precision, Smith put the Americans out in front with his 11-9, 6-2, 6-3 triumph over the disgruntled Romanian.

Gorman became the victim of some disgraceful stalling and gamesmanship from Tiriac in the second match, squandering a two-sets-to-love lead and falling in five. Then Smith and Erik Van Dillen cut down the firm of Nastase and Tiriac in straight sets as the Romanians succumbed tamely. On the last afternoon—despite outrageous line calls by the Romanian officials and reprehensible court conduct from Tiriac—Smith ignored the bedlam and halted Tiriac 6-0, in the fifth set to win the cup for his country.

Smith told friends later that night, "I never thought when we came here that I could beat

---

Tiriac orchestrates a war of nerves which ends in defeat.

Nastase, and that we would then win the whole thing. It's an unbelievable feeling." His sense of accomplishment traveled well beyond the tennis court. The American squad had lived precariously during their entire stay in Bucharest.

A few months before, the Black September movement had threatened the U.S. contingent because, presumably, it included two Jewish players, Harold Solomon and Brian Gottfried. Every precaution had to be taken. As a result, twenty-five Secret Servicemen accompanied the American players, and their captain, Dennis Ralston, throughout their visit. Ralston and the players ate all their meals in their rooms and took a different route to the courts every day.

At the end of 1972, Smith and Nastase clashed on one more momentous occasion, this time in the final of The Masters indoors at Barcelona. Nastase always seemed to save his most inspired tennis for that tournament—he won it four times in all—and he stopped Smith in a stirring five set final after the American recouped from two sets to love down. This was the last year before the advent of the official ATP computer rankings, but all the experts concurred at the end of 1972: Stan Smith was unequivocally No. 1 in the world, while Ilie Nastase stood indisputably at No. 2.

Nastase was at his peak. In 1973, he had another banner year. He secured a second Grand Slam singles championship by taking the French Open in Paris. Seeded second behind Smith, Nastase was so far superior to everyone else that he had no reason or time to become disputatious. In seven clean and impeccable matches, he did not drop a set, crushing Pilic, 6-3, 6-3, 6-0, in the final. He had his share of successes and failures thereafter, but he made it to the top by claiming the Masters crown again, this time gaining the victory in Boston. He won a first rate, four set final from the "Flying Dutchman," Tom Okker. He was recognized at the end of that year by the ATP computer, and the experts, as the No. 1 player in the world.

As for Smith, his 1973 season began in the fashion he wanted. He played perhaps the best tennis of his career from the winter months into the spring. In that challenging span, he recorded six tournament triumphs in eleven appearances, and was a worthy winner of the WCT Finals in Dallas, which remained an elite event. In the Dallas final, he defeated Ashe in four arresting sets.

On that form, Smith seemed destined to retain his ranking. He was so respected after Dallas that the players regarded him almost across the board as the man to beat. Smith lost in the fourth round of the French Open on his least favorite surface in a spirited five set contest with Okker. He hurried to London to get ready for Wimbledon, but the player boycott on behalf of Pilic prevented him from defending the title he might well have won again.

Smith was seeded first at the U.S. Open, and expected to win his second championship at Forest Hills. He was eager to demonstrate that he still belonged at the top of his profession. Smith was on course when he faced the 1971 U.S. Open finalist and three-time Grand Slam titlist Jan Kodes in the semifinals. Kodes had been outclassed by Smith in the 1971 Forest Hills final, and when the American moved ahead two sets to one on this occasion, history seemed likely to repeat itself.

Smith, however, seemed to lose his authority and took only one game in the fourth set. He recovered and went on to one point from the final in the tenth game of the fifth set. With Kodes serving at 4-5 and match point down, Smith was crouched and poised in the advantage court, anxious to make the kind of return that might close out a hard fought battle. The sky was darkening, the remaining light fading rapidly, when Smith tried to make contact with his backhand return. Kodes's deep serve had taken a bad bounce, and Smith barely got a racket on it. An emboldened Kodes went on to win, 7-5, 6-7, 1-6, 6-1, 7-5. Smith was justifiably distraught. Shortly after it was over, he sat on the steps outside the clubhouse at the Westside Tennis Club, looking down at the ground searchingly, wondering how it had happened.

Smith finished 1973 at No. 5 in the world behind Nastase, Newcombe, Connors, and Okker. During that year, he lost two agonizing, final set tiebreakers to a much improved Connors, including a round-robin defeat in

---

For Smith the 1973 season brought mixed results.

Boston at The Masters. Despite the disappointment of sharing the No. 1 American ranking with the feisty Connors for the year, Smith headed into 1974 full of optimism, still believing he was the better player.

His 1974 WCT results were lackluster compared to 1973. This time, the big man captured only two of twelve events, and had his WCT Finals crown taken away from him by Newcombe in the semifinals. Newcombe toppled Borg in the final, and at that stage of the year—before Connors took over with his Wimbledon and U.S. Open triumphs—Newcombe was seen as the best tennis player in the world.

Trying to reassert himself in his return to Wimbledon, Smith marched to the semifinals and took a two-sets-to-love lead over an evergreen Ken Rosewall, the graceful and indefatigable Australian. Smith served for the match at 5-4 in the third, poised on the edge of a decisive triumph. Surprisingly, the American's volleying let him down and he dropped that critical game. He revived from 0-4 down in the tiebreak to reach 6-5, match point. Rosewall served to Smith's weaker backhand wing and the 1972 champion tentatively drove the ball into the net. The compact thirty-nine-year-old Australian now had the measure of the tall man from the United States. Rosewall prevailed, 6-8, 4-6, 9-8, 6-1, 6-4.

That loss marked a pivotal moment in the career of Stanley Roger Smith. Only a single point away from a final round meeting with Connors, Smith had faltered. As was the case in the Kodes match ten months earlier at Forest Hills, Smith had been wounded—perhaps permanently—by his lost chances. When he lost to the big serving left-hander Roscoe Tanner in the quarterfinals of the U.S. Open—thus depriving himself of another opportunity to confront Connors on grass—the signs were increasingly evident: Stan Smith was no longer the player who had once reached the top.

The following year, in 1975, a severe elbow problem further weakened Smith. He fell in the first round at Wimbledon, then lost in the opening round of the U.S. Open, which had shifted surfaces to the green-gray Har-Tru, known in some circles as "American clay." Smith battled on and as he approached the age of thirty-one in 1977 he had a brief resurgence, pushing Connors into a suspenseful five set showdown before bowing in the round of sixteen at Wimbledon.

Commenting on the decline in his fortunes, Smith said, "I played my best tennis in 1973 and

Stan Smith (jumping over net) and Ilie Nastase

then I kept playing more and more. I played too many tournaments at that time and lost some zest for the game. But when I look back on matches like the Kodes U.S. Open loss, or Rosewall at Wimbledon the next year, I realize that you have to lose sometimes in situations like that. You have your missed opportunities, but I feel fortunate about doing as well as I did. Being the best in the world for a time makes me proud. And winning Wimbledon over Nastase was the culmination for me of my four goals: making the Davis Cup team, becoming No. 1 in the U.S., getting to No. 1 in the world, and winning Wimbledon, which were almost synonymous at the time."

In the 1980s, Smith was enlisted by the United States Tennis Association to spearhead their player development program, although he was not selected as a Davis Cup captain. By the 1990s, his two sons were playing college tennis at Duke and Princeton respectively.

Nastase had a number of good years left in

him as Smith began to descend. The Romanian did not win another Grand Slam championship, but remained in the world's top ten from 1974-77, finishing the 1976 season at No. 3 behind Connors and Borg. Nastase had another chance to win Wimbledon in 1976, reaching his second final four years after his memorable meeting with Smith. But Borg routed him in straight sets. He was nearly thirty by then. His best was behind him.

Meanwhile, the Romanian's propensity for foolish imbroglios did not diminish. In 1975, he faced Ashe in a round robin match at The Masters in Stockholm. Nastase was on the brink of defeat, serving at 1-4 in the final set, down 15-40. With Ashe waiting to receive serve, Nastase resorted to mockery. "Are you ready, Mr. Ashe," he said more than once. The umpire should have admonished him, but timidly backed away.

Ashe took matters into his own hands. He gathered his belongings and left the court in a quiet rage, and said later he viewed his actions as a "citizen's arrest" of Nastase. The tournament committee knew that under ordinary circumstances Ashe should have been defaulted, but they sensibly acknowledged the negligence of the umpire and awarded the match to Ashe. Nastase, regretting the embarrassment, sent Ashe roses as an apology. What is more, he went on to win the tournament by beating Borg. It was his last eminent prize.

The following year—on his way to his last Grand Slam tournament semifinal at the U.S. Open—Nastase provoked one uproar after another. His second round win over the German, Hans Jurgen Pohmann, was played with so many transgressions that Nastase should not have been permitted to complete the match. He ranted at his opponent and the officials, spat at photographers, and turned the tennis court into something resembling a bullring. A fight broke out in the stands as fans argued heatedly about Nastase's conduct. Tournament referee Charlie Hare had disqualified Nastase during a Palm Springs match six months earlier for much lesser offenses. Asked why he had not removed him from this fiasco of a match, the dignified Englishman replied, "You must understand that what was happening on the tennis court today was a great human drama. And for me to interrupt it and throw Nastase out would have been wrong."

Nastase was at the center of another U.S. Open fracas. In a 1979 second round match, he faced John McEnroe. The Romanian was in one of his fractious moods during this nighttime clash. Umpire Frank Hammond reluctantly disqualified Nastase for his disruptive behavior, but tournament director Billy Talbert feared a "potential riot" in the stands. He told referee Mike Blanchard to take Hammond's place and continue the match. Play resumed, and McEnroe won in four sets. Nastase may have meant no harm, but Hammond's career as a leading umpire was unjustly diminished.

Nastase began playing senior events in the 1980s. In 1996, he ran unsuccessfully for mayor of Bucharest. As it was, he and Smith both concluded their careers with two major singles titles. Both were underachievers in different ways, but Smith at least had done his best with what he possessed. Nastase, on the other hand, willfully provoked controversy while squandering his vast potential.   •

BILLIE JEAN KING VS. EVONNE GOOLAGONG

U.S. OPEN, FINAL, SEPTEMBER 9, 1974

In the last American Championships to be contested on the grass courts of the Westside Tennis Club, King and Goolagong produced some of the most spectacular points ever played in a match of this importance.

PROLOGUE

In a match against an American top-twenty player named Mona Schallau at an obscure Australian tournament, Evonne Goolagong was given an unexpectedly difficult time. She was pressed into a third set. She needed to save several match points. Her followers felt she was fortunate to escape. One of them approached her after the match and asked how she had remained so calm when she confronted match points against her. Goolagong deadpanned, "What match points? I didn't know she had any."

Goolagong's on court demeanor was markedly different from other modern champions. She was more disciplined and driven than was commonly understood, but was not obsessed with winning big matches or collecting major titles. All through her career, Goolagong was seemingly oblivious to pressure or expectations. She played the game with an old-fashioned mindset, treating every match as an adventure, pursuing her objectives earnestly, yet without much stress.

Born into a poor family in New South Wales, Goolagong was one of eight children. Her father was an itinerant sheepshearer and a descendant of an Aboriginal tribe. As a young girl, she learned to play tennis at the War Memorial Tennis Club next door to her home. When Evonne was thirteen, she went to live with her tennis coach, Vic Edwards, and his family in Sydney. He became not only her mentor but her surrogate father. By the time she was eighteen, Goolagong was appearing in women's tournaments and making her mark. The following year, in 1971, she was still an unpolished player in many ways, but her brilliance brought her victory at the French Open and Wimbledon.

Many of the leading women—including Billie Jean King—were not present in Paris. Goolagong was seeded third after coming close to defeating Margaret Court in the Australian Open final at the start of that year. In the French quarterfinals, she ousted 1967 titlist Francoise Durr, 6-3, 6-0. She lost no sets on her way to the championship match. Determined and confident in the final, she revived from 2-5 down in the second set to defeat countrywoman, Helen Gourlay, 6-3, 7-5.

Despite recording that first major success of her career, Goolagong was not given a serious chance of winning Wimbledon the next month. She was seeded third again and respected by the experts as a player of long range possibilities. But with Court and King in her path, it seemed certain that Goolagong would not be visiting with British royalty at the end of the fortnight.

That widespread notion was way off the mark. Goolagong was timing her ascent carefully, playing serenely as if in a world of her own. She already possessed several important attributes that carried her gracefully through her career: a versatile backhand ground stroke hit with topspin or slice, an astonishing backhand volley, and a superior backhand overhead to back it up. She also had a first serve of high quality. Her weaknesses then—and for the remainder of her career in tennis—were a short and inviting second serve, and an erratic and unreliable forehand ground stroke.

Exploiting her strengths regularly and not often exposing her weaknesses, Goolagong turned Wimbledon upside down with apparent ease. She stopped the formidable American, Nancy Richey, 6-3, 6-2, in the quarterfinals. In the semifinals, she accounted for King, 6-4, 6-4, perhaps her strongest showing. That left only

---

The women at the top frequently changed places.

Court in her way, and Goolagong came through that match convincingly, 6-4, 6-1. Goolagong did not turn twenty until more than three weeks after Wimbledon. Neither she nor her adviser

Edwards had anticipated the twin successes in Paris and London. She did not appear at the U.S. Open despite her revised status as a champion.

Over the next couple of years, Goolagong refined her skills, won some significant matches, lost a number of others, and kept growing as a player without changing her attitude. She made it back to the final of the French Open in 1972, losing in straight sets to a better prepared King. She overcame Chris Evert in their inaugural meeting in the 1972 Wimbledon semifinals, taking that celebrated match, 4-6, 6-3, 6-4, after trailing, 3-0, in the second set. King was waiting for her again, and the American posted another victory over the Australian, taking this final by the identical scores—6-3, 6-3—with which she had won in Paris.

Goolagong's performances in 1973 were much the same. She was a semifinalist at Wimbledon, falling in three hard sets to the redoubtable King. Since her big win over the American at the 1971 Wimbledon, Goolagong had lost to her talented rival three times in the Grand Slam events. At the U.S. Open, her consistency in the major events was revealed again when she got to the final. Goolagong played with her usual panache, but Court was better on the big points and prevailed in another three set duel.

Heading into 1974, the best players were King, Evert, and Goolagong. They were clearly the "Big Three" in the women's game. Goolagong started that season impressively with a victory over Evert. She toppled the Floridian, 7-6, 4-6, 6-0, in the final of the Australian Open to secure her first title at that major event. Evert took the French Open title with remarkable baseline strength. At Wimbledon, both King and Goolagong were defeated surprisingly in the quarterfinals. King was ousted by the Russian Olga Morozova. Goolagong bowed out against Kerry Melville.

Evert was moving into high gear, and she took the tournament with a convincing win over Morozova in the final. By the time the leading players assembled again two months later at Forest Hills, Evert had not lost since late March. But in a semifinal that began late on a dark, cloudy afternoon and concluded on a bright, balmy Sunday—rain washed out play in between—Goolagong snapped Evert's fifty five match winning streak with a 6-0, 6-7, 6-3 semifinal victory. That win enabled the Australian to set up a final-round appointment with Billie Jean King.

RUSS ADAMS

Billie Jean King

THE MATCH

King had been consumed for much of that season by the formation of a new league called World Team Tennis, which she had established with her husband's help. She had played that spring and summer for the Philadelphia Freedoms while Goolagong represented the Pittsburgh Triangles. The American's tournament form had been top of the line early in the season when she captured five tournaments. And yet, she had not appeared in Australia, had missed Paris because of World Team Tennis, and had played an undistinguished match against Morozova at Wimbledon.

The U.S. Open represented the last chance for King to salvage something substantial from the season, the final opportunity to seize one of the majors. She was seeded second behind Evert, three places above Goolagong. In the semifinals, the feisty thirty-year-old avenged her 1973 defeat by Julie Heldman. That year, King had walked off the clubhouse court in the middle of her round of sixteen match against Heldman, who had complained to the umpire that King was taking too much time between points. Incensed by her opponent's strict reading of the rules, King told Heldman, "If you want it that badly, you can have it."

This time, King had recouped admirably for a 2-6, 6-3, 6-1 win over Heldman. She was not at her best, but was on her way to a higher level. Goolagong was approaching the top of her game. She had settled a score with Melville, winning their Wimbledon rematch 6-4, 7-5 in the quarters before defeating Evert in one of their typically absorbing struggles.

On form, Goolagong appeared to have a slight edge coming into the final against King. That was balanced by the American's grittiness on big points. The two supreme serve-and-volleyers came at each other aggressively from the start. Both exhibited some nervousness in the early games. Goolagong was broken in the opening game, but broke right back. They stayed on serve until King stood at 2-3. She saved five break points. On the sixth, the American served a double fault to hand the advantage to the Australian.

Evonne fully exploited that opening. She held for 5-2, then held again to close out that chapter, 6-3. King was not discouraged. Her serve began functioning with increasing efficiency. Her returns became sharper and better directed. Breaking Goolagong at love in the fourth game of the second set, she built a 3-1 lead. King was punishing Goolagong's second serve without hesitation. She held for 4-1, and twice more to win the set, 6-3, and thus force Goolagong into a third set.

That final set was a spectator's delight. There were so many rousing points that the Forest Hills fans sounded at times like an audience from another sport. They could not contain themselves during dramatic exchanges between

Evonne Goolagong

the two peaking players. Goolagong was superb in building a 3-0 lead, winning twelve of sixteen points in that span, breaking King in the second game. The penultimate point in that game featured Goolagong in full flow. She rolled a topspin backhand pass down the line to place King on the defensive, then drove another tough topspin shot off that side, crosscourt. King barely got a racket on the volley. On the next point, a deep, defensive lob from Goolagong backed Billie Jean up on break point, and the American was unable to make the overhead. Goolagong had the break, and consolidated it.

That 3-0 lead was not nearly as large as it looked. King gained more than a measure of pride in the following game. At 0-3, 15-15, she released an inside-out overhead winner off a high, tantalizing lob. On the next point, Goolagong directed a penetrating bounce smash crosscourt and seemed certain to take the point. King chased the overhead and answered with a running topspin forehand crosscourt passing shot produced from far behind the baseline. She had lifted her own spirits and created doubts in Goolagong's mind. Goolagong served at 3-1, 30-15. She double faulted for 30-30, then double faulted again, cautiously pushing that second delivery into the net.

King found the mark with four consecutive first serves to hold at love for 3-3. In her three-game run, she had taken twelve of fifteen points. In responding for a 4-3 lead, Goolagong had large segments of the audience shaking their heads in disbelief. Opening up a 30-0 lead, she reached behind herself for a King lob over her backhand side. Goolagong wheeled around, snapped her wrist, and put the backhand overhead away at an unimaginable angle crosscourt. King applauded with her racket.

King was pressed persistently by Goolagong in the eighth game. Twice, the score was knotted at deuce. King needed three game points to hold. She succeeded with nine out of ten first serves and managed to reach 4-4. Both women probed nearly identical weaknesses in each other's games. Goolagong directed deep and wide first serves to King's vulnerable forehand. King had the same plan. Furthermore, King and Goolagong went for each other's forehand volleys if given an option. They had the two best backhand volleys in the business, and their backhand ground strokes were almost equally polished.

At 4-4, Goolagong trailed, 0-30, but won the next three points. King should have advanced to 0-40. She attacked Goolagong's second serve, stationed herself at the net, and had a wide open space available for a forehand volley winner. King deposited that crucial volley into the net. Goolagong got to 40-30 but King took the next two points. Break point down, Goolagong missed her first serve and hung back behind the second. King drove her backhand return crosscourt with good depth, and Goolagong netted her reply under pressure.

Time and again both players had to recover from break points.

King was at 5-4, serving for the match. Goolagong followed her return of a first serve in, made a forceful forehand half volley crosscourt to put King in a bind, then put her backhand volley past Billie Jean into the open court. At 0-15, King's second serve kicked up too high and Goolagong laced the backhand return at her feet—0-30.

The third point of that game was surely one for the ages. King served-and-volleyed behind the first delivery. She tried an angled forehand volley crosscourt but Goolagong was quickly upon it. Evonne scooped her forehand crosscourt, seemingly out of King's reach. As King chased it, another ball fell out of her dress pocket, but in the frenzy no one realized what had happened. King somehow got to Goolagong's shot near the service line and whipped a topspin forehand down the line.

At that stage of the point, the crowd was shouting in excitement. It seemed as if King had the point sealed with her forehand, but Goolagong ran back diagonally across the court and, with her back to the net, sliced a backhand crosscourt. King covered that and, from a deep position, approached down the line off her backhand. Goolagong lifted a remarkable flat lob off the forehand forcing King back to the baseline again. King ran it down furiously, wheeled around, turned her shoulders, and drove an explosive flat backhand down the line. Goolagong was trapped in "no man's land" but instinctively flicked a forehand half volley crosscourt and retreated to the baseline. King came under her forehand, chipping the approach into the dangerous territory of the Goolagong backhand.

Goolagong sent her topspin pass down the line. King had an immense space open for the crosscourt forehand volley. It was right in her range, not too high or low. King made contact. She volleyed over the baseline. The crowd had been bursting with every stroke in that unfathomable rally. When it ended, they rose and cheered both players with wild applause. It hardly mattered who won that point in the end. Both players had triumphed with the wide range of their shotmaking, with their speed and athleticism, with their courage and composure. It was 0-40. Perhaps shaken by her errant forehand volley at the end of that critical point, King missed another volley to drop her serve at love. Goolagong was at 5-5.

King might have been distraught, but she refused to show it. With Goolagong serving at 5-5, 15-15, the Australian missed a forehand volley wide at full stretch. At 15-30, King came in behind her return and confronted Goolagong at the net. A first-rate reflex volley off the forehand was a clean winner and took King to 15-40. She broke on the following point with a forehand crosscourt passing shot off a midcourt ball.

Serving for the match a second time at 6-5,

King did not falter. She made three out of four first serves. Goolagong missed narrowly with two passing shots. King held at love to complete a 3-6, 6-3, 7-5 triumph. She had won eight of the last nine points. She had played better tennis matches before, from a purely technical standpoint, but she had never shown more gumption under such trying circumstances. King had captured the championship of her country for the fourth time, and for the third time in the Open Era. In the nature of her victory, she had defined her competitive character. Goolagong had also revealed much about her high personal standards with both her fighting spirit and her reaction to the verdict.

"My greatest high," Goolagong would say years later, "was to hit a ball well, to try to do it perfectly, to try different things with my shots whether they came off or not. I can think back to matches I lost where I played one or two points perfectly, and that gave me a thrill. The most exciting match I ever played was the 1974 U.S. Open final against Billie Jean, and I lost it. What I recall most about that match was standing there in the Forest Hills stadium. Billie Jean and I had just had a great point. I looked down at my arms and there were goosebumps."

EPILOGUE

Ten months later, in July 1975, King and Goolagong met again in a major final. When they stepped out on Centre Court for the championship match at Wimbledon, it was expected by those who had been at Forest Hills that the two rivals would play another splendid match. It did not work out that way at all. King won her sixth and final singles title on the Centre Court with a display of disciplined and irresistible tennis. She was flawless in her execution, concentrated in her attack, certain of her chances. Goolagong never found her form. King routed her, 6-0, 6-1. Knowing that she would turn thirty-two four months later, King announced that she was retiring from big-time singles competition. She had conquered Goolagong with such decisiveness that it seemed appropriate to retire from singles and devote herself to doubles and administrative endeavors. But that was a promise she could not keep.

Goolagong reached the finals of the 1975 and 1976 U.S. Opens. The tournament had shifted for a three-year period from grass to clay (Har-Tru) courts. With her exceptional mobility, Goolagong was an accomplished clay-court player. Nevertheless, she had the misfortune to meet Evert on a surface where the Floridian was nearing invincibility. In the 1975 title match, Goolagong gave a good account of herself in a 5-7, 6-4, 6-2 defeat. The following year, she lost, 6-3, 6-0. For four consecutive years, Goolagong had reached the finals of the U.S. Open. Nevertheless, the ranking trio of Court, King, and Evert stopped her on all of those occasions.

It was during this lively period that Goolagong's rivalry with Evert had reached new heights. They had staged one scintillating showdown after another in 1976, meeting no fewer than seven times over the course of that season. The best of all those clashes was the Wimbledon final of 1976, when both women

were performing powerfully. In their closest ever big-match contest, Evert beat Goolagong, 6-3, 4-6, 8-6.

The Australian had her first child in 1977 and missed that season. In the ensuing years, she traveled with her husband and her daughter all over the circuit. She finished 1978 at No. 3 in the world, ended 1979 only one place lower, and remained fleet of foot and gifted on the court. And yet, it seemed likely that Evert and Martina Navratilova had permanently overtaken her.

Billie Jean King and Evonne Goolagong

Furthermore, the Californian, Tracy Austin, had emerged, becoming the youngest ever to win the U.S. Open when she was sixteen, in 1979.

Could Goolagong ever come through again to win a major championship? She had won the Australian Open for the fourth time in 1977 over a mediocre field. Winning Wimbledon or the U.S. Open would be a much taller order. Having lost in the semifinals in

---

King wanted to retire but Goolagong and Evert intensified their rivalry.

1978 and 1979, she returned in 1980. In a rousing semifinal, the fourth-seeded Australian surprised Austin, 6-3, 0-6, 6-4. On the other half of the draw, Evert had toppled Navratilova to join Goolagong in the final.

When the Australian took on Evert that dark, damp afternoon, she played an outstanding match. She coasted to a 6-1, 3-0 lead, then moved on to an impressive 6-1, 7-6 victory. The Australian had secured her second Wimbledon singles title nine years after her first, also becoming the first mother to realize that feat since Dorothea Lambert Chambers in 1914. Goolagong recalled in 1998 her Wimbledon journey of 1980, saying, "I wanted to prove to myself and other people that I could do it. Because of the challenge of coming back after having a baby, I probably worked harder than I had for a long time. I didn't want to have any regrets about my career. . . . I had been in the final three times since winning in 1971 so I thought in 1980 that I still had a good chance. I had lost to Chris a few weeks before Wimbledon in a three set final, but I felt quietly confident about Wimbledon. I kept telling myself that I was not going to lose. It was exciting to be out there that entire tournament."

Taking her seventh and final major singles title was inevitably a "last hurrah" for the congenial Australian. Recurring leg injuries made it impossible for her to compete in that territory any longer. She played sporadically for a few more years, and gradually withdrew from competition. She returned in the 1990s to play selected senior events.

King skipped the singles at Wimbledon in 1976 but she came back from 1977 to 1983. In the latter year, she reached her last major semifinal at thirty-nine, losing to eighteen-year-old Andrea Jaeger. Four years earlier, King joined Martina Navratilova to take the women's doubles championship. With that success, she broke the record for Wimbledon titles collecting twenty in all (six in singles, ten in women's doubles, four in mixed doubles). She had shared that record with Elizabeth Ryan. Ryan, at the age of eighty seven, collapsed on the grounds of the All England Club the day before the 1979 doubles final and died on her way to the hospital. King would say with sympathy later, "I think deep down, she didn't want to see her record broken ."

King concluded her career with twelve Grand Slam singles championships in her collection and thirty-nine major trophies altogether. But her contribution to the game transcended her triumphs on court. While she clearly earned a place for herself among the all-time great players—somewhere among the top ten in the minds of most experts—she made a larger impact as a crusader for causes, as a major leader for women. Nevertheless, tennis fans would celebrate her most for her litany of great performances throughout the 1960s and into the 1980s. In many ways, none of her competitive victories matched her triumph over Goolagong at Forest Hills in 1974.   •

ARTHUR ASHE VS. JIMMY CONNORS

WIMBLEDON, FINAL, JULY 5, 1975

Ashe was nearly 32 when he confronted the heavily favored defending champion. This strategic masterpiece was one of the most analyzed matches of the modern era.

PROLOGUE

Walking onto Centre Court at Wimbledon in 1975 for their legendary final, Americans Arthur Ashe and Jimmy Connors represented conflicting philosophies and personalities, separated not only by age but by ambition, distinguished not simply by the color of their skin but by the range of their interests. Ashe was African American, less than a week shy of his thirty-second birthday, and in many ways a vast underachiever. He had taken the first U.S. Open in 1968 and the Australian Open two years later, but had never fully explored or expanded his talent because his mind too frequently was far away from the confines of the court.

Beyond that, Ashe was the master of restraint. Often a daring shotmaker and superior server, he placed sportsmanship on the highest plane, and contained his emotions no matter how trying the circumstances. He had been taught by his highly motivational coach, Dr. Robert Walter Johnson, during his boyhood in Virginia to call any shot even remotely close to a line in favor of his opponent. Johnson also admonished Ashe not to succumb to anger on

the tennis battlefield, telling his well-mannered pupil, "Those whom the gods wish to destroy, they first make mad." Ashe carried that message with him wherever he went, never forgetting the value of self control. He was unfailingly polite and dignified, always a cool voice of reason.

Ashe had been brought up in Richmond by his widowed father, who was a policeman, and a strong disciplinarian. He explained to author John McPhee, "I told Arthur I wanted him to get an education and get himself qualified so people would respect him as a human being." It is not surprising that Arthur was an "A" student throughout his schooling.

Connors came from Belleville, Illinois, not far from St. Louis. He was metaphorically a street fighter, unashamedly demonstrative as he moved through his professional career, encouraged from the outset to stand up vigorously for his rights, told not to let anyone or anything get in his way on the tennis court. His mother Gloria—a former player of modest success on the national level—and his grandmother, whom he called "Two Mom," taught him how to play the game.

The two women built his style around solid, flat, ground strokes including a two-

Jimmy Connors

handed backhand that became his trademark. Connors left for California in his teens to polish his skills with Pancho Gonzales and Pancho Segura, who gave him the benefit of their experience and lifted him to another level.

The combative Connors looked at life almost entirely through the lens of his tennis aspirations, believing he was born to prove his worth in this particular sport, knowing he could beat back bigger and stronger men with a killer instinct for triumph. As he prepared to play Ashe at the premier tournament of tennis, Connors was close to the peak of his powers. At twenty-two, he was the game's most acclaimed player, the top seed and defending champion at the All England Club. The previous year, he had pursued success in a manner few players have ever known, capturing three of the four major championships, winning a startling ninety-nine

of 103 matches, claiming fourteen tournament titles in a steady, dramatic campaign, always intimidating his opponents.

Earlier in 1975, Connors had shown some fleeting signs of vulnerability, most notably in a four set loss to John Newcombe in the final of the Australian Open on the grass courts of Melbourne. But the left-handed American had restored himself during the following winter and into the spring, rising to extraordinary heights in nationally televised challenge matches against Rod Laver and Newcombe in Las Vegas. Those "Winner Take All" contests— a label later exposed as false although the matches themselves were bruising battles featuring top-flight tennis—drew excellent ratings on television and revealed Connors as authentically, though unofficially, "The Heavyweight Champion of Tennis." He carried himself convincingly like a man who genuinely believed he was larger than the sport he played, strutting around the court as if he owned it, treating even his most revered adversaries as if they were insignificant. He always seemed confident that anyone who confronted him was going to be conquered.

While Connors isolated himself and relished his image as a maverick, Ashe was a universally popular figure among the players and the public. He was challenging himself in 1975 to perform as he never had before, to play his most productive and intelligent brand of tennis before it was too late. Over the course of that season, at a time when most world class players in his age bracket were gradually descending from eminence and falling short of their former standards, Ashe was moving beyond his chronological age to an unexpected proficiency.

In the months leading up to Wimbledon, he had played perhaps the finest tennis of his career. Among his signature moments that season was a carefully crafted, tactically sound four set triumph over Bjorn Borg in the championship match of the WCT Finals in Dallas, one of the foremost indoor events of that era. Ashe had come from behind to oust Borg for the title on that well remembered May afternoon. With Wimbledon commencing in less than two months, the win in Dallas over a player of Borg's caliber told Ashe everything he needed to know about what he could accomplish if he maintained his unprecedented drive and discipline.

He had been seeded No. 6, although he had demonstrated over the recent months and years that he could handle all of the men placed above him when he was in form, with the exception of the overwhelming fellow at No. 1.

He had played Connors on three previous occasions, with Connors prevailing each time. In the 1973 final of the U.S. Pro Championships in Brookline, Massachusetts, a surging Connors had stopped Ashe in five tumultuous sets on a sweltering summer day. That was a convincing test for both players which arguably could have gone either way.

Not so in the 1973 and 1974 South African Open finals in Johannesburg, when Connors checked Ashe decisively in straight sets on autumn afternoons one year apart. Those were historic events for Ashe because he was appearing in South Africa where apartheid was enforced. He knew his presence in that country as a proud representative of his race transcended

The symbolism of playing in South Africa meant much to Ashe.

whatever happened in the matches. But his off-court activities and distractions did not diminish his desire to make positive statements in professional combat, and he was fully committed to toppling Connors on the hard courts in both of those tournaments. Connors's ground stroke control and depth had neutralized the power Ashe was able to summon. Most telling, Ashe had been unable to find a suitable answer to Connors's incomparable return of serve.

Ashe took considerable pride in his ability to disconcert almost all of his rivals with the force and variety of his first serve. But in the two Johannesburg clashes—and to a lesser extent in the Brookline battle—Connors had wounded Ashe beyond repair with his searing returns off both sides, taking away Arthur's primary weapon, reading the delivery with crushing effect.

Through the first half of the 1975 season, Connors and Ashe had not competed against each other. They had played on different circuits, Ashe appearing on the WCT tour with the likes of Laver, Rosewall, Stan Smith, and Newcombe. Connors kept himself in the com-

---

Ashe needed an imaginative strategy to upset Connors.

---

pany of much lesser competitors on a circuit run by his tempestuous manager Bill Riordan. Connors had seldom encountered difficulty in these relatively lightweight events, but he was delighted to be the center of attention in every city, celebrating his status as the top player of them all, handling most of his assignments with consummate ease.

Connors had thrived in the relatively relaxed atmosphere of the Riordan circuit, but had marched through the draw at Wimbledon against a much more accomplished cast, demolishing them all without the loss of a set. Meanwhile, Ashe survived some strenuous tests including a four set win over Borg in the quarterfinals, and a hard fought, five set contest with 1968 Wimbledon finalist, Tony Roche, in the semifinals. The tension surrounding the two finalists on Centre Court went well beyond the contrasting paths they took to get there.

The previous year, Connors had been barred from competing at the French Open by the French Tennis Federation along with all other participants in the new World Team Tennis league, an endeavor that the sport's power brokers believed was in direct competition with tournament tennis and, therefore, detrimental to the health of the game. When Connors was prevented from playing in Paris, his absence did not seem to be particularly significant despite his triumph at the start of that season in the Australian Open. But then Connors won Wimbledon and the U.S. Open later in that summer of 1974. His camp made the case that he could have won a Grand Slam if he had been allowed to appear on the red clay courts of Roland Garros, and thus would have become only the third man in tennis history to realize that phenomenal feat.

The combative Riordan convinced Connors to wage a number of lawsuits against the tennis authorities for millions of dollars based on an alleged injustice. Among the many targets of Connors's charges was the Association of Tennis Professionals (ATP). The ATP president was none other than Arthur Ashe. Riordan was an arch political enemy of Ashe's close friend and lawyer Donald Dell, a prime mover behind the inception of the ATP in 1972, and the lawyer for that organization. Furthermore, Riordan was at odds with Jack Kramer, a loyal Dell ally and the first executive director of the ATP.

Connors was too young and politically tone deaf to fully realize what he was doing with what many considered irresponsible lawsuits. By engaging in legal action of that kind against colleagues in a small professional universe, Connors had created an unmistakable distance between himself and most of the people he played against. He found himself—unwittingly or not—caught up in conflicting actions while Ashe stood progressively on the side of the establishment.

And so, as Connors and Ashe took the court, insiders looked at this encounter as much more than another big match between famous tennis players in a major final. It was a philosophical struggle, a meeting of sharply contrasting strategies, a confrontation extending far beyond the lines on the manicured grass.

THE MATCH

When Ashe woke up on the morning of his historic appointment with Connors, he found himself filled with an inner security he could not fully explain. At breakfast with his friend, Dr. Doug Stein, Ashe revealed, "I have this strange feeling that I just can't lose today."

How could Ashe have been that sure of himself against a great rival he had never beaten? Connors, after all, was blazing. He obliterated the big left-handed server Roscoe Tanner in a straight set semifinal conquest, returning serve with such awesome consistency and conviction that he appeared to be a player in a league above anyone in the field of 128. The oddsmakers not only picked Connors to defeat Ashe, but many of them predicted that the left-hander would come through decisively without the loss of a set. He was too confident, too cocky, too good.

Ashe was not by nature an overconfident man, not a player prone to an exaggerated view of his chances. He quietly sensed that this was his time. And he knew that he had prepared himself with meticulous care. The night before the contest Ashe went to dinner with Dell—his former

captain on the United States Davis Cup team— and fellow players and friends, Charlie Pasarell, Marty Riessen, and Fred McNair. He telephoned his former doubles partner and Davis Cup coach Dennis Ralston for last minute advice. As Dell recalled later, "Arthur brought along that night a list of ten or twelve things he thought would be important for him to do in the match against Connors. He left the dinner with five or six key points which he wrote down on a small piece of paper. At the changeovers when he played Connors, he

Arthur Ashe

pulled that piece of paper out of his racket cover and it looked to some people like he was meditating, but he was really concentrating on the five or six key points."

That analytical approach to playing Connors clearly fueled Ashe, but few were prepared for how dramatically he would alter his normal grass court gameplan in this supreme effort to throw the heavy favorite off guard. Ashe's strategy was unexpected by his followers. They had grown accustomed to his adventurous, but sometimes reckless, tactics. They had watched him lose many excruciating matches over the years by hurting himself with careless gambles at the wrong times, with questionable shot selection in the crunch, with a low regard for percentage tennis. At one stretch in the early seventies, he had lost sixteen of twenty-two finals.

This time, Ashe unsettled Connors from the outset with a masterpiece of strategic acumen, baffling his opponent with a wide array of spins and speeds, exchanging his usual potent ground strokes for subtle variations of pace, swinging his slice serve wide to Connors's two-handed backhand to pull him off the court, and refusing to allow his adversary any rhythm. Ashe had sweepingly altered his game to suit the opponent and the occasion, displaying a discipline and flexibility in his thinking, cutting into the core of Connors's confidence with an exquisite mixture of chips, dinks, slices, and some of the most superbly crafted backhand underspin lobs of his career. Most surprising of all, Ashe was rarely missing, making astonishingly few unforced errors, and consistently clicking on the low forehand volley, a critical shot that had cost him numerous vital points (and matches) over the years.

The match had commenced shortly after 2 P.M. on a pleasant afternoon, but with Ashe's strategy working sublimely and Connors way off the mark, the first two sets were finished rapidly. Ashe seized them, 6-1, 6-1, shocking the spectators with the speed of his progress. The allegedly invincible Connors was induced by Ashe, time and again, to beat himself, and the favorite was obliging. Ashe was exposing the weakness in the Connors arsenal—the low forehand ground stroke—particularly on the approach. Ashe cunningly exploited that shortfall. Connors typically was trying to hit his way out of danger, but his shotmaking was not working.

After Connors held in the opening game of the match, Ashe refused to look back. In the last four games of the first set, he swept sixteen of twenty-one points with a superb display of controlled aggression. With Connors serving at 1-5, 15-30, Ashe chipped one of his teasing lobs off the backhand, directing it over the right shoulder of Connors. All the left-hander could do was tamely poke a high backhand volley back to his opponent. Ashe read the reply easily, driving a forehand passing shot into an open court. His ball control had never been better.

Ashe executed his game plan studiously most of the way.

The older American sustained his cutting edge in the early stages of the second set. In establishing a 3-0 lead, he took twelve of fifteen points. Connors ended a nine game slide when he held in the fourth game. He did not collect another in that set, although his play was much cleaner and crisper toward the end as he fought hard in the process of losing a pair of demanding deuce games.

Ashe looked up at the Centre Court clock for the first time during a changeover with his comforting two sets-to-love-lead behind him. He was momentarily thrown off stride by the speed of the match. He thought at that juncture, "Hey, I'm not supposed to be beating Connors so easily. But I couldn't believe it because the clock told me it was only 2:41. I thought it had

The brief letdown might have been fatal but Ashe adjusted.

to be at least 3:15 or 3:20. I really think if I had not looked up at that clock, I would have beaten Connors in straight sets. That snapped me out of a time warp."

Undoubtedly it did. But, conversely, Connors was not willingly going to relinquish his title. He may well have recalled the 6-1, 6-1, 6-4 triumph he recorded over Ken Rosewall in the 1974 final on the same court. Aroused and contentious, Connors had not become a champion without unwavering self confidence. An agitated fan had screamed out during the early stages of the match, "Come on, Connors." Looking up briefly to the stands, Connors snapped back, "I'm trying for Chrissakes."

By the middle of the third set, with Ashe losing some of his edge, Connors at last translated effort into reward. Ashe had inexplicably strayed from his winning playbook, and could not resist the impulse to explode at full force with some flat first serves. Connors answered those deliveries emphatically with returns of the highest order, blasting the ball past Ashe with almost blinding speed and precision. Buoyant and flowing, his spirits soaring along with his game, Connors forced his way back into the match. He dropped his delivery to trail

3-2, then broke Ashe for the first time in the match in the following game. Connors was firing away freely, going for his shots with grunting aggressiveness, aiming almost arrogantly for his targets. Nonetheless, Ashe was making his rival work laboriously for every service game. Connors escaped two break points en route to 4-3, needed four game points to reach 5-4, then saved two more break points in holding for 6-5. In the twelfth game, he broke Ashe once more, advertising his growing intensity with two crackling forehand return winners in a row to seal the set.

The complexion of the contest was changing rapidly as Connors regained his momentum. The 1974 champion moved to a 3-0 lead in the fourth set with a break in the second game, and a fifth set seemed virtually certain as Connors served at game point for 4-1. He was heading inexorably toward the style of play he liked best, recapturing all of his resources in an attempt to overcome the inspired Ashe.

Ashe knew that he faced a crisis. A fifth set would plainly favor an opponent nearly ten years his junior, and he could not afford to allow such a tenacious opponent to regain level ground. Ashe made up his mind to stick assiduously to his original set of tactics, hoping his guile would carry him through in the end.

But could he contain Connors now that the younger man was accelerating? Ashe responded with the imagination required of him. When Connors stood at 40-30 in the critical fifth game, he had served-and-volleyed, drawing his opponent awkwardly into midcourt with a low volley. Ashe came under his forehand and chipped it low over the highest part of the net. Connors leaned to his left, lunged, and poked his forehand volley wide. It was deuce. Two points later, Ashe broke for 2-3, snapping his forehand passing shot with surprising pace down the line, coaxing Connors into an error. He then held for 3-3.

Ashe desperately wanted to avoid a fifth set.

With Connors serving at 4-4, Ashe allowed his adversary only a single point, releasing a cluster of impeccably crafted backhand returns. Now he had a two-sets-to-one lead, a 5-4 advantage in the fourth set, and a chance to serve out the match in the following game. He exploited the same patterns that had already taken him to the edge of an exhilarating victory. Ashe's wide slice serve was unreturnable for 15-0. Connors then sent murmurs through the crowd, moving across the court swiftly, connecting with an astounding forehand passing shot. It was 15-15. Ashe pressed forward behind his first serve, punched a firm crosscourt first volley, and Connors attempted another forehand pass. He caught the net tape; 30-15 for Ashe, two points from the title. Now Ashe intelligently took something off his first serve. His offspeed delivery confounded Connors, who netted a seemingly simple backhand return. It was 40-15, double match point, and Ashe swung one more wide slice serve to the Connors two-hander, opening up the court for a routine forehand volley. Sweeping five of the last six games, coming through with inspiration and confidence, Ashe secured one of the monumental upsets of the Open Era, toppling Connors, 6-1, 6-1, 5-7, 6-4, with the most powerfully persuasive performance of his career.

When he put away that last volley to conclude the contest, Ashe raised a fist in celebration, glancing over to the box behind him where Dell beamed and his wife Carole wept in jubilation. A despondent Bill Riordan walked out of the stands, shocked by the defeat. In the crowded Centre Court, and all over the world, most tennis fans were euphoric in their appreciation of Ashe's triumph. He had silenced the critics who said he could not win the matches of consequence, and had overcome the scrappy, self-assured James Scott Connors when it mattered most.

EPILOGUE

By virtue of that triumph in the world's most prominent tournament, coupled with overcoming Connors in the single most important match of the season, Ashe was universally accorded the No. 1 world ranking for 1975 by the experts. The two top Americans did not meet again that year, and so the Wimbledon showdown took on added significance when the authorities analyzed the best in the business and selected Ashe as the premier player in the world for the first and only time. Connors remained the top-ranked player on the ATP computer because he boasted a stronger week in, week out record than Ashe, but the southpaw failed to collect any of the Grand Slam championships during a frustrating year. Following his losses to Newcombe in the final of the Australian Open, and against Ashe on Centre Court, Connors had one more chance to secure a major prize when he reached the final of the U.S. Open. But in another notable upset, Spain's clay-court wizard Manuel Orantes upended Connors on Har-Tru at Forest Hills after surviving a

Arthur Ashe

marathon five set collision with Guillermo Vilas that ended near midnight of the previous evening. Orantes had saved five match points and had apparently exhausted himself with that heroic effort, but somehow he revived the following afternoon and he took an error prone Connors apart, 6-4, 6-3, 6-3, for the title.

Ashe later concluded that he had been responsible to a large degree for Connors's problems in the late 1970s. Connors took two more U.S. Opens during that decade—becoming the first player ever to win the tournament on three different surfaces—but he was not the same indomitable player he had been before the Ashe defeat. He revived briefly again with a dazzling run in 1982 and 1983 that included a second championship at Wimbledon and two more U.S. Open successes, but he was no longer the overpowering force he had once been. Connors would not acknowledge the depth of his disappointments in public. After the Ashe loss, he characteristically asserted, "I came in here with my head held high, and I will leave the same way."

As Ashe commented in 1985 on the one decade anniversary of his Wimbledon win over Connors, "I think that had I lost to Jimmy at Wimbledon in 1975, Bjorn Borg might not have gone on to do what he did by winning five Wimbledons in a row and six French Opens. If Connors had beaten me, he might have gone on to beat Orantes at the U.S. Open final. Jimmy might have staved off Borg for a few more years. But losing to me and then Orantes at Forest Hills rattled Connors just long enough for Borg to get in the front door."

As for Ashe, his life was permanently altered by his Wimbledon triumph, a singular success that enabled him to claim a much larger place for himself in the hearts of fans and the minds of historians. He never had another year like 1975, nor did he win another major title or appear in subsequent Grand Slam finals. He lost his last three meetings with Connors to finish with a 1-6 record against his arch foe, but he continued to compete at a remarkably high level into his mid-thirties. In fact, he had some impressive performances when he was thirty-five against the younger brigade of Americans, including a final round appearance at New York's Madison Square Garden with nineteen-year-old John McEnroe. Ashe had two match points before losing that blockbuster to the young New York upstart.

In the summer of 1979, seven months after his great struggle with McEnroe, Ashe suffered a heart attack only three weeks into his thirty-seventh year. He was still ranked No. 7 in the world at the time and hoped to attenuate his career a little longer, but it was not to be. Four years later, he had another heart attack. In 1988, when he was forty-five, he lost all motor function in his right hand, which led to brain surgery, and the fateful discovery that he had AIDS. He had contracted the disease from blood used during one of his open heart operations, presumably the second, in 1983.

In 1992, Ashe publicly acknowledged his predicament and became an outstanding spokesman for the fight against AIDS during the last year of his life. On February 6, 1993, the illness claimed him and he died at forty-nine, leaving behind a loving wife Jeanne Moutoussamy and a devoted daughter Camera, who was only six. In 1997, the new U.S. Open primary court was appropriately named "Arthur Ashe Stadium" in his honor.

The win at Wimbledon had a long and multifaceted life.

The Wimbledon match with Connors was a defining moment in his career, a watershed event that touched the lives of countless tennis fans around the world. As Ashe recalled, when asked about the public response to that unique triumph, "I might be standing in an elevator or walking down a street somewhere, and somebody always seems to come up to me and says something about that Wimbledon win. Among whites they say it was one of their most memorable moments in sports. Among blacks, I've had quite a few say it was up there with Joe Louis in his prime and Jackie Robinson breaking in with the Dodgers in 1947. Once a month somewhere, somebody brings up that Connors match to me." •

JIMMY CONNORS VS. BJORN BORG

U.S. OPEN, FINAL, FOREST HILLS, SEPTEMBER 12, 1976

Connors and Borg enlarged their reputations with a clay court engagement of superb rallies and shifting fortunes.

PROLOGUE

When he burst into prominence in the middle of the 1970s, he broke new ground on many surfaces. Sweden's Bjorn Borg carried himself with admirable composure no matter what the score, no matter how dire the circumstances. He had immense appeal to tennis fans worldwide because he maintained unwavering dignity in the public arena. Borg had been brought up by strict parents who taught him to control his emotions. His father won a tennis racket as a prize at a Ping-Pong tournament. He gave the racket to his son, but could not have imagined the consequences of that gesture.

Borg achieved his many successes at a time when tennis was soaring in popularity and attracting colorful rivals who fired the public imagination with their explosive personalities. But Borg was not going to be swayed, even by colleagues whose company he enjoyed off the court. He went about his business entirely on his own terms, building his reputation with the consistency of his character, earning the respect of his peers and the public with his high standards and unfailing sense of fair play.

Borg's arrival as a champion was nourished by his strong code of conduct. He was a persuasive contributor to the evolution of the two-handed backhand along with the Americans, Jimmy Connors and Chris Evert. The impact of this powerfully influential trio in the seventies carried on through the rest of the century as young players everywhere emulated their playing styles and copied their distinctive two-handed shots. Borg's two-handed backhand, however, was a different type of weapon than either of the great Americans possessed. While both Connors and Evert took traditional straight backswings and produced essentially flat strokes with their two-handers, Borg employed his stroke with a contrasting technique.

The stoic Swede was taught to come over the ball with heavy topspin, making his shots dip at the feet of those who dared to attack him from close range at the net. And while Connors and Evert damaged their opponents with their unrelenting depth during rallies, Borg presented other problems to his rivals with topspin trajectories never seen before in the upper levels of the game. What Connors, Evert, and Borg all had in common was the stunning deception of

RUSS ADAMS

Jimmy Connors

their two-handed backhands and all three were nearly impossible to read when they went for passing shots.

Furthermore, Borg had a devastatingly efficient western topspin forehand that many authorities believed was even better than his backhand. And while he never became a first-rate volleyer, he developed one of the best first serves of his era, exploiting that skill with exquisite purpose on grass courts. His preferred surface was clay, where he would wear down his foes with his fitness and ball control. As he came into his decisive meeting with Connors at Forest Hills, he had been gathering momentum in the major events, winning back-to-back French Opens in 1974 and 1975, then defying the predictions of his critics by winning at Wimbledon earlier in that summer of 1976.

Connors, meanwhile, was on a crusade to move back to the top of the tennis rankings he had dominated in 1974. Having lost three of the four major finals in 1975 after he put on twenty excess pounds and drifted into an overconfident style, Connors had rekindled his intensity. He had not played at the French Open, and had faltered surprisingly during a quarterfinal loss to compatriot Roscoe Tanner at Wimbledon, but his form over the course of the year had been increasingly effective. He had defeated Borg twice during his 1976 campaign, ousting his adversary in the final of the U.S. Pro Indoor at Philadelphia, and again on the hard courts at Palm Springs. Altogether, Connors had clipped Borg five consecutive times since losing their first head-to-head duel in a final set tiebreaker at Stockholm in 1973. His crackling flat ground strokes had been the perfect foil for Borg's severe topspin. The piercing shots Connors made off both wings were too much for the Swede, who was forced frequently into defensive positions during the rallies, and asked too often to produce superb passing shots under pressure as Connors attacked without inhibition on every short ball.

As both Borg and Connors approached Forest Hills, they fully realized the dramatic significance of the occasion. If Borg were to win, he would have taken the two most prestigious tournaments of them all, and his status as the top-ranked player would be established unequivocally among the experts—if not on the ATP computer. As for Connors, the challenge of grasping the championship of his country was in some respects even larger. He did not want to endure a second straight season without gaining a major tournament title, and he wanted to make certain he displayed his most inspired brand of tennis in the tournament he loved like no other.

THE MATCH

Curiously, despite the fact that the Har-Tru claylike surface seemed much more favorable to Borg with his greater margin for error off the ground, Connors had a much easier time reaching the final. The top seed did not drop a set in six matches on his way to the appointment with Borg. Most impressively, Connors crushed the superb clay-court player Guillermo Vilas of Argentina, 6-4, 6-2, 6-1, in the semifinals, with a breathtaking exhibition of back-court skill, punch, and precision. The No. 3 seed Vilas—a left-handed topspin shotmaker reminiscent of Borg—would topple Connors a year later in the Forest Hills final. But he had no chance in this confrontation. Borg, meanwhile, struggled in five-set collisions with No. 15 seed Brian Gottfried, and defending titlist Manuel Orantes of Spain. But when he cut down Ilie Nastase clinically in a straight set semifinal—repeating his victory over the Romanian in the Wimbledon final two months earlier—Borg demonstrated emphatically that he was ready to conquer a man who had been his superior in their four-year rivalry.

Despite the previous encounters, many thoughtful observers expected Borg to overcome Connors on this occasion. He had lost against the left-handed American on clay courts—at the 1974 U.S. Clay Court Championships and on the same court at Forest Hills in the semifinals the year before—but Borg was clearly the more comfortable of the two performers on the green-gray surface at Forest

Hills. Connors was well aware that Borg was not going to give anything away.

Furthermore, Connors realized that a best-of-five-set final favored Borg to some extent on a slow surface. The twenty-year-old Swede thrived on matches where his patience and extraordinary persistence could enable him to prevail. A case in point was his 1974 French Open final against Orantes. Borg had fallen behind two sets to love, but he staged a stunning recovery and eliminated his Spanish adversary, 2-6, 6-7, 6-0, 6-1, 6-1. Connors wanted to establish an edge from the start and lock

Bjorn Borg

Borg out of the match. The twenty-four-year-old American had the heart and the conditioning to fight Borg convincingly to the finish and stay with the Swede in a five set struggle, but the longer the match transpired the larger the danger that Connors might falter on his low forehand approach shot.

The preceding matches and the surface influenced the result.

Predictably, Connors went on the attack from the beginning. He broke Borg in the third game of the opening set to take a 2-1 lead, bruising the Swede with a brilliant barrage of flat backhands. In turn, he made two timely visits to the net, concluding that game with a crosscourt approach off his two-hander that Borg could not counter. Borg broke back in the following game with some remarkable retrieving, but the tone had been set. Connors would largely control the tactical agenda.

After Borg cast aside a pair of break points to reach 3-2, Connors resumed command. On his way to 5-3, the American collected twelve of fifteen points, breaking Borg in the seventh game at love. The left-hander then served for the set at 5-4, and did not grant his adversary a single point in closing out the set convincingly. At triple set point, he scampered forward from deep behind the baseline to catch up with a Borg half volley. With one hand, he guided a gentle backhand past Borg. The crowd applauded admiringly.

Borg was behind, but not rattled. He had a game plan and despite his first-set failure, he was going to stay with it. Trying to avoid the Connors backhand at all costs, Borg picked away purposefully at the forehand side. He played a surprising number of sliced backhands crosscourt to break the rhythm of the American. That policy was rewarding. Borg took a 3-1 second-set lead, breaking Connors in the fourth game when the American pressed on a backhand approach and sent it into the net. Borg did not lose his serve in that set. In the ninth game, he served to get even at one set all. At 5-3, 40-30, he reached that destination. Connors directed a forehand approach down the line. His timing was flawed, his execution rushed. The shot landed long. Borg had the set.

But the key to the contest was the third set. Connors marched to a 4-2, 40-0 lead. Had he held here and converted on any of his three game points, he would almost surely have closed out the set safely and the entire course of the match might well have been different.

Instead, Connors hobbled himself inexplicably. He was guilty of five consecutive flagrant errors. At 40-0, Borg caught him off guard by rushing the net behind an ordinary backhand approach. Connors drove his passing shot over the baseline. Thereafter, the American was way out of sorts. He netted a high backhand carelessly, then stepped a yard inside the baseline in an attempt to cut off a deep return from the Swede. His low percentage play resulted in a netted backhand volley. It was deuce. Two errant high forehands cost Connors that game and complicated his task. Rather than going to the changeover with the 5-2 lead he urgently wanted, Connors had lost his break and a pleasantly surprised Borg—a master at exploiting unexpected vulnerability from an opponent—was not only back on serve, but very much back in the heart of the match. Borg surged to 4-4 and then had Connors down 0-30 in the ninth game. On that pivotal point, Borg struck his forehand

Bjorn Borg

of fourteen thousand pulsatingly gripped by every moment of the contest.

A rare Connors double fault—only his second of the match—allowed Borg back to 2-2. When Connors missed a high forehand volley by a whisker, the Swede proceeded to 4-2. Serving the seventh point, Borg was guilty of a forehand unforced error. Connors revived to 4-4, and seemed certain to win the ninth point on his serve. Connors advanced to the net behind an exceedingly deep forehand approach. Borg was on the run. He prepared early, whipped over the ball with moderate topspin on his two-hander, and clipped the sideline for a clean winner. Borg had moved to 5-4. At 6-4, 6-5, 8-7, and 9-8, Borg was within a single point of sealing the tiebreaker for the set. True to his cautious instincts, he played not to miss and dared Connors to make the big shots under intense pressure. A composed Connors was up to that task. He attacked audaciously on all four set points against him. Once, his sidespin forehand approach went behind Borg for a winner, and the other three times his approach shot was so forceful that Borg could not counterattack with any authority.

In command each time he got up to the net, Connors put away two easy overheads and knocked off a high backhand volley emphatically. After fighting off four set points, Connors was level at 9-9 in this lengthy playoff. From behind the baseline, he sent a searing backhand crosscourt for a clean winner. In a gesture that would become his trademark in the years ahead, Connors pumped his fists as he looked up animatedly toward the sky. Connors came through 11-9 in that tiebreak as Borg tamely missed a backhand. The American had seldom, if ever, been better with his back to the wall. As

passing shot with heavy topspin down the line. Connors was seemingly stranded. He lunged to his left, volleyed into the clear, then held.

From there, the players proceeded to a crucial tiebreak. After his mid-set collapse, Connors could not afford to come apart again and fall behind two sets to one. As for Borg, emerging from this set with the lead would have given him such an immense boost that even the unrelenting Connors would have been hard-pressed to halt him. So the protagonists put all of their resources into as dramatic a ten minutes as they would ever share on a tennis court together. Incentive was high on both sides of the net, the juices were flowing, the audience

Connors recalled years later of that frantic sequence of points, "That tiebreaker is probably the best tennis that I will ever play under such pressure conditions."

Having lifted that burden and left it behind him, Connors broke Borg for a 3-2 fourth set lead and it went with serve the rest of the way. But there remained some last moments of anxiety for the champion. With Connors serving for the match at 5-4, the left-hander directed a forehand volley into a vacant spot for his first match point. Then he followed his serve into the forecourt. Borg's dipping return would have been awkward to volley. Connors let it bounce, then sent a piercing backhand crosscourt and closed in on the net. Borg took his shot on the rise and passed Connors cleanly crosscourt off the forehand. Deuce. Connors was unruffled. He attacked again off a fierce, flat forehand. Borg missed the passing shot. Match point to Connors for the second time. Borg's return this time was a deep crosscourt to Connors's forehand. The American's apprehension was painfully evident. He came under the ball and sliced it wide. Deuce again. Once more, Connors pressed forward. Coming in off the backhand, his approach was magnificent. Borg lobbed long off his backhand. Match point No. 3 for the American. The pattern was familiar. Connors got the short ball he wanted. He hit a penetrating forehand crosscourt and came in. Borg tried his patented two-handed crosscourt passing shot. His reply found the net. Match and title to Connors, 6-4, 3-6, 7-6 (11-9), 6-4. He had won his second U.S. Open. An instant after Borg missed the final stroke, Connors wheeled around with arms upraised, turning to share his triumph with longtime mentor Pancho Segura, who stood behind the court applauding unrestrainedly.

Afterward, Connors downplayed his long wait for the first major title he had won since his Forest Hills triumph on grass in 1974. "If the sun rose and set only on Wimbledon and Forest Hills," he reflected, "there would be a lot of guys without tans." That was a fair comment, but Connors fully realized that he could not settle for minor triumphs. He had built his reputation

---

Connors had not won a major tournament in two years.

---

on getting the job done when the stakes were high, and this triumph over Borg on a landmark occasion was one of the shining moments of Connors's career. His tan that evening was unmistakable.

EPILOGUE

After losing that agonizing battle with Connors at Forest Hills in 1976, Borg was discouraged, but not for long. They did not meet again in an official match until Wimbledon in 1977. In that memorable final, Connors was down, 0-4, in the fifth set and Borg had break points to establish a 5-0 lead. Had he converted in the fifth game, the Swede would likely have taken that final set, 6-0. But Connors saved the break points, held for 1-4, and then put on a burst of brilliant shotmaking, reaching 4-4 as an appreciative crowd at the All England Club cheered him on with unreserved enthusiasm. Serving at 4-4, Connors reached 15-0 but a rare double fault "came out of nowhere," as he explained later. The resurgence from Connors was over and Borg quickly collected eight straight points to win, 3-6, 6-2, 6-1, 5-7, 6-4.

That was the turning point of the Borg-

Connors rivalry. After losing six of his first seven clashes with Connors, Borg won fourteen of the last sixteen, including the last ten in a row, for a 15-8 career edge. The critical difference during the last five years of their series was Borg's capacity to deliver unreturnable first serves on big points. He could call on that strength nearly always. In turn, Borg added more elements to his game, demonstrated more flexibility, and altered his tactics on the faster surfaces. It was another case of a reversal of fortunes, but their matches remained superb spectacles until the conclusion of their rivalry at the U.S. Open in 1981. In their earlier confrontation in the Wimbledon semifinals of 1981, Connors had played perhaps his best ever tennis against Borg during the early stages, but he could no longer sustain the accelerated pace against the Swede, and he bowed, 0-6, 4-6, 6-3, 6-0, 6-4, in a sparkling showdown.

No one competed with more intensity than Connors.

Connors, however, performed more productively much longer than Borg, who retired from big-time tennis after the U.S. Open in 1981. Connors remained a force until early in the following decade. After beating Borg in that earlier 1976 U.S. Open final, Connors celebrated his last victory over the Swede in the 1978 Open final on hard courts and thus became the only player ever to win a major championship on three different surfaces (grass, clay, and hard courts). Borg was constantly cutting Connors down at Wimbledon, adding wins over Jimmy in the 1978 final and the 1979 semifinals before that incomparable triumph in the 1981 semifinals.

Those losses clearly cut into the core of Connors's confidence during big matches. When John McEnroe emerged in the late 1970s, Connors had another nettlesome rival on his hands. From 1979 through 1981, Connors did not capture a single major championship, and as he approached the age of thirty it seemed entirely possible that he would not capture any more Grand Slam titles. But Borg's unexpected departure after the 1981 season altered everything, and Connors was reawakened.

In 1982—for the second time in his career—he was victorious at both Wimbledon and the U.S. Open in the same season. With Borg gone, Connors took a terrific five set final from McEnroe at Wimbledon, and then removed a rising Ivan Lendl in a four-set U.S. Open final only days after turning thirty. The following year, he defended his U.S. Open championship with another surprise victory over Lendl. Over the remainder of the 1980s, Connors gradually declined, but he remained among the top-eight players in the world every year from 1973-88. For five straight years (1974-78), he was No. 1 on the official ATP computer. From 1973-84, he did not finish a single year lower than No. 3 in the world.

When Connors had wrist surgery in 1990 at thirty-eight, his time in top-flight tennis seemed certain to be over. But the obstinate left-hander was not through. At the 1991 U.S. Open, he not only celebrated his thirty-ninth birthday, but he strung together a series of inspiring matches and made it to the semifinals of the U.S. Open before losing to French Open Champion, Jim Courier. Connors could not help but be reminded—as were countless players and members of the press—of Ken

Rosewall's remarkable runs to the finals of Wimbledon and Forest Hills in 1974 when the stylish Australian was also thirty-nine. On each occasion Rosewall was overwhelmed by

---

Connors, at 39, makes a final run.

---

the mighty power of the Connors ground stroke arsenal, winning only eight games in a total of six sets. Eight years later, on the eve of the 1982 U.S. Open, Connors stood in the bright sunlight on the stadium court at Flushing Meadow talking to the Englishman John Lloyd as he prepared to practice. He told Lloyd, "Rosewall more than anyone taught me how important it was to get down low for my ground strokes. He kept the ball so low all the time that he forced you to keep digging and it was a great lesson for me."

But after his "last hurrah" at the Open of 1991, Connors wisely rearranged his priorities and, despite sporadic appearances on the men's tour, he moved on to establish a senior tour that revolved largely around him. Right up to the end of the century, he stayed in excellent shape and was the player fans most wanted to watch. He remained, as always, a ferocious competitor who stood by a statement he made in his prime. "I hate to lose more than I love to win." He carried that attitude with him on the senior circuit, dominating Borg and other marquee players for many years with his overwhelming appetite for success and the fierce combativeness of his play. Observing him on court in his mid-forties, it was hard to imagine that anyone could summon so much energy and enthusiasm.

The joy in putting himself on the line was always unmistakable, and he had demonstrat-

ed that quality against different generations of great players. When he first came into prominence at seventeen, he had toppled the renowned Roy Emerson at the Pacific Southwest in Los Angeles, and he had won and lost against the great Pancho Gonzales, one of his early coaches and his doubles partner (once) at the U.S. Open. Connors continued his inexorable march to the top when he confronted the Australian superstars Rosewall, Rod Laver, and John Newcombe. Then he took on Borg, McEnroe, and Lendl in the most colorful rivalries of his career, but it did not stop there.

After his salad days were over, he was not reluctant to struggle with much younger men moving up and through their primes. He had stirring clashes with Boris Becker and Stefan Edberg—routing the Swedish star only a year before Edberg reached No. 1 in the world. And his unflinching latter-day journey even included two meetings with Pete Sampras in the early 1990s. There were times when his behavior was embarrassing, when his crudity toward linesmen and umpires was unacceptably obscene, when his abrasive actions overshadowed his clean and elegant shotmaking. But despite the complex facets of his personality, Connors was a man the fans could not ignore. The record reveals that McEnroe at his best was a better player, that Borg was superior on the crucial occasions over time, that Lendl won the same number of major championships. But over the last third of this century, no male tennis player did more than Jimmy Connors to boost the game's popularity. He was an indispensable figure.

As for Borg, after his difficult setback against Connors in their tense 1976 U.S. Open

Jimmy Connors

final, he produced a long sequence of sterling achievements. He won Wimbledon five years in a row from 1976-80, a feat never matched since the abolishment of the "Challenge Round" system in 1922. Borg was also victorious at the French Open six times between 1974 and 1981, leading many observers to the conclusion that he was the best men's clay-court player of all time. He won at least one Grand Slam championship a year for eight consecutive years from 1974-81, amassing eleven in that span.

In his era, Borg created an almost discernible aura around himself as the unfailingly cool man in a crisis, as the man you could depend upon when the chips were down. He would be beaten during this period by players who peaked on particularly auspicious afternoons, but he seldom beat himself. He was the quintessential match player and a surprisingly adaptable competitor, taking the French Open and Wimbledon in succession for three consecutive years (1978-80) as he shifted his objectives from the slow clay of Paris to the fast grass of Wimbledon. •

BJORN BORG VS. JOHN McENROE

WIMBLEDON, FINAL, JULY 5, 1980

In this match of endurance and suspense, perhaps unequalled in its athletic splendor, the Swede and American produced the most gripping tiebreaker ever played.

PROLOGUE

As a new decade dawned in 1980, Borg remained the preeminent player in tennis, and his mastery of the big points made him virtually unassailable. He had firmly overtaken Connors, and his majestic performances in the major championships set him apart from anyone else in his field. But in all his time at and near the top of his profession, he had encountered no one quite like John Patrick McEnroe of New York.

McEnroe was a dynamic left-hander with an explosive temperament and a spontaneous style of play that contrasted with Borg's much more meticulous, programmed patterns. McEnroe had grown up in Douglaston, just outside New York City, and had been coached as a teenager by former Australian Davis Cup captain, Harry Hopman. While Hopman had worked largely with conventional Australian serve-and-volleyers who seemed to have followed the same systematic guidelines, McEnroe was raised at the opposite end of the spectrum.

His service stance was so fashioned that his opponents saw as much of his back as his face.

He seemed dead set against bending his knees when he was up at the net, but he volleyed brilliantly and his touch in the forecourt was often astonishing. His ground strokes were uncommonly well produced. He frequently took the ball on the rise but he was not a big hitter off either side; instead, he was a master at playing off an opponent's pace and rushing them into mistakes with his adroit, subtle variations of speed and direction. Almost across the board, McEnroe broke the rules of conventional wisdom with his approach to playing the game. He was one of the few great innovators ever to step on a tennis court.

McEnroe had a distinguished junior career but it was not until he was eighteen, in the summer of 1977, that he made his mark. That year he went to Wimbledon for the first time, where he had to work his way through the qualifying rounds at Roehampton just to earn the right to make his debut at the All England Club. Even when he won his three qualifying matches, no one expected him to strike a spark in the main event, but McEnroe was rising into another realm as a competitor and the grass court surface was suited to his aggressive serve-and-volley game.

John McEnroe

RUSS ADAMS

Furthermore, McEnroe's disarming volatility caught the establishment off guard. He seemed to have little respect for the leading players and even less for the officials. He wore what seemed to be a permanent scowl and seldom smiled at his good fortune. No matter how well he was playing, McEnroe seemed incapable of finding satisfaction in his gifted shotmaking. He was so talented that he progressed through the draw at his first Wimbledon with almost bemused assurance, surprised by his success on one level, unimpressed with his opposition on the other. He toppled No. 13 seed Phil Dent, a former Australian Open finalist, in the quarterfinals, then lost his semifinal appearance to Connors in a first-rate, four-set comeuppance.

Nevertheless, McEnroe was now indisputably a rising star. He attended Stanford University for a year, won the NCAA Championships in 1978, then turned professional and went to work with unbridled passion and persistence. By the end of 1978, when he was only nineteen, he became the No. 4 ranked player in the world, and he closed that season with a display of impressive poise under pressure. Facing his esteemed countryman Arthur Ashe in the final of the Masters at New York's Madison Square Garden, McEnroe led 5-4, 40-0 in the opening set, then double-faulted three times in a row to allow Ashe back into the set. Ashe pounced on the opportunity and won a tiebreaker to move out in front. Later, in the third and final set, Ashe had two match points with McEnroe serving at 4-5. A deliriously pro-Ashe crowd of seventeen thousand cheered their man vociferously, but McEnroe kept his nerve and went on to win, 6-7, 6-3, 7-5.

He seemed to draw upon that outcome over the next three years. In 1979, McEnroe won the championship of his country for the first time. In the semifinals, he cut down the defending champion Connors in three convincing sets, then took apart his friend and fellow New Yorker, Vitas Gerulaitis, 7-5, 6-3, 6-3 for the title. He had won his first major championship only a few miles from his boyhood home in New York, and he had shown that he would be difficult for anyone to handle as the leading players took their talent and ambitions into the 1980s.

Borg, however, was going strong as Wimbledon approached in 1980. In both 1978 and 1979, he had captured the French Open and Wimbledon. He wanted to keep his chances for a Grand Slam alive by winning the U.S. Open in both of those years. He had lost to Connors in the 1978 Open final and to the big-serving American, Roscoe Tanner, the following year in the quarterfinals. But the month before the 1980 Wimbledon, Borg ruled at Roland Garros on the clay for the third consecutive year, and the fifth time in all, winning the clay court championship of the world without the loss of a single set in seven matches, crushing Gerulaitis, 6-4, 6-1, 6-2, in the final.

McEnroe, who had risen past Connors to No. 2 in the world with Borg ahead of him, had lost in the third round at Paris to the Australian, Paul McNamee. That may have

---

John McEnroe made his mark early and then briefly stumbled.

---

been a hidden blessing because it gave him more time to adjust to grass courts and prepare for Wimbledon. McEnroe plainly wanted to make amends for his last two Wimbledons, which had paled in comparison to his first in 1977. In 1978, he had lost on an outside court to countryman, Erik Van Dillen, a much better player in doubles than singles. For McEnroe, it was a very disappointing five-set, opening-round defeat. The next year he was beaten in straight sets by fellow American, Tim Gullikson—who later coached both Martina Navratilova and Pete Sampras—in the round of sixteen. McEnroe was surely a better player than he had shown on either of those occasions. By 1980 he was also more sure of himself as a person and a competitor.

THE MATCH

There was a quiet sense among the cognoscenti all through Wimbledon in 1980 that Borg and McEnroe would meet in the end to play for the title. Borg had become an immensely intimidating adversary for everyone competing on the grass of the All England Club. He was seeking to establish himself as the first man in the modern era to win the game's most coveted crown five years in a row. He had survived so many stern tests on Centre Court that he seemed invincible in that setting. After taking the title without the loss of a set in seven impeccable matches in 1976, he had been stretched to five sets six times in the following three years but had won them all. He was by now the master of the defining moments at the All England Club, a player who treated adversity as a minor annoyance.

McEnroe, meanwhile, was the stylistic counterpart to Borg. No one in the Swede's dominant years at Wimbledon had played a better brand of grass court tennis. Furthermore, McEnroe had demonstrated in his rivalry with Borg that he could compete successfully against the Swede on any fast surface. In their initial battle two years earlier, McEnroe had toppled Borg in straight sets indoors at Stockholm. They had been trading victories and defeats ever since. Borg took their second confrontation at the WCT Richmond event early in 1979, and McEnroe prevailed in a final-set tiebreak a few months later in New Orleans. Borg got back to 2-2 in the series with a 6-4, 6-2 triumph in Rotterdam. McEnroe retaliated with a four-set triumph over Borg in the WCT Dallas Finals in May 1979. Borg made it 3-3 in that summer of 1979 with a win over McEnroe on hard courts at

Toronto. Then in January 1980 at The Masters in New York, Borg got by his tenacious adversary, 6-7, 6-3, 7-6.

Coming into Wimbledon, Borg held a narrow 4-3 edge and the Swede had posted two wins in a row in this scorching personal series. Seeded first and second, they took their places in the final as expected. Borg dropped only two sets along the way and was never seriously tested. McEnroe was pressed hard in a five set, second round match with the Australian, Terry Rocavert, but he struggled from two-sets-to-one down to pull out the victory. In the semi-

Bjorn Borg

finals, Borg accounted for the unseeded American, Brian Gottfried, 6-0, in the fourth set, while McEnroe rallied from 2-4 in the fourth to oust Connors in a high-tension contest, 6-3, 3-6, 6-3, 6-4.

McEnroe was magnificent at the start of his eagerly awaited battle with Borg. He glided through the first set, 6-1, conceding only seven points in four service games, breaking Borg twice by attacking diligently as Borg stayed back on his second serve. Borg remained cautious and somewhat out of sync in the second set. But he sedulously held on to his serve time and again as McEnroe looked for a way to claim a decisive two-sets-to-love lead. With Borg serving at 4-4 in the second, McEnroe raised the stakes and went after a service break full force.

Three times in that critical ninth game, McEnroe reached break point by pressing forward at every opportunity and volleying with awesome control and touch. Yet on all three of these big break points, Borg produced surgical first serves that were unreturnable. The Swede held for 5-4, and then again for 6-5. Until this juncture, McEnroe had been too much for Borg on serve as the Swede stood 10 to 15 feet behind the baseline to make his returns. But with the New Yorker serving at 5-6, Borg finally found the range with his heavy topspin shots, making them dip at McEnroe's feet as the left-hander came in for the first volley. After McEnroe netted a low backhand approach volley at 5-6, 30-30, Borg was able to make it one set all.

Emerging from that late second set crisis raised Borg's spirits considerably and carried him stubbornly through the third. Borg charged to 3-0, stood firm in a seven deuce game in which he saved five break points to reach 5-2, then served his way smoothly to a 6-3 third set verdict and a two-sets-to-one lead. Borg was proceeding methodically toward his goal in the fourth set. He broke McEnroe in the ninth game with a plummeting backhand crosscourt return winner, off a trademark McEnroe slice serve wide in the advantage court, and took a 5-4 lead.

He served for the match in the tenth game and proceeded rapidly to 40-15, double match point. As he paused at that moment before attempting to finish his business, Borg seemed certain to prevail in four sets. The clock behind his right shoulder read 4:53 in the afternoon. The match was two hours and thirty-four minutes old. Everything was neatly in place for Borg to enhance his record by vanquishing McEnroe with calm assurance. On the first match point, a deep first serve to the backhand was narrowly off the mark, and then when Borg attacked during a short exchange, McEnroe passed him cleanly down the line off the backhand. A second match point was still available.

The tie-breaker became a match in itself.

The top seed tried to put away a backhand volley but he popped it up slightly and McEnroe advanced to cut it off. On the run, McEnroe released a forehand drive volley past Borg for another winner. The tension was palpable. At deuce, McEnroe forced Borg into a forehand passing shot error and then hit a winning service return. It was 5-5. McEnroe was resurgent. Borg was incredulous. How had it all slipped from his grasp? Why was he still on the court? Could he possibly recoup?

Both players held to set up a tiebreaker. They proceeded to play a sequence of points that enthralled the British audience, and kept people around the world in front of their television sets. Both men were so good with their backs to the wall that the fabric of emotion among the fans was torn by conflicting, changing loyalties. The two contrasting competitors raised the level of play far beyond expectation. In this excruciatingly close tiebreak, Borg reached match point with McEnroe serving at 5-6, but the left-hander lunged for Borg's dipping forehand return and produced a brilliant forehand drop volley winner. Borg immediately responded with a vintage crosscourt backhand passing shot and served at 7-6, arriving at match point for the fourth time.

A conservatively played high backhand volley from Borg opened up a wide window of opportunity for McEnroe, who whipped a backhand pass down the line for an outright winner. McEnroe came up with another dazzling passing shot to reach 8-7 and his first set point, only to be halted by a winning forehand return from Borg off a deep first serve.

Then McEnroe stormed in behind serve to knock off a high backhand volley. He led, 9-8, but Borg served his way out of that precarious moment and connected with a winning volley of his own. A penetrating first serve deep to McEnroe's backhand forced an error, and brought Borg to 10-9—a fifth match point.

Neither man was buckling. McEnroe's service winner to the backhand lifted him to 10-10. Borg's forehand pass beyond the reach of a diving McEnroe gave the Swede an 11-10 lead on serve and a sixth match point. McEnroe was in mid-court when he tentatively struck a backhand approach shot. It clipped the net cord and fell over for a very dicey winner. Internally, Borg had to be distressed by that improbable point, but he concealed his emotions and forced McEnroe into a low forehand volley error with a sharply struck two-hander.

Borg thus moved to 12-11, and a seventh match point. Surely he would seal it all here. But McEnroe rejected that possibility. Borg ran around a return of a second serve and hit his forehand hard with heavy topspin. McEnroe had closed in tightly and his crosscourt backhand first volley was well beyond Borg's reach. It was 12-12. The players now changed ends for the fourth time in this agonizingly suspenseful struggle. McEnroe again came in behind his second serve and punched a forehand volley behind Borg for a winner and a 13-12 lead and for him, a third set point.

Then Borg came in swiftly behind a deep first serve to the backhand. His backhand volley floated deep toward the baseline. It seemed to be going out, but fell an inch inside the line and McEnroe could not handle the bounce. Then Borg missed a low backhand volley to give McEnroe a 14-13 lead that the New Yorker flagrantly squandered with a forehand volley wide of the sideline despite an open court. Then McEnroe charged to 15-14. A service winner from Borg to the backhand made it 15-15. The players changed sides for the fifth time as the audience lustily applauded both men. Such extraordinary tennis under stress, over so many climactic points, was unimaginable.

Borg served the thirty-first point and failed to "stick" his crosscourt backhand volley. McEnroe easily chased it down and drove a forehand pass into an open space to lead at 16-15. McEnroe served and volleyed again but overplayed a high backhand volley. It was 16-16. Borg

missed a forehand return placement by a hair. He was serving at 16-17. Borg charged behind a solid first serve but dumped a forehand drop volley into the net. Centre Court erupted thunderously. The appreciation was non-partisan. Two valiant young men had fought for a glory both deserved. Set to McEnroe, 18-16, in a tiebreak that would never be replicated. McEnroe had saved seven match points—five of them in this stupendous tiebreaker. The New Yorker had needed seven set points of his own before he could force a fifth set.

Borg had to put the tiebreaker behind him, and did.

Borg sat in his chair at the changeover understandably dismayed, and deflated by his many lost opportunities. A reinvigorated but not overconfident McEnroe reflected briefly on his good fortune. Then both men went back to work. In the opening game of the fifth set, Borg trailed, 0-30. He was not going to recover easily if he lost his serve here, not after the demoralizing conclusion of the fourth set. A perfectly placed first serve deep to McEnroe's backhand forced an error, and three more solid points lifted Borg out of that bind. He held for 1-0. Now McEnroe trailed, 0-40, in the second game. He double-faulted to fall behind break point for the fourth time, but resolutely held for 1-1. At 3-4 in the fifth, McEnroe did it again. Down 0-40, he summoned the best that was left in him and held on gamely for 4-4.

Borg had been through it all now, but he kept plodding on. By the time he reached 7-6, he had finally taken too much out of McEnroe at last. From 0-30 in his opening service game, Borg had won twenty-eight of twenty-nine points on his serve in the fifth set. He had served five love games. He had kept leading his foe into trouble by directing his first serve deep and wide to the American's backhand, and McEnroe could not defend himself against that tactic. At 6-7, 15-15, McEnroe was caught off guard by an inside out forehand return winner from Borg. Then Borg's whipped topspin backhand passing shot provoked a netted forehand volley from McEnroe. It was 15-40 and Borg was at match point for the eighth time. McEnroe came in gamely on serve and punched a forehand volley down the middle of the court. Borg lined up his backhand and rifled it crosscourt. McEnroe turned to watch the shot land safely inches inside the sideline. Borg fell to his knees with relief and exultation. After three hours and fifty three minutes—nearly an hour-and-a-half after he had reached match point for the first time—Borg had persevered as only he could.

As Borg walked off the court following his 1-6, 7-5, 6-3, 6-7 (16-18), 8-6 triumph, he was asked by NBC broadcaster Bud Collins where he placed his victory in a historical context. "It has to be one of the best matches I have ever played," he said, "and I think probably the best I have ever played at Wimbledon. I thought after I lost the fourth set I would lose the match. I was exhausted, especially after losing all of those match points, but I didn't give up."

Nearly two decades later, when he was in New York for a press conference announcing his 1999 induction into the International Tennis Hall of Fame, McEnroe did his best to put this unprecedented match into perspective. Despite the hard reality of losing an epic battle, McEnroe maintained that no match had meant more to him as he looked back on his illustrious career.

"The one thing I hear about the most is the match with Borg at Wimbledon in 1980," he said. "In some ways I would have to pick that. It showed me, and hopefully showed a lot of other tennis players, that in losing, actually that could elevate your status. And even if you are not necessarily the winner every time, if you are part of history like I felt there, it makes it okay. Being part of that match was perhaps the most exciting thing in my career. The vibrations and goodwill I get from people from that match are incredible. It is far and away my most talked about match."

EPILOGUE

Two months after their monumental encounter at Wimbledon, Borg and McEnroe met again in the final of the U.S. Open. For the third straight year, Borg had a chance to win a third consecutive Grand Slam title and a first U.S. Open. Had he realized that goal, he would have gone to Australia at the end of those years in an attempt to complete the Grand Slam. But it was not to be. He lost to McEnroe, 7-6, 6-1, 6-7, 5-7, 6-4, in a bizarre final at Flushing Meadow. It was a contest that did not approach the level of the Wimbledon extravaganza. At the U.S. Open, Borg twice served for the first set but threw it away. Quietly angered by his failure, he was taken apart in the second set by a resolute McEnroe. Before he knew it, Borg was down two sets to love but he slowly worked his way into the match with meticulous determination in the third and fourth sets. By the time he reached 3-3 in the fifth, Borg looked highly likely to succeed. But on the first point of the seventh game, McEnroe approached on a backhand that the linesman called good on the baseline. Borg stood there staring at the official for an exceedingly long moment, but the call was not altered. McEnroe broke him for 4-3 and ran out the match.

A year later, the major championships were essentially a showcase for Borg and McEnroe to display their rivalry and their supremacy. After Borg took a five set final from an evolving Ivan Lendl at the French Open—making him the only man in history to win at least one Grand Slam title for eight consecutive years—the Swede and the American squared off in the finals of both Wimbledon and the U.S. Open for the second year in a row. At Wimbledon, Borg had made a remarkable recovery from two-sets-to-love down against Connors in the semifinals to lift his winning streak to forty-one matches, but after taking the first set of the final from McEnroe, Borg bowed, 4-6, 7-6, 7-6, 6-4.

Two months later, Borg bowed in four sets to McEnroe in the U.S. Open Final. He had failed again in New York, falling for the fourth time in a championship match of a major tournament he never won.

When that match was over, the normally imperturbable sportsman was so distraught that he did not stay for the presentation

Bjorn Borg (back) and John McEnroe

Bjorn Borg vs. John McEnroe, 1980 • 169

ceremony. He sadly picked up his belongings and left the stadium. Without realizing it at the time, he was in the process of quitting the game. The following year, he obdurately refused to adhere to the rules imposed by the game's governing authorities who wanted him to commit to ten tournaments outside of his Grand Slam participation. Borg had already sharply reduced his schedule in the previous two years. He played a few scattered events thereafter, but never again appeared in a major tournament. His loss to McEnroe in New York was his last match at a Grand Slam event.

Borg would later concede that one of the primary reasons he left the game was his pessimistic view of how he would fare in the future against McEnroe, who had taken away his No. 1 ranking by winning the two most coveted titles in tennis during the 1981 season. Borg believed then that McEnroe was too versatile for him and assumed he would keep confronting his nemesis time after time in the years ahead. But he may have been well off the mark with that assessment. In 1982—with Borg having stepped out of the picture—McEnroe did not retain his major titles. He lost to Connors in a five-set Wimbledon final, then fell to Ivan Lendl in a straight-set U.S. Open semifinal. Connors, the man who had not beaten Borg since 1978, elevated his game brilliantly and won Wimbledon and the U.S. Open in 1982.

McEnroe, for his part, acknowledged that he missed having Borg around to push him on to greater heights. He was not as comfortable as he should have been occupying the lofty terrain as the best player in the world. In retrospect, Borg would almost surely have won at least one major championship in 1982 and perhaps more. But he had lost his taste for tough competition, and once he stopped training as he had for so long, his determination crumbled.

Nearly a decade later, in 1991, Borg plotted a comeback. He was approaching thirty-five by then and he had waited far too long. The ill-advised return to tennis never got off the ground, and he was unable to win a match in his main tour appearances from 1991-93. He sensibly stopped playing in the men's game once and for all. In the years ahead he did make a credible return on the senior tour where he played some lively matches against Connors and McEnroe in the late 1990s.

Bjorn Borg had a relatively brief but remarkable career. In the Open Era, he won more men's major championships than anyone except Pete Sampras. His footwork and mobility were unsurpassed in his time—and perhaps ever. He gave the game a good name with his dignified demeanor and admirable court behavior. He may well be remembered most for his splendid series with McEnroe. After the 1980 season, Borg led, 7-4, but following the three 1981 setbacks, they stood even at 7-7, and that is how it ended.

McEnroe's best tennis was still ahead of him. He, too, would suffer from a mid-career burnout, but he played successfully into the early 1990s. Somehow it was never the same for the stormy left-hander without Bjorn Borg.   •

CHRIS EVERT VS MARTINA NAVRATILOVA

AUSTRALIAN OPEN, FINAL, DECEMBER 6, 1981

With the wind blowing unrelentingly, the two great rivals of contrasting styles and temperaments closed out their 1981 campaign with a captivating contest.

PROLOGUE

During the last quarter of the twentieth century, there were no series of matches more engaging than those played by Martina Navratilova and Chris Evert. These superb clashes pitted a demonstrative, left-handed volleyer against a patient, disciplined baseliner. They met in head-to-head competition eighty times between 1973 and 1988. They collided at least four times in every major championship. They battled gamely indoors and out, on slow and fast surfaces, in good and bad conditions, throughout their careers. Their rivalry was regarded by the vast majority of authorities as the greatest in the history of the game—not excluding the men. Others placed their confrontations in an even grander category as the most compelling rivalry produced in any sport.

From the outset, the Evert-Navratilova matchup had everything working for it. As Evert herself said when she reflected on the rivalry for this book, "What made it interesting all along was the contrasts between Martina and me. If you have two players with the same kinds of games and personalities, it can be boring and repetitious. But we had so many things about us that were different. She came from Czechoslovakia and I was from Florida. She was left-handed and aggressive. I was right-handed, with a two-handed backhand, and a counterpuncher. I internalized things and she did not. We both brought our own set of fans into each match we played."

The contrasts did not end there. Navratilova was sturdily built and over time became muscular and ruggedly athletic. Evert was known as "The Girl Next Door," and was a model of womanly grace and elegance. Navratilova was often outspoken and emotional; Evert was diplomatic and polite in the public arena. Evert turned her restraint and dignity into enduring attributes; Navratilova used her passion to engender popularity with her audiences. Navratilova would protest questionable line calls genuinely but sometimes caustically; Evert would simply register her disapproval with a stern glare at the officials.

And yet, there were some subcutaneous similarities. Their respect for each other as professionals was visible and sincere. Both women were highly intelligent in person and as players.

They would become better at their craft because of the demands they placed on each other with such different brands of play. Finally, Chrissie Evert and Martina Navratilova stayed at or near the top of their profession for much longer than they could have imagined when they started their climb up the ladder.

Chris was one of five children raised by Fort Lauderdale teaching professional Jimmy Evert, a strict taskmaster. Jimmy Evert was once ranked eleventh in the United States and won the Canadian Championships in 1947. He stressed sound ground stroke fundamentals and a consistency of commitment. Each one of his five children—three daughters and two sons—reached at least the final of a national championship during their junior careers, but Chrissie had the greatest drive and the highest hopes.

She was well ahead of the game during her junior days, moving into women's tennis precociously in her teens. When she was fifteen, she sent signals to the tennis world of her immense promise, toppling world No. 1 Margaret Court in a pair of tiebreakers at a small tournament in Charlotte, North Carolina. Less than a month before, Court had completed a Grand Slam by capturing the U.S. Open.

At sixteen, in the summer of 1971, Chrissie

Evert's youthful start was aided by a family of tennis players.

---

became the youngest ever to reach the semifinals of the U.S. Open. She recorded a string of stirring, come-from-behind triumphs in that tournament. A pivotal victory was her round of sixteen success against countrywoman Mary Ann Eisel. Confronting a seasoned serve-and-volleyer on the fast grass courts at Forest Hills,

the Floridian saved six match points in a remarkable three-set win. Although she lost decisively to Billie Jean King in the semifinal round, Evert had arrived as a celebrated player.

By 1974, when she was nineteen, she was the best woman player in the world. She won her first two Grand Slam championships at the French Open and Wimbledon that year. Evert would stay at the top for seven of eight years in that span. She had tested herself against a cluster of commendable rivals through the seventies and into the eighties, winning nine of thirteen matches against Court, taking nineteen of twenty-six meetings with King, and overcoming Goolagong in twenty-five of thirty-eight battles.

Other than Navratilova, the only major adversary to cause serious problems for Evert was the Californian, Tracy Austin. Austin was a virtual clone of Evert from the baseline, solid and assertive off both sides, seldom making careless mistakes, always probing for flaws. She would have her career cut short in the early eighties by back problems, but not before she defeated both Navratilova and Evert to establish herself as the youngest-ever U.S. Open women's champion in 1979 at sixteen. Austin took the crown again two years later.

Evert recorded one of the most significant triumphs of her career when she stopped Austin, 4-6, 6-1, 6-1, in the semifinals of the U.S. Open in 1980. She had lost to the Californian five consecutive times leading up to that battle. Evert collected her fifth Open title the next day, and restored her confidence and authority with that triumph. She then had an excellent first half of 1981, winning her third Wimbledon singles title and expanding her game under the expert guidance of a new coach, Dennis Ralston, a former U.S. No. 1 player.

Navratilova had developed her game in Czechoslovakia. She was two years younger than Evert, and much more of a risk taker. Her parents divorced when Martina was three. Her father committed suicide when she was about ten, although Martina did not know until much later. Meanwhile, her mother married Mirek Navratil. They lived in a village called Revnice. Martina regarded Mirek as her father—not stepfather. Both her mother and grandmother were versatile tennis players, though they did not make a career of it. Her mother's family lost nearly everything they had during the 1948 takeover by the communists. Nonetheless, Martina was able to pursue her tennis career. After losing to Evert in the semifinals of the U.S. Open in 1975, she defected from her native land and took up residence in the United States. By then, Navratilova was already entrenched among the top five in the world.

The athletic left-hander joined Evert to win two major tournaments in doubles, including the 1976 championship at Wimbledon. Over time, they gave up playing as a team because their singles competition took precedence. In 1978, Navratilova came of age when she won her first Grand Slam singles title at Wimbledon. At twenty-one, she rallied from 2-4 in the final set to oust Evert, 2-6, 6-4, 7-5. The following year, Navratilova toppled Evert again in the Centre Court final. She was the top-ranked player for the year.

Navratilova seemed to be peaking after enduring a couple of difficult years. She did not win a major title in 1980, and her confidence was

Chris Evert

wavering in the spring of 1981. During the clay court final at Amelia Island, Florida, Evert was letter-perfect and Navratilova was way out of sync. Evert won, 6-0, 6-0. But that loss made Navratilova realize that she needed to get back to work.

It was in that period that basketball player Nancy Lieberman took over as a fitness coach and mentor for Martina, and later in the year transsexual Renée Richards became her tennis coach. As Evert recalled, "I remember Nancy Lieberman coming to Amelia Island and watching me beat Martina love and love. Nancy had an edge and a toughness about her and she influenced Martina with those characteristics. Nancy convinced Martina to get more serious about her conditioning. Right after Martina lost that match to me at Amelia Island, Nancy took her out to the basketball court."

Between then and the U.S. Open, Navratilova trimmed her weight and approached each match with a growing professionalism. As Evert observed, "By the U.S. Open, there was a big change in Martina's body. She was much stronger and fitter. She went through rigorous workouts, changed her eating habits, became a better athlete, and it all helped her tennis. In a sense, she was brainwashed. Nancy Lieberman kept reinforcing that she was the strongest and the best one out there. Together with Renee Richards, they were a very good combination for the fitness and the tennis."

At the U.S. Open of 1981, Navratilova was rejuvenated in many ways. She had become a U.S. citizen after a six-year wait. In the semifinals, she and Evert played a stupendous match, a contest filled with splendid points and brilliantly pursued rallies. Navratilova was behind, 2-4, in the final set, but stopped Chrissie, 7-5, 4-6, 6-4. They had not played since Amelia Island. The hard courts at Flushing Meadow provided a neutral surface, and both players shined. Navratilova lost a wrenching 1-6, 7-6, 7-6 match against Austin in the final.

As the year came to a close and the leading players assembled at the Australian Open for the last major of the season, both Evert and Navratilova looked at Melbourne as the chance to finish the Grand Slam season on a high note. Navratilova had not won a "Big Four" singles title since Wimbledon two years earlier. Evert wanted to add Australia to her victory list—it was the only major title she had not secured. At Kooyong Stadium on the grass courts of Melbourne, they would confront each other in yet another epic clash.

THE MATCH

The rivalry was eight years old when Martina and Chrissie came into Melbourne. This would be their first meeting at the Australian Open, but they had played many classic matches over the years in and outside the major events. In their overall series, Evert led 29-15. In the Grand Slam events, Evert held a slim 4-3 edge. It was apparent, however, that Navratilova was making sizable strides. She had been beaten in twenty of their first twenty-four clashes between 1973 and the middle of 1978. In that time frame, Evert was much

Evert and Navratilova had never before met at the Australian Open.

stronger mentally, more consistent off the ground, and better as a match player.

With her comeback triumph over Evert in the 1978 Wimbledon, Navratilova demonstrated a tenacity she had seldom shown before. She would drift away from her finest form again in the years ahead, but on balance she was moving in the right direction. In any case, after their extraordinary U.S. Open battle three months earlier, Navratilova had ousted Evert that autumn in Tokyo. But the week before

Martina Navratilova

while Navratilova conceded only one—to the American, Kathy Jordan. The second-seeded Austin was upset by countrywoman Pam Shriver in the quarterfinals; Navratilova accounted for Shriver in a straight-set semifinal.

In their forty-fifth career confrontation, Evert and Navratilova stepped onto the stadium court at Kooyong on a windy afternoon. "I felt going into the match," said Evert, "that Martina had the momentum with her. She was in great shape and I knew she had not won a Grand Slam title for a long time. She had a lot of pride. As a champion, she did not want to go without a Grand Slam title that year. By the time we played at the end of the tournament, the stadium court at Kooyong was pretty chewed up, so your best bet was to get to the net. That also favored Martina."

Nevertheless, Evert stood her ground ably in the first set. She had the best ground strokes of her era, and they served her well on any surface. On both the forehand and her revered two-handed backhand, she hit the ball basically flat with incomparable depth. She kept her returns solid and low when Navratilova charged in behind her heavily spun serve. And no one could disguise the lob better than Evert, particularly off her backhand side.

Martina was on her way to demonstrating that she was the greatest grass-court player in the history of the game. With so many slow and irregular bounces, Navratilova's slice backhand approach was a deadly weapon, paving the way for open court volleys and crisp smashes. Her mobility all over the court was strikingly impressive, but she excelled with her lateral movement at the net. There were times when Evert seemed certain to have driven a ball past her on her right side, and yet Martina would

Melbourne and the "Big Four" showdown, Evert had stopped Navratilova in the grass court warm-up event, winning 6-1 in the third set at Sydney.

Seeded first and third, respectively, at the Australian Open, Evert and Navratilova reached the final without much difficulty. Evert did not drop a set on her way to the title match

lunge with alacrity and make astounding back-hand volley winners at full stretch from near the sideline.

Evert knew the importance of a high first-serve percentage when she faced Martina on grass. Chrissie did not want to present Navratilova with the opportunity to chip and charge off her second serve, although she had unflagging confidence in her ability to counter-attack. No one could match her in that depart-ment. It was not Evert's agility that gave her such an edge on her passing shots off both sides; it was her intuitive anticipation, her unerring court sense.

The first set was fought intensely all the way. Evert had to work harder to hold serve, but her concentration was a strong asset. She knew precisely what she wanted to do against Navratilova from the backcourt, and her exe-cution was nearly flawless. "It was tough playing Martina on grass," she recalled, "but it was predictable. She would hit big fore-hands and that was her dangerous side because she could do anything and go any-where with that shot. But her backhand was also a great shot for her on grass because she would keep it so low and deep, and then be on top of the net so quickly that I would have to hit a perfect passing shot. Her serve was ver-satile and she gave me problems pulling me off the court to my backhand."

That was essentially the pattern of play. Navratilova applied the pressure; Evert tried to shift the burden back to her rival with her uncanny precision. Navratilova attacked relent-lessly on serve and closed in swiftly to the net; Evert answered with a marvelous mixture of passing shots and lobs. The players battled furi-ously in that first set and were level at 5-5, then again at 6-6. They moved on to the tiebreak, and were locked there at 4 points all.

Evert collected three points in a row to take the tiebreaker, 7-4, and it gave her an inevitable lift. She went down a break at 3-2 in the second set, then broke back in the sixth game with pinpoint returns and held for 4-3. She sensed then the possibility of a straight-set win. If she could break in the next game, she would be serving for the match. The soon-to-be-twenty-seven-year-old Floridian was eager to finish the job in style.

Navratilova was not obliging. As Richard Yallop observed in the Melbourne newspaper, *The Age*, "Navratilova met fire with fire, pro-ducing her best service game to date, with two winners, and although she was passed twice by Evert's forehand, she held serve with a back-hand volley." Martina was at 4-4 and she was soaring. She granted Evert only two points in the next two games to close out the set and level the match, finishing with an emblematic ace on set point in the tenth game.

The twenty-five-year-old left-hander was ignited by her second-set resurgence. She moved

---

Navratilova rescued the second set with the strength of her serve.

---

firmly to 2-0 in the third set, having won five games in a row. With Chrissie serving in the third game, Martina reached break point six times. An obstinate Evert would not yield, giving nothing away, forcing Martina to sustain a very high standard of attacking play. The Floridian held for 1-2 after a long and strenuous game.

A composed Navratilova resumed her con-trol of the contest. She held on safely for 3-1, broke for 4-1, and held again for a seemingly

insurmountable 5-1 lead. "At that stage," Evert said eighteen years later, "you are frustrated. You are so mad that you just find yourself going for your shots more stubbornly. Shots were hit-

---

Evert recovered from 5-1 down with an inspired run.

---

ting the lines and I was connecting with the ball as well as I could have."

In a scintillating recovery that captivated the crowd, Evert came back into the match. She held on for 2-5, broke for 3-5, held again, and broke once more. Navratilova had twice served for the match but had never advanced to match point. Evert had displayed her determination when it counted. She was serving at 5-5, looking to complete a spirited comeback, knowing she was on a very good roll.

And yet, she was not convinced she could keep flowing. As she recalled, "Martina didn't panic when I got to 5-5. She just stuck to her game plan and kept trying to get in. She had the attitude that if she was going to lose, she would lose playing her game. By then I think I had probably exhausted my supply of passing shots."

At 5-5, 30-30, Evert served into a heavy wind. She wanted to maintain her length off the ground but did not gauge the wind correctly. She drove a flat forehand long for 30-40. She decided she had to make a move, beat her opponent to the net, and strike from close range. Chrissie came in, but Navratilova worked her way in as well. They had an exchange of volleys, but the left-hander pressed forward to put away a backhand volley.

Navratilova was serving for the match a third time at 6-5. She reached 40-15, double match point, only to squander the first with a netted low forehand volley. Navratilova attacked again, made a remarkable half volley, and forced Evert to miss one last passing shot attempt. Martina Navratilova was the Australian Open champion, defeating Chrissie Evert, 6-7, 6-4, 7-5. She had captured the third Grand Slam championship of her career, having defeated her foremost rival and friend on every one of those final round occasions. Evert had narrowly missed out on an opportunity for a thirteenth "Big Four" title.

EPILOGUE

By virtue of that triumph over Evert in a major final, Navratilova had altered the course of her career irrevocably. Although Evert finished 1981 as No. 1 in the world, for the seventh time in eight years, and Navratilova concluded her campaign at No. 3 behind Tracy Austin, the prodigious left-hander would take over the game in the first half of the 1980s the way Evert had controlled the second half of the 1970s.

In the five years that followed her breakthrough in Australia, Navratilova was beaten only fourteen times. From 1982-86, she won seventy of eighty-four tournaments, including twelve Grand Slam singles championships. In 1982, the Richards-Lieberman team gave her the regimen on and off the court to make major advances as an athlete. The following year, Richards stepped aside and was replaced by former world-class player, Mike Estep.

Estep—who remained Navratilova's coach through the 1986 season—took full advantage of the hard work done by Richards in the year-and-a-half preceding his arrival. Richards had revamped Navratilova's ground game comprehensively. She urged her pupil to come over the forehand with heavier topspin, providing a platform for Martina to gain greater margin for error with that shot while still attacking. Richards also had worked diligently on the development of a topspin backhand, a shot Martina needed primarily to pass her opponents.

Martina's revamped ground strokes made her less vulnerable from the backcourt. Her forehand remained a potent stroke, but there were days when it went off the mark. The topspin backhand was still suspect at times, but it made Martina a much better counterattacker. When Estep appeared on the scene in 1983, he tinkered with Navratilova's serve and worked on other aspects of her game, but primarily he devoted his energies to strategy.

Ralston, meanwhile, was devoting his time to encouraging Evert to be a more well-rounded player. He added kick to her second serve. He gave her the confidence to take more chances to volley. He helped her develop sting in her smash. He worked with Chrissie to develop a topspin lob off the forehand to match her two-handed backhand topspin lob. Across the board, in subtle and sensible ways, without devaluing her superb ground strokes and enormous consistency, he helped Evert to become a more complete tennis player.

Evert and Navratilova—the two great champions—divided the four Grand Slam titles between them in 1982. Navratilova won her first French Open and a third Wimbledon; Evert secured a sixth U.S. Open and avenged her loss to Navratilova in a repeat Australian Open final, finally adding that title to her résumé. In 1983 and 1984, Navratilova swept six of the eight majors, with Evert taking the other two.

Over that period, Navratilova was virtually flawless in her meetings with Evert. They were in a class of their own as the two best players in the women's game, but from the end of 1982 through the 1984 season, Navratilova defeated her chief rival thirteen consecutive times. The last of those losses was particularly painful for Evert. In the final of the U.S. Open, Evert earned a standing ovation from the capacity crowd at Flushing Meadow when she took the first set from Navratilova.

The crowd sensed a watershed moment for Evert and so did she. Chrissie seemed set to break back for 5-5 in the second set when she had Martina down 15-40. Navratilova stayed back behind a second serve, but Evert was too careful on the return and sent it long off the forehand. Her chance was gone. Navratilova prevailed, 4-6, 6-4, 6-4. Evert found a vacant room outside the stadium court, where she wept over a golden opportunity lost. "If I had won this match," she lamented to friends, "it would have been the perfect time to retire. I wish I could have done it."

Three months later, Evert captured the last Grand Slam title of the season, taking her second Australian Open title over the tall Czechoslovakian, Helena Sukova. Sukova had toppled Navratilova in a three-set semifinal, ending a record seventy-four-match winning streak by the world No. 1, and preventing Martina from capturing a Grand Slam. This time, it was Martina who was in tears as a significant goal eluded her grasp. •

JOHN McENROE VS. MATS WILANDER

DAVIS CUP, ST. LOUIS, JULY 11, 1982

In a rousing Davis Cup match, the veteran McEnroe, and the newly crowned 17-year-old French Open titlist, played the fifth and final match between their nations with a patriotic passion.

PROLOGUE

With the unexpected departure of Bjorn Borg from the major championships after the 1981 U.S. Open, when he was only twenty-five, it seemed safe to say that no one of his skill would emerge from Sweden or anywhere else for a long while. But in a peculiar twist of fate, a teenager did emerge from Sweden—almost as if by design—the following year. In 1982, Mats Wilander struck down one established, frontline player after another at the French Open, the tournament Borg had ruled so thoroughly for six of the previous eight years. Wilander, who as a boy played ice hockey along with his two brothers, was the son of a factory foreman. He became a virtual replica of Borg on the tennis court, wearing down his rivals with exasperating patience from the backcourt, coolly sizing up the opposition before systematically dismantling their games. He rarely allowed himself to be thrown off stride by players with a much wider range of experience.

In 1982, Wilander was unseeded at Roland Garros, seventeen years old, and a semifinalist at the recent Italian Open in Rome. He had never won a professional tennis tournament before, though only one year earlier he had been the French Open junior titlist. With a temperament much like Borg's, a two-handed backhand of similar quality, and a flair for match play, he became the youngest ever to take this championship and the first unseeded winner as well. In the round of sixteen, he trailed second-seeded Ivan Lendl two sets to one, but came through in five exhausting sets. Fifth seeded Vitas Gerulaitis of the United States was his next victim in a four-set quarterfinal. He then recorded a four-set triumph over Argentina's Jose Luis Clerc—the No. 4 seed—in the semifinals. In the final, Wilander completed a startling run by upending third-seeded Guillermo Vilas of Argentina in four sets. Vilas had won the tournament in 1977.

With this cluster of fine wins, Wilander established a place for himself among the world's top-ten players. He also earned the right to represent his nation against the United States in St. Louis that summer, when the two countries collided in a Davis Cup quarterfinal. He had shown unequivocally that he belonged among the elite by defeating four of the top five seeds in one stirring sequence on the slow red clay at Roland Garros. After watching that

John McEnroe

the weekend after Wimbledon. He did not have the luxury of time to heal the wounds of his loss. He had to come right back to represent the United States. He knew how much captain Arthur Ashe and his teammates were counting on him.

The strain of competing at the loftiest levels had clearly taken its toll on McEnroe. His 1981 season demonstrated indisputably that he was a player made for great moments. Not only had he toppled Borg in both the Wimbledon and U.S. Open finals from a set down each time, but he had been the chief architect of the U.S. Davis Cup triumph as well. He had scored a critical five-set victory over Argentina's Jose Luis Clerc in the Cup final at Cincinnati, and joined Peter Fleming to capture a five-set doubles match from Clerc and Guillermo Vilas. With his tactical acuity and shot selection, McEnroe was considered by many to be the greatest doubles player in the history of the game. In terms of his on court heroics, he had done everything he could possibly have asked of himself, perhaps more.

But the fact remained that he had withstood an untold amount of deep personal pain which must have diminished his successes as he weighed them later in his mind. During the Davis Cup semifinals against Australia, he was coasting along with Fleming, leading two sets to love against Phil Dent and Peter McNamara when he became embroiled in a needless dispute. Both Fleming and McEnroe railed at their captain, Arthur Ashe, in an embarrassing courtside episode when the captain refused to intervene on their behalf. Although order was restored and McEnroe and Fleming completed a routine triumph, severe damage was done in the process.

In the weeks that followed, Ashe received

string of unanticipated successes, Don Budge returned from Paris to New York and confessed that he was thoroughly impressed with what he had witnessed. He told a reporter in New York, "You know what this guy Wilander is. He is another Borg. He is just like Bjorn in so many ways."

As the United States-Sweden confrontation neared, John McEnroe was going through a rough patch in his career. Most significantly, he had lost the Wimbledon final to Connors in five sets after coming within three points of a four-set victory. That discouraging defeat was fresh in McEnroe's mind as he headed for St. Louis

numerous letters from leaders in the tennis community urging him to remove McEnroe from the team, believing that was the only remedy for his unacceptable behavior. The letters were responding to a number of incidents, including McEnroe's first-round contest at Wimbledon against Tom Gullikson. He had caused such uneasiness on that occasion that the committee at Wimbledon wanted to disqualify him retroactively for his conduct during that match. ATP Executive Director Butch Buchholz persuaded the Wimbledon officials that they would be making a serious mistake if they took that action. They concurred. McEnroe remained in the tournament and won it. Moreover, Ashe stood by him against many revered members of the tennis establishment because he was convinced McEnroe sincerely wanted to stop demeaning himself by behaving so inappropriately.

In any case, the scars of 1981 were still haunting McEnroe as he stumbled through 1982. This was painfully evident when the Wimbledon title slipped from his grasp against a revitalized Connors. Connors, on the edge of thirty, was an immensely popular player who had left behind most of his troublesome times. He was not only a superb shot-maker but also a brilliant orchestrator of an audience. His gesticulations became a familiar trademark. Arm-raising, fist-shaking, air-punching exhortations brought the crowd to its feet when he needed their support. That was a role which suited Connors's theatricality, but McEnroe was not nearly as skilled or as natural in that posture. Connors, with the fans whooping, rallied from two sets to one behind and three points from defeat to prevail in five tempestuous sets.

McEnroe was a man in utter misery, knowing he had been outplayed, recognizing that Connors was the overwhelming sentimental favorite of the fans. McEnroe's despondency was visible after that loss, and the Davis Cup schedule gave him no time to heal.

THE MATCH

When the Wimbledon finalist and French Open titlist were scheduled to meet each other on the closing afternoon of the United States-Sweden Davis Cup quarterfinal, the players, press, and performers were all in accord that McEnroe was the overwhelming favorite. With the two nations deadlocked at 2-2, the intensity surrounding this match was heightened by the circumstances. McEnroe was a renowned Davis Cup veteran who had represented the United States in the 1978 final at Palm Springs, when he took two singles against the British as the Americans completely outclassed their rivals from across the Atlantic. Now, in his fifth year of Davis Cup duty for his

McEnroe without much time seeks revival in Davis Cup play.

country, McEnroe had developed a genuine pride in his participation. That was precisely why he was willing to put himself on the line so soon after Wimbledon, a sacrifice Connors refused to make. He had joined McEnroe the week after Wimbledon in 1981 when they collaborated to oust Ivan Lendl's Czechoslovakian squad at Flushing Meadow.

This time, however, McEnroe's task was more burdensome. He had defeated Anders Jarryd on the opening day, but Wilander

Mats Wilander

brought Sweden to 1-1 with a five-set win over the Californian, Eliot Teltscher (or "Teliot Eltscher," as Connors playfully referred to him). McEnroe then took the doubles alongside Fleming to give the United States a 2-1 lead with a straight-set win over Jarryd and Hans Simonsson. When Teltscher was injured, Brian Gottfried had to step in and substitute in the fourth match of the series against Jarryd. Gottfried had once been ranked third in the world, but he was now a few years past his prime. He bowed in straight sets.

The pressure was back on McEnroe to prevent a stunning American defeat. The match would be played on a medium-fast supreme court carpet. McEnroe's chances seemed excellent against the Swedish teenager, who had made his debut in cup competition against the Russians earlier in the year. Confronting McEnroe in his rookie season representing

Sweden was a daunting prospect for Wilander, even if he did mask his emotions in a manner strikingly reminiscent of Borg. Despite playing away from home on a court much faster than he preferred, Wilander demonstrated early that he was not about to surrender passively.

While McEnroe had the advantage of sealing points with relative ease by packaging his first serve with solid first volleys, Wilander had to work considerably harder to hold his place. Spinning the first serve in deep to McEnroe's backhand, he did a fine job of pinning the American deep in the backcourt, forcing him to wait for just the right midcourt ball to attack. Even then, Wilander often had the appropriate answers, finding even the smallest spaces to pass the hard-charging New Yorker at the net with his precise shots off the backhand side.

Wilander moved ahead of McEnroe to take a 3-1 opening set lead before the American broke back. The Swede stayed stubbornly with McEnroe until 7-7, but was broken in the fifteenth game and McEnroe happily served out the set in the following game. The final point

---

Wilander, like Borg, stayed back until he had an opening.

---

featured a classic move from the left-hander. He closed in confidently behind his serve, then opened his racket face purposefully to produce a delicate drop volley off his forehand side. Leaving the burden of that long set behind him, McEnroe escalated his attack and he swept through the second on the strength of two service breaks, 6-2. When McEnroe raced to a 4-2 lead in the third set with four break points for 5-2, he seemed about to complete his mission with swift resolution.

In fact, the battle in many ways had just begun. Wilander's court behavior was virtually identical to Borg's. He was never demonstrative, but he was determined to make a full and forceful effort. As he slid precariously close to a decisive straight-set defeat, his body language was telling McEnroe in essence, "You are going to have to beat me because I won't give this match to you."

Wilander made his move at the right time. He held on for 3-4, then broke for 4-4 at the cost of only a single point. A grinding struggle developed as both men gave all they had to taking the set. It lasted for an astonishing two hours and thirty-nine minutes. A crowd of 15,103 in St. Louis cheered on the American through the marathon set, but Wilander seemed oblivious to the sentiment of the fans. The Swede saved break points at 8-8 and 10-10 with a pair of superb volleys. He plodded on and salvaged a measure of self-respect when he broke McEnroe in the thirty-second game to take the third set, 17-15, as the American double-faulted into the net at 30-40. What had once seemed a mere formality was now a tennis match of the highest order.

Quietly buoyant after finally sealing the third set, Wilander had the advantage of starting the fourth on his serve. His counterattacking was increasingly accurate and a somewhat exasperated McEnroe was missing ground strokes with distressing frequency. At this stage, his serve had lost some sting, and the pattern of play was slowing down as Wilander skillfully prolonged the points. The Swede got the break he needed in the eighth game, served for the fourth set at 5-3, and held. He had now rescued himself from a routine defeat to force a fifth and final set, and the momentum was inescapably on the Swede's side.

McEnroe, however, had other notions and still held the bedrock belief that he was going to win. And yet, his tightly strung personality was becoming a problem. After smacking a ball in the direction of a linesman who had given him a questionable call, McEnroe was assessed a point penalty. The violation allowed Wilander to advance to break point, and placed McEnroe two steps from disqualification. Nevertheless, he responded characteristically. He took three straight points with verve, two of them unreturnable serves, and held on for 1-0. He broke Wilander in the following game, but Wilander had not resurrected himself by accident. He broke back in the third game with consecutive backhand placements, held in the fourth, and it was 2-2. With both men competing unyieldingly down the stretch, they got into a holding pattern until 6-6. In that crucial thirteenth game,

Wilander reached 15-30 with two superb returns. McEnroe retaliated with two aces down the "T" for 40-30, only to steer a forehand volley out of court. Wilander was two points away from gaining a break, which would have given him a chance to serve for the match. McEnroe had been pushed to his emotional limits.

With the match in such jeopardy, McEnroe somehow composed himself and refused to succumb. He pulled off a magnificent forehand volley into the corner when Wilander appeared to have him beaten with a well-struck forehand pass. At game point for the second time, McEnroe directed a slice serve into his opponent's body. Wilander was handcuffed and netted his response. McEnroe had escaped. He had the edge, 7-6. In the following game, the American collected the first point on a net cord service return that fell into the forecourt on Wilander's side, well out of reach. The New Yorker surged to 15-30 by attacking a first serve and following his return in for an emphatic forehand volley winner. The Swede then seemed to have connected with a forehand crosscourt passing shot, but was chagrined

---

McEnroe once again had to face long, exasperating rallies.

---

when the linesman signaled wide. McEnroe was at 15-40, double match point. Wilander saved the first one with a cleverly placed serve into McEnroe's body. At 30-40, he was set up for a routine forehand crosscourt, a shot he had hardly missed all through the contest. His high trajectory topspin off that side had served as a safety net in rally after rally. This time, however, he did not give himself his customary margin for error. He drove the ball into the net.

McEnroe had won, 9-7, 6-2, 15-17, 3-6, 8-6, to give the Americans a 3-2 triumph. It had taken a record-breaking six hours and twenty-two minutes to complete this unforeseen drama. Both players had tapped into resources only defiance can produce. McEnroe had not lost his nerve when the match seemed to be slipping inexorably from his control. And Wilander had come gallantly close to a major upset on a surface and in a setting he hardly knew.

EPILOGUE

Over the rest of the 1982 season, Wilander reaffirmed his status as a worthy top-ten player. In Barcelona that fall, he repeated his French Open triumphs over Lendl, Vilas, and Clerc to take that tournament title. He finished the year at No. 7 in the world. He had set himself up for a productive future and made the most of it. Altogether, from 1982-88, he spent seven consecutive years among the top ten, the last six in the top four. He expanded his shot making steadily, developing a vastly improved one-handed slice backhand that complemented his two-hander handsomely. He improved his volleying off both sides minimally, but his tactical game was greatly enhanced when he learned to serve-and-volley on fast courts at opportune times.

In that impressive seven year run, Wilander collected seven Grand Slam singles championships, including three French Opens, three Australian Opens (on two different surfaces), and one U.S. Open. But while he celebrated many victories in that span, his best season by far was in 1988, when he won three of the four Grand Slam titles, a feat last achieved by Connors fourteen years earlier. Wilander in

1988 held back the aggressive serve-and-volley specialist, Pat Cash, 8-6 in the fifth set, to begin the year with a triumph at the Australian Open. Then he won the French Open, overcoming a rising eighteen-year-old Andre Agassi in a five-set semifinal. Then he crushed Frenchman, Henri Leconte, in a straight-set final, connecting on a remarkable 97 percent of his first serves.

Wilander was upended by the crafty Czechoslovakian Miloslav Mecir in the quarter-finals of Wimbledon, but he more than made up for that defeat at the U.S. Open where he recorded an inspiring five-set, final-round conquest over three-time titlist, Ivan Lendl. That victory provided the key to Wilander's unexpected rise to No. 1 in the world for the year, as

Mats Wilander

he lifted himself deservedly past Lendl, the man who had occupied that slot for the previous three seasons. In a four-hour-and-fifty-five-minute clash on the stadium court at Flushing Meadow, Wilander deployed a more versatile game plan than Lendl, but he needed courage as well to come through.

The inscrutable Swede led by a set and 4-1, but Lendl rebounded to one set all. Then Wilander led two sets to one, 4-3, 30-0, but Lendl broke back and worked his way into a fifth set. When Lendl held for 3-2 in the fifth and had Wilander at 0-30 in the sixth game, he seemed ready to win a fourth Open in a row and thus repeat his triumph over Wilander in the 1987 final. But Wilander gathered himself for one last surge to the finish line, and he succeeded, 6-4, 4-6, 6-3, 5-7, 6-4. He had approached the net no fewer than 131 times (winning seventy-six points) over the five sets, and had connected with 86 percent of his first serves. Wilander was at the peak of his game, and there seemed no reason why he could not contend for major titles and the No. 1 ranking for several years to come.

Oddly, after his superb 1988 season, Wilander was through as a frontline player. He slipped to No. 12 by the end of 1989, and played only sporadically thereafter. He did not appear again in the latter stages of a Grand Slam event. He lost his spark and initiative, not anticipating how little would be left of his competitive zeal after reaching the top. He did make a modest comeback in 1995, finishing that season at No. 45 in the world. He was not, however, a formidable player anymore. Asked early in the 1988 season if there was a danger that he might burn out in his mid-twenties as had happened to Borg—a prediction ESPN commentator and former player Cliff Drysdale had made—Wilander answered, "I don't think Borg quit because of his style of play. He won what he thought he should win and then he didn't enjoy playing tennis anymore, so he left. I don't see myself playing at thirty-five like Jimmy Connors. But, for sure, I'll be playing another four, five, six years at least."

Drysdale's vision of the future was sharper than Wilander's. Perhaps if the Swede had taken a few months off after the end of his 1988 campaign, he might have found a way to remain in the upper echelons much longer. Instead, he faded too fast from the center of the tennis universe, and he was missed by fans and players alike. For those who cherished the fierce rivalries between the leading players, the Wilander-McEnroe series was surely a big loss.

In their prime years together on the tour—1982-87—they confronted each other on twelve occasions with each man prevailing six times. And many of these meetings were in the prestige events. After their initial epic match at the Davis Cup in 1982, Wilander posted victories over McEnroe at the 1983 French Open—winning in four sets after taking twenty-three points in a row at one stage—and again at the Australian Open in a surprise grass-court win later that year. McEnroe routed Wilander indoors at the 1983 and 1984 Masters events indoors at New York. Wilander upended McEnroe at the 1985 French Open in the semifinals, but was defeated by his American adversary on a scorching afternoon later that summer in the semifinal round of the U.S. Open. They had one more major meeting in 1989, when McEnroe ousted Wilander on his way to the semifinals of Wimbledon.

McEnroe's career turned in different directions after his superlative struggle with Wilander in 1982. Despite not winning a major championship that season and losing decisively in the semifinals of the U.S. Open to Lendl, he remained No. 1 in the world for the second year in a row by taking six singles championships, including four consecutive titles at the end of

Wilander maintained a remarkably good record against McEnroe.

the year when he built a twenty-four-match winning streak. But he fared much better in the big championships of 1983, extending his run as the game's top ranked player to four consecutive seasons.

In 1983, he secured a second singles championship at Wimbledon, and that was the primary reason why he stayed at No. 1. In 1984, he dominated the game in a fashion few have equaled. He was victorious in thirteen of fifteen tournaments, winning eighty-two of eighty-five matches, losing only to Lendl in the French Open final, to the gifted Indian, Vijay Amritraj, in Cincinnati, and to Sweden's Henrick Sundstrom in the Davis Cup final. In examining the Open Era from 1968-99 when all of the best players competed against each other, McEnroe's 1984 ranks not far behind Laver's 1969 Grand Slam season, and alongside Connors's 1974 when he, too, was nearly invulnerable in winning ninety-nine of 103 matches. McEnroe's most masterful performance was his dissection of Connors in the Wimbledon final. Two years after he lost that agonizing five set, final round contest against Connors on Centre Court, he balanced the books by beating

Connors with shocking ease, 6-1, 6-1, 6-2, in the 1984 title match.

Not since Budge had beaten Bunny Austin in the 1938 final had there been such a one-sided final on Centre Court. It was 102 degrees Fahrenheit that afternoon at the All England Club, and McEnroe's shotmaking shimmered with the same intensity as the glaring sunlight on court. He was on target with forty-three of fifty-five first serves (78 percent). Facing the game's greatest returner, McEnroe allowed Connors a mere eleven points in eleven service games. Connors was unable to secure a single break point. The match lasted only eighty minutes. McEnroe had released the full range of his talent, tantalizing his countryman with topspin lobs off both sides, delicate drop volleys disguised brilliantly, and passing shots that Connors could not read.

Two months later, McEnroe and Connors collided again and this was an entirely different and more competitive match. In five sets, Connors broke McEnroe seven times, but McEnroe still managed to win. He went on to top Lendl in a straight-set final that was almost as impressive as his Wimbledon shutout over Connors. Nonetheless, when the year was over,

---

McEnroe and Connors would rise and fall during a splendid series of matches.

McEnroe would have traded half a dozen of his thirteen titles to have reversed the result of his French Open loss to Lendl.

He had started that match irresistibly, taking the first two sets, seemingly on his way to a swift success. But Lendl persisted single-mindedly. He won the third, recovered from 4-2 down in the fourth and 3-3, 15-40 in the fifth,

and toppled a distraught McEnroe, 3-6, 2-6, 6-4, 7-5, 7-5 in a splendid comeback. McEnroe was at a loss to explain how he had failed to prevail, but Lendl had found both the confidence and the power to take the day.

When McEnroe produced the most persuasive tennis of his career at Wimbledon and the U.S. Open later in 1984, he seemed to have many great years ahead of him and was a expected to add to his collection of four U.S. Open titles and three Wimbledons. But he was never the same player again, not by a wide margin. He would not win another major championship. When Lendl trounced him in a straight-set U.S. Open final in 1985, both men knew that McEnroe would be hard-pressed from then on. At the end of that season, McEnroe elected to take a seven-month sabbatical from the game.

The time off cleared his mind in many ways as he took care of matters in his personal life, but as a player he did not return with force or conviction. He concluded 1986 at an unimaginable No. 14 in the world, then finished 1987 at No. 10 and 1988 one place lower. In 1989, McEnroe sought a higher level again, reaching the semifinals of Wimbledon, achieving consistently impressive results all year, climbing back to No. 4 in the world. The following year, he reached his last U.S. Open singles semifinal, losing a four-set encounter to Pete Sampras. In 1992, he joined forces with Sampras as the United States regained possession of the Davis Cup. McEnroe and Sampras were victorious in the doubles against the Swiss tandem of Jackob Hlasek and Marc Rosset. Earlier that year, McEnroe made it to the semifinals of Wimbledon before losing to the eventual champion, Andre Agassi.

These modest successes were rewarding to

McEnroe in the autumn of his career, but he was nothing like the man who had reached five consecutive Wimbledon finals in the 1980s. He was not in the same league as he had been when he won his four U.S. Opens. He had probably not done complete justice to his rare talent despite winning seven major championships, but that

McEnroe could still deliver admirably, but not consistently.

assessment must take into account his luminous Davis Cup accomplishments.

In matches he played for the United States Davis Cup contingent, he won forty-one of forty-nine singles assignments and eighteen of twenty doubles matches. It was his intuitive quickness in doubles that gave him a special niche among the great players of his era. Overall, across his entire career, he won as many doubles championships as singles (seventy-seven of each). In the major championships, his credits were even greater in doubles as he won five Wimbledon titles (four with Fleming in the 1970s and 1980s, one more with Michael Stich in 1992), and four at the U.S. Open (three with Fleming, one with Australian Mark Woodforde in 1989). Adding the French Open mixed doubles title with Mary Carillo in 1977, he took ten major doubles championships compared to his seven in singles.

In the ultimate analysis, no expert would place him at the top of the list as the greatest ever to play the game of singles. But many would rate him an inspired titan among doubles players, possibly the finest ever. He will be remembered above and beyond anything else as a personality. The most provocative performer of his time, he angered some observers, delighted others, fascinated even more. And he was brutally honest in many cases about himself. After flirting with disqualification at many tournaments over the years, he was finally disqualified officially at the 1990 Australian Open during a fourth round meeting with Sweden's Mikael Pernfors.

After it was over, he freely admitted that the only reason he had been thrown out of that tournament was his ignorance about the new rules. He thought he would get one more penalty before removal, but he had not been familiar with the new standards. He also conceded some time later that being removed from a match for unacceptable behavior should have happened to him years earlier when it would have been more damaging and instructional.

As the century closed, McEnroe was named Captain of U.S. Davis Cup team, a position he had wanted for a long time. He had also taken on a new role as a color commentator for a number of networks including NBC and USA at the French Open and Wimbledon, and CBS and USA at the U.S. Open. Easily able to detach himself during the matches while he was in the television booth, McEnroe emerged as an excellent analyst, offering his pungent and informative commentary to a large audience. In that capacity, he continued to give his share of incisive performances.   •

MARTINA NAVRATILOVA VS. CHRIS EVERT

FRENCH OPEN, FINAL, JUNE 8, 1985

This was perhaps their most absorbing match in a major championship. Out of an incomparable rivalry, spanning 80 matches, none surpassed the suspense and inspiration of this struggle.

PROLOGUE

At the start of 1985, Chrissie Evert was at a crossroad. She had spent the three previous years at No. 2 in the world behind Martina Navratilova. Her thirteen match losing streak against Martina was an unprecedented sequence of disappointments in her career. Although she had been beleaguered by Tracy Austin during her five-match losing streak against the Californian, those losses had been contained in a brief five-month period. Three of the defeats took place in eleven days in the winter of 1980. No one but Navratilova had plagued her for as long and as thoroughly as Austin.

Martina had lost only three matches in her vintage 1983-84 seasons, recording twelve of her thirteen consecutive victories over Evert in those campaigns. Four of her wins were in major finals, including two at the U.S. Open, one at Wimbledon, another at Roland Garros.

The French Open final of 1984 was the most surprising of the showdowns. Navratilova was a 6-3, 6-1 victor on the red clay. She was in complete command of the court, winning long rallies with verve and spontaneity. She saved her visits to the net for propitious moments, and served with great spin and variety. It was arguably the most comprehensive display she would ever present on a tennis court, and easily the best slow court performance of her career. She had picked apart Chrissie on the Floridian's favorite surface—a surface on which Evert had amassed an awesome twenty-four-tournament, 125-match winning streak from 1973 to 1979. Navratilova went on to win the next two Grand Slam finals over Evert at Wimbledon and Flushing Meadow.

In late January 1985, the two veteran adversaries opened their campaign against each other in the final at Key Biscayne, Florida. Appearing about half an hour away from where she grew up in Fort Lauderdale, Evert snapped the losing streak decisively, defeating her nemesis, 6-2, 6-4. But that victory provided only a temporary reprieve from Navratilova's mastery. Martina avenged the loss with two more wins in the finals at Delray Beach, Florida, and again in Dallas.

Martina Navratilova

As the two best women players in the world faced the first Grand Slam championship of the season in Paris, Evert remained psychologically stranded by Navratilova. She had lost fifteen of their last sixteen meetings. She realized that the red clay of Roland Garros offered probably her best chance to regain momentum, but her pride had been severely wounded by the accumulation of losses.

"I remember how I felt going into the French," she recalled in 1999. "I thought 'Why should this time be any different?' I didn't have much confidence going into the match. Dennis Ralston talked to me a lot about believing in myself, and told me Martina was vulnerable on clay and I could beat her. But as a player you

have to believe that yourself, and I still had a lot of doubt in me. It was funny in a way because I knew I was a champion, yet I had those lingering doubts that were hard to wipe out of my mind."

THE MATCH

The top-seeded Navratilova reached their final-round appointment without the loss of a set. Navratilova took her semifinal from the tall German, Claudia Kohde-Kilsch, 6-4, 6-4. Evert knocked out Gabriela Sabatini—the top-spin artist from Argentina—in straight sets.

The time had come for Navratilova-Evert match number sixty-five, with Martina leading 33-31 in the career series. This would be their fifth final-round collision in the last six Grand Slam tournaments. Since Austin had taken the 1981 U.S. Open, Navratilova had won eight of the "Big Four" events while Evert had secured four. No one had threatened their authority during that time.

The morning of the final, the weather was disruptive. A bright sun was shining at dawn, but a few hours later it was pouring rain. The precipitation was accompanied by strong winds sporadically throughout the day.

The conditions changed frequently as the final unfolded. The sun would emerge briefly, then slip behind the clouds, then reappear. The wind whipped across the stadium court at Roland Garros with substantial force for minutes at a time, then subsided, returning again intermittently all afternoon.

The slow court and gusty wind were allies for Evert. Navratilova much preferred the calm conditions indoors with no sun or wind. She could synchronize her service toss, gauge easily how hard to hit off the ground, and punch her volleys without fearing they would float out of her control.

Evert was not daunted by the capricious conditions. She had played all through her youth on windswept afternoons at Holiday Park in Fort Lauderdale, a public facility that was named after her father in 1997. He had worked as a teaching pro there for four decades. Chrissie's classic ground strokes were groomed on days when the wind became something like a third player on the court. She was so adaptable, and her racket preparation was so reflexive, that she kept hitting freely and precisely both with and against the wind. She selected her strokes with tactical effectiveness, making good use of her sidespin forehand, raising the trajectory of her two-handed backhand for more safety, figuring out a way to keep the pressure on her opponent without going for too big a shot herself.

The Floridian was ready from first point onward to accept the challenge of both Navratilova and the wind. Down 15-40 in the opening game of the match, she collected herself quickly. A forehand drop volley winner saved the first break point, and then Evert used a sizzling two-hander crosscourt off a short ball for the second. When Navratilova's forehand approach carried over the baseline, Evert was at game point. She lofted a backhand crosscourt lob high into the wind. An apprehensive Martina hit an overhead wide, and Evert had held for 1-0.

Navratilova reached 40-30 in the second game. She took her case to the forecourt but a running forehand passing shot crosscourt from Evert forced Martina into a backhand volley error. Then Evert connected with a backhand

return winner into the corner for break point. The next point would produce a pattern repeated frequently for the rest of the match. Navratilova chipped her favorite backhand approach shot down the line to Evert's backhand side. On the run, Chrissie laced another two-hander crosscourt on the sideline. She led 2-0, then held for 3-0.

Martina found her range at that juncture. She worked her way back to 3-3, breaking Evert in the fifth game. Unshaken by Navratilova's recovery, Evert regained the upper hand, took three games in a row, and closed out the set,

Chris Evert

6-3, with gusto. She had broken serve twice, lost her serve only once, and competed with an equanimity she had not been able to muster for years against Martina.

The No. 2 seed sustained her edge into the middle of the second set. She moved ahead, 4-2, 15-40. With success on one of the next two points, she would have served for the match with an extra break in hand. But Navratilova held in that critical seventh game and got back on serve. Evert broke again in the eleventh game and served for the match at 6-5.

Navratilova kept coming forward. She broke Evert to force a tiebreaker. The favorite was highly focused. She sparred well with Evert from the backcourt, served skillfully on the big points, and seized the tiebreak, 7-4.

Having been on the verge of a straight-set triumph, Evert found herself locked at one set all, needing to start all over again. She was not discouraged by that prospect. "I never gave up mentally in that match," she said. "In many of those losses in my losing streak against Martina, I did not give up, but I thought I lost some of my fighting spirit. This was a seesaw match, but I just played each point as it came

Chris Evert shakes off the ghosts of past defeats.

and stayed in the moment. I didn't look ahead and I didn't look back."

At the start of the third, Evert shifted to a higher level. She answered a backhand drop shot from Martina with a forehand drop shot winner of her own to hold for 1-0. In the next game, she produced two splendid backhand passing shots on her way to break point, then took the game with a daring forehand drop vol-

ley along the sideline. The fleet-footed Navratilova dashed forward swiftly and had a chance to make the forehand passing shot, but she directed her shot over the higher part of the net and hit the tape. The ball fell back on Martina's side. Evert went ahead, 2-0, in the final set.

Chrissie moved to 40-15 at 2-0, seemingly ready to establish a 3-0 lead. Navratilova was steady despite the danger. On Evert's second game point, she outlasted the baseline expert in a long rally. Chris netted a backhand to lose the point. Evert had one more game point. Martina drew her in with a backhand drop, then drilled a backhand crosscourt to provoke an errant volley. When Chrissie punched a high backhand crosscourt volley wide at break point down, Martina closed the gap to 2-1.

This was not a day for holding serve, not for either player. In the fourth game, Evert found the range with another beautifully struck backhand passing shot to reach 15-40. She broke for 3-1 when Navratilova overplayed a backhand approach, chipping it long. This time, Evert was absolutely determined to consolidate her break and widen her lead. In a five-deuce game, she persisted, and had two game points. But Navratilova broke back for 2-3 with a first-rate backhand pass of her own. Evert had come in on a solid, down-the-line backhand approach, but Martina unleashed a passing shot with topspin. The shot grazed the top of the net, but landed out of Evert's reach for a well-deserved winner.

In the sixth game, Navratilova delivered her best service game of the match. She found her mark with four consecutive first serves and held at love for 3-3. The opening point of that game was a tribute to Martina's talent and ingenuity. She played a backhand drop shot cross-court to Chrissie's forehand. Sensing that Evert would not be able to do much with that shot, Martina moved into "no man's land" and sent off a perfect backhand volley down the line into a vacant court.

In the seventh game, Evert served at 30-40 after Navratilova had read her passing shot on the previous point, closing in again for a fore-hand volley winner. Chrissie served deep to Martina's forehand, got the short ball she want-ed on the forehand, and came in with sidespin to the left-hander's forehand. Navratilova—perhaps thrown off guard by Evert's approach to the net—missed the passing shot. Evert came in again on Navratilova's forehand and elicited another error, then held for 4-3.

Serving in the eighth game, Navratilova proceeded to 30-0 with her trademark serve-and-volley combination, sending her backhand volley crosscourt crisply for a winner. Evert stuck with her task, responding with another stinging backhand passing shot, then reaching 30-30 when Martina hit a looping crosscourt forehand long with the wind at her back. The defending champion came in behind a kick serve to Chrissie's forehand but the hard hit return was too good. Break point. Martina approached the net behind a well-executed backhand crosscourt. Evert was on the dead run. She whipped over the ball with topspin, and Navratilova had no chance to cover it. Evert had moved to 5-3 with an incredible shot.

Serving for the match a second time, Evert did not miss a first serve in five points. Nevertheless, Navratilova was too good in this game. The left-hander concluded the sixteen-stroke first point with a backhand drop volley winner. An instant before Evert made contact with a crosscourt backhand on the second point, the wind gathered sudden force. Her shot flew inches long over the baseline, making it 0-30.

Navratilova knew she needed to apply the pressure. She came forward confidently, made a

Navratilova's attacking style brings her to the very edge of victory.

penetrating backhand volley crosscourt, and Chrissie netted her forehand pass on the run for 0-40. Evert got to 15-40 with a bold backhand drop volley winner at full stretch, but was bro-ken when Navratilova got some extra bite on her backhand approach. Evert's lob was short. Navratilova devoured it with an overhead from close range.

Martina was back to 4-5 and serving. She passed Evert off the backhand for 15-0, came up with a quick forehand volley winner for 30-0, and passed Chrissie again with another slice backhand for 40-0. Navratilova then found her mark with a first serve and held at love for 5-5.

As Evert served in the eleventh game, Navratilova continued to attack. Chrissie missed the first serve and then double-faulted as a menacing Martina moved in closer to pro-voke the mistake. Martina rolled a forehand passing shot with accelerated pace crosscourt. Chrissie barely got a racket on it. It was 0-30. Somewhat shaken, Evert made a rare backhand unforced error for 0-40. After all of her leads, she found herself in a desperate position, triple break point down at 5-5 in the final set.

"At that point," Evert said, "I did not have complete faith that I could win the match but I had so much desire. I still wanted it and the juices were flowing. But I also remember that I didn't have my normal tunnel vision where I would block everything out as I was used to doing. I opened up my senses and was aware of the crowd's response to our tennis. I didn't lose my focus but I allowed myself to enjoy the suspense of the match and the excitement it was bringing to the fans. They were completely involved in that match."

Serving at 5-5, 0-40, Chrissie benefited from a brief lapse from Martina, who drove a forehand topspin crosscourt wide, allowing her rival to reach 15-40. Down to a second

Chris Evert

serve as she had been on the previous point, Evert took full advantage of a relatively short return from Navratilova. She stepped in as if it were 2-2 in the opening set and directed a two-hander crosscourt. Clean winner. 30-40. The next point was the single most critical exchange of the match.

Navratilova waited for her opening, releasing a well executed backhand drop shot. Evert scampered forward and had to scrape the ball back. Unintentionally, she hit the ball with sidespin. The spin surprised Martina, who lifted her forehand higher than she would have liked. Both women were at the net. Evert needed to make a forceful high backhand volley. She struck it hard and kept it low. Navratilova could not respond. Deuce.

When Martina netted another attempted backhand drop shot, Evert had climbed back to game point. Martina was not yielding. With Evert in the forecourt again, Navratilova chipped a lob over her backhand. Evert chased it down but could not make the play. Deuce for the second time. Navratilova unwisely tried another backhand drop shot. Evert anticipated it early, moved forward rapidly, and drove her two-hander with extra pace for a winner. At game point for the second time, Evert came through as Navratilova netted a forehand approach.

It had seemed certain that Navratilova was going to serve for the match in the twelfth game. Instead, she served to save it at 5-6, knowing that a triple break point opportunity had eluded her. Even so, the left-hander was not unduly rattled. She had come from behind throughout the match. She would try to do that again one more time.

Martina got to the net on the first point,

coming in behind a crosscourt forehand with good depth. Evert responded with a magnificent backhand topspin lob winner, making it 0-15. Martina rallied to 15-15. She closed in on the net again; Chrissie made her stretch for a low forehand volley. Martina handled it reasonably

---

Borrowing from each other's strategies, Martina and Chris played spectacularly.

---

well, but Evert struck a flat forehand pass down the line through a narrow slot. The crowd raised the level of their applause excitedly. It was 15-30. Evert was two points from triumph.

Navratilova got her first serve in, covered the return with customary swiftness, and knifed a backhand volley crosscourt into the clear—30-30. Martina charged in again and sensed Chrissie would go crosscourt off the backhand. She moved forward to cut it off, and her forehand volley was a winner down the line—40-30. Martina served-and-volleyed but Chrissie took the net away from her, coming in behind a forehand crosscourt deep to Martina's backhand. Martina sliced her lob crosscourt. Chrissie could not cover it, but thought it might go long. Both players waited in suspense for the call. Out. Deuce.

Evert looked up at the sky and rolled her eyes, appreciating her good fortune on a big point. Again Martina came in behind her first serve to the forehand. Chrissie's return was low. Martina poked her backhand volley long. It was match point for Evert.

Martina went for an ace down the middle in the advantage court, but her serve landed well wide. The favorite stayed back behind her second serve. On a high ball off the forehand, Chrissie went crosscourt but her shot lacked

depth. Martina moved into her backhand approach with authority and chipped down the line. Chrissie had a lot of court to cover. She got her racket back early. Martina seemed to have the entire net covered. Somehow, from well outside the sideline, Evert found the space to drive her backhand down the line. Navratilova turned, knowing it was over. The passing shot was perfect. In two hours and fifty-two minutes, Evert had triumphed, 6-3, 6-7 (4), 7-5.

"Nobody gave me a chance going into that match," said Evert. "I don't think people thought it was going to be an epic Navratilova-Evert match. When I won, that was the happiest I ever felt after winning a Grand Slam title. I was thirty at the time and everybody had counted me out. Beating her near the end of my career, when everybody including myself was beginning to doubt if I would ever do that again, was very rewarding. I beat the odds and broke through my negativity. Winning that match with Martina spurred me on. That title alone prolonged my career for another four years. I honestly have never felt better after winning a tennis match."

EPILOGUE

Thereafter, the rivalry took on added dimensions. After Roland Garros in 1985, Navratilova took ten of their last fifteen head-to-head encounters. That is a misleading statistic because Evert recorded two more major triumphs over her foremost opponent. In 1986, back on the same court at Roland Garros, Evert registered a 2-6, 6-3, 6-3 victory over Navratilova to collect a record seventh French Open crown.

That match was of a higher technical quality

Martina Navratilova

and men that might well stand forever. Her win over Martina at Melbourne in 1988 enabled Chrissie to make her thirty-fourth and last appearance in a major final.

She would lose to Steffi Graf in the German's Grand Slam season. But she would still conclude her career with eighteen Grand Slam titles, setting a standard for consistency that no one has equaled in the modern era of the game. In fifty-six Grand Slam events, she was at least a semifinalist in fifty-two. Furthermore, in nineteen consecutive U.S. Opens beginning in 1971, she never failed to reach the quarterfinals.

She appropriately appeared in her last tournament at the U.S. Open in 1989. In many ways, that was where it all began for her—at Forest Hills when she was sixteen in 1971. On a remarkable Sunday afternoon in the middle of the event, she played one of the great matches of her career, dissecting the fifteen-year-old Monica Seles, 6-0, 6-2. If she had beaten Zina Garrison in her quarter-final match, Evert would have squared off one last time against Navratilova. She lost to Garrison in straight sets.

on a calmer afternoon in Paris. Evert trailed 0-2 in the third before taking six of the last seven games to win the match. For dramatic content, however, it was not as compelling as the 1985 final. In 1988, Chrissie upstaged Martina, 6-2, 7-5, in the semifinals of the Australian Open on the hard courts. In those latter stages of her career, she had no trepidation about facing Martina. The Roland Garros battle of 1985 had revived her belief in herself.

The 1986 final at Paris marked the thirteenth consecutive year that Evert had won at least one Grand Slam title, a record for women

"I came along at a good time," said Evert in 1999 as she reflected on her eighteen-year run among the top four in the world. "It was good timing and hard work. I came along at a time when very few players really had ground strokes. You needed to be able to handle pressure and you had to be a great tennis player, but you didn't have to be a great athlete. When people compare players from different eras, I always say you are as good as your competition. It comes down to how hard they push you, and that is how good you become. When I beat Monica Seles at that last U.S. Open, I was a better player than when I won Wimbledon the first two times. What I feel great about is that for eighteen years I stayed with the competition. I improved as they improved."

So, too, did Navratilova. She would conclude her career with the same number of Grand Slam singles titles as Evert. Her tally of eighteen was differently distributed. In 1990, at thirty-three, she won a record ninth Wimbledon singles title, defeating Garrison in the championship match. Chrissie was a three-time Wimbledon champion, losing seven of nine times she played Martina on Centre Court, falling five times to the left-hander in the finals. In the end, it was the edge Navratilova had at the All England Club that made the difference in her overall series with Evert.

Navratilova retired from singles at the end of the 1994 season when she was thirty-eight. Little more than three months shy of that birthday, she very nearly took a tenth singles championship at Wimbledon, losing in three sets to the Spaniard, Conchita Martinez. Just as Evert had built a strong case for herself as the greatest clay court player of all time, Navratilova had the all-time supremacy on grass.

Historians will differ in their assessment of the two enduring champions. Navratilova may well have been the most complete woman player in history and the best at the peak of her powers. Evert played the game at a high level longer than anyone who ever competed in the field of women's tennis. Together, their rivalry surpassed any other series of matches between champions in the twentieth century, and by a wide margin. At its conclusion, Navratilova had the edge—43 to 37— including victories in 14 of 22 Grand Slam confrontations.

As Evert concluded, "In our era, I felt Martina was the best athlete and the strongest and fastest we had. Physically, she was better than anyone else. In that era, I was the best athlete mentally and maybe the best under pressure, possibly the best match player. When we played each other, it came down to whose

---

The two champions developed a synergy that may never be equaled.

---

strengths were better on that day. She forced me to develop the physical side of my game and made me a better shot maker and athlete. Because of her I was a more versatile, well-rounded player and I improved my mobility. And in my way, I guess I forced her to get stronger mentally.

"On the negative side, the frustrating part for me was that Martina could be very arrogant on the court and that got to me at times. I am sure I got to her at times with my coolness and concentration when she could not read what I was thinking. But on the positive side, it was great that we had one another. If she had not been around, I am sure I would have won more titles, and if I had not been there I'm sure she would have won a lot more tournaments. But I think we would have gotten bored and we would not have had the drive to go to the next level. That is what kept us going." •

IVAN LENDL VS. STEFAN EDBERG

AUSTRALIAN OPEN, SEMIFINAL, DECEMBER 8, 1985

Lendl was firmly established as the best player in the world at 25. Edberg was on the rise at 19. In a superb grass court duel, one used dazzling groundstroke power, the other startling volleys.

PROLOGUE

Over the last third of the century, only an elite cast of competitors reached the level long occupied by Ivan Lendl and Stefan Edberg. Between them, they secured fourteen Grand Slam singles championships. Lendl celebrated four years as the No. 1 ranked player in the world, and Edberg took that position for two consecutive years. Both men were earnest craftsmen who conducted most of their business with dignity and restraint. They worked hard and played fair. They earned their triumphs with a sense of honor. They respected the highest standards of court behavior.

Lendl established himself first. He came out of Czechoslovakia, tall and confident, ready to shape a new modern style of play that would affect the future of men's tennis. His parents were tennis players—his mother was ranked second in his country; his father was ranked No. 15 and became president of the Czech Tennis Federation. Lendl was primarily a back-court player who built his game around a potent semi-western forehand, and a heavy first serve. He introduced a brand of power tennis that had not been demonstrated before.

As he ascended, top notch players like Connors and McEnroe were hard-pressed to contain him. Lendl hit through them, drove the ball by them, and overwhelmed them at times with the immense pace and precision of his shots. He reached his first major final at the French Open of 1981, losing in five sets to Bjorn Borg on the Swede's best surface. In 1982 and 1983, Lendl reached the finals of the U.S. Open. He lost both to an enduring Jimmy Connors. At the end of 1983, he fell in a fourth Grand Slam final to Mats Wilander at the Australian Open.

He was gaining a reputation during that stretch as a player who collapsed under pressure. In 1982, he had won 106 of 115 matches and fifteen of twenty-three tournaments, but could not record a Grand Slam title. He took seven more tournament titles in 1983, still falling short at the tournaments that counted the most. The following year, in 1984, he altered his reputation for folding in big matches when he recouped from two-sets-to-love down and 4-2 in the fourth to oust John McEnroe, 3-6, 2-6, 6-4, 7-5, 7-5, for the French Open title.

Ivan Lendl

before his eighteenth birthday. When he completed that sweep of the eighteen-and-under majors, Edberg's semifinal victim at the U.S. Open was McEnroe's younger brother Patrick.

Edberg's first full year on the men's circuit in 1984 developed favorably for the Swede, who was ranked No. 20 in the world. He would make substantial progress in 1985. But he clearly saved his best tennis of the season for the last of the big events, playing brilliantly in Melbourne on the surface that suited him more than any other.

Edberg's game was designed for fast court play. With his slender frame (6' 2", 165 pounds), he was strikingly fleet of foot. A strict serve-and-volleyer, he was faster than anyone in his time at getting to the net for the first volley, although he was always precariously close to foot-faulting. Once, in a five-set loss at the U.S. Open against the American, Aaron Krickstein, he foot-faulted no fewer than twenty-five times. He would close in so tightly behind his kick first serves that it took an almost impeccably low or well-placed return to stop him.

Although his forehand volley was first rate—crisp, decisive, and sound—it paled in comparison to his backhand volley, the best the men's game had seen since Tony Roche. In many ways, Edberg's volley off that side was

Fifteen months later, Lendl trounced McEnroe again in the U.S. Open final to take his second major title. With that win, and a good autumn to follow, he supplanted the New Yorker as the best tennis player in the world. As he headed into Melbourne for the Australian Open, he was near the top of his game, hoping to add another Grand Slam title to his collection, knowing he had little left to prove.

Edberg was just beginning his move toward the upper strata of the game. His father was a detective in the Swedish police force, but it was his mother who taught him to play tennis. He captured a junior Grand Slam in 1983,

even more graceful than Roche's. While Roche was probably every bit as good on medium to high backhand volleys, Edberg could pick them off from the level of his shoestrings. Agile and very athletic, he could retreat convincingly for a smash as well.

Off the ground, Edberg had a weakness on the forehand side. His grip forced him to steer the ball off that side. He could be pressured into mistakes by the best of his opponents. Be that as it may, Edberg protected himself ably. As Lendl once remarked, "Everybody said Stefan's forehand was so shaky, but it was fine when he was moving well. You would serve wide to his forehand and he would just push it back down the line. If you then volleyed back to his forehand he would be standing there ready because if

---

Lendl found it difficult to test Edberg's forehand.

---

you went to his backhand he was deadly. It was hard to get to Edberg's forehand."

His backhand ground stroke was a graceful, free-flowing, penetrating weapon. Edberg would turn his shoulders unfailingly, accelerate the racket head with extraordinary timing, then pass his opponents at will or force them into mistakes from the baseline. In his early days as a junior, he had a two-handed backhand in the Swedish tradition of Borg and Wilander, but his switch to a one-hander gave him more flexibility and was better suited to his attacking pattern of play.

Edberg's game contrasted interestingly with Lendl's. Lendl was more scientific in his approach to playing matches, and was far more comfortable in the backcourt. He had persistent problems with his low forehand vol-

ley. Lendl was a supreme counterattacker; Edberg was a superb aggressor. Lendl won with his awesome power; Edberg flourished with finesse and quickness.

The meeting in Melbourne would be their first of many collisions in major championships. It was arguably their best match ever in terms of dramatic content.

THE MATCH

At Kooyong in Melbourne, the fifth-seeded Edberg was pushed to the limits on his way to Lendl. In the third round, the American, Matt Anger, had him down a set and 6-1 in the second-set tiebreak before bowing in four sets. In his next match against the Australian, Wally Masur, Edberg was required to save two match points as he rallied from two-sets-to-love down for the triumph. Although he won his quarterfinal easily, Edberg had put himself through some excruciatingly strenuous psychological tests.

The top seeded Lendl had been in an aggravated frame of mind all through the tournament. Grass-court tennis forced a departure from his normal pattern of play. He felt he had to serve-and-volley on every point—a tactic he pursued rarely on other surfaces—and he was not happy with the low bounces that diminished his return of serve in many instances.

Lendl dropped sets in every round before a straight-set conquest of the Englishman, John Lloyd. That put him into the penultimate round against a tried-and-tested Edberg. At this stage of their careers, Lendl was vastly more experienced in the tensions of the Grand Slam game. But that advantage for the favorite was balanced by Edberg's grass court skill.

The two competitors waged a stern service battle across the first set. Edberg's kick serve bounded high to Lendl's backhand, forcing the top seed into a quandary. He preferred to sweep over the ball with heavy topspin to dip his returns at the incoming server's feet. But the Swede's serve forced Lendl to miss too many returns. Lendl frequently returned much too high over the net, giving Edberg an open invitation to clip easy approach volleys into wide open spaces.

Lendl struggled to win his serve during the opening set. He saved six break points in three service games during that stretch before controlling the tiebreak, 7-3. Lendl's match-playing prowess was showcased as he took the lead.

Edberg responded admirably in the second set. He replicated Lendl's first-set feat, saving six break points at different junctures to keep himself firmly in contention. Lendl's prime opportunity occurred in the sixth game. Edberg served at 2-3, 0-40. With a break there, Lendl could have served for a 5-2 advantage, and conceivably could have distanced himself conclusively from the Swede.

In his account of that critical game, Richard Yallop of the *Melbourne Age* commented, "As in so many moments of the match, Edberg could thank his serve for getting him out of the crisis. Arching his back like a long bow, he kept firing it at impossible heights and angles."

Edberg held on for 3-3 and stayed persistently with the No. 1 seed. Serving at 5-5 in that crucial second set, Lendl had not been broken, and he clearly held the

upper hand. He was fully committed to taking a two-sets-to-love lead. But he faltered at this fateful moment, delivering consecutive double faults from deuce to drop his serve. Edberg was reprieved. Rather than serving to save the

RUSS ADAMS

Stefan Edberg

set, he served for it. The Swede converted, holding for one set all, demoralizing Lendl in the process.

Briefly, Lendl lost his initiative. Bothered by a sore knee and a wounded psyche, he won only a single game in the third, calling for the trainer near the end of that segment. Edberg broke him twice. The two protagonists were locked at 4-4 in the fourth when rain forced a seventy-five-minute postponement. When they returned, Lendl was rejuvenated, raising his game markedly.

Lendl began connecting with one probing return after another. He broke Edberg for 5-4 in the fourth, served out the set, then got an immediate break for 1-0 in the fifth. He was back on form, breaking Edberg down methodically, building momentum to carry him through the rest of the match. Once more, however, Lendl's serve let him down.

Serving for 2-0 in the fifth, he double-faulted at break point down. Edberg was back in business. He returned to his customary serve-and-volley strength, moving in swiftly for the telling shot, making it nearly impossible for Lendl to pass him. Having squandered his service break, Lendl was always serving from behind. He held on at 3-4, but at 4-5 he found himself down match point three times. On the last of those match points, Edberg was set up for a backhand passing shot. He had the court wide open but overplayed the shot. Lendl survived for 5-5.

The Australian Open rules allow no fifth-set tiebreakers, a judgment shared by Wimbledon and the French Open. Only the U.S. Open elected to play tiebreaks in every set. And so the players proceeded to 6-6, then to 7-7. In the fifteenth game, Edberg stood at 30-30 on his serve. Lendl had a sizable opening to pass the Swede on the next two points but missed them both. Edberg moved to 8-7.

Serving to save the match for the fourth time, Lendl took the first two points for 30-0. He double-faulted substantially long, making it 30-15, and was unable to put an overhead out of Edberg's reach on the next point. He was caught out of position by Edberg's get, making it 30-30. Lendl served his way to 40-30, needing one more point for 8-8.

Edberg answered that challenge with a vintage backhand down the line pass. On the next point, Lendl seemed to have the net covered thoroughly but Edberg drove a brilliant topspin backhand past him on the dead run to reach match point for the fourth time. Casting aside his earlier apprehension, Edberg came through with a forehand passing shot to close the four-hour account on a high note. The Swede had toppled the No. 1 player in the world, 6-7 (3), 7-5, 6-1, 4-6, 9-7.

Edberg was asked in his press conference how he had missed that backhand at match point in the tenth game of the fifth set. He answered, "I stopped looking at the ball. I

The young Swede made mistakes, but avoided the ultimate loss.

---

looked at Lendl instead. I kept thinking about that, although I know you're not supposed to. If I hadn't won this match, I don't know what I would have done. I don't think I've ever played so well in such an important match as I did in the fifth set."

EPILOGUE

Edberg did not rest on the laurels of his major triumph over Lendl. He took apart countryman, and two-time defending champion, Mats Wilander in a straight-set final to garner his first Grand Slam singles title. The Swede—still considerably shy of his peak—was on the rise, finishing 1985 at No. 5 in the world.

As for Lendl, he was undaunted by his failure against Edberg. He stayed at No. 1 in the world in 1986 and 1987, winning the French and U.S. Opens both years. He was replaced at the top in 1988 by Mats Wilander, who ousted him in an engrossing five-set U.S. Open final. But bolstered by the strategic acumen of former world No. 2 Tony Roche, his talented coach, Lendl remained positive.

Lendl returned to No. 1 for the fourth and last time in 1989 when he triumphed at the Australian Open for the first time, coming through on the Rebound Ace hard courts in the second year of the tournament's transformation to a new site and surface. He was fortunate to regain the No. 1 ranking because Becker won both Wimbledon and the U.S. Open, defeating Lendl in both tournaments.

Winning his eighth and last Grand Slam championship in 1990 at the Australian Open, Lendl defeated Edberg in the final. Lendl remained in the upper echelons of the game through the 1992 season, his thirteenth consecutive year among the world's top ten. Bothered increasingly by an aching back, he retired after the U.S. Open of 1994 when he was thirty-four. It was appropriate that his last match was contested at Flushing Meadow, where he had appeared in a record eight consecutive finals from 1982-89.

RUSS ADAMS

Ivan Lendl

Edberg was hitting his stride as Lendl declined. The Swede won a second Australian Open in 1987, beat Becker in the finals of Wimbledon in 1988 and 1990, and took back-to-back U.S. Opens in 1991 and 1992. In the first of these, he played the best tennis of his illustrious career, cutting down the American, Jim Courier, 6-2, 6-4, 6-0, in a mind-boggling demonstration of skills. Always taciturn and understated, Edberg was bolstered throughout the middle and latter stages of his career by the motivational skills of his outspoken coach, Tony Pickard, a former British Davis Cup player.

Stefan Edberg

In 1992, Edberg indefatigably provided a series of remarkable performances as he defended his U.S. Open crown and captured his sixth and last Grand Slam singles title. Before he stopped Pete Sampras in a four set final, Edberg rallied from a service break down in the fifth set of three consecutive matches. The first of those victories was against the Dutchman Richard Krajicek, who won Wimbledon four years later. The last was a five-hour, twenty-six-minute win over the steadfast American, Michael Chang. In between, he overcame Lendl after his old adversary unsuccessfully served for a 5-3 final-set lead.

Edberg retired in 1996 at the age of thirty, four years after he had last won a major championship. For a decade—from 1985 through 1994—he finished every season among the top seven players in the world. That record of enduring consistency was not quite as impressive as Lendl's, nor were his Grand Slam results. Edberg was a two-time champion at Wimbledon, the U.S. Open, and the Australian Open. Lendl won two more major titles than Edberg.

Early in 1999, Lendl reflected on his battle with Edberg at Melbourne in 1985. "Stefan was always very difficult for me to play on grass," he recalled. "He was such a good mover and such a good server. At Kooyong the way he moved in behind his kick serve and volleyed was tough to handle. He wasn't at his very best yet, but he was already very good. I had questions then like everybody else about Stefan's mental toughness, but he was able to overcome it and that is why he became No. 1 in the world. He was a great fighter. For a player who was questioned for his guts, he became a very gutsy player."

Lendl could have said essentially the same thing about himself. He was stricken by nerves during the early stages of his career but developed into a first-rate competitor. In the end, he stretched his talent as long and as far as it would go, into something of lasting value. The only regret his followers had was that Lendl never realized his dream of winning Wimbledon, where he twice reached the final.

But he was not sorrowful about missing that milestone. "I don't have any regrets. When I look back at Wimbledon, and the way the tournament did not suit my game, I did really well there. But overall I have no feelings about not reaching my potential. To the contrary, I am proud of what I did. I don't sit around and think about it. That was one chapter in my life and now I am going on with the rest of it." •

STEFFI GRAF VS. MONICA SELES

FRENCH OPEN, FINAL, JUNE 6, 1992

Two big hitters battled methodically on the clay of Roland Garros with the outcome uncertain until the closing points.

PROLOGUE

Groomed for greatness on the tennis court, propelled by an obsessive but savvy father, Steffi Graf was a central player in the women's game over the latter stages of the twentieth century. She came out of Germany as a slender teenager, determined to stake her claim swiftly as a champion, admiring but not in awe of those who stood in her path.

Graf was well ahead of the game during her formative years. She turned professional at thirteen in 1982. She had first picked up a racket at the age of four. It had been sawed off for her by her father Peter who created a mini-court inside the house by fastening a cord between two chairs. A year later, she played in the seven-and-under "Bambino" Tournament in Munich. After that, Steffi's mother Heidi drove her to tournaments until her father decided to become a teaching professional at the tennis center in their hometown, Bruhl.

She was only fifteen in 1984 when she took the Olympic demonstration singles title and reached the round of sixteen at Wimbledon the same year. Displaying arguably the most explosive and the best forehand in the history of women's tennis, she moved quickly toward her goals.

In 1985, still only sixteen, she became No. 6 in the world and was a U.S. Open semifinalist. The following season, while rising to No. 3, she played world champion Martina Navratilova in the semifinal round of the U.S. Open and had three match points before conceding defeat in an absorbing struggle. From that moment on, Graf was not to be contained.

She won her first Grand Slam singles title at the French Open in 1987, lost only twice all year, and became the No. 1 player in the world. In 1988, only nineteen, still far short of her peak, she became the third woman to win the Grand Slam as she garnered the Australian Open, French Open, Wimbledon, and the U.S. Open titles. She validated her arrival among the elite by beating Chris Evert in the Australian Open final and Navratilova in the Wimbledon final.

Graf played with triumphant verve, guided every step of the way by her sometimes overbearing but always attentive father. She captured three of the four majors in 1989, winning eighty-three of eighty-five matches. In her three years at the top, she had suffered a mere seven defeats in forty-three tournaments. With Evert retiring and Navratilova beyond her prime, Graf seemed capable of dominating the game for many years and perhaps securing another Grand Slam.

But the quality of women's tennis was enhanced in 1990 by Monica Seles, who challenged Graf for the top ranking. Seles had been born in Yugoslavia, moving with her family to Florida to train at the Nick Bollettieri Tennis Academy when she was thirteen, in 1986. Bollettieri, a master motivator, had been the coach for many of the world's leading players. While Seles was at his academy, Andre Agassi and Jim Courier were among the pupils. In future years, Bollettieri would work with Boris Becker. By all accounts, Bollettieri devoted more of his time in the late 1980s and early 1990s to Seles than anyone else.

As Bollettieri wrote of the young Seles in his illuminating book, *My Aces, My Faults* (with Dick Schaap), "She worked hard from the moment she stepped on the court. She was tireless, persistent, dogged. From the first ball to the last, she was always focused. She would hit the same shot over and over until she had it down. Not for an hour. Not for a day. For weeks. She would hit nothing but two-handed backhands for two or three weeks, then nothing but two-handed forehands for two or three weeks, followed by nothing but overheads for two or three weeks. She practiced for three or four hours at a stretch. She wouldn't leave the court until she had hit the perfect shot."

After Seles and Bollettieri had a parting of the ways in 1991, Seles insisted he had never been her coach, a baffling stance to all who had watched Bollettieri in consultation with her over the years. But Monica Seles said her father Karolj was her first and only coach.

Steffi Graf

Karolj had a career as a cartoonist, but saw Monica's tennis as a serious matter. She burst into the top ten during her debut professional year in 1989, finishing that season at No. 6, pushing Graf surprisingly hard while losing a three-set semifinal at the French Open.

Seles was a seminal player, a teenager who shaped and elevated the sport with her revolutionary style. A left-hander, she produced devastatingly potent, two-handed strokes off both sides, going boldly for the lines with every invitation, taking the ball unfailingly on the rise, driving opponents into submission with her unrelenting backcourt attack. She revealed her inimitable talent at the 1990 French Open when she made a stirring recovery to oust Graf. Trailing 6-2 in a first-set tiebreaker, Seles struck back with immense power and courage. She took six points in a row and overcame the German, 7-6, 6-4, to collect her first major crown and become the youngest ever to take that title.

Graf plainly had a new rival. At the end of that year—after Navratilova had won

---

Seles explosively hit with two hands off both sides.

Wimbledon and Gabriela Sabatini took the U.S. Open—Seles stopped Sabatini to win the season-ending Virginia Slims Championship at New York's Madison Square Garden. While Graf retained her official WTA Tour No. 1 ranking on the computer, Seles overtook the German in the minds of many experts. She did not turn seventeen until the season was over.

The following year, in 1991, the "changing of the guard" was ever more apparent. Graf won Wimbledon for the third time with a spirited comeback against Sabatini, after the Argentine served for the match twice in the final set. Seles mysteriously pulled out of Wimbledon a few days before the big event, citing an injury, but refusing to discuss her withdrawal with the media. Everywhere else of importance, Seles was the victor. She took the Australian Open for the first time over Jana Novotna, after Novotna eclipsed Graf in the quarterfinals. In Paris, Seles defended her crown with a well-deserved, final-round triumph over 1989 titlist Sanchez Vicario. And, at the U.S. Open, Seles succeeded for the first time, defeating Navratilova in the final. Navratilova had upset Graf in the semifinals.

As Graf approached the age of twenty-three in 1992, Seles seemed to be soaring above and beyond her, and everyone else. The left-hander was victorious at the Australian Open with Graf injured and absent. As the players focused their attention on the French Open, Seles was an eighteen-year-old competitor who did not often doubt herself. She was controlling the course of the women's game with the same force and persuasion Graf had shown from 1987-89. Seles was seeking a third-straight title in Paris. She had a preference for faster surfaces which gave her greater rewards for the enormous pace of her strokes. But she was more at home on the clay courts of Roland Garros than Graf, who too often had been her own worst enemy, self-destructing under an avalanche of errors.

After her twin successes in the 1987-88 French Opens, Graf did not sustain her mastery in the next three French Championships. Seles was a shade unlucky losing to Graf at Roland Garros in 1989 before posting a prodigious win over her rival in 1990. All of the signs pointed to another Seles victory on clay. It even seemed possible that Graf would fall before the final. She didn't.

THE MATCH

Both the top-seeded Seles and No. 2 Graf overcame considerable hurdles on their way to a final-round confrontation. In the semifinals, the immensely popular Sabatini did everything short of beating Seles. She delivered an imposing array of heavy topspin shots off both sides to take Seles out of her rhythm in the rallies. She attacked at the right moments, volleying handsomely when she had the openings. She played skillfully to and for the crowd, who celebrated her every move with boisterous approval. Sabatini led 4-2 in the final set. It took all of Seles's resolve to pull her through, 6-3, 4-6, 6-4.

In her semifinal, Graf got off to a dismal start. She was being out-maneuvered by Sanchez Vicario. The German seemed uncomfortable and troubled. Then, almost abruptly, she found her range and turned it around in a 0-6, 6-2, 6-2 victory over the Spaniard.

On clay the bounce seemed to favor Seles.

It was time for the Graf-Seles rivalry to be renewed. This was their fourth major meeting, with Graf leading 2-1. Seles believed she was the better player. She had not lost in a Grand Slam event since the 1990 U.S. Open. In fact, Seles had won four majors in a row.

In the opening set of the final, Seles seemed to be in another league. Her intensity and immense firepower were evident from the outset. She attacked Graf's stronger forehand wing in the early stages with great precision. In her gallop to 3-0, Seles collected twelve of fourteen points, breaking Graf at love in the second game. Graf's fearsome forehand—a flat, penetrating, go-for-broke stroke—was misfiring and Seles wasn't missing. Seles served an authoritative love game to reach 4-1, then coasted to a 6-2 first-set win behind her boldest hitting.

In essence, Graf had been diminished in the first set, denied the opportunity to dictate the tempo of play. And yet, the fundamental question remained: Could Seles sustain her awesome standards without some sign of vulnerability?

In the fifth game of the second set, with the score locked at 2-2, Graf began raising her game markedly. When Seles served a double fault to give Graf a second break point, the German seized the moment. A series of piercing fore-

hands put Seles on the defensive. Graf gained the break for 3-2 by blasting a forehand that forced Seles into a backhand error.

Graf then appeared to have squandered her momentum. She lost her serve immediately for 3-3 with a pair of backhand unforced errors. Grimly, she fought on. The seventh game stretched into three deuces. Seles escaped two break points before Graf took the third when Seles drove a backhand long. The German had the lead at 4-3, and this time made the most of it.

In another exceedingly hard-fought, four-deuce game, Graf trailed 15-40, saved three break points, and held on grimly for 5-3. She closed out that game with two morale boosting shots. First, she angled a backhand approach volley crosscourt with sharp efficiency, then followed with a crushing inside-out forehand winner. Even the resilient Seles was shaken by Graf's furious stand. Serving at 3-5, the top seed was broken at love as Graf accelerated. Set to Graf, 6-3. One set all.

The supreme competitive qualities of both champions were on view all through the stormy final set. After Graf had held easily for 1-0, Seles struggled through two deuces and finally held on her fourth game point, stepping in confidently to drive a forehand down the line for a winner. In the third game, Seles regained the initiative after Graf double-faulted for 0-30.

Graf managed to cast aside three break points, but on the fourth Seles produced an untouchable backhand to get the break for 2-1. Seles needed four game points before she held for 3-1—winning that game with a startling forehand down the line placement that caught the German completely off guard. Nonetheless, Graf was still holding her ground and giving

Monia Seles

three forehands, all of them unforced errors. But both players knew that those mistakes were errors of execution and not of judgment; Graf was not going to beat Seles by being conservative.

At 2-4, Graf was in another precarious position. She served an ace for 40-15, only to miss two first serves in a row. Seles exploited that opening. Graf struck back with a service winner for a third game point, then watched helplessly as Seles clipped the sideline with a forehand down the line. On the next point, Seles sent a series of superbly directed drives off both sides to the distant corners, moving the German around at will, controlling the point from start to finish. Graf ran around her backhand at the end, missed a forehand, and was down break point.

This one was imperative for the No. 2 seed. She could not afford to go two breaks down. She had to stay within range of the front-running Seles. Graf stepped around again and attempted another forehand winner. It worked. Graf finally held on her fifth game point with a service winner. She had closed the gap to 4-3. The effort was swiftly repudiated by Seles, who was feeling the physical strain. She held at love for 5-3, saving her energy for the following game.

With Graf serving to save the match, the

little away. In making it 2-3, the German played an excellent game, including an ace, a forehand winner, and a clean smash.

Every game was becoming a statement of authenticity for both players. Neither one was allowing tension to interfere. The two highly charged competitors were going at full force, playing to win, refusing to lose. As Seles held at love for 4-2, Graf was off the mark with

battle became even more remarkable at both ends of the court. Four times in that game, Seles stood at match point. On the first of those opportunities, Graf's crosscourt forehand seemed certain to go long as it traveled through the air. When it landed, it hit the baseline and forced a stunned Seles into an error on the backhand. On the second championship point for Seles, Graf attacked unhesitatingly, angled a backhand volley crosscourt, then knocked off a gift overhead close to the net.

One point away from the title for a third time, Seles lost length on her ground strokes and Graf waited for the right ball to wallop her forehand reverse crosscourt for a gutsy winner. On the fourth match point against her, Graf knifed a backhand slice crosscourt and low. It skidded off the court just near the service line and never came up. With the crowd almost entirely on her side, raising their level of support with every shot, Graf held for 4-5 by forcing Seles into an error with an unexpected forehand down the line.

Despite the enormity of that disappointment, Seles was still serving for the match in the tenth game. But she had thrown such a big part of her stamina into the previous game that she was too drained to close out the account in this service game. A rare, wild unforced error off the forehand from Seles put her down 0-15, and another sorely misdirected forehand put her in a 15-30 hole. Graf sensed her chance, breaking serve for 5-5 by pulling a weary Seles off the court with an acutely angled crosscourt forehand.

Graf was soon in a bind again in the eleventh game, serving at 30-40. Seles drove a crosscourt forehand return deep toward Steffi's backhand corner. She thought she had the win-

ner, headed for the changeover, then looked up and was told by the umpire that her shot had been called out. Graf celebrated with a service winner down the middle in the deuce court. Seles followed with an errant backhand, inches over the baseline, making it 6-5 to Graf.

Fatigue and willpower played key roles in this match.

From the enviable position of a 5-3 lead with four match points to follow, Seles found herself serving to save the match at 5-6. She was baffled by her predicament, but undaunted. She served a perfect love game to hold for 6-6. After Seles won the first point outright, Graf helped her with three preventable mistakes. Despite a double fault at 40-15, Graf held serve for 7-6. At 40-30 down in that game, Seles recklessly tried for an outright winner on the return. Her shot landed in the net, not even coming close.

Once more, Seles served to save the match in the fourteenth game. Graf missed a routine backhand return on the first point, and netted a backhand drop shot from too deep a position on the last. Seles held for 7-7. From 30-30 in the following game, Graf could not connect with two critical forehands. She drove the first one long off a deep backhand return, then missed the next one from very close in, anxiously overhitting with an open court.

Seles was again back in positive territory, serving for the match at 8-7. She moved to 15-0, then came in for a short forehand. Had she gone crosscourt to Graf's backhand side, she would surely have found a winner for 30-0. But Seles chose the wrong side. Graf recovered, and as Seles backed away from the net, Graf passed her with a backhand. A brilliantly concealed backhand drop shot winner gave Graf 15-30, and she made it to 8-8 when Seles hit an ill-advised backhand drop shot into the net from behind the baseline.

Having served for the match a second time and failed, Seles was an exhausted and confused competitor. The next game was crucial for both players. Graf did not miss a first serve. She reached 30-30. She had the Roland Garros spectators cheering her raucously, willing her on. At 30-30, she stepped around her backhand, drove through the forehand, and watched it sail inches long. Seles then went to work, moving Graf from side to side with searing strokes from both flanks. She got a midcourt ball on her backhand, lined it up, and drove it crosscourt out of reach. Graf was stranded. Seles had the break for 9-8.

Seles served for the match again, and reached 40-15. Graf saved a fifth match point with a clean forehand down the line for a winner. It was 40-30. Graf exploded again from

---

An emotional finish to an extraordinarily close encounter.

---

the forehand, looking to send it out of reach on Seles's backhand side. The ball caught the tape on top of the net. Then it fell back on her side. Seles was triumphant, 6-2, 3-6, 10-8. It had lasted for two hours and forty-three riveting minutes.

Reduced to tears at the presentation ceremony, Graf was overwhelmed by the affectionate crowd that almost carried her to a victory. "I've never played for a crowd like this before. Never," she said. Of Seles, she added, "Even when it's close, even when she's tired, she's going for it. She's tough."

Seles responded in kind, "Both of us deserved to win." No one there could disagree.

EPILOGUE

With Seles the victor at both the Australian and French Opens of 1992, she was halfway to matching Graf's Grand Slam feat of 1988. Be that as it may, she knew that winning Wimbledon would inevitably be a difficult challenge. She had only played on the grass courts of the All England Club twice before, losing in the round of sixteen to Graf in 1989 and falling in the quarterfinals the following year to Zina Garrison of the United States. The skidding, low, grass-court bounces were a major deterrent to Seles's rhythmic, ground-stroking style.

Graf was just the opposite. Her footwork was one of her reliable attributes. Her first serve—a powerful weapon that won her countless free points—was particularly effective on grass. And her slice backhand was a shot made for the lawns, coming through fast and biting, forcing opponents into defensive positions. Seles and Graf—the top two seeds—advanced to the final, their first such meeting outside Paris.

Despite Graf's greater ease on the grass, another titanic battle seemed likely. But their first Centre Court title match did not live up to expectations. Graf's performance was immaculate. She subdued Seles, 6-2, 6-1. Seles, however, was devoid of spirit, shaken by accusations made against her by the Frenchwoman, Nathalie Tauziat (a future finalist), and Navratilova (her semifinal victim) that her loud grunting had become unbearably intrusive on court and was breaking their concentration.

Deeply disturbed by the comments of her colleagues—most reporters interpreted the griping of Tauziat and Navratilova as sour grapes—Seles could not muster anything near

---

The Seles poise was weakened by a "grunt" controversy.

---

her customary intensity. Her grunting was unmistakably softer. Her tennis suffered irreparably. Making matters worse, the fifty-nine-minute match was delayed by rain four times. They started at 2 P.M., but it did not conclude until five hours later. By then, the fans were listless. Only a month after the French Open epic, this was a disappointing sequel for the two best players in the world.

Seles recouped remarkably in New York, winning the U.S. Open for the second year in a row, defeating Sanchez Vicario in the final. The Spaniard had ousted an erratic Graf in the quarterfinals. Seles had secured three of the four major championships, replicating her 1991 feat. As was the case in 1991, Graf had won only Wimbledon—no small consolation.

As 1993 commenced, Seles and Graf collided for the third time in four major championships. They met in the Australian Open final. The tennis was played at the lofty level they had reached in Paris seven months earlier. Graf won the first set and pressed her adversary staunchly to the end. Seles succeeded, 4-6, 6-3, 6-2, but the match was much closer than the numbers.

The Seles-Graf rivalry of the 1990s was notable, but did not inspire the passion of those who followed the Evert-Navratilova series played during the seventies and eighties. Graf was closing in, gaining confidence, threatening

Seles in serious fashion. The feeling grew among the experts that the two combatants would share the most celebrated prizes and that Graf would hold her own with her younger rival.

Both women appeared in Hamburg at the German Open, preparing for the 1993 French Open, which was less than a month away. Seles was playing the Bulgarian, Magdalena Maleeva, in the quarterfinals on April 30. She was seated in her assigned chair at a changeover when a deranged man came up from behind her with a knife and stabbed her in the back.

The assailant, Gunther Parche, was an obsessed Graf fan who wanted his heroine to regain the No. 1 world ranking from Seles. Seles was rushed to the hospital and was visited by Graf the next day. The two strong-minded women, who so seldom showed emotion during matches, both burst into tears. Graf may have felt some guilt for what happened in her country as a direct result of her crazed fan. She also felt immense sympathy for an opponent she respected above all others.

The wound to Seles's back was minimal; the wound to her psyche was considerably deeper. She would not return to tennis for nearly twenty-eight months. The game lost a unique and admirable player. Meanwhile, Graf came back resolutely into her own. She took the rest of the major championships in 1993. In the French Open final, she recovered from a break down at 4-3 in the third to beat Mary Jo Fernandez. At Wimbledon, she played Jana Novotna in the final. Novotna had a game point for 5-1 in the third, double-faulted, and lost five games in a row. Graf then came through at the U.S. Open in less dramatic fashion, beating Helena Sukova in the final.

The German was indisputably back on top. But it was impossible not to wonder what might have happened if Seles had been able to play. Could Graf have been so secure and successful? Was she simply the beneficiary of a tragedy, or was she destined for these triumphs anyway?

That kind of speculation served no useful purpose. Undoubtedly, Graf's inner game was altered substantially by the absence of Seles. Nevertheless, that could not diminish what she had done. Graf took the first Grand Slam event of 1994 to record a fourth consecutive major championship victory. Thereafter, she faltered and did not win another big title the rest of the year. She remained No. 1 on the official WTA computer for the second year in a row, and the sixth time overall, but her year was less than stellar.

Graf missed the Australian Open of 1995 with an injury, but won the French Open and Wimbledon. As she trained in the summer before the U.S. Open, Seles made a dramatic return to tournament tennis at the Canadian Open. In that tournament, Monica lost a mere fourteen games in five matches and romped smoothly through the field. Her timing was as precise as ever. Her shotmaking remained strikingly self-assured. She looked like the Seles of old.

Coming into the U.S. Open final, Seles was sharper than Graf. She competed with the same all-out authority as she had displayed in Canada. Her ball control was dazzling. On "Super Saturday" at the U.S. Open—after Pete Sampras had beaten Jim Courier, and before Andre Agassi had removed Boris Becker in the

Steffi Graf

men's semifinals—Seles and Graf renewed their rivalry, sharing a court for the first time since the Australian Open of 1993. They staged one of their highest quality encounters. The first set went into a tiebreak. Seles narrowly missed an ace on set point and lost the playoff, 8-6. She struck back passionately to take the second set at love, but Graf served splendidly throughout the third set and won, 7-6, 0-6, 6-3. The two players embraced genuinely at the net. This had been more than another major tennis match; it had been a healing moment for two young women who had shared a traumatic experience.

With Graf absent again from the Australian Open of 1996, Seles collected her first major crown since 1993 and her ninth overall, taking the title over the German, Anke Huber. Then Graf won the French Open and Wimbledon. At the U.S. Open, she took on Seles for the first time since the 1995 title match. In this final, Graf won, 7-5, 6-4. Seles—set back by injuries, absent her old gusto—was not nearly as good as she needed to be.

Seles suffered severe shoulder and psychological problems throughout 1996. Some believed she should have taken the time off for surgery. Seles elected to keep competing, and she did so at a reasonably high level.

Many would wonder how Seles might have fared without the injury.

One Grand Slam title and another final in that season was respectable. All the same, her comeback was still in the early stages. The force of her will and the scope of her talent would be felt by all her rivals in the immediate years to come.   •

PETE SAMPRAS VS. ANDRE AGASSI

U.S. OPEN, FINAL, SEPTEMBER 10, 1995

In a defining moment for the careers of both players, the two highest ranked players in the world pursued the American Championship.

PROLOGUE

After the accomplished pair of champions named Jimmy Connors and John McEnroe had moved into the autumn of their careers in the second half of the 1980s, key leaders of tennis in the United States began to drift into a malaise. It appeared then to most of the authorities that it would be a very long time before anyone emerged to take over the mantle of supremacy from the two enduring superstars. The United States Tennis Association announced the formation of a player development program in 1987 to address the issue of future aspirants to the championship level.

What few people recognized was that the wheels of progress were already in motion. As the 1980s concluded, a promising group of American players reached the upper tier of tennis. The indefatigable Michael Chang became the youngest-ever French Open and men's Grand Slam singles titlist, when he won at seventeen in 1989. Jim Courier sealed four major singles titles between 1991 and 1993.

More compellingly in many ways, Andre Agassi and Pete Sampras took their talent to the top with eminently successful runs. Agassi

broke into the top three in the world in 1988, appeared in three major finals during the 1990-91 seasons, and captured Wimbledon majestically in 1992. Unconventional and charismatic, possessed of perhaps the best hand-eye coordination of any player of his time, exploding with supreme confidence one moment and sinking into deep insecurity the next, he fired the imagination of the public. Andre's father was a former Iranian Olympic boxer who defected to America and lived in Las Vegas. When Andre was an infant, his father hung a tennis ball on a string over his crib. By the time Andre was four, the family put a ball machine in the backyard. Mike Agassi estimated that his son Andre, even as a small boy, hit fourteen thousand balls a week.

Sampras was an entirely different personality and player. While Agassi had grown up in Las Vegas—a city that seemed the ideal setting for his brashness—Sampras had his upbringing in California. His father Sam was born in the United States to parents of Greek ancestry. His mother Georgia emigrated to the United States from Greece. They were married in Maryland, where Pete was born. Sam worked for the Department of Defense, but moved to

RUSS ADAMS

Pete Sampras

California in 1977 when Pete was almost six years old. It was there that the Sampras interest in tennis began to flower. Sampras's game was essentially free flowing and his ability to hit every kind of shot definitively was apparent early. When he was only a month past his nineteenth birthday, Sampras became the youngest-ever U.S. champion. He took the U.S. Open with wins over three-time former titlist, Ivan Lendl, four-time former winner, McEnroe, and the heavily favored Agassi.

By then, Sampras had developed one of the best serves in the history of the sport. He had been taught by his boyhood coach Pete Fischer to produce different spins—primarily the kick and slice—from the same toss position. That lesson in deception was invaluable, enabling him to keep the opposition guessing rather than anticipating. Deuce court or advantage court, Sampras was a master at moving his serve around the box tantalizingly.

But the speed of his delivery on serve was an essential ingredient in his success. His

motion was pure and economical, graceful and fluid. In nearly effortless fashion, without visible strain, Sampras would serenely serve his way through long afternoons or swift encounters. He backed up his serve with as complete a fast-court game as the sport had yet seen. Sampras had the entire package of skills on any given day, but his vulnerabilities were his fitness, his concentration, and his shot selection.

After the 1990 U.S. Open triumph, it took Sampras time to settle into his heady status. He had been seeded only 12th at that landmark event. He thought his time to take a major crown was at least a year away. He spent a large part of 1991 either injured or indifferent. But he finished that campaign productively with a victory at the season-ending ATP Tour World Championships in Germany. In 1992, he took his place among the top three in the world, reaching the semifinals of Wimbledon, then the final of the U.S. Open.

His loss in that U.S. Open final changed his career irrevocably. Beaten in four sets by Stefan

Edberg, Sampras had served for a two-sets-to-one lead before falling. He had been bothered by a stomach virus that had plagued him since the end of his semifinal win over Jim Courier. And yet, Sampras refused to use his ailment as an alibi. He felt he should have taken that Grand Slam final, and detested the taste of failure on such an important occasion.

Fueled by a new intensity and ambition, Sampras won Wimbledon and the U.S. Open in 1993. He took the Australian Open and Wimbledon in 1994. In 1995, as he began his quest for a third straight year as the No. 1 ranked

---

The undemonstrative Sampras usually veiled his emotions.

---

player in the world, he confronted an inspired Agassi in the Australian Open final. Known for his calm court demeanor, Sampras had broken down in tears during his quarterfinal win over Courier. Trailing two sets to love in that match, Sampras gamely rallied to win in five.

The day before, his coach Tim Gullikson had been sent home with brain tumors for treatment at a hospital in Chicago. Sampras was shaken by the reality of a life-threatening illness afflicting his friend. A fan called out early in the fifth set of the Courier match, "Do it for your coach!" Sampras concealed his tears behind a towel at the next changeover, but could not stop during the following game. Courier half-jokingly shouted across the net to his rival and old doubles partner that they could continue the match the next day.

Angered by what he considered an insensitive goading, Sampras collected himself and won the match, his second-straight comeback from two-sets-to-love down in that tournament.

In the semifinals, he stopped the scampering Chang. Agassi, meanwhile, had raced through his matches without the loss of a set. Much fresher than his adversary, he stopped Sampras in a well-played, combative four-set final.

The two leading Americans, and two best players in the world, met three more times en route to their historic U.S. Open showdown. Sampras conquered Agassi at Indian Wells, California, but Agassi was the victor in the Key Biscayne and the Canadian Open finals. Sampras remained a cut above everyone else in the world in 1995, but Agassi was playing the kind of explosive tennis he had not attained earlier in his career.

The great ground stroker from Las Vegas had fallen upon some hard times after his Wimbledon breakthrough in 1992. He had wrist surgery at the end of 1993, a procedure that could have threatened his career. In fact, he came back stronger and more secure than ever. After an uneven late start to that season, he entered the U.S. Open unseeded, but emerged as a colorful winner of the 1994 American Championship. He stopped 1991 Wimbledon champion Michael Stich in the final.

With his win over Sampras at the 1995 Australian Open, Agassi had collected a second straight Grand Slam title. He would fall in the quarterfinals of the French Open to eventual champion Yevgeny Kafelnikov, and then surprisingly bow out against Boris Becker in the semifinals of Wimbledon. But nothing could dismay Agassi at that stage of the season. Over the summer, he was invincible. He won four consecutive tournaments in Washington, Montreal, Cincinnati, and New Haven.

That string of impressive hard-court successes solidified Agassi's status at the time as the best player in the world. But he fully realized that a successful defense of his title at Flushing Meadow was the only way he could belong at No. 1 for the year. Sampras had struggled through much of the season. He had won only three tournaments. One of those titles happened to be the most important championship of them all.

After Agassi had been beaten by Becker in the semifinal at Wimbledon, Sampras eliminated the burly German in a four-set final on Centre Court, becoming the first American man ever to sweep three consecutive Wimbledon singles titles. That key victory had kept Sampras very much in the struggle for supremacy.

Despite a lackluster summer following Wimbledon—his best showing was a final-round loss to Agassi in Montreal—Sampras was pointing toward New York and the U.S. Open. That was where he wanted to play his best tennis of the year. He was not worried by his failures in the weeks leading to the Open. He prepared himself carefully for the next threshold.

Agassi, too, wanted more than anything else to show his best on the hard courts at the National Tennis Center in New York. He had not expected to win every tournament he entered during the summer. Good fortune had simply fallen into place. His return of serve—certainly the best the game had seen since Connors and arguably even better—was flourishing. His construction of points from the baseline was remarkable. He was wearing everyone down on stifling days, keeping his opponents running from corner to corner with his ball control off both sides, celebrating his efficiency in the heat.

As Agassi and Sampras approached the U.S. Open in that exceptional summer of 1995, all signs pointed to a landmark battle between the two finest players of the day. The consequences of their meeting were clear to both champions. If Agassi could prevail, he would raise his record against Sampras to 4-1 for the season, collect a second major championship,

---

Expectations were at their highest whenever Sampras and Agassi met.

---

and affirm that he could lift his game when the stakes were high.

As for Sampras, a triumph over Agassi at the U.S. Open could restore his eminence, and demonstrate that there was no better big-match player in the business. A victory over Agassi in the American Championships would more than make up for his loss to his foremost rival back in Melbourne. This was the last major championship of the season. This was their nation's showcase tennis tournament. Sampras and Agassi were certain that the 1995 edition of the U.S. Open would have lasting implications for both of them.

THE MATCH

Agassi was seeded first and Sampras second. The two favorites were both tested at different stages of the tournament. In the second round, under the lights, Agassi trailed two sets to one against the spry Spaniard, Alex Corretja, a skillful strategist. Corretja, however, could not sustain his clay-court tactics on the hard-court surface. He began cramping, lost a significant amount of speed, and collected only two games in the last two sets as Agassi survived, 6-2, in the fifth. The top seed was pushed hard in subsequent four-set collisions with the gifted Petr Korda—the

1998 Australian Open titlist—and Boris Becker.

Sampras progressed through the draw with relative ease, although he was tested in a four-set triumph over the Australian eighteen-year-old powerhouse, Mark Philoppousis, who would beat him four months later at the Australian Open. In the semifinals, Sampras took on Jim Courier, who provided useful preparation for Agassi. Sampras overcame a fiery Courier—1992 world No. 1—in a lively contest, 7-5, 4-6, 6-4, 7-5. In many ways, Courier's backcourt game strongly resembled Agassi's. His two-handed backhand was not nearly as good, but his inside-out forehand was perhaps more potent, and he served much

bigger. The Floridian made his opponent work diligently. Sampras was suitably challenged, and came away in good shape.

At 4 P.M. on Sunday afternoon, September 10, 1995, Sampras and Agassi walked onto the stadium court at Flushing Meadow. They were given an appreciative round of applause by the capacity crowd. Many in the audience recognized that both men were close to their peaks. As they played perhaps the most momentous match of their lives, Sampras was twenty-four, Agassi twenty-five. They had taken over the game that year. Their rivalry was not only the talk of the tennis establishment, but it was examined by the media around the world. The *New York Times Magazine* featured a lengthy pro-

Andre Agassi

file on the two men the day before the U.S. Open commenced.

On the day of the final, Sampras woke up with a feeling of exhilaration. As he recalled a few weeks after the match, "I am usually a pretty good sleeper, and I get up at 9 or 10 in the morning for a 4 o'clock match like this one. But for some reason, I woke up at seven that morning and I couldn't get back to sleep. Boom: I immediately thought of the match. I thought about the fear of losing and how great it would be to win, and I realized just how big this match would be."

The best server confronted the best returner.

Agassi was not as fresh. While Sampras had played the opening semifinal men's match on "Super Saturday" the previous day—finishing his business by 2 P.M.—Agassi had waited until the women's final between Steffi Graf and Monica Seles was over for his match with Becker to begin. He played on into the evening. He had less time to recover from the rigors of a hard fought contest than Sampras.

In any case, both men were taut and eager as they stood in the sunshine of the stadium court on a windy day. "It seemed like we had been building up for this match the entire year," said Sampras.

Despite the persistent wind, the two players gave good accounts of themselves in the first set of the final. They knew each other's games all too well. This was their seventeenth meeting in a series that began six years earlier. Each man had won eight times. The style and content of their meetings attracted passionate crowds. Sampras, the game's greatest server,

was pitted against the outstanding return-of-serve artist. Sampras's brilliant blend of attacking tennis—he loved the options a hard court presented to him as he picked his net rushing opportunities—was matched by Agassi's backcourt acumen. As a confirmed, big-hitting baseliner, Agassi's strategy was less complicated. He would look to open up the court by placing immense pressure on Sampras's weaker backhand wing. He would pound away relentlessly from the baseline and counterattack with his customary automatic responses, particularly his impeccable two-handed backhand.

Sampras served first, and his deep resolve was apparent. He opened the first game of the match with an unreturnable thunderbolt to Agassi's backhand in the deuce court, then connected with his favorite first serve down the middle in the advantage court, forcing an errant forehand return from his toughest opponent. Sampras did not miss a first serve and held for 1-0.

Agassi nevertheless asserted himself in the second game. When Sampras chipped-and-charged off a backhand return of a second serve, Agassi passed him cleanly with a two-hander crosscourt. He cracked a potent inside-out forehand to force an error from Sampras for 30-0, then hit a blazing forehand crosscourt winner for 40-0. Agassi held at love for 1-1. The battle was brewing.

The next two games were on serve as the players proceeded to 2-2. In the fifth game, Sampras faced his first dilemma. He had advanced rapidly to 30-0—boosted by two big first serves—but then double faulted twice on his way to a 30-40 deficit. Agassi was at break point. This point alone could settle the set, and perhaps heavily influence the outcome of the match.

Sampras fired his first serve down the middle to Agassi's forehand. The ball exploded off his racket at 123 miles per hour. Many players would have been aced, but not Agassi. With his extraordinary eyes and racket preparation, he made solid contact with the return. Sampras was moving in quickly behind his serve. Agassi's shot hit the net tape, and fell back. Deuce.

Buoyed by that point, Sampras produced a superb slice serve wide to Agassi's forehand in the deuce court. Agassi handled the return with dexterity, making a first-rate, low return down the line. Sampras—knowing he needed to serve-and-volley—stretched athletically for the low backhand first volley and punched it sharply crosscourt near the sideline. Agassi had been pulled out of court by the serve. He could not cover that much ground. Sampras's winning volley gave him game point. When Agassi netted a forehand passing shot, Sampras moved to 3-2.

Agassi remained confident. Serving in the sixth game, he started with a service winner to the backhand, then fired an ace for 30-0. He held for 3-3. The level of play was rising as both players invested all they had in the contest. Serving a love game for 4-3, Sampras delivered three first serves that Agassi could not get back into play. Agassi answered with an unexpected display, approaching three times successfully on Sampras's backhand to provoke passing shot errors, winning another point with a dazzling forehand winner off a high ball. It was 4-4.

Sampras struggled with his serve in the ninth game, as only two of six first serves found the mark. He had reached 40-15 with a one-two punch only he could produce. Sampras kicked his serve high to Agassi's backhand and his

adversary made a short, defensive return. Sampras was serving-and-volleying but he recognized that the volley would be awkward. He pulled up behind the service line, used a short backswing off the backhand, and rolled a topspin winner crosscourt. At 40-30, his typically deep and intimidating second serve was sufficient to make Agassi hit a forehand return inches long. Sampras was in the lead at 5-4.

Serving in the tenth game to save the set, Agassi seemed at last to feel the pressure. On the first point of that critical game, Sampras accelerated the pace off his forehand. His deep, penetrating crosscourt shot caught Agassi on his heels. Agassi met the ball late, and his forehand fell meekly wide. He took the next point to reach 15-15. Then Sampras sent another scorching forehand crosscourt, and Agassi's response jumped off the net cord. The ball waited perfectly for Sampras, who took it on his backhand and rolled it out of Agassi's reach for 15-30.

Two points from winning the set, Sampras sliced a backhand long. At 30-30, Sampras's

---

The interplay of power and strategy stirred the crowd.

---

forehand approach hit the net cord and dribbled over the net. Agassi chased it down, but his contact point was too low for comfort. He netted his forehand to give Sampras set point. That opportunity was swiftly erased when Sampras cautiously chipped a forehand return off a first serve into the net. Set point saved. Deuce.

Agassi took control of the next point, driving a forehand approach deep to Sampras's backhand. Sampras was rushed and his down the line passing shot hung up in the air. Agassi was near the sideline, anxious to put the ball away with one of his patented forehand drive volleys. He took a big swing, seeking the open court, but it was too big a swing, and perhaps he took his eye off the ball for just an instant. The shot was well out. Sampras was at set point for the second time.

The next point lasted twenty-two strokes. Both competitors played that rally as if their lives depended on it. The pace was furious. They were covering the court with amazing agility, chasing down every high-velocity shot and replying with gusto. Time and again, Sampras had Agassi in jeopardy with running forehand crosscourt drives. Agassi got those back with interest. Sampras would start all over again. Neither player was going to lose this point.

With the crowd reacting wildly to their frantic exchange, Sampras pulled Agassi off the court one last time with a furious forehand crosscourt on the run. Agassi could not send this one back over the path it had taken. He had to direct it down the line. Sampras was ready. He drove a topspin backhand crosscourt, making certain to exploit the open territory. Agassi tried to get there, but the ball was well out of reach. Sampras had come up with an irretrievable winner. It was his set, 6-4. He clenched his fists, fully charged by the atmosphere, feeding off the crowd's appreciation.

Sampras concluded the long set point with a winner.

There was a long way to go, and Sampras knew it. In all three of his 1995 losses to Agassi, Sampras had won the opening set but had been unable to sustain his standard. Agassi had been calm and professional in all of those matches, sticking to his baseline aggression, raising the quality of his service returning, rescuing himself with gutsy stubbornness.

In the opening game of the second set, Agassi tried to negotiate a service break. Sampras had inadvertently invited Agassi back into that game with a careless topspin backhand unforced error at 40-30. Sampras looked to rectify the situation when he swung Agassi wide with the slice serve at deuce, moving in behind that serve to close off the court. Agassi stung him with a forehand down the line return that forced Sampras into a backhand first volley error.

It was break point for Agassi. This was how and why he had turned so many of his encounters with Sampras around. He had been opportunistic and focused in the opening games of second sets after Sampras had established leads. Agassi knew he could make this an entirely different match by breaking serve at this moment, and taking advantage of Sampras during an emotional letdown.

The letdown did not last. Sampras was stationed right where Agassi wanted him after staying back on a second serve. A few feet behind the baseline, Sampras ran around his backhand. He had no alternative but to drive this shot into Agassi's vacant forehand corner. There was no room to spare. The shot had to be perfectly timed and executed. Sampras was off the ground when he made contact with the ball. It came off his racket like a laser. His shot landed in the corner. It was as timely a placement as he would make in the match.

Now, at deuce, Sampras gathered himself. He missed his first serve but moved to game point with a backhand slice down the line eliciting a forehand crosscourt error from Agassi. That down the line backhand was an avenue he

Andre Agassi

explored with growing conviction throughout the match. At game point, Sampras aced Agassi down the middle. He had a 1-0 lead. He retained his grasp, refusing to allow Agassi room for encouragement.

Dismayed by his lost chances, Agassi served at 0-1 in the second. He led, 40-30, but committed his third backhand unforced error of the game. Agassi reached game point for the second time, then was wounded by a deep slice backhand down the line from Sampras, driving a forehand wide in response.

Sampras realized he was on a roll. He blasted a forehand crosscourt to set up a forehand down the line winner. At break point, Agassi

made a delayed approach behind his serve when he saw Sampras play a defensive backhand return crosscourt. Agassi closed in on the net but swung wildly. The drive volley let him down again. His shot went into the net. Sampras had a 2-0 lead, which he stretched easily to 3-0 by holding with an ace.

Agassi managed to take the fourth game—ending a sequence of five-straight games for his opponent—but Sampras raced to 4-1 with another love game on serve. He opened that game with a backhand drop volley winner, then followed with three consecutive aces. With early evening approaching, the shadows began forming across the stadium court, complicating Agassi's task in returning Sampras's serve.

Agassi held from 0-30 for 2-4, but Sampras delivered two more aces and lost only one point while making it 5-2. Agassi played a better game on serve to hold for 3-5. Sampras was now serving for a two-sets-to-love lead in the ninth game. He had lost only two points in his last three service games. He was soaring.

The next game was stubbornly contested by both combatants. Sampras hit the outer edge of the sideline with a forehand down the line to reach 40-30, set point. He served-and-volleyed on the second serve, punching his backhand volley with good depth down the line. Agassi was on the run but his forehand passing shot was angled elegantly crosscourt. Sampras dove for the volley but could not make the play.

It was deuce. Sampras released a superb forehand down the line, making Agassi respond with a weak one-handed slice backhand. Sampras came in on a forehand crosscourt, picking off Agassi's forehand passing shot easily. Moving virtually on top of the net, Sampras emphatically put away a forehand volley to arrive at set point for the second time. Perhaps unwisely, Sampras stayed back on a big first serve. Agassi had control of the point, took over the net, and put away a solid smash.

Both players escaped from break points.

Agassi then advanced to break point when Sampras made a forehand unforced error.

Sampras thus found himself in another bind. Having been in such devastating form for much of the set, he wanted to avoid at all costs the loss of this critical service game. He needed firepower on this break point, but did not want to gamble recklessly. He cracked a 125-mile-per-hour first serve deep to Agassi's backhand. Agassi was stifled. His return was wide. Sampras pulled him wide again in the deuce court with another biting slice serve. At set point for the third time, Sampras missed his first serve. Knowing that Agassi would be looking for a deep second serve to the back-hand side, Sampras went down the middle. Agassi was leaning the other way. A second serve ace for Sampras. He had a two-sets-to-love advantage. He shouted, "Yeah" as he walked to his chair, delighted to have built such a commanding lead.

Agassi knew the full dimension of his predicament. He had never come back from two sets to love down in his career, but his incentive to realize that feat had seldom, if ever, been more aroused. This was going to be a defining challenge, an opportunity to prove that he could beat his arch rival when it required the most effort.

Conversely, Sampras was in no mood to squander such a comfortable lead. Because Tim Gullikson remained at home all year fighting brain cancer—unable to join his prized player on the professional tour—Sampras had seemed distracted during much of the season. "Winning Wimbledon saved my year," he would say in the aftermath of that triumph.

That was true. And yet he was not resting on the laurels of his success at the All England Club. A U.S. Open win would not only turn a good year into a great one, but by defeating Agassi he would overcome a rival who had haunted him all season. In essence, this match was for No. 1 in the world, and both players agreed on that fundamental point.

Agassi opened the third set with a strong service game, holding at love with an ace for 1-0. Sampras was still in full swing. He held with ease, then broke Agassi in the third game to register a 2-1 lead. At 30-30 in that game, Agassi double faulted tamely to fall behind break point, and then was damaged by a piece of hard luck. His solidly struck forehand clipped the net cord and hung in the air. Sampras had the court completely at his disposal. He ran around the backhand, turned his shoulders, and waited for Agassi to commit. Agassi moved to his right to cover the fore-hand, and Sampras hit a reverse crosscourt winner behind his stranded opponent.

It seemed likely at this stage that Sampras would replicate his 1990 U.S. Open final round against the same man. Sampras had taken that meeting, 6-4, 6-3, 6-2. With a break in hand in this battle five years later, he seemed more than capable of reproducing that finishing touch. Had he held in the fourth game, he might well have glided to his goal and won with hand-somely.

That did not happen. Agassi broke him for

the first time in the match to reach 2-2. After Sampras led 15-0 in that game, he double faulted on successive points for 15-30 before Agassi forced him into mistakes on a low backhand volley and a forehand half volley. Agassi got to 3-2, closing that service game with a trademark backhand crosscourt winner off a short backhand return from Sampras.

The next four games were dominated by the server. Sampras conceded only two points in his two service games while Agassi lost four. Agassi was finding the range with increasing effectiveness, hitting through the wind magnificently, giving his strokes an almost contemptuous edge as he attacked the ball uncompromisingly. At 4-4, 30-15, he aced Sampras wide to the backhand side. Despite a double fault on the following point, he marched to 5-4 with a deep, forcing forehand down the middle crowding Sampras into an error.

Serving to save the set at 4-5, Sampras took a 30-0 lead, only to miss a forehand volley at close range. A backhand unforced error allowed Agassi to reach 30-30, and then Sampras's second serve bounced long off the net cord. The double fault gave a rejuvenated Agassi a set point, but Sampras erased it abruptly with a superb first serve deep to the backhand. Agassi netted the return.

When Sampras mishit a backhand topspin wide at deuce, Agassi was back where he had been moments before, one point away from salvaging the set. Sampras played serve-and-volley, directing his approach volley deep to Agassi's forehand down the middle. Agassi turned, picked his target, and gave the ball a mighty wallop. He went with the reverse crosscourt angle. Sampras knew it was a winner as soon as it left his opponent's racket. Set to

Agassi, 6-4. Agassi raised his fists. He was pumped up, his energy refueled.

With his lead cut to two sets to one, Sampras was concerned but not apprehensive. He had played one bad game on serve early in the third, and was unlucky to lose the last game of the set. In his mind, he still believed he was the better player. With Agassi serving the first game of the fourth set, Sampras improved his service returns, hoping to distance himself permanently from his aroused opponent. After Agassi arrived at 30-0, Sampras looped a high trajectory topspin backhand return into Agassi's backhand corner, came in behind it, and put away a high volley. On the following point, Agassi belted a potent inside-out forehand deep to Sampras's backhand. Sampras was ready, answering with a deceptive topspin backhand down the line into an empty corner, making it 30-30. Agassi's service winner took him to 40-30, but he double faulted for deuce.

Sampras went to break point. He wanted the early break, knowing he could build substantial momentum with a quick fourth-set lead. Agassi approached behind a strong forehand but was caught in an awkward position as Sampras sent a backhand at his feet. Agassi half-volleyed ineffectually down the middle of the court. Sampras stepped around to clout his

---

Agassi wanted to prove he could come back from two sets down.

---

forehand passing shot. He aimed over the higher part of the net. Agassi was at his mercy. The shot from Sampras had too little margin for error, hit the tape, and refused to go over.

Agassi was heartened by the reprieve. When Sampras missed a forehand return at deuce and followed with another errant fore-hand, Agassi had held for 1-0. He had avoided disaster. Sampras was disappointed but not distressed. He cracked two aces in holding for 1-1, concluding that game with his most dazzling stroke of the match. Agassi had him on the run. Sampras moved to the corner at full speed. He drove a flat forehand down the line with great velocity. No one in the world could surpass Sampras on the running forehand. Clean winner for 1-1.

Agassi held at love for 2-1. Sampras held at 30 for 2-2. When Agassi held for 3-2 at love, he released three outright winners, two off the forehand, one off the backhand. It was his best service game of the match. Agassi was relaxed, hitting freely off both sides, looking fresher and faster than he had at the outset of the match. He had every reason to be bolstered by his progress.

In the sixth game, Sampras responded in kind. He held at love with four simple swings of the racket, striking four consecutive aces. His first untouchable delivery was down the middle in the deuce court. The second landed in the corner down the middle in the advantage court. The third was wide to Agassi's forehand in the deuce court. The last was down the middle again on the other side of the court. Sampras allowed himself the brief luxury of a smile as he finished that jewel of a service game. He was even at 3-3.

Agassi retaliated, though not as spectacularly. He aced Sampras for 40-15. On game point, Sampras stepped around his backhand and boldly ripped a forehand reverse crosscourt. Agassi would have been troubled had the shot gone in, but it clipped the net cord and fell in the alley. Did Agassi rattle Sampras with his improved play and his growing passion?

Apparently not. Sampras held at love for 4-4 with three more unreturnable serves including an ace. Serving in the ninth game, Agassi appeared to have committed a double fault which would have put him in a 0-30 predicament. His second serve looked wide. Sampras

Four aces in a row was a rare feat against Agassi.

was clearly surprised by the lack of a call. He played the point and was coaxed into a backhand error by Agassi. Agassi took his good fortune and ran with it, holding for 5-4 as Sampras overhit a topspin backhand return on game point.

Sampras found himself, at 4-5, serving to save the set, determined to avoid the tension of a fifth set. He took command from the middle of the court, drove a flat, piercing forehand into Agassi's backhand corner, then moved in for a forehand volley winner crosscourt. A kick serve high to the backhand enabled Sampras to get well inside the service line for his first volley, which he directed down the line for a winner—30-0. Agassi made a rare backhand unforced error as Sampras rolled on to 40-0. Sampras closed out that game with another ace (this one wide to the backhand) making it 5-5. He had lost only one point in that critical game.

It seemed nearly certain that the two proud competitors would settle the fourth set in a tiebreaker. They were holding confidently, giving little away, capitalizing on their forcing shots with consistency. The crowd sensed the provocative possibility of the tiebreak. Agassi served at 5-5, having lost only three points in his previous four service games.

The first point of the eleventh game was

pivotal. Sampras inventively angled a topspin backhand crosscourt, his shot landing well in front of the service line and just inside the sideline. Agassi was drawn dangerously out of court. He replied with a crosscourt backhand, but Sampras was able to chip his backhand and approach the net. Agassi had too much court to cover. On the run, he overplayed a forehand topspin lob. It was 0-15. Sampras clipped a thundering forehand crosscourt that Agassi netted— 0-30. Agassi double faulted to make it 0-40.

The murmur of the crowd was unmistakable. They sensed the end of the match. Agassi then aced Sampras wide to the backhand for 15-40, and served his foe wide to the forehand to provoke a cautious error. It was 30-40. Agassi had saved two break points and was still facing a third. He missed his first serve. Sampras ran around his backhand for a forehand return but played it carefully down the middle. Agassi took the high ball on his forehand and went for broke. He hit his shot at full force. It landed long. Sampras pointed to the mark to clarify for Agassi that the call was correct.

A silent message to the absent coach.

Serving for the match at 6-5, Sampras was serene. He aced Agassi down the middle for 15-0, then followed his serve in on the next point. Agassi made him half-volley, then drilled his forehand crosscourt. Sampras lunged to his right and played his forehand volley with surprising force. Agassi was trapped in no-man's land and could barely get a racket on the ball—30-0. Sampras spun a second serve wide to the forehand and Agassi went for the down the line winner. His return was wide. Sampras was at triple match point. He took his time before directing his serve down the middle. It was an ace.

Match to Sampras, 6-4, 6-3, 4-6, 7-5. He had served eleven of his twenty-four aces in the fourth set. He had swept sixteen of his last seventeen service points, winning half of those points with aces. He had won the single most important tennis match of his career. Sampras raised his arms to acknowledge his supporters, shook hands warmly with Agassi at the net as they exchanged a few quiet words, tossed his racket gently into the crowd, and sat down in his courtside chair.

Realizing that the CBS camera was directed at him, Sampras leaned forward and addressed his absent, stricken coach Tim Gullikson, who had been replaced by Paul Annacone, another former player. "That was for you Timmy," Sampras seemed to silently mouth the words. "Thanks for all your help." (Gullikson died eight months later.)

Six weeks after his triumph, Sampras talked about the high value he placed on it. "That was the biggest match of the year for me," he reflected, "and one of the biggest in my career. Everyone was talking about Andre being the favorite and saying how well he was playing. To beat him in the final was certainly extra special for me. Andre had given me more problems than anyone else this year, so to beat him added a lot to winning the U.S. Open. The serve was the shot that won it for me. Andre returns so well he forces me to serve that big to beat him. In the fourth set, I was in a zone with my serve. I peaked for the semifinal and the final and everything worked out the way I would have planned it. You have a good, but not a great, summer and then leave your best tennis at the U.S. Open."

Before the match, Agassi had said almost

prophetically, "When you get to the end of the tournament like this, Pete is playing some great tennis. You are going to see his best, and nothing shy of it, I am sure."

EPILOGUE

The consequences of that contest were farreaching for both players. Sampras was inspired by the effort. He was ranked first in the world for the third consecutive year. In the Davis Cup final, with Agassi injured, Sampras carried his nation to victory over Russia almost all by himself. He took two singles matches and shared in the doubles victory alongside Todd Martin. His series of important victories over the second half of 1995 propelled him through 1996 and beyond.

Agassi was another story altogether. He was deeply scarred by his loss to Sampras in the championship of their country, almost permanently wounded. The all-consuming commitment he had made to the game from the summer of 1994 to the same point in 1995 was over. He was listless in 1996 despite a spirited effort in taking the gold medal at the Olympic Games in Atlanta. He slipped to No. 8 in the world, did not advance beyond the semifinals in any of the major championships, and lost all three of his meetings with Sampras decisively in straight sets.

The following season, Agassi skipped three of the four majors, and lost to eventual champion Patrick Rafter in the fourth round of the U.S. Open. His ranking plunged as low as No. 141. He finished the year stationed at No. 122. He concluded that campaign by appearing in a pair of minor league "Challenger" tournaments in an effort to raise his game and his stock again.

He was rewarded for his dedication,

conducting an energetic 1998 campaign, rising to No. 6 in the world, even defeating Sampras in two of three meetings (all outside the majors). And yet, he was not the same player he had been before his crucial appointment with Sampras at the Open of 1995.

Sampras could see and feel Agassi's deep disappointment in the weeks and months that followed, and he understood why his rival had taken the defeat so hard. "It really would have crushed me to lose that match. It is a great effort to get to the final of majors but unfortunately in sports, only one name gets on that plaque. I could see a few weeks after the Open that he was deflated and I was still riding high."

Despite Agassi's revival in 1998, he still did not appear to be near his former standards. In 1999, however, the unpredictable American confounded his critics by capturing his first Grand Slam title in four years. He had strongly considered skipping the French Open after suffering a shoulder injury the previous week at the World Team Cup matches in Dusseldorf. Despite low expectations, he came to Roland Garros and proceeded to play his way into surprisingly good form during the fortnight in Paris. He had divorced his wife—the actress Brooke Shields, granddaughter of 1931 Wimbledon finalist, Frank Shields—less than two months before Roland Garros.

In the fourth round of the world's premier clay-court tournament, he staged a remarkable recovery from a set and two service breaks down in the second set to oust defending champion, Carlos Moya. Buoyed by that triumph, he moved on to the final, where he collided with a resurgent former top-five player named Andrei Medvedev. Medvedev obliterated Agassi in the first two sets as heavy winds disrupted the

American's big hitting game. Then Agassi found his range with deeper and more daring ground strokes. Inspired by a capacity crowd of sixteen thousand cheering his every move, Agassi recovered brilliantly for a 1-6, 2-6, 6-4, 6-3, 6-4 triumph.

That victory seemed fated. He himself called it "sheer destiny." Agassi had lost in the finals of the 1990 and 1991 French Opens. He was defeated in the former battle by Andres Gomez of Ecuador, and faltered in the latter against Jim Courier. He knew he should have secured at least one, if not both, of those meetings. But this time around, in 1999, he seemed to be blessed by extraordinarily good fortune, and made the most of his openings. He became only the fifth man in the history of tennis to win all four Grand Slam tournaments, and the first to do it on three different surfaces. In this elite category, he stood alongside Fred Perry, Don Budge, Roy Emerson, and Rod Laver. Laver had been the last man to collect the four most prestigious championships, winning them all in 1969 for a second calendar year Grand Slam. Therefore, it was appropriate that the Australian presented an emotionally overcome Agassi with his trophy in Paris, although it was regrettable that Agassi made no mention of Laver in his victory speech.

Be that as it may, Agassi redeemed himself in many ways by rounding out his career résumé with the Roland Garros win at the end of the century. Did he rise to the historical level of Laver or Sampras with his French Open victory? Not so. Nevertheless, he validated his standing as one of the great players of the Open Era, demonstrating a mastery of all the surfaces on the major occasions. Furthermore, he came through characteristically against heavy odds.

When he had won his first Grand Slam title seven years earlier at Wimbledon, Agassi had been seeded 12th. In 1994, when he won the U.S. Open, he had been unseeded. The only time he had secured a major tournament as one of the primary favorites was in 1995 at the Australian Open, when he was seeded second.

Agassi joined a small company of Grand Slam winners.

Most important about Agassi's French Open win of 1999 was the boost it gave the game of tennis. In the days following his success, sports radio talk shows in the United States featured an astonishing number of calls from listeners who wanted to comment on Agassi's final against Medvedev. Most of these calls came from people who normally would have paid scant attention to tennis. And yet, Agassi appealed to this breed of sports fan as no other tennis player could. In that sense, he transcended tennis as an athlete recognized by a much wider constituency.

Fueled by his stunning run at Roland Garros, Agassi went at full force after another major title at Wimbledon two weeks later. He wanted to become the first man since Bjorn Borg in 1980 to take those two Grand Slam tournaments back-to-back. Agassi was returning serve with his customary crushing efficiency over the fortnight. He removed U.S. Open champion, Patrick Rafter, convincingly in the semifinals. A surprising number of authorities picked Agassi to upset Sampras in the final. But in their first major meeting since Flushing Meadow four years earlier, Sampras was impeccable on the grass courts of the All England Club. From 3-3, 0-40 in the first set, he swept majestically to victory, and did not lose his serve in a 6-3, 6-4, 7-5 triumph. He had set himself apart with his sixth championship at Wimbledon—a men's record for the century—and the success also marked the twelfth Grand Slam title win of his career, tying Roy Emerson's record.

Two weeks later, in a press conference conducted by the ATP Tour, Sampras said of his Wimbledon win over Agassi, "It was the best tennis I think I've ever played on that court. From a tennis standpoint, I think when Andre and I are both playing well it's the best tennis, maybe ever. He's made me a better player over the years." Agassi did not disagree, saying of his revered opponent, "He walked on water today."

Over the summer of 1999, Sampras extended his winning streak against Agassi to three matches in a row by defeating his chief rival in the final of Los Angeles and the semifinals of Cincinnati. The two Americans seemed almost certain to meet again in the U.S. Open final, to reprise their 1995 battle. But Sampras was forced to withdraw from the century's last Grand Slam event with a herniated disc in his back. Agassi marched into the final, then overcame the towering Todd Martin in a compelling five set showdown. Not only had Agassi taken a second Open, but he had won two Grand Slam events in one year for the first time. And by appearing in three Grand Slam finals and suceeding in two, he was certainly the Player of the Year for 1999 in the men's game.

Their lively gilt-edged series of matches

Pete Sampras

peaked at Flushing Meadow in 1995 when they clashed at the U.S. Open. Sampras took his triumph over Agassi in one of the decade's most meaningful matches, and used the success as a motivation toward other goals and titles. Agassi wavered for a long while, but recovered his competitive zeal in time to close out the century in style.   •

BORIS BECKER VS. PETE SAMPRAS

ATP TOUR WORLD CHAMPIONSHIP, FINAL, HANOVER, GERMANY, NOVEMBER 24, 1996

In an atmosphere resembling a heavyweight boxing match, the German audience cheered Becker thunderously but treated his rival with much respect. When it was over, the players embraced at the net in a rare gesture of mutual admiration.

PROLOGUE

After Gottfried von Cramm drifted out of tournament tennis in the late 1930s, Germany did not produce another world championship player until the arrival of Boris Becker in the middle of the 1980s. Boris was raised in a small German town called Leimen. He dropped out of school to play competitive tennis. His father was an architect who helped to build a tennis center near the Becker home. Though he had played soccer as a boy, Becker was determined to make his mark in top-flight tennis. As a teenager, Becker was notably muscular and fit. Burly and imposing, he was surprisingly mature for his age, on and off the tennis court. Becker burst into greatness when he was seventeen.

Unseeded and unknown to all but the cognoscenti, Becker cut down one veteran performer after another at the All England Club in the summer of 1985. He became the first unseeded, and the youngest-ever, men's singles titlist at seventeen, vanquishing four seeded competitors, and stopping the big-serving

South African, Kevin Curren, in a four-set final.

An explosive player in every facet of the game, Becker quickly earned the nickname "Boom Boom," a vernacular tribute to the speed and impact of his shots. He would over time be recognized as one of the strongest servers of the modern era, and probably of all time. Becker's serving style featured a pronounced knee bend, which helped him spring up and out at the ball. He used an eastern forehand grip for his serve, an adjustment few if any of his competitors emulated. Off the ground, his muscle power separated him from nearly everyone else.

Becker won Wimbledon again in 1986, toppling the world No. 1 Ivan Lendl in a straight-set final. In 1989, he took his third crown at the All England Club, securing that championship with a triumph over Stefan Edberg, the same player who defeated him in the 1988 and 1990 finals. Later in the summer of 1989, Becker defeated Lendl for his lone U.S. Open title. The win in New York was sufficient for the International Tennis Federation to honor him with the title of "World Champion," although Lendl was ranked No. 1 in the world on the ATP

Boris Becker

his seventh final, defeating Andre Agassi for the first time in six years in a scintillating semifinal match. In an ironic twist, Becker was supported by the presence of Nick Bollettieri as his coach. Three years earlier, Bollettieri had sat in the same "friend's box" and cheered for his longtime pupil, Agassi. The master motivator elected to end his ten-year coaching association with Agassi in 1993, joining forces with Becker the following year, much to the dismay of Andre.

Becker lost the 1995 Wimbledon final to Sampras, and handled his defeat with unusual grace. Paying tribute to a rival he had come to revere, Becker said, "This court used to belong to me in the 1980s. Now it belongs to Pete Sampras." Becker was a semifinalist at the U.S. Open that year. He was back again among the elite. Settled and motivated, he won the Australian Open, at the start of 1996, over Michael Chang, dedicating that triumph to his wife Barbara, who had never seen him capture a major championship.

He injured his wrist at Wimbledon that year and did not return until the autumn segment on the ATP Tour. He was twenty-nine. He had been a formidable force in the game for twelve years. He had conquered the field in Melbourne at a time when many knowledge-

computer. The ATP did not place as much emphasis on the major championships.

The gifted German briefly took his place at the top of the rankings early in 1991 when he halted Lendl yet again in a major final, prevailing in a four-set Australian Open title match. A man of many facets, strong willed and more interested than most of his peers in the world at large, Becker lost some of his zest for the game from 1992-94, only sporadically displaying his best tennis.

In 1995, he recovered his enthusiasm, raised his standards, and was rewarded for his wider commitment. At Wimbledon, he reached

able observers believed he could no longer play that well. It had been five long years since he had last won a Grand Slam singles title.

Becker seemed to revive his competitive zeal indoors at the end of 1996. At the Stuttgart "Super Nine" event, he played Sampras in the final and prevailed in a splendid five-set match, recovering from two-sets-to-one down. That triumph was crucial in enabling him to join the field as one of the top-eight players in the world at the season ending ATP Tour World Championship at Hanover. Having missed ten weeks of competition—including the U.S. Open—it was no small feat for Becker to make the roster.

Sampras, meanwhile, was enjoying another banner season at the top. He had endured a year with a wide range of emotions. His friend and coach, Tim Gullikson, had passed away in May. He played the French Open less than a month later, and reached the semifinals at Roland Garros for the first time on the strength of three five-set victories before exhaustion set in. At Wimbledon, he lost for the first time since 1992, bowing in the quarterfinals against Richard Krajicek, the towering Dutchman who went on to win the tournament.

The U.S. Open was a fortnight of heightened significance for Sampras. He had won two major tournaments in each of the previous three years; this was his last chance to salvage one Grand Slam crown for 1996. In the quarterfinals, he faced the cunning Alex Corretja of Spain. Sampras miscalculated the starting time of the match and did not eat a full meal on schedule. This he would greatly regret.

Corretja forced the favorite to play a match of protracted points, turning the contest into something resembling a clay-court struggle. By the latter stages of the third set, it was apparent that Sampras had little energy left. He trailed, two sets to one, labored to win the fourth, and somehow willed himself into a fifth-set tiebreak. Early in that tiebreaker, he lowered his head behind the court and threw up. The umpire gave him a warning for time abuse.

Sampras was in a terrible bind. He was playing solely on adrenaline and grit, stretching for his shots, making astonishing placements. Between points, he would lean over his racket, shoulders sagging, drained, listless. The New York crowd was chanting, "Pete, Pete, Pete" almost metronomically. Sampras saved a match point with a lunging drop volley for 7-7 in the tiebreak. He followed with an incredible second serve ace, then abruptly, anticlimactically, he won the match when Corretja double-faulted. The crowd stood and cheered both players. At the net, Corretja embraced Sampras, offering generous recognition of an extraordinarily plucky performance.

After a day off, Sampras stopped Goran Ivanisevic and Michael Chang back-to-back for his fourth U.S. Open title. That success carried him through the fall and into Hanover. The Open had been a make-or-break challenge for Sampras, and he refused to be broken. As he headed into Hanover, he had sealed the No. 1

Sampras and Becker competed with warm mutual respect.

world ranking for the year. He was playing chiefly out of pride, seeking to enhance his standing at the end of the season, knowing that his most obstinate adversary in that setting on a fast indoor court would be Boris Becker.

THE MATCH

As fate would have it, Sampras and Becker were placed in the same round-robin group of four. After Sampras had ousted Agassi in his opening match, he took on Becker in a grueling dramatic showdown. The German— boosted by his win over the American in Stuttgart—overcame Sampras again. He won in two tiebreaks. The first tiebreaker was settled by a 12-10 score, and the second was seized by Becker, 7-4. Sampras had served for the second set, but Becker broke back and went on to victory.

Despite the loss, Sampras still qualified for the semifinals by overcoming his French Open conqueror, Yevgeny Kafelnikov. He took on Ivanisevic in one semifinal while Becker faced Krajicek in the other. Both matches were high-quality contests. Sampras edged Ivanisevic, 6-7 (6), 7-6 (4), 7-5, surviving thirty-five aces from the Croatian left-hander. Becker withstood a powerful performance from the Wimbledon champion Krajicek, but came through efficiently 6-7 (4), 7-6 (3), 6-3.

The battle of the heavyweights was on. The players walked from their entranceway a level above the court at Messe Halle 2. As they were making their way to the stage, the theme from Rocky was reverberating in the arena. In other venues, that kind of a pre-match buildup would have been regarded as nothing more than hype, but not for this encounter.

The thirteen thousand fans and both players were exhilarated by the music and the moment. Here were two of the game's all-time greatest players confronting each other in the final of the most coveted men's event outside the Grand Slams. Becker was buoyant about performing for an audience understandably eager for his success. Sampras relished the challenge of trying to overcome a fellow champion who was at his best indoors in his homeland.

"It is tough playing Boris anywhere, but especially in Germany," Sampras would say

---

The atmosphere was charged with pride and anticipation.

---

later. "He really feeds off the emotion from the crowd. Indoors I find him extremely difficult to play because he is so powerful and hits the ball so big. I remember telling my coach Paul Annacone right before we walked on the court that this was going to be fun to go out there and hear the crowd going bananas. For me, this is what it is all about."

Sampras took a 9-7 career edge over Becker into this battle. From the start, he knew he was up against an inspired player at the top of his form. Becker served the opening game of the match. Sampras never made contact with the ball. Becker aced him four consecutive times in holding at love. On the first point, he went wide to the forehand. He followed with an untouchable delivery down the middle, then another one out wide, then one more wide to the backhand in the advantage court. The crowd was delirious.

Sampras served a love game himself for 1-1, then had Becker down, 0-30, in the third game. Becker blasted his way out of that corner with three unreturnable serves in the next four points. He broke Sampras for 3-1 at the cost of only a single point, producing a forehand return winner, a backhand return placement, and a stinging forehand return at break point that Sampras could not handle. In the fifth game, Becker trailed, 15-30, as Sampras found the range with a backhand return crosscourt winner and a stupendous running forehand out of Becker's reach.

Becker responded with two more timely aces and an effective kick serve into the body on the backhand side. The German advanced to 4-1. Both men held at love in their next service games as Becker increased his lead to 5-2. He was playing his best tennis in perhaps seven years, serving superbly, striking his first volleys with certainty, returning with power and panache.

At 5-3, Becker served for the first set. Sampras pressed him hard. A forehand service return winner took him to 0-15. A low return set up a backhand pass by the American down the line for 15-30. Becker was composed and ready to deal with the resistance from the American. He served another ace down the middle for 30-30, then benefited from a piece of good fortune.

Sampras drove a backhand passing shot down the line, making the ball dip with top-spin. Becker lunged, made contact off the edge of his frame, and that freakish volley fell over the net. He had hit an accidental drop volley for 40-30. Becker then sealed the set with an amazing winning shot on the run. Racing to his left for a backhand, he snapped it with topspin and left Sampras helplessly stranded. Set to Becker, 6-3. The crowd was chanting, "Boris, Boris, Boris."

It took all of Sampras's immense resolve to keep him in the match. He had played a respectable first set, but Becker had simply played maddeningly inspired tennis. Sampras served first in the second set, and built a 3-2 lead. He had two break points against Becker in the sixth game. Becker erased those opportunities abruptly. He forced the American wide to the forehand with a deceptive serve to save the first, then delivered a searing ace to escape the second.

At 4-5, Becker served to save the set and held at love with complete assurance. Sampras held for 6-5 employing one of his patented plays. Serving and moving in, he sensed the return would be awkward to volley. The American stopped, took a short backswing, and drove an inside-out forehand into the clear for a winner. Becker was behind 5-6, serving to save the set a second time. He released three more aces in a love game—two of them down the

Pete Sampras

middle in the deuce court—and took the match into a tiebreak.

Sampras was strikingly unruffled during this critical sequence. After Becker aced him on consecutive points for 2-1, Sampras calmly took over. He served and played his first volley deep to the backhand to force a passing shot error, then connected with an elusive first serve to the backhand that Becker netted on the chipped return. Sampras was ahead, 3-2. He reached 4-2 when a slightly mishit forehand return pulled the German over to the sideline. Becker's forehand first volley crosscourt lacked penetration, and Sampras whipped a forehand passing shot into the clear space. Becker took the next point with a well-placed wide serve to the forehand.

Sampras got to 5-3 when Becker netted a topspin backhand return off a second serve. He reached triple set point at 6-3 with a percentage play, punching the first volley to Becker's backhand, forcing the German into an error as Becker went down the line. Becker took both of his service points to close the gap to 6-5, but Sampras had a third set point in hand.

The American directed his first serve deep to the German's backhand. Becker lifted his return tamely. Sampras charged in for the backhand volley, sending it down the line safely for the winner, taking the set, 7-5, in the tiebreak. Pumping his fists, the world No. 1 sat down for the changeover with a renewed spirit, relieved and delighted to be level at one set all.

In the sixth game of the third set, Sampras served at 2-3, 15-40. He needed two clutch aces to come out of that crisis, holding on for 3-3. Both men were serving prodigiously, finding ways to keep each other off guard. Sampras served at 4-5, and lost only a single point in that game. He reached 5-5 by backing up a big

serve with a crisp backhand volley winner crosscourt.

The two titans traded love service games for 6-6. They moved into another tiebreak. Becker revealed a lurking apprehension for the first time in the match. He stayed back behind a second serve and Sampras looped his return high to the German's backhand side. Becker anxiously drove the ball into the net. Sampras played a forehand approach on the next point dangerously close to the baseline. Becker wanted a call but did not get it. Sampras slipped in and deposited an elegant forehand drop volley winner for 2-0. An unnerved Becker complained to the umpire, to no avail.

Sampras soared to 3-0 after a forehand reverse crosscourt winner off Becker's return of serve. Sampras moved to 4-2, but Becker connected confidently with a backhand passing shot down the line to make it 4-3.

Becker again stayed back after his second serve, got the short ball to his backhand, and came in behind a deep approach. He had closed off the court, punching a backhand volley winner down the line for 4-4. Becker missed his first serve, paused, and attempted a deep second serve. The ball was out. Double fault. 5-4, Sampras.

The American served wide to the German's backhand, near the sideline. Becker could not

---

The tiebreaker mystique depends on the serve. Both men excelled at it.

---

answer. That ace gave Sampras a 6-4 tiebreak lead. Sampras now stayed back behind a second serve. Becker rolled his return of serve and came in on the American's backhand. The approach was not sharply hit. Sampras swung freely from low to high, and passed Becker easily down the line. With that shot, he took the lead, two sets to one. His fortunes were rising.

In the first game of the fourth set, Sampras found himself in a 15-40 predicament, but he steadied and held on for 1-0. The two players proceeded to 3-3, knowing service breaks would be nearly impossible to find. By the middle of the set, both men were in a kind of

---

The burden was on Becker to stay in the match.

---

rhythm on their deliveries. Sampras held confidently for 4-3. Becker answered with a love game on another ace for 4-4. The American conceded only one point on his way to 5-4.

In the tenth game, serving to save the match, Becker was in trouble. Sampras lined up a backhand passing shot and drove it with unexpected velocity, forcing Becker into a backhand volley error for 0-15. Becker took the next point, but he then netted a crosscourt forehand for 15-30. The American was two points away from the championship. Becker cracked a menacing first serve down the middle and Sampras could not return it—30-30. Becker worked his way in on a heavily sliced backhand approach shot to the Sampras forehand. The American netted the difficult pass. Then the German aced Sampras wide to the backhand. He was alive at 5-5.

Both players held at love to set up a third consecutive tiebreak, with Becker smacking two more thundering aces on his way to 6-6. Inexplicably, the first four points of the tiebreak went against the serve before Sampras broke that pattern to reach 3-2.

Becker took the next three points for a 5-3 lead. Serving on the ninth point, Sampras bold-

ly played his backhand first volley to Becker's forehand side. The German created an acute angle crosscourt. His forehand passing shot looked successful, but Sampras leapt to his right and opened his racket face to bring off a drop volley winner. Becker was still ahead, 5-4.

Becker sent a forehand crosscourt wide off a service return hit down the middle for 5-5. When the German was off the mark with another first serve, Sampras hit an extraordinarily deep forehand return. Becker got to it, but Sampras approached behind a low backhand chip. Becker's attempted forehand passing shot was wide. It was 6-5, Sampras. Match point for the American.

He hit a heavily spun second serve down the middle that Becker could not attack off the forehand, but Sampras rolled a backhand narrowly wide to lose that point. It was now 6-6. The German crowd had lost some of their intensity as Sampras had marched to the edge of triumph. They raised the volume once more as the players changed ends.

Sampras swung his second serve wide to Becker's forehand. The German snapped the return with great pace, forced a weak response from the American, then whipped another forehand for a winner. 7-6 for Becker. Set point for the German.

Becker served-and-volleyed behind a second serve. Sampras dipped a forehand return at his feet. Becker could not handle it. It was 7-7. Becker took control after a stinging first serve to lead 8-7 and reach set point for the second time. Sampras retaliated with an unplayable first serve to the backhand to make it 8-8. The American directed another serve to Becker's backhand, closed in on the net, and put a backhand volley out of reach. Sampras, at 9-8, had a match point for the second time. On his second serve, Becker stayed back and gave Sampras the opportunity to trade ground strokes with him. They had a fourteen-stroke rally. Becker stood his ground. Sampras concluded it by going for too big a forehand. His shot landed well over the baseline. Becker, at 9-9, moved Sampras out of position, then came in on the American's backhand. Sampras netted the passing shot. 10-9, Becker. Set point to the German for the third time.

Sampras was unforgiving on serve, going deep to the German's backhand to tie it at 10-10. Sampras then served-and-volleyed but he played with caution. Becker would not let him get away with it. His backhand pass was a clean winner. Set point number four for the German, 11-10.

Becker stayed back on his second serve, then approached behind a deep crosscourt forehand. On the run, Sampras whipped a forehand crosscourt winner. The crowd sat in nearly silent awe as the score went to 11-11. Becker served a bomb to the Sampras backhand, came in behind it, put away a high forehand first volley for 12-11. Set point number five for the German.

Sampras served and Becker's backhand return was unexceptional, but the American

---

The spectators were balancing admiration with sentiment.

---

had run out of heroics. He moved around his backhand volley to play an inside-out forehand volley. He opened the racket face too much. The ball flew well out of court. Tiebreaker to Becker 13-11. Set to the German. Two sets all. The fans showered Becker with prolonged applause.

Sampras sat quietly at the changeover, reviewing missed opportunities, wondering if he had the will or resources to win the fateful fifth.

Becker opened the final set by connecting on four out of five first serves, for 1-0. Sampras double-faulted on the first point of the second game, then netted a backhand first volley to dig a 0-30 deficit for himself. He could not afford to lose this service game. Three unreturnable first serves took him to 40-30 before Becker struck back for deuce. Sampras had a second game point but Becker was reprieved when the American ran around his backhand and caught the tape with a blazing forehand.

It was deuce for the second time. Sampras missed his first serve, but rolled the dice on his second. It was hit as hard and as close to the sideline as his first delivery. Becker's return was wide. Game point for Sampras. When Becker lost a spirited rally, Sampras held on for 1-1. He had survived another crisis.

In the third game, Becker aced Sampras down the middle in the advantage court. It was his thirty-first untouchable delivery of the match. But he followed with two consecutive double faults for 30-30. He held for 2-1, but not before revealing weakness. Sampras served a double fault into the net for 30-30 at 1-2, but he came through this test unscathed after putting away a leaping overhead and then serving an ace. It was all even, 2-2.

Becker served brilliantly in the fifth game, opening with his thirty-second ace down the middle, holding at love for 3-2. The tension was mounting. The fans had high expectations that Becker would complete his task. The players were visibly exhausted, but the suspense seemed unending. Sampras was off target with three out of four first serves in the sixth game,

Pete Sampras

but he held at love as Becker's ground game seemed to unravel.

At 3-3, Sampras probed as much as possible on his returns. He reached 30-30, but Becker used a big serve down the middle to set up a backhand down the line for a placement. He served-and-volleyed forcefully at 40-30, and Sampras netted a backhand down the line pass under considerable pressure. Becker, 4-3.

On the first point of the eighth game, Becker struck his backhand return so deep that Sampras could not play it. A service break would permit Becker to serve for the match. Calmly, Sampras fired a first serve down the middle, making Becker stretch too far for the forehand. At 15-15, Sampras serve-volleyed successfully again, going behind the German

with the approach volley. An ace wide to the forehand gave Sampras 40-15. Becker saved the first game point, but Sampras made it 4-4 with a sidespin backhand volley provoking an error.

At 4-4, Sampras and Becker invested most of what energy they had left. It was a crucial game. A chipped backhand return from the American was answered by a backhand volley from the German. Sampras was waiting for that response and he flicked a forehand passing shot down the line for a winner. Becker double-faulted for 0-30, but rallied to 30-30.

Sampras again chipped a low backhand return. Becker was a step too slow moving into the forecourt. He punched his forehand volley crosscourt. Sampras was ready. He curled another forehand passing shot down the line for a winner. It was 30-40. Break point for the American. Becker responded with all-out aggression. A first serve deep to the backhand was too strong. Sampras floated his return too high. Becker spiked the forehand volley to reach deuce. Sampras rolled a high return of serve off the forehand down the line. Becker may have had too much time to think. He mishit a backhand crosscourt wide.

At break point for the second time, Sampras seemed in control. Becker had hung back at the baseline. But the American overplayed a forehand. It was deuce again. Becker served wide to the American's forehand and fielded a difficult low return with a backhand volley crosscourt. As Becker retreated to the baseline, Sampras rolled his backhand down the line. Becker did a terrific job reaching that ball and drove a forehand crosscourt. Sampras responded with a flat forehand, but not too deep. Becker had to lunge laterally as he moved forward and his slice backhand found the net.

It was break point number three for Sampras at 4-4 in the fifth. It must have seemed as if he had played several tennis matches on this one long afternoon. He had been out there for nearly four hours. He had lost his serve only once in five sets, but had not yet broken the German's big delivery. He had waged this debilitating battle in a Davis Cup atmosphere, feeling to some extent that he was playing not only Becker but the entire German nation. Pete Sampras knew he was an American competing on his own, not representing his country in any official capacity. More than anything else, he wanted this match as a personal reward for a demanding year.

Becker connected with a first serve to the backhand. Sampras chipped low down the line to Becker's forehand. Becker had to lift the volley but he placed it with good depth. Sampras read it early, and propelled his backhand with exceptional topspin. It left his racket and gathered speed. Becker turned. He knew at once that he had lost the game. Sampras had hit a perfect backhand passing shot to break for 5-4. As a stunned audience applauded politely, Sampras released his tension with a barely audible "Yeah." His fists were clenched. His mind was focused on the next game.

Sampras served for the match in the tenth game. He aced Becker down the middle for 15-0. Becker took advantage of a loose backhand drop volley to reach 15-15, but the American moved to 30-15 with a backhand at Becker's feet. Sampras served to the backhand, played a deep, low volley into the German's backhand corner, and Becker put up a short topspin lob. Sampras was in place, and easily put away a high backhand volley.

It had all come down to 40-15, double match point for the American. Sampras served-and-volleyed. Becker hit a backhand passing shot crosscourt. Sampras lunged but could not make the play—40-30. Sampras missed the first serve, stayed back behind his second, and the two gladiators had their longest and best baseline exchange of the match. Sampras had Becker on the run. He sent a barrage of forehands into the corners, and Becker ran them all down. His replies to every big shot from Sampras were powerful strokes of the same high quality.

Having hit Becker with everything in his arsenal, Sampras finally tried a change of pace. He looped a forehand down the line with heavy topspin. Becker now had to generate his own pace. He unleashed a backhand but drove the ball into the net. Sampras staggered briefly behind the baseline, raising his arms and looking as if he might collapse under the weight of victory and the length of the struggle. Becker walked up to the net and leaned over it, a thoroughly depleted figure. Sampras came up to greet him. They embraced for a long moment, and exchanged congratulatory words. In the tennis world of the 1990s, there was no more poignant moment than that.

The electric atmosphere had driven the players to perform at a level they did not think existed. When it was over, Becker said,

---

It was a contest of such high quality that victory was shared.

"I can't play any better than that. It was the most incredible feeling I have ever had walking on a tennis court. That was the ultimate match for me. By the end, I didn't really care who won." (Sampras: 3-6, 7-6, 7-6, 6-7, 6-4.)

Sampras was largely in accord. He reflected

a month later, "I have never really been in a match like that one anywhere in the world. I have been in my share of U.S. Open and Wimbledon finals but this was very special. You

---

Becker and Sampras brought out the best in each other.

---

couldn't even talk because the noise was so deafening. It was a huge match for me. Thirteen million people saw the match in Germany, one of the biggest television audiences ever. It was a phenomenal experience. . . . After I won they gave me a good ovation, which I appreciated. That match with Boris will always stick out in my mind. I have enough money, I have my ranking. It is playing those great matches that matters to me."

British writer Richard Evans has probably witnessed more magnificent men's tennis matches from the early 1960s until the end of the century than any other reporter. He wrote in *Tennis Week*, "Had Boris Becker managed to beat Pete Sampras in one of the greatest matches of modern times, Hanover might never have recovered from its hangover. This was a pulsating encounter between the two best indoor players of their generation."

EPILOGUE

Eight months later, Sampras and Becker clashed again in the quarterfinals of Wimbledon. It was their third Centre Court meeting. Sampras defeated his gifted rival in four sets. When it was over, Becker walked up to Sampras at the net and said, "This was my last match here. I just want you to know it has been a pleasure playing against you."

Sampras was astonished by the announcement, and thanked the German sincerely for the compliment. Becker believed then he was on his way out of the game. He did not plan to compete again in the major championships, preferring to stick with one-week tournaments on a part-time basis. Two years later, however, in 1999, the German could not resist returning to Wimbledon one more time. He reached the round of sixteen, but was soundly beaten by Patrick Rafter in straight sets.

Becker had enjoyed a fine career as a full-time competitor. Between 1985 and 1996, he had finished all but one year among the top six. He had won six Grand Slam singles titles, had briefly resided at No. 1 in the world, and had shown in particular respects that he was larger than the game he played. He had galvanized tennis in Germany, and had become an immensely popular player around the world.

As for Sampras, he moved on from his battles with Becker to conquer other rivals and collect more major titles. In 1997, he won the Australian Open for the second time. At Wimbledon, he was the winner for the fourth time. In seven matches in that tournament, Sampras held serve in 116 of 118 games.

In 1998, the American returned to Wimbledon after an undistinguished first half of the season. At the All England Club, he was revitalized. He won his fifth singles title in six years, besting Ivanisevic in his first-ever five-set Grand Slam final. He had confirmed that no one in the modern game was better when the stakes were highest. One year later, Sampras did it again. In a devastatingly potent display, he defeated Andre Agassi in a straight-set Wimbledon final. He had triumphed for the twelfth time in fourteen major finals. He had won Wimbledon three years in a row for the second time. He had set a men's record for the century with his six singles titles on Centre Court. One more major tournament and he would break Roy Emerson's coveted record of twelve Grand Slam championships.

Over the second half of 1998, Sampras had gone after a different record. No man had ever been ranked No. 1 in the world for six consecutive years since computer rankings were introduced in 1973. Bill Tilden was the only man ever to achieve that feat in the history of the game. Sampras reached his goal in 1998 after playing six consecutive tournaments in the autumn, pushing himself almost past his physical and emotional limits to remain the best in his profession.

That achievement added substantial weight to the claim that Sampras should be considered the greatest tennis player of all time. His critics argued that the self-effacing American needed to round out his record with a French Open title. His supporters countered that he had been so far superior on faster sur-

Sampras may yet surpass his and all other records.

faces that a failure to take the world's premier clay-court championship should not disqualify him. Those who stood on middle ground admired Pete Sampras for his supreme skill and dignity. He is clearly the best tennis player of his generation.   •

MONICA SELES VS. MARTINA HINGIS

FAMILY CIRCLE MAGAZINE CUP, FINAL, HILTON HEAD, SOUTH CAROLINA, APRIL 6, 1997

In a tense meeting between the current and former No. 1 ranked players in the world, Seles and Hingis traded high velocity shots and guileful changes of pace.

PROLOGUE

When she was born, her mother decided to name her after Martina Navratilova. She was born in Slovakia, moving to Switzerland when she was eight. Raised on a steady program of tennis competition, Martina Hingis precociously demonstrated her talent during her childhood years. Her mother Melanie Molitor was a former Czech tennis champion who put a racket in her daughter's hand when Martina was two years old. Two years later, she was playing in children's tournaments in and around her hometown of Trubbach.

The rewards from an early start came steadily. When she was twelve, in 1993, she became the youngest ever to capture the French Open junior title at Roland Garros. In 1994, she was the world junior champion, winning at Roland Garros again, taking the Wimbledon junior girls title, and reaching the final of the U.S. Open juniors.

Hingis made her mark convincingly. The time had come to turn professional and test herself in the women's game. She did so in October 1994, two weeks after turning fourteen. Despite sparse appearances, Hingis had the poise to finish that season among the top 100 in the world. She was well on her way.

In 1995—her first full year as a professional—Hingis broke into the top 20 and concluded the year at No. 16. The next year, she made substantial strides. She ascended to No. 4 in the world, had her first big win over Steffi Graf at the Italian Open, and won the women's doubles crown at Wimbledon alongside Helena Sukova. The last of those achievements was a landmark moment for Hingis. She became the youngest ever to secure a Wimbledon title at fifteen years, 282 days. She broke a record held by the English prodigy, Lottie Dodd, who captured the singles when she was three days older than Hingis in 1887.

As 1997 began, a significant number of authorities expected Hingis to make her move toward the top of women's tennis. She had demonstrated that she was on the verge of a breakthrough when she reached the semifinals of the U.S. Open the previous September. After Hingis had lost a spirited, 7-5, 6-3, match to Graf, the victor was asked if she was reminded of herself as she looked across the net at another fifteen-year-old champion in the making.

"Not really," replied Graf. "With Martina, the way she has been playing, you can't really look at her as a fifteen-year-old. She has been playing so well and the way she plays the points, it doesn't seem like you have got somebody really that young on the other side of the net. I am sure I wasn't as consistent at that age."

That extraordinary consistency from Hingis blossomed into something more substantial in 1997. She took her first Grand Slam singles title at the Australian Open, sweeping through the tournament without the loss of a set, dissecting the Frenchwoman, Mary Pierce, with consummate ease in the final. She thus became the youngest Grand Slam singles titlist of the century.

Hingis was flowing, enjoying every match, cutting down all who crossed her path. She brought very different tools to her craft than either of her immediate predecessors at the top. Graf had subdued her rivals with unprecedented power off the forehand and a big serve to boot. Seles had brought a unique blend of double-handed strokes off both sides that she hit with great velocity.

Hingis was a new breed. She was much closer in style and substance to Chrissie Evert. Her game was largely about ball control and strategic prowess. She could take control of the center of the court with her open stance forehand and move her opponents around with precise placements. She could catch her foes off guard with her backhand down the line, the best shot in her versatile repertoire which included a very effective overhead. She could volley capably off both sides, benefiting enormously in that department from her doubles participation.

The Swiss upstart—a remarkably mature sixteen as she played the 1997 season—was utterly confident in the aftermath of Australia. She had prevailed in Sydney before taking the first of the year's Grand Slam crowns. After Melbourne, she was victorious in Tokyo, the Paris Indoor, and the Lipton Championships in Key Biscayne, Florida.

In the final of the latter event, she met Seles, who had been out since the previous November nursing her sore shoulder and other injuries. On paper, the matchup was perfect: former world No. 1 versus the newly established top player; left-handed powerhouse against a cool, counterattacking right-hander; experience opposed by youth. Hingis tore up all those comparisons with a superb performance. She won, 6-2, 6-1, showing cool calculation on a humid afternoon. The only time they had played before Key Biscayne, Hingis had obliterated Seles, 6-2, 6-0, indoors in Oakland.

In two matches, Seles had managed to win a total of five games over the course of four sets against the Swiss stylist. Furthermore, Hingis had been overwhelming the other leading players with apparent invulnerability. As the two champions left the hard courts of Key Biscayne for the slower, softer clay of Hilton Head Island, South Carolina, Seles was making only her second tournament appearance of the year. Hingis had not been beaten all season. She had five tournament wins in her collection and it was only April.

THE MATCH

The Family Circle Magazine Cup at Hilton Head Island was inaugurated in 1973 and had always featured the leading names in women's tennis. Over the years, the great players of the modern era had appeared in this event. Evert had won it eight times in the 1970s and 1980s. Tracy Austin took it twice. Graf had won her first tournament there as a professional at sixteen, in 1986, when she ousted Evert in the final. Navratilova, Sabatini, and Sanchez Vicario were others who recorded Hilton Head tournament triumphs across the years.

The top-seeded Hingis and No. 3 seed Seles advanced to the final methodically. Hingis dropped only one set in five matches while Seles did not concede any. Hingis came from behind to defeat the big-serving Brenda Schultz McCarthy, 5-7, 6-3, 6-2, in her semifinal for her thirtieth consecutive match victory in 1997. Seles accounted for Germany's Anke Huber and former champion Conchita Martinez despite battling the flu during the week.

Eight days after their Key Biscayne final, Hingis and Seles were challenging each other again. With Hingis having come through so overwhelmingly indoors at Oakland and on the hard courts in Florida, she had every reason to like her chances against Seles as they clashed on a third surface. Skeptics wondered why Seles had not pursued shoulder surgery in 1996 when she seemed to have no alternative. Players and press alike wondered whether Seles would ever be anything like the player she had once been before her stabbing in Germany.

Briefly, after her potent return in the sum-

Russ Adams

Martina Hingis

mer of 1995, Seles had seemed much like her old self. There were moments during her 1996 Australian Open title run when she attacked the tennis ball in a manner resembling her former authority. But, by and large, Seles seemed diminished by uncertainty and inhibition. Her sense of abandon was missing when the pressure was on. She had given up almost two-and-a-half years in the middle of her career, and the cost of that withdrawal was incalculable.

In any case, Seles was not consumed by psychological issues as she faced Hingis at Hilton Head. She simply wanted to make amends for her two previous contests with the premier player in the world. She had lasted only forty-four minutes in Key Biscayne. Hingis would be more than willing to replicate that effort.

From the instant the battle began, it was apparent that Seles was playing with well remembered panache. Hingis led, 40-30, in the first game of the match, then heard a champagne cork pop in a nearby box at courtside. The favorite smiled, paused, then released her second serve. Seles cracked a forehand return winner down the line. A backhand crosscourt driven at an extreme angle lifted Seles to break

---

Seles was reminding the spectators of her former self.

---

point. Shaken, Hingis netted a backhand drop shot from behind the baseline. Seles was off and running, 1-0.

In holding for 2-0, Seles went for winners off both wings. She struck a forehand down the line to take the first point, clipped the sideline with a forehand approach for 30-0, and closed out that game by drawing Hingis into the forecourt with a drop shot. Hingis covered it but could merely pop up her reply off the back-

hand. Seles swooped in to cut it off with a backhand drive volley for 2-0.

Serving at 30-30 in the third game, Hingis double-faulted and then missed a routine forehand. Seles surged to 3-0, then held for 4-0. On game point, Seles punished a short ball from Hingis with a backhand crosscourt approach and followed with a forehand drive volley winner.

Seles was not stopping, not for a moment. She broke Hingis easily for 5-0, collecting all four points with outright winners. She was displaying every stroke in her game, including a one-handed forehand winner down the line off a drop shot, and an untouchable forehand return winner taken early off a short second serve.

The set was over—or was it? Seles served for the set at 5-0, recouped from 0-40 to 30-40, then missed a forehand by inches over the baseline. Hingis was finding improved form, trying to lengthen the rallies, looking for ways to move Seles from side to side. Serving at 1-5, the Swiss girl revealed her range. A well-directed forehand approach shot deep to Seles's forehand corner set up an overhead for Hingis, and she put the smash away effortlessly. At the cost of only one point, Hingis held for 2-5.

Both players put immense effort into the next game. Serving for the set a second time, Seles attempted in vain to close the account. She saved two break points and moved to set point, only to be caught flat-footed by a neatly executed drop shot from an increasingly self-assured Hingis. Seles was on the run. Hingis was probing, moving her adversary around skillfully, making Seles work much harder in longer backcourt exchanges. Down break point for the third time, Seles was stretched wide on her backhand. She poked at the ball awkwardly with one hand, and her shot floated long.

Hingis was back in the set, serving at 3-5, gathering momentum in the process. At 0-15, however, she outfoxed herself. Lined up for a forehand from mid-court, she should have made an assertive shot and moved in behind it. Instead, Hingis rolled her forehand softly at a sharp angle wide to Seles's forehand. Monica chased it and connected with a winner down the line past a stranded Hingis. At 15-40, Seles brought Hingis into the net on her terms again, then passed her cleanly with a backhand crosscourt. Set to Seles, 6-3.

The extra work required to finish off that set hurt Seles considerably in the second set. She lost much of her energy and initiative as Hingis gained length off both sides and took command of the court. She closed out the second set, 6-3, and served her way to a 4-1 final-set lead. Seles had lost her sting and Hingis had found the right formula. The match was fading away from the former world No. 1 who appeared helpless.

Serving at 1-4 in the third, Seles stood at 15-30 after Hingis stepped around for a backhand reverse crosscourt winner. The loss of this game would surely be irreparable for Seles. She knew a 5-1 deficit would be too deep to overcome. The left-hander rolled the dice with a daring backhand drop shot down the line. It worked for 30-30. On the swing point of the game at 30-30, Hingis drove a reasonably good backhand crosscourt.

Monica Seles

Seles answered emphatically with a brutally delivered forehand crosscourt out of reach. Confident after getting to game point, Seles swung her slice serve wide to Hingis's backhand, the classic play against the two-handed brigade. Hingis stretched but could not control the return. Seles was back to 2-4.

Hingis figured the seventh game would be essential, as it often is. If she could hold for 5-2, she would be tangibly close to the victory she had fought so hard to achieve. If she was broken, Seles would be serving for 4-4. The difference was great. Hingis played perhaps her best game of the match. She came in behind an authoritative forehand approach, then put away a solid smash for 15-0. After progressing to 40-0, she delivered a forceful first serve deep to Seles's forehand. Realizing that the return was high and weak, Hingis moved in to make a forehand drive volley. She timed it precisely, whipping it crosscourt for a winner. She had held at love for 5-2.

Seles was cornered. She could not afford an unforced error. Serving in the critical 2-5 game, she was two points away from defeat at 30-30. Hingis controlled a baseline exchange and had Seles on the defensive for almost the entire point. Seles chased down a barrage of deep, down the line drives from the purposeful Hingis. Finally, Seles slipped out of the defensive with a sudden burst. She forced Hingis back on her heels, playing deep to the teenager's forehand. Hingis netted it. Seles held for 3-5 with a running forehand down the line winner.

Serving for the match at 5-3, Hingis handled a deep, defensive lob from Seles with surprising efficiency. The favorite got behind the ball, took her racket back early, and made the overhead on the bounce. Her smash was perfect, landing inches inside the opposite baseline behind a stranded Seles. Match point for Hingis. She saw her opening, went for the backhand winner down the line, and overhit it. Deuce.

Hingis reached match point for the second time, and played it safer. In her dominant days,

---

Hingis was showing a vulnerability that was unexpected.

---

no one had ever used the width of the court as productively as Seles. Her implementation of deep drives off both sides mixed with sharp crosscourt shots landing just beyond the service line made Seles nearly impossible to stop from the baseline. On the second match point down against an expectant Hingis, Seles angled her forehand crosscourt with great accuracy, then stepped in to drive a backhand crosscourt into an open space.

Hingis kept trying to press her advantage. She reached match point for the third time. Hoping to catch Seles back too far, Hingis threw in a drop shot crosscourt. Seles came forward slowly but confidently, and smacked a forehand winner down the line. The capacity crowd cheered for a comeback as Seles stayed staunchly in the battle. Hingis had been a point away from the title three times, and unable to convert. She was frustrated by her difficulty, and mishit a backhand wide to present Seles with a break point. Hingis elected to send her next forehand down the line. The shot caught the tape and fell back on her side. Break to Seles.

As she came around after the changeover to serve at 4-5, the audience bathed Seles in a prolonged ovation, appreciative that she had played with such mettle in the previous game. Hingis was rattled. She made four consecutive forehand unforced errors as Seles held at love for 5-5. Seles then broke at love for 6-5—boosted by a double fault from the tiring Swiss girl at 0-30—and served for the match in the twelfth game.

Solid and thoughtful through this revival, Seles connected with two first serves on her way to a 30-0 lead as Hingis testily missed a backhand down the line long, and drove a poorly produced forehand over the baseline. Seles was two points away from an astonishing triumph. From the time she saved her third match point in the ninth game, Seles had taken thirteen points in a row. All she needed was two of the next four points to complete her mission.

Suddenly, but not inexplicably, Seles lost her edge and discovered how much she wanted the win. Hingis, conversely, had virtually conceded the match in her mind. She became engaged in an intense fifteen stroke rally with Seles. Had she erred at any time in that sequence, Hingis would have found herself down triple match point. She refused to allow that to happen, adding velocity to her two-hander, directing it crosscourt, forcing Seles into a one-handed forehand mistake from out of position.

Seles discovered that Hingis would not give in.

Still two points away from the victory at 6-5, 30-15, Seles looked for an opening with her backhand down the line. She drove it narrowly long, inches over the baseline—30-30. Hingis pinned Seles behind the baseline with another well-struck crosscourt backhand. Falling back uncharacteristically, Seles mishit a forehand long—30-40. Hingis was reprieved. She played a safe service return at break point. Seles netted

her backhand tamely. It was 6-6—and time for the tiebreak.

Both players were well aware of their missed chances in the third set. They realized they needed to channel everything into the next critical sequence of points. The player who could take seven points by a margin of two would walk away with the title. The player who could not accomplish that task would leave with a wounded psyche, knowing the opportunity had been there for the taking—and not just once.

Hingis opened the tiebreaker with trepidation. She double-faulted long to lose the first point. The favorite rebounded to 1-1 with a backhand approach volley down the line for a winner. Seles answered with a service winner to the forehand to take a 2-1 lead, then widened her lead to 3-1 when Hingis's heavy topspin forehand down the line landed long.

Both competitors played every point in this tiebreak with desperate passion. Hingis added velocity to her first serve to force an ineffectual return, then came through again with a solid, bounce smash winner. It was still 3-2 for Seles. Seles sensed she could now take the match firmly into her own hands. She used a running forehand crosscourt to pull Hingis out of position. Seles did not hesitate, releasing another vintage backhand crosscourt placement for 4-2.

Hingis played a conservative return of serve down the middle and Seles responded with a hard-hit, inside-out forehand. The shot was wide, 4-3. The next rally was first rate on both sides of the net. Seles finished it off with a bounce smash winner for 5-3, once again two points away from victory.

Before serving the next point—knowing she could face triple match point if she did not win it—Hingis took extra time. She grinned, looking over at Seles as if to say, "You have played a great match, but I dare you to beat me now!"

The contemplative pause seemed to make Seles uneasy, shifting the burden of pressure. Hingis found her range at a propitious moment, probing one side, then the other. She mixed up her down the lines with suitable crosscourts, keeping Seles in a quandary. When Hingis got the two-handed backhand she wanted, she hit it crosscourt with terrific pace. Seles netted her forehand. She still had the lead, 5-4.

Seles could serve out the match by winning the next two points. But Hingis was once again inspired. She would not give anything away from here. She would force Seles to produce the big shots under pressure. Hingis sent a teasing, high topspin return of serve down the middle. It was a semi-lob. Seles had no angle to work with but could not resist attempting a conclusive shot. She was off the mark. It was 5-5.

In the tiebreaker, Seles was two points from victory.

Seles missed her first serve, spun in her second, and Hingis made another solid return. Seles tried for a forcing two-handed backhand, driving it long. Hingis had regained the advantage, moving in front, 6-5, reaching match point for the first time. She sensed that Seles was more suspect off the forehand, and served her first delivery to that side. Seles answered with her favorite forehand down the line return. This shot had won her numerous points across the three sets as she found the corner time and again. At match point against her, it failed. Seles hit it solidly, and the ball hit the net cord. It refused to go further.

Hingis had prevailed, 3-6, 6-3, 7-6 (5). She remained unbeaten in 1997. This was clearly not the final of a major championship. The players knew it did not have those kinds of consequences. But they competed with the intensity and pride usually reserved for the Grand Slam events. They supplied sparkle and suspense, grit and guile. The crowd was amply rewarded.

Outside of the major events—beyond the boundaries of Melbourne and Paris, London and New York—a match of this kind is seldom contested. Two of the best-ever female tennis players shared a couple of fascinating hours with a nationwide television audience, and gave tennis fans a match to be remembered.

EPILOGUE

Two weeks after her Hilton Head triumph over Seles, Hingis went horseback riding in Switzerland. She fell off her horse and damaged her left knee, which required arthroscopic surgery. She was off the circuit for seven weeks, and came into the French Open cold. Despite the predictable rustiness in her game, she reached the final in Paris. But she played too defensively in a straight set loss to Croatia's Iva Majoli, suffering her first defeat in thirty-eight matches.

The world No. 1 recouped to win Wimbledon, striking back from a set down to oust doubles partner Jana Novotna in the final. Two months later at Flushing Meadow, she beat a rapidly improving Venus Williams, 6-0, 6-4, to win the U.S. Open. Hingis ended the year with victories in twelve of seventeen tournaments, winning seventy-five of eighty matches, securing three of the four major events.

The pressure to perform at that level—or to

move beyond it—was too much for Hingis in 1998. Her mother was still at her side, not only as a parent but as her coach, and insiders believed Hingis needed someone else with a sharper lens to look after her strategies. Her quick mind and point playing acumen were still sizable assets, but Hingis found herself getting attacked by bigger hitters including Williams, and another able American, Lindsay Davenport.

She did manage to take her second Australian Open in a row in 1998. Thereafter, however, she did not win another major title. Seles played a stupendous match to beat Hingis in the semifinals of the French Open. Novotna stopped her in the same round at Wimbledon. At the U.S. Open, in the most important match of the year, Davenport defeated Hingis, 6-3, 7-5, in the final. Although Hingis overcame Davenport at the end of the season indoors at New York's Madison Square Garden in the final of the Chase Championships, the American had taken over the No. 1 world ranking for the year, with Hingis slipping to No. 2.

Dismayed but not discouraged, Hingis opened 1999 in style, collecting a third consecutive Australian Open title, defeating the promising Frenchwoman, Amelie Mauresmo, in the final. Still only eighteen, she already had five Grand Slam singles titles in her possession. Moreover, she won a doubles Grand Slam in 1997, taking three of the four majors with Novotna.

Seles stalled to some degree after her battle with Hingis at Hilton Head. She finished fifth in the world for the year. In Paris, she confronted Hingis in the semifinals, came close again, but bowed, 6-7 (2), 7-5, 6-4. Seles lamented her loss. "I had so many chances," she reflected later.

"Martina would come up with unbelievable shots and put me on the defensive. I don't have the strength and intensity on my strokes that I used to. I am missing too many."

In the spring of 1998, Seles suffered a much larger loss. Her father Karolj who had remained her trusted adviser and coach, died of cancer less than two weeks before the start of the

Her father's death motivated Seles to play in Paris.

French Open. She pondered whether or not to play in Paris, but went ahead with her plans. As if it were fated, she played some of the best tennis of her career. In the semifinals, she overcame Hingis for the first time in six career meetings. Seles won, 6-3, 6-2, with a flurry of dazzling shots, dictating the entire course of the match.

Based on that glowing performance, it seemed entirely possible that Seles would win a fourth crown in Paris. She had lost only twice in sixteen career clashes with Sanchez Vicario, including a straight-set win in the 1991 Roland Garros final. In the first set of this final, Seles was visibly apprehensive, tightening up at critical moments, squandering leads and chances. She served for the first set at 5-3 and was two points away from victory. Sanchez Vicario hung on and rejected Seles, 7-6 (5), 0-6, 6-2.

"I was up so many times on her serve in the third set," said a dejected Seles later. "Those games just slipped away from me. You can't expect that to happen three times against someone like Arantxa and win. But that's a lesson learned. Every time that I lose I'm disappointed. I'm really happy that I got this far, but no matter what, it is tough to take."

Seles endured a string of more difficult

defeats the rest of the year. She fell in the Wimbledon quarterfinals against Natasha Zvereva, and lost to Hingis decisively in the semifinals of the U.S. Open. When the year concluded, Seles stood at No. 6 in the world.

And yet, her heart was as large as ever. At the start of 1999, she stopped Graf in the quarterfinals of the Australian Open, winning eight straight games after the German served for the first set at 5-4. Seles romped, 7-5, 6-1, with a display nearly as dynamic as her showing in Paris against Hingis seven months earlier. But the pattern persisted. Seles lost in straight sets to Hingis in the semifinals. She could peak for one big match, but could not keep it up in those that followed.

Nonetheless, Seles set the pace for the women's game in the early nineties with courage and ingenuity. She inevitably would have taken more major titles had she not become a victim of a deranged fan. But Seles had her share of brilliant, isolated afternoons in the second half of the 90s. And one of those was that soul-stirring defeat at Hilton Head against the redoubtable Martina Hingis, a player cut from the same high quality cloth.   •

MARTINA HINGIS VS. STEFFI GRAF

FRENCH OPEN, FINAL, JUNE 5, 1999

Before a vibrant partisan crowd at Roland Garros, Hingis wanted to win the only major title to elude her grasp, while Graf resolutely sought another major crown in the twilight of her career.

PROLOGUE

Martina Hingis headed into her 1999 Roland Garros title battle with Steffi Graf propelled by a seemingly unshakable confidence. She would not turn nineteen until three months later, but already she had recorded five Grand Slam tournament victories. Having taken her third consecutive Australian Open five months earlier, the Swiss teenager had established herself as a player who was always primed for the occasion. The last time she had not been at least a semifinalist in a major tournament was at Wimbledon in 1996. After relinquishing her No. 1 world ranking to Lindsay Davenport for the 1998 season, she had taken back her place at the top in the early months of 1999. But as she looked forward to her confrontation with Graf on the clay in Paris, Hingis was driven by a larger goal. Roland Garros was the lone "Big Four" tournament she had not captured. She wanted it passionately, was fully committed to taking it, and firmly believed it was her turn to claim the crown.

Graf's inner view was radically different. She came to Paris expecting very little from herself. She had not won a major event since the U.S. Open of 1996. In 1997, her season came to an end after a quarterfinal loss at Roland Garros. Knee surgery was performed on the German immediately following that tournament. Not until Wimbledon in 1998 did Graf compete again in a Grand Slam event. She had lost in the third round there, and bowed in the round of sixteen later that summer at the U.S. Open after securing a morale-boosting title in New Haven the week before.

At the close of 1998, Graf played brilliantly in winning two tournaments and reaching the semifinals of the season-ending Chase Championships at New York's Madison Square Garden. The resurgence was brief. On her way to Roland Garros in 1999, the German's instability surfaced repeatedly. She did not win a tournament. She squandered a 4-2 final-set lead against the surging Serena Williams in the championship match at Indian Wells. She was thoroughly blasted off the court by the advancing Venus Williams at Key Biscayne. Her clay court results en route to Paris were not encouraging.

Graf hoped she could win some matches in Paris to toughen herself up for Wimbledon

Martina Hingis

a hitch. She did not concede a set, defeating defending champion Arantxa Sanchez Vicario of Spain in a one-sided, straight-set semifinal. In that match, Hingis had displayed the full range of her talent. She made some surprise serve-and-volley attacks, catching the Spaniard off guard. She used the drop shot judiciously. She improvised with the lob volley. She used every inch of the court to her advantage. Hingis was close to the top of her game, and was convinced she was going to win the tournament no matter whom she faced in the final. She had completed her semifinal triumph before Graf and Seles stepped on court. Hingis was asked about which woman she would rather play for the title. She did not hesitate. She said she preferred to play Steffi Graf in the final.

THE MATCH

Graf held a 6-2 career edge in her series of matches against Hingis, but that statistic was misleading. Most of those wins had been posted when Hingis was developing her game, and Graf was the best player in the world. Nevertheless, in the year leading up to this clash at Roland Garros, the two champions had each won once against the other. These two matches were played indoors. Graf still had the weapons and the energy to stand her ground against a player eleven years her junior. Be that as it may, the slow court conditions in Paris were much in Hingis's favor. Graf would have more difficulty concluding points with penetrating forehands. She would have to work harder to earn her keep. She would need to make certain her sliced backhand was working

and the grass courts that suited her game much better. And yet, seeded only sixth, she was surprisingly sharp and solid over the early rounds. Her first major test was against the precocious Russian, Anna Kournikova, in the round of sixteen. Kournikova had cut down Graf on the grass courts of Eastbourne the previous year. When her big-hitting game was clicking, she had shown just how formidable she could be. In this encounter, Graf recouped from 5-6, 0-40 in the second set to prevail, 6-3, 7-6. In the quarterfinals, she stopped the second-seed Davenport in three sets. That set the stage for a semifinal against the No. 3 seed Seles. Graf was apprehensive at the outset, but came on strong for a three-set victory and a well-deserved place in another major final.

Hingis made her way to the final without

at full efficiency. She would need to serve with sting and authority.

Anything less than a top-of-the-line performance from Graf would cause the German to fall short of victory. Hingis had not done herself justice at Roland Garros the previous two years, sliding indifferently to a final-round loss against the Croatian, Iva Majoli, in 1997, falling almost petulantly in straight sets against Seles in the 1998 semifinals. Despite those failures, there was no logical way to explain why she had not succeeded on a surface that suits her style so well.

At the start of her duel with Graf, Hingis seemed to be saying, "This is my time. This is my tournament. No one—not even Steffi—is going to stop me." The eighteen-year-old was precise and assertive as she broke Graf in the opening game. The Swiss player reached 15-40 by driving her two-handed backhand return deep crosscourt and following it into the net. Graf anxiously sliced her passing shot wide. The German recovered to deuce but hurt her cause with consecutive backhand unforced errors to drop that game. Hingis confidently held at love for 2-0, closing that game with a flourish. A forehand placement lifted her to 40-0, and then she confounded Graf by following her serve to the net, punching a backhand volley into an open court.

When Graf drifted to 15-40 with a double fault in the third game, her chances appeared bleak. It was here, however, that the twenty-nine-year-old realized she had to go for bigger and bolder shots and thus take Hingis out of her rhythm. Steffi released a piercing reverse crosscourt forehand that Hingis could not manage with a one-handed backhand stab. The German took charge of the next point, came in forceful-

ly, and put away a smash. It was deuce. Two more scintillating forehands enabled Graf to hold on for 1-2. She broke Hingis easily in the following game, then had three game points for 3-2. Graf sorely needed to maintain her momentum and hold her serve, but Hingis was not yielding. The Swiss girl hit winners on two of Graf's three game points, and provoked a backhand mistake from Steffi on the other. Another errant backhand from Graf—this one unforced—cost her the game. Hingis was back in front, leading 3-2.

Martina's mind was not muddled. She was ably breaking down Graf's weaker backhand wing, and preventing Steffi from getting enough opportunities to produce punishing forehands. Hingis took the next two games, breaking Graf again for 5-2. Steffi

---

Hingis was the superior player in the first set.

---

double-faulted for 15-40, saved the first break point with a potent serve and forehand combination, but surrendered the seventh game when Hingis sliced a forehand that dipped at the German's feet. Graf attempted to half-volley into an empty court, but could not bring it off.

Hingis served for the set at 5-2. She reached 30-30 with an impeccable topspin forehand down the line winner off a short sliced backhand from Graf. Had Hingis applied herself and raised her intensity, she would have closed out the set with relative ease. Instead, she became careless and complacent. An ill-advised drop shot from the Swiss girl served as an invitation for Graf to explode. The German did just that, driving her backhand with topspin down the line. The shot was out of her opponent's reach. Graf broke with a booming forehand crosscourt that Hingis could not control. Reprieved, Graf held at love for 4-5. Her form had been fluctuating, but she kept her resolve.

Hingis, meanwhile, was in a bind. She knew she should already have sealed the set. Serving for it a second time at 5-4, the teenager was strikingly vulnerable. She rolled a two-hander into the net, then double-faulted for 0-30. Then Hingis gathered herself, drove a forehand deep into the corner, and moved in swiftly for a drive volley winner. She proceeded to 40-30 and her first set point. Graf sliced a backhand that clipped the net cord, and fell over. It was deuce. Hingis responded remarkably well, defending skillfully from the backcourt, then stepping in with authority to crack a backhand winner.

Graf was not giving in. Her forehand approach was too powerful and accurate for Hingis, who missed a backhand pass. It was deuce for the second time. Martina swung her serve wide with a slice to Steffi's forehand, opening up the court for a backhand crosscourt win-

---

The crowd was emotionally favoring Steffi on each point.

---

ner. Set point to Hingis for the third time. Graf retaliated once more with all-out aggression. She drove her reverse crosscourt forehand return with great pace. It was untouchable. The score was deuce for the third time. The German seemed poised to make an effective backhand return, only to slice it over the baseline, giving Hingis a fourth set point. Martina whipped a forehand crosscourt. Graf was made to play a running forehand at full stretch. She missed. Set to Hingis, 6-4.

Having withstood the challenge of Graf's comeback late in the first set, Hingis started the second set warily protecting her territory. The opening game was hard fought by both players, with Graf determined to establish an early lead, and Hingis equally determined to stay ahead. There were three deuces and Hingis needed three break points before she got the early advantage. Martina had altered her game plan, working persistently to pull Graf wide on the forehand side, taking Steffi out of her comfort zone. Rather than allow Graf to control the court with her inside-out forehand, Hingis shrewdly kept Graf on the run with a calculated combination of sharply angled crosscourt forehands, and well disguised backhands down the line.

When Hingis held at the cost of only one point for 2-0, she seemed safely back in command, closing in rapidly on the title she coveted above all others. But on the first point of the third game, she lost her bearings. All along, the crowd had been fervently behind her opponent, cheering with wild enthusiasm for Graf, giving Hingis little more than reserved rounds of applause. In a dangerous lapse in judgment, Hingis changed the emotional texture of the match irreversibly. When her forehand return of serve was called out, Hingis irritably questioned the call. Umpire Anne Lasserre got out of her chair and conferred with the linesman, then reaffirmed the decision.

Hingis was not willing to move on and play the next point. She walked around to Graf's side of the court to check the mark herself, a blatant violation of the rules. Lasserre stood by her decision. The Roland Garros capacity crowd of sixteen thousand began chanting, "Steffi, Steffi, Steffi." Hingis sat down on her chair, waiting for WTA supervisor Georgina Clark to arrive. The crowd was booing Hingis, frustrated by the delay. Hingis spoke with Clark. Hingis—who had earlier been given a warning for racket abuse—was now assessed a point penalty. Graf was rewarded with a 30-0 lead. The German held for 1-2 to the crowd's delight, but Hingis came through with a pinpoint forehand crosscourt passing shot to reach 3-1.

Despite a 40-15 edge at 3-2, Hingis did not hold. On her second game point, she outsmarted herself with an ineffectual serve-and-volley tactic. Graf read the plan early and responded with a backhand return winner. With Hingis at game

Steffi Graf

point for the third time, the two competitors waged a superb battle of crosscourt forehands. Graf prevailed in that hard-hitting exchange as Hingis faltered in the end. Another damaging crosscourt forehand brought Graf to 3-3. Steffi saved a break point on her way to 4-3. She sensed a chance to take control of the match. So, too, did the animated crowd.

With Hingis serving at 3-4, 30-40, she saved a break point for deuce. Then both players produced the best exchange of the match. In the middle of this tense exchange, Graf angled a drop shot crosscourt off her backhand. The Swiss star answered with a backhand angled sharply crosscourt, which Graf handled with a deep backhand chip down the line, forcing Hingis again to the baseline. Hingis put up a high defensive lob off the forehand, and Graf replied with an indecisive overhead. Hingis had time to set up a strong two-handed response crosscourt. Steffi was stretched low and wide at the net on her backhand side. She tried a drop volley crosscourt, but Hingis read it early. She scampered in swiftly for a backhand down the line. Graf was trapped. She could not make a volley. All she could do was chase the shot down. The ball was almost behind her, but Graf managed to make a wonderful lob over the incoming Hingis. She lofted it crosscourt, deep into the corner, and Hingis was hard-pressed to even get there. She chased it down and managed a high defensive lob. Graf let the ball bounce. Steffi was standing well inside the service line and in the alley. She picked her target, swung hard, and smashed the ball straight into the net. The crowd rumbled a collective moan. Hingis smiled at her good fortune. Graf held her head in despair, astounded that she had lost the point.

Hingis held on for 4-4, then broke a still-dazed Graf for 5-4. Hingis lost only the first point of the ninth game, then swept the next four. She got that break with one of her patented backhand down the line placements. Hingis was only a single game away from the championship. She served for the match in the tenth game. On the first point, Hingis reached 15-0 when her forehand skidded off the baseline and provoked an error from her opponent. The eighteen-year-old was three points from her goal. Then she missed a routine backhand, driving the ball over the baseline, squealing in disappointment over her unnecessary error. It was 15-15. Graf got to 15-30 with a topspin backhand crosscourt pass, then delivered another thundering forehand, rushing Hingis into a backhand error with the force of her shot. When Graf netted a backhand slice, Hingis was back to 30-40, but the teenager's shot selection on the next point revealed that she was both tense and tired. She attempted a backhand drop shot from just behind the baseline. The ball did not clear the net. Graf was level at 5-5.

Graf was revitalized. Hingis was rattled. The fans were galvanized behind the German. Graf took the next two games, sweeping eight of nine points. Graf had the set 7-5. She also had the momentum and the crowd. Graf held quickly for a 1-0 third-set lead, and then Hingis left the court for a bathroom break. Graf followed her rival off the court, but returned long before Hingis. As Graf sat at courtside, the crowd broke into a spontaneous "wave," and Graf joined in the fun. The chants of "Steffi, Steffi, Steffi" echoed around Roland Garros stadium. When Hingis returned with a clean, white outfit, the jeers increased in volume.

With Hingis seemingly devoid of energy, and despondent about her lost opportunity, Graf glided to 3-0 in the third. The German had

collected six games in a row, winning twenty-four of twenty-nine points in that span. It was apparent that her Swiss adversary was not only depleted but demoralized. She could not comprehend what had happened to her. She had invested nearly all of her resources in an effort to finish the job in two sets. Fighting to salvage her cause in a third set was a task she did not want. Nevertheless, she had too much pride and professionalism to acquiesce. She summoned her waning resolve, moving well and striking the ball with vigor.

When Hingis held her serve for 1-3, the audience responded with a combination of boos and cheers. On the first point of the following game, Graf double-faulted. Hingis pounced. A

RUSS ADAMS

Martina Hingis

running forehand winner off a drop shot from Graf made it 15-30. Graf sliced a backhand wide under pressure for 15-40, and Hingis took the next point with another sparkling forehand out of Graf's reach. Hingis had broken back for 2-3. She was leaving her disappointments behind her and getting on with her business.

The next game was pivotal. Hingis slumped to 15-40, but then took the following three points. She was a point away from 3-3. Her shots were flowing again. Her concentration and confidence were reviving. Graf realized she had to raise her intensity and start dictating the tempo again. She moved around her backhand and hit a scorching forehand, sending that shot deep to the Hingis backhand. Martina was on her heels. She was stretched wide, forced to play the stroke with one hand. It was off the mark. The score was deuce. Graf quickly advanced to another break point. She then took

---

Hingis had to overcome her doubts and the hostile crowd.

---

a high ball off her backhand and knifed it cross-court, short to Hingis's backhand. Martina was rushed. She could not deal with the low ball, netting a backhand. Graf was at 4-2.

The match was essentially over. Graf and Hingis both knew it. The crowd sensed it. Graf connected with three out of four first serves to hold at love for 5-2. As she walked to her chair at courtside for the changeover, the crowd resumed chanting, "Steffi, Steffi, Steffi."

In the eighth game of the third set, Hingis was a forlorn figure, baffled and frustrated by the crowd's bias against her, infuriated by her earlier wasted chances. She drifted to 2-5, 30-40, match point down. Astounding the crowd and

her opponent, Hingis released an underhand serve. She confounded Graf completely with the surprise tactic. Furthermore, she put heavy sidespin on that serve. Graf lunged to make the return, and could only produce a weak shot. She had been pulled so far forward that she had no alternative but to approach the net behind her return. Hingis had no trouble hitting a backhand passing shot down the line that Graf could not cope with.

The hostile fans booed Hingis vociferously believing, as many critics in the media did, that an underhand serve was a shameful display of bad sportsmanship. Graf, however, did not agree. She would say after the match, "I thought it was a hell of a serve. I mean, for her to do it for the first time at match point down was very good. I had the feeling the crowd thought it was an insult. Obviously it shook things up a bit and she won the point. It was a good decision from her point of view."

Hingis got to game point, then missed an awkward low forehand when Graf hit another biting slice backhand. Graf moved to match point for the second time with an unintentional backhand drop shot winner, acknowledging her luck with a wave of the hand toward Hingis. For the second time, Hingis tried the underhand serve, but this one was out. With the fans now baiting Hingis with loud disapproval, the Swiss girl approached the chair umpire, asking for quiet. Graf then walked up to the umpire herself, saying, "Let's play tennis." Order was restored. Hingis produced a conventional second serve. The two players had a brief baseline exchange. Graf sent her last emphatic forehand deep to the Hingis backhand, and Martina meekly netted her response in defeat.

Graf had come through, 4-6, 7-5, 6-2, to

Steffi Graf

claim her sixth French Open title, only one shy of the record held by Chris Evert. Hingis had lost her bid for a first championship at Roland Garros. The tennis had been exciting, the theater even better. It was a watershed event for both competitors.

When it was over, a tearful Hingis left the court for the locker room, booed by the sixteen thousand fans in the stadium. They continued to shower Graf with affectionate applause, saluting her spirit and fortitude, recognizing her enduring stature in the history of women's tennis. A few minutes later, Hingis returned to the court for the presentation ceremony, walking arm in arm with her mother (and coach) Melanie Molitor. Hingis was fighting in vain to hold back her tears, consoled by her mother. It was the most poignant moment in a long afternoon.

At the post-match ceremony, Hingis regained some of her composure, speaking in French, congratulating Graf and recognizing her rival as a "great champion." The crowd applauded her warmly, appreciating her grace under the pressure of a shocking defeat. When Graf stepped up to the microphone, she was presented with the trophy by five-time former French champion, Margaret Court of Australia. It seemed particularly appropriate because Court remained the only woman to win more major championships than Graf, by the slim margin of twenty-four to twenty-two.

"I feel French," was Graf's heartfelt opening remark. "I've played all over the world, but I've never had a crowd like this one—ever."

Later in her press conference, Graf said, "This is the biggest win I've ever had, for sure. I've had a lot of unexpected ones. I have to admit that. But this is by far the most unexpected. I really came into this tournament without belief. This has been incredible. This was one of the craziest matches ever. It had everything."

Hingis was asked if there was one key reason why she lost the match. She replied, "There were a few things. I was not fighting against Steffi only, but the whole crowd, the referee, the line calls. It was not always the way I would like it to be. But if you're better, you win anyway."

Hingis had made many miscalculations. Her actions were inflammatory, inviting the crowd to treat her with increasing disapproval. Nevertheless, the audience was willing to tolerate Graf's excessive questioning of line calls. Umpire Anne Lasserre lost control of the match and did not exert her authority with any conviction. She got down from her chair too many times to check marks, and should have set a tougher tone.

In the end, the controversy and the unpredictability added to the drama of the occasion, and made it a more memorable match. Both players had given powerful performances and played inspired tennis. Graf, fired by the crowd, was the victor because of her immense will and her ability to draw upon the resources of past triumphs.

EPILOGUE

Two weeks later, Hingis and Graf came into Wimbledon as the top two seeds. The tennis world eagerly awaited another dramatic meeting between the two champions. But Hingis had still not recovered from her wrenching loss in Paris. And something had gone fundamentally wrong in her professional and personal relationship with her mother. In her opening-round match, Hingis was beaten soundly by an Australian qualifier named Jelena Ducic, a sixteen-year-old ranked No. 129 in the world. Ducic upended the 1997 titlist, 6-2, 6-0. The Australian played inspired and inventive tennis, overpowering Hingis from the backcourt, looking uninhibited from start to finish. It lasted fifty-four minutes. Hingis gave a desultory display.

In the press conference following the match, Hingis revealed that her mother had not been with her at the match and had gone home. She was bombarded with questions by reporters who wanted to know why Melanie Molitor had not been by her side for the first time at a major tournament. Hingis said that she and her mother had mutually decided they needed time apart. She explained, "With this tournament, my mother and I decided to have a little bit of distance from each other to work a little more on our private lives. We'll see how it goes in the future."

As she approached her nineteenth birthday in September, Hingis was enduring the inevitable growing pains, coming to terms with a world where nearly everyone expected and almost demanded unbridled success from her year in and year out. Inevitably, Hingis would remain a player of considerable importance in the early stages of the twenty-first century. Graf would not. The thirty-year-old German played her ninth Wimbledon final in 1999, scoring an

---

The loss to Graf in Paris was still festering.

---

impressive, three-set triumph over the gifted athlete, Venus Williams, along the way. In the final, however, Graf was unable to repeat what she had done in Paris. She lost to Lindsay Davenport of the United States, 6-4, 7-5. Her chance for an eighth singles title on Centre Court was not realized.

Graf announced her retirement in late summer, withdrawing from the U.S. Open. Her career was winding down after eighteen years as a professional. She was the only player—male or female—to win every major championship at least four times.

Graf departed at the right moment, when she was still a great player, but no longer invincible. She had overcome a multitude of injuries, illnesses, and personal stress to become a champion of the highest order. Graf had begun her career competing against Evert and Navratilova. She ended her tenure in the era of Hingis and the Williams sisters. Through it all, she reflected the dignity and competitive resolve that has marked the highest standards of tennis in the twentieth century. •

RANKING THE GREATEST MATCHES OF THE TWENTIETH CENTURY

For the purposes of this book, I have listed the selected matches chronologically. Readers thus have an easier time tracking the different eras of tennis, and placing these matches in historical context. But, as a writer and tennis historian, I have decided to rank the matches themselves. This ranking is based on a wide range of factors: the importance of the match; the significance of the occasion; the lasting implications of the results on the lives of both players; the level of play from both combatants.

Any ranking list is highly subjective. Mine is no exception. Be that as it may, I have tried to balance the best matches of different eras, so as to produce a list that reflects the appearance of new players in each decade.

1. *Bjorn Borg d. John McEnroe*, 1-6, 7-5, 6-3, 6-7 (16-18), 8-6, final, Wimbledon, grass, 1980.

2. *Suzanne Lenglen d. Helen Wills*, 6-3, 8-6, final, Cannes, France, clay, 1926.

3. *Don Budge d. Baron Gottfried von Cramm*, 6-8, 5-7, 6-4, 6-2, 8-6, Davis Cup, grass, Wimbledon, 1937.

4. *Ken Rosewall d. Rod Laver*, 4-6, 6-0, 6-3, 6-7, 7-6, final, WCT Dallas Finals, indoor, 1972.

5. *Chris Evert d. Martina Navratilova*, 6-3, 6-7, 7-5, final, French Open, Paris, clay, 1985.

6. *Pancho Gonzales d. Charlie Pasarell*, 22-24, 1-6, 16-14, 6-3, 11-9, first round, grass, Wimbledon, 1969.

7. *Henri Cochet d. Bill Tilden*, 2-6, 4-6, 7-5, 6-4, 6-3, semifinal, Wimbledon, grass, 1927.

8. *Monica Seles d. Steffi Graf*, 6-2, 3-6, 10-8, final, French Open, clay, Paris, 1992.

9. *Margaret Court d. Billie Jean King*, 14-12, 11-9, final, Wimbledon, grass, 1970.

10. *Pete Sampras d. Boris Becker*, 3-6, 7-6, 7-6, 6-7, 6-4, final, ATP Tour World Championships, Hanover, Germany, indoor, 1996.

11. *Lew Hoad d. Tony Trabert*, 13-11, 6-3, 2-6, 3-6, 7-5, Davis Cup, Melbourne, grass, 1953.

12. *Martina Navratilova d. Chris Evert*, 6-7, 6-4, 7-5, final, Australian Open, Melbourne, grass, 1981.

13. *Rod Laver d. Tony Roche*, 7-5, 22-20, 9-11, 1-6, 6-3, semifinal, Australian Open, Brisbane, grass, 1969.

14. *Helen Wills Moody d. Helen Jacobs*, 6-3, 3-6, 7-5, final, Wimbledon, grass, 1935.

15. *Jimmy Connors d. Bjorn Borg*, 6-4, 3-6, 7-6, 6-4, final, U.S. Open, Forest Hills, clay, 1976.

16. *Pancho Gonzales d. Lew Hoad*, 3-6 4-6, 14-12, 6-1, 6-4, final, U.S. Pro Championships, indoor, Cleveland, 1958.

17. *Billie Jean King d. Evonne Goolagong*, 3-6, 6-3, 7-5, final, U.S. Open, Forest Hills, grass, 1974.

18. *John McEnroe d. Mats Wilander*, 9-7, 6-2, 15-17, 3-6, 8-6, Davis Cup, St. Louis, indoor, 1982.

19. *Jack Kramer d. Don Budge*, 6-4, 8-10, 3-6, 6-4, 6-0, semifinal, U.S. Pro Championships, grass, Forest Hills, 1948.

20. *Maria Bueno d. Margaret Smith*, 6-4, 7-9, 6-3, final, Wimbledon, grass, 1964.

21. *Pete Sampras d. Andre Agassi*, 6-4, 6-3, 4-6, 7-5, final, U.S. Open, Flushing Meadow, hard courts, 1995.

22. *Steffi Graf d. Martina Hingis*, 4-6, 7-5, 6-2, final, French Open, Paris, clay, 1999.

23. *Stan Smith d. Ilie Nastase*, 4-6, 6-3, 6-3, 4-6, 7-5, final, Wimbledon, grass, 1972.

24. *Maureen Connolly d. Doris Hart*, 8-6, 7-5, final, Wimbledon, grass, 1953.

25. *Arthur Ashe d. Jimmy Connors*, 6-1, 6-1, 5-7, 6-4, final, Wimbledon, grass, 1975.

26. *Martina Hingis d. Monica Seles*, 3-6, 6-3, 7-6, final, Hilton Head Island, S.C., clay, 1997.

27. *Sarah Palfrey Cooke d. Pauline Betz*, 3-6, 8-6, 6-4, final, Forest Hills, grass, 1945.

28. *Stefan Edberg d. Ivan Lendl*, 6-7, 7-5, 6-1, 4-6, 9-7, semifinal, Australian Open, grass, 1985.

29. *Fred Perry d. Ellsworth Vines*, 7-5, 3-6, 6-3, 6-4, Pro Tour Opening, Madison Square Garden, New York, indoor, 1937.

30. *Althea Gibson d. Darlene Hard*, 3-6, 6-1, 6-2, final, Forest Hills, grass, 1958.

HONORABLE MENTION MATCHES OF THE TWENTIETH CENTURY

Included here are matches (listed chronologically) that narrowly missed inclusion among the top thirty of the century.

1. *SUZANNE LENGLEN d. DOROTHEA DOUGLASS LAMBERT CHAMBERS*
      10-8, 4-6, 9-7, final, Wimbledon, 1919.

The Frenchwoman never lost a match at Wimbledon and was beaten only once in her entire amateur career. This was her closest call. Lambert Chambers—a seven time Wimbledon singles titlist—was nearly 41. She served for the match at 6-5 in the third set and had two match points in that game. Lenglen survived these tests, and never looked back.

2. *BILL TILDEN d. BILL JOHNSTON*
      6-1, 1-6, 7-5, 5-7, 6-3, final, U.S. Championships, Forest Hills, 1920.

Tilden took the championship of his country for the first time over the rival who had beaten him in the final the previous year. " Big Bill" would overcome "Little Bill" in five of his seven finals at the U.S. Championships. This was perhaps their highest quality clash.

3. *RENE LACOSTE d. JEAN BOROTRA*
      6-3, 2-6, 6-0, 2-6, 8-6, final, French Championships, 1929.

In this collision between two of the famed " Four Musketeers", the cunning Lacoste, who had fashioned a five set victory over Bill Tilden in the 1927 final, triumphed this time over his countryman. Lacoste narrowly escaped after Borotra staged a couple of spirited comebacks. Having been beaten by Henri Cochet in the title match of 1928, Lacoste regained his title in a superbly contested match.

4. *FRED PERRY d. DON BUDGE*
      2-6, 6-2, 8-6, 1-6, 10-8, final, U.S. Championships, Forest Hills, 1936.

Budge served for the match three times in the fifth set, and had two match points, but the Englishman refused to concede. Perry had won his third consecutive Wimbledon earlier in the summer. This triumph gave him a third American Championship as he concluded his amateur career with one of his best wins.

5. *ALICE MARBLE d. HELEN JACOBS*
    6-0, 8-10, 6-4, final, U.S. Championships, Forest Hills, 1939.
Collecting her third of four singles titles at Forest Hills, Marble was challenged persistently in the second and third sets by her countrywoman. Competing on a windy afternoon, Jacobs led 3-1 in the third set. The final game of the match produced seven deuces. Jacobs had five game points for 5-5 and saved two match points before bowing gamely. Marble was the first female player to be described as "playing like a man". She attacked brilliantly behind her serve with searing approach shots. Her aggressive style was developed on the hard courts of California.

6. *PANCHO GONZALES d. TED SCHROEDER*
    16-18, 2-6, 6-1, 6-2, 6-4, final, U.S. Championships, 1949.
Allison Danzig, of *The New York Times*, wrote of Gonzales following this epic clash: " One can hardly give the champion too much praise for his moral fiber." Both Americans were aware of the stakes—the winner would inevitably move on to a career in professional tennis while the loser would be held back. Gonzales toppled Schroeder in another of his seemingly impossible comebacks. The outcome remained in doubt until 4-4 in the fifth set. Schroeder had won Wimbledon, coming through four times in five set matches. On his way to this battle with Gonzales, he won two more five set contests—over Frank Sedgman and Billy Talbert. On this day, Gonzales was stronger down the stretch.

7. *ROBERT HAILLET d. BUDGE PATTY*
    5-7 7-5 10-8, 4-6, 7-5, fourth round, French Championships, Paris, 1958.
In one of the most closely fought matches in the history of international tennis, Haillet upended the 1950 Roland Garros champion. Patty had a 5-0, 40-0, lead in the fifth. Then, in one of the most improbable turnarounds ever recorded, Haillet took seven straight games and climbed all the way back to victory.

8. *MARGARET SMITH d. LESLEY TURNER*
    6-3, 3-6, 7-5, final, French Championships, Paris, 1962.
In this dramatic meeting of two Australian women, Smith struck back boldly from 3-5 and match point down in the final set to beat Turner in a compelling final for her first of five French Champioship titles. Turner—who took the tournament the following year— was better suited to the slow clay court surface, but was conquered in the end by a superior all around player.

9. *ROY EMERSON d. CHUCK McKINLEY*
    3-6, 6-2, 6-4, 6-4, Davis Cup Challenge Round, Cleveland, 1964.
Emerson's win clinched the Davis Cup for Australia in a thrilling 3-2 finish. After his

teammate Fred Stolle had stopped Dennis Ralston to even the score between the two nations at 2-2, Emerson rallied from a set down against the formidable McKinley, who was the 1963 Wimbledon champion. At 28, Emerson was at his peak, performing with characteristic athleticism, displaying his patented "rocking motion" as he set up for his powerful serve.

10. *MARIA BUENO d. ROSIE CASALS*

6-2, 10-12, 6-3, semifinal, US Championships, Forest Hills, 1966.

Bueno was on her way to claiming her fourth and last title on the grass courts at the Westside Tennis Club. Casals was 17, and a rising star. Their clash was brilliantly played on both sides of the net. It was thought then that Casals would win her share of major prizes, but she fell just short of that standard.

11. *NANCY RICHEY d. BILLIE JEAN KING*

4-6, 7-5, 6-0, semifinal, Madison Square Garden International, New York, 1968.

The two top women in the United States had not played each other in a singles match for four years. In this classic confrontation between the net charging King and the counter-attacking Richey, a dramatic reversal of fortunes took place. Richey lost the first set and trailed 5-1 in the second. In the ninth game of that set, she saved a match point. The determined Texan completed a run of 12 consecutive games to prevail against her greatest rival. Less than three months later, Richey ousted King in the semifinals and went on to win her second and last major title—the French Open.

12. *KEN ROSEWALL d. CLIFF RICHEY*

6-8, 5-7, 6-4, 9-7, 7-5, quarterfinal, Wimbledon, 1971.

Like his sister Nancy, Cliff Richey became the top ranked player in American tennis. He had achieved the No. 1 U.S. ranking in 1970 by stopping Stan Smith in the semifinals of a California tournament. In that stunning encounter, Richey and Smith reached simultaneous match point at 4-4 in a fifth set, "Sudden Death" tie-break. Richey made an almost miraculous diving forehand volley to win. But in this battle with Rosewall, Richey was less fortunate. He led two sets to love, went up a break in the third, but could not sustain his authority. He was twice up a break in the fourth, but could not hold on to the advantage. In the fifth, he had the determined Australian at 15-40 in three different service games, but Rosewall prevailed.

13. *JOHN NEWCOMBE d. BJORN BORG*

4-6, 6-3, 6-2, 6-3, final round, WCT Dallas Finals, 1974.

Newcombe was one of the finest fast court players of the modern era. He won seven Grand Slam singles championships, including three at Wimbledon. Had he not been involved in the 1972 and 1973 boycotts of that event, he would surely have won at the All England Club at least one more time. In this meeting with the 17-year-old Borg, Newcombe was mesmerized at the beginning by the Swede's heavy and well disguised topspin. The Australian fell swiftly behind 4-0. From that juncture, however, he put his highly observant mind to work, and picked Borg apart superbly. The score does not begin to do justice to the quality of the tennis.

14. *MANUEL ORANTES d. GUILLERMO VILAS*

4-6, 1-6, 6-2, 7-5, 6-4, semifinal, U.S. Open, Forest Hills, 1975.

In this evening clash under the lights on " Super Saturday", Vilas was in command. He led two sets to love, and later built a 5-0 fourth set advantage. Then he saw five match points erased by the Spaniard in this battle of left-handers. Orantes managed to construct a victory from what appeared to be certain defeat. The next day, exploiting his superior clay court skills, Orantes dismantled Connors 6-4, 6-3, 6-3 to claim his only major title.

15. *CHRIS EVERT d. EVONNE GOOLAGONG*

6-3, 4-6, 8-6, final, Wimbledon, 1976.

Of all the delightful duels between the American and the Australian, this was their most memorable. Evert had never beaten her seemingly carefree rival on grass before. Their rivalry had begun on the same Centre Court four years earlier when Goolagong had recouped from a set and 3-0 down to win in three sets. In this confrontation, Evonne's instinctive grass court game lifted her to a 2-0 final set lead. Evert served for the match at 5-4, only to drop the next two games. But from 5-6 in that gripping final set, Evert demonstrated her mental toughness and came away with the second of her three Wimbledon singles titles.

16. *JIMMY CONNORS d. ADRIANO PANATTA*

4-6 6-4 6-1, 1-6, 7-5, fourth round, U.S. Open, 1978.

In the first year of the Open on hard courts, Connors overcame ain inspired and gifted rival on a day when he was often outplayed. Panatta—the Italian and French Open winner of 1976—attacked Connors diligently. He served for the match at 5-4 in the fifth set, reached 30-30, but was beaten there by two scorching returns from the American. Panatta, serving at 5-6, recovered from 0-40 and saved four match points. In that high tension game Connors provided one of the most astonishing shots of his career, curling a one handed backhand passing shot around the netpost for a winner. Panatta double faulted on the fifth match point to conclude an exhilarating contest. Buoyed by that triumph, Connors marched to the title without the loss of a set in his last three matches.

17. *JOHN McENROE d. JIMMY CONNORS*

    6-4, 4-6, 7-5, 4-6, 6-3, semifinal, U.S. Open, 1984

This match was played on a history-making day. Stan Smith had opened the program by defeating John Newcombe in a closely contested Men's 35 final. Ivan Lendl won his men's semifinal from match point down against Pat Cash. Martina Navratilova came from a set down to beat Chrissie Evert in the women's final. McEnroe and Connors finished their business after 11 o'clock that evening, but not before waging perhaps their best ever battle. Connors missed a large opening when he did not convert a 3-1 third set lead. Despite connecting with 70% of his first serves, McEnroe was broken seven times by a highly charged Connors. Four years earlier—despite losing eleven straight games at one stage—McEnroe had beaten Connors in another epic five setter at the Open. It was a riveting encounter, but not the equal of the standard set in this 1984 meeting.

18. *HANA MANDLIKOVA d. MARTINA NAVRATILOVA*

    7-6 (3), 1-6, 7-6 (2), final, U.S. Open, 1985.

Mandlikova was an immensely gifted shotmaker who could produce winners from anywhere on the court. The Czechoslovakian possessed a rare combination of power and touch. She would win four major championships in her sporadically brilliant career, taking all the big titles save Wimbledon, where she was twice a finalist. Mandlikova's triumph in this match was her finest performance. She wasted a 5-0 first set lead before holding on at the end. Navratilova was in top form in the second set, but Mandlikova served for the match in the third. Ultimately, she played a magnificent tie-break to conclude a battle of constant attacking tennis. Having ousted Chrissie Evert in the previous round, Mandlikova became the first woman in the Open Era to defeat two former titlists in the process of winning the U.S. Open.

19. *MONICA SELES d. JENNIFER CAPRIATI*

    6-3, 3-6, 7-6 (3), semifinal, U.S. Open, 1991.

Seles, 17, was a near the top of her game. Capriati, 15, was seemingly on her way to a long and distinguished career. The two teenagers produced a bruising backcourt battle, featuring corner to corner rallies of the highest caliber. Twice in the final set—at 5-4 and 6-5—Capriati served for the match. She was two points away from victory at 30-15 in the twelfth game. Somehow—through a combination of immense willpower and groundstroke skill—Seles staved off defeat and achieved one of her grittiest triumphs by taking the tie-break 7-3. The following year, Capriati took the gold medal at the Olympic Games, ousting Steffi Graf in a hard fought final. But then, beset by personal problems, the Floridian lost her way. She made some brief comebacks, but was never close to attaining her former world top ten status.

20. *STEFFI GRAF d. VENUS WILLIAMS*

6-2, 3-6, 6-4, quarterfinal, Wimbledon, 1999.

In her 14th and final Wimbledon, Graf met a player who seemed likely to capture the title in the early stages of the next century. The match was delayed several times. The players started an hour late at 1PM, and did not finish their business until near darkness after three more rain delays. Nevertheless, the 30-year-old German and 19-year-old American played with striking power and control under difficult conditions. Graf gave an inspired performance against a player with remarkable spark and agility. It was a battle worthy of a final, but it was experience triumphing over youth. At the U.S. Open later that summer, Venus Williams lost another hard fought encounter to Martina Hingis in the semi-finals. But her younger sister, Serena, still 17, claimed the crown by defeating Hingis in the final, becoming the first African American female since Althea Gibson in 1958 to win a major title. As the century came to an end, it was apparent that the Williams sisters were beginning to show the promise of dominating women's tennis in the next decade.

THE TWENTY BEST PLAYERS
OF THE TWENTIETH CENTURY

Comparing the top players of different generations is a complex task. Could "Big Bill" Tilden have held his own against Rod Laver? How about Helen Wills Moody facing Steffi Graf? Imagine Jack Kramer and Pete Sampras going full force against each other if both were at their best. All of the experts share the feeling that each decade in this century has showcased a new cast of top-notch players. Early round matches—once a formality for the leading competitors—have become increasingly challenging assignments for the favorites. The level of play across the board on both the men's and women's tours is better than it has ever been before.

Nevertheless, it does not automatically follow that the champion of today would defeat yesterday's champion, or that tomorrow's top player will surpass today's leading player. For example, Pancho Gonzales toppled Rod Laver twice only months after Laver's second Grand Slam. Pancho was forty-two when he pulled the latter upset, Laver not yet thirty-two. Ken Rosewall reached the finals of Wimbledon and the U.S. Open when he was thirty-nine. Jimmy Connors remained a major force deep into his thirties, and made it to the U.S. Open semifinals when he was thirty-nine.

The great players must be judged by the scope of their accomplishments, by their consistency as frontline competitors, and by their ability to produce their best under pressure. In making my assessment of the top ten men and women of all time, I have graded these players primarily on the strength of their records, on their consistency over long periods of time, and by examining their peak performances in the summertime of their careers. In compiling these rankings, I have attempted to do justice to the great players of every era.

MEN

1. PETE SAMPRAS

His dominance of the entire decade of the 1990s was an extraordinary feat. Winning a twentieth century record six Wimbledon singles titles, reaching another milestone by finishing six consecutive years (1993-98) as the world's top ranked player, tying Roy

Emerson's record by securing twelve Grand Slam singles championships, he was a prolific achiever who lifted his game to great heights when the top titles were on the line. He was victorious in twelve of fourteen major championship finals. In my view, Sampras at his best was better than anyone else who has achieved eminence on a tennis court.

2. ROD LAVER

The only player, man or woman, to capture two Grand Slams, the Australian left-hander's sweep of the majors in 1969 was majestic. His many admirers point to Laver's absence from the Grand Slam events from 1963 through 1967 when he was limited to only professional tournaments. Historians project that Laver would have taken half a dozen more major titles had he been eligible. The fact remains that six of his eleven "Big Four" titles were taken as an amateur when he was not forced to confront the top professionals. Be that as it may, Laver was a magnificent competitor with a multi-faceted game of surpassing excellence.

3. JACK KRAMER

Surely he was the most underrated of all the great tennis champions. He did his finest work in professional tennis after capturing only three major singles titles as an amateur. Kramer performed in a league of his own for five years as a pro. He introduced the "Big Game" to tennis, and during his time at the top no one could come close to touching him. He was overwhelmingly efficient. He could break down even his most formidable opponents systematically, and he was a master percentage player. Kramer deserves a higher place in history than most critics have accorded him.

4. BILL TILDEN

Taking his ten major titles between 1920 and 1930, Tilden may have been the game's best-ever match player. Tilden took tennis to another level in his time with a wide range of strokes and an unparalleled strategic sense. As a young player his backhand was vulnerable. Once he perfected that stroke, Tilden became the supreme player of his day. His performance on court was always dramatic because he liked to toy with opponents, risking defeat before taking control.

5. BJORN BORG

Displaying surprising versatility for a confirmed baseliner, Borg not only won a men's record of six French Opens, but he altered his game admirably to suit the lawns of Wimbledon and secured that title five years in a row (1976-80). The implacable Swede failed in four U.S. Open finals and left the game too soon at twenty-five. Nevertheless, he won at least one Grand Slam tournament for eight years in a row. In the Open Era, only Sampras claimed more major championship titles.

6. DON BUDGE

The first player ever to record a Grand Slam (1938), he had a well designed, all-court playing style. His backhand may have been the best ever in tennis, and he carried himself as only a champion could. What Tilden was for tennis in the twenties, Budge was for the thirties. Many authorities, including Jack Kramer, place Budge at the top of the list of the all-time great players because he had such a well-proportioned game with no apparent weaknesses.

7. PANCHO GONZALES

The fiercest competitor of them all and one of the most durable of top players, he turned professional at twenty-one and could not compete again in the majors until he was forty. In the intervening years, he would undoubtedly have collected a cluster of large prizes. His eight triumphs at the U.S. Pro Championships demonstrates just how remarkable he was at the height of his powers.

8. JIMMY CONNORS

The only player ever to capture the U.S. Open on three different surfaces—grass, clay, and hard courts—he had more emotional determination than any other player in the century. Borg was too good for him at one stage of his career, and McEnroe got his measure in another, but Connors was indefatigable and he played top-quality tennis longer than any of his rivals.

9. JOHN McENROE

A Davis Cup stalwart who played on five championship American squads between 1978 and 1992, McEnroe did not do himself full justice on his own. He secured four U.S. Opens in singles and won Wimbledon three times, but with his unique playing style featuring exquisite touch on the volley, he could have taken many more big tournaments had he mastered his own temperament.

10. IVAN LENDL and FRED PERRY

Both men won eight major championships. Perry is one of five players in the history of the men's game to collect all four majors. Lendl was a three-time French and U.S. Open champion and twice came through at the Australian Open. Although Lendl was unable to break through at Wimbledon, he was the best player in the world for four years and a major force much longer. Both men stamped their authority on an era. In my view, neither man can be excluded from a place in the top ten of the century.

WOMEN

1. STEFFI GRAF

The game's greatest female player for eight years, she recorded twenty-two major championship victories, beginning in 1987 and ending in 1999. She became only the third woman to win a Grand Slam (in 1988), and yet her presence was felt for more than a decade thereafter. Although Margaret Court won more major titles, Graf was the only tennis player in the twentieth century to take all of the Grand Slam tournaments at least four times. Her incomparable forehand, her extraordinary coordination, and an unmatched zest for competition lifted Graf to her own preeminent level.

2. MARTINA NAVRATILOVA

No woman in the century had a more complete game. She was the best fast-court player, the most skillful volleyer, and a magnificent athlete. For five years, from 1982 to 1986, she was virtually unbeatable, losing only fourteen matches in that span. She won a record nine Wimbledon singles titles, accounting for half of her Grand Slam crowns on that celebrated ground. No woman packaged the serve with the first volley so unremittingly.

3. CHRIS EVERT

Her durability and determination set Chrissie apart from all rivals. In fifty-six career Grand Slam tournament appearances, she missed the semifinal cut only four times. In nineteen consecutive U.S. Open appearances, she never failed to advance at least to the quarterfinals. For thirteen consecutive seasons—1974 to 1986—she was the winner of at least one Grand Slam singles title. She collected a record seven French Open singles titles, and won 125 consecutive matches on clay courts to establish herself as the premier slow-court player of them all. No woman in the century played the game better for longer than Evert.

4. HELEN WILLS MOODY

In a much honored career, she won nineteen Grand Slam tournaments, one more than both Navratilova and Evert. Her eight Wimbledon singles triumphs were eclipsed only by Navratilova. Although the majority of critics placed Suzanne Lenglen above her as the best player of the first half of the century, she is the better player in my book because she sustained her talent in top-flight tennis for longer than Lenglen or any other rival.

5. MARGARET SMITH COURT

The best Australian female tennis player of all time, she took more Grand Slam events than any man or woman over the century, securing twenty-four majors between 1960 and 1973. Eleven of those triumphs were at her native Australian Championships however, where her opposition was often undistinguished. Nevertheless, this towering serve-and-volleyer managed to rule on the clay courts of Roland Garros five times, demonstrating her versatility and resolve undisputably.

6. SUZANNE LENGLEN

A fragile and emotional competitor, she never lost a match at Wimbledon or her native French Championships. But in her only appearance at Forest Hills, she retired after losing the first set to Molla Mallory, and did not return to the U.S. Championships. A ballerina on the tennis court, she soared gracefully past one opponent after another through a glorious career. Most who saw her during her prime, including the esteemed critic Ted Tinling, were convinced she was the greatest of all woman players in the twentieth century.

7. MAUREEN CONNOLLY

The first woman to win a Grand Slam (1953), she seemed destined then to dominate the game for as long as she wanted. An accident when she was riding a horse the following year ended her career, but did not diminish her stature. A hard-hitting baseliner, she cut down her foes with powerful shots off both sides and an immense will to win.

8. BILLIE JEAN KING

Much like Gonzales in men's tennis, she was the competitor you would select to play for your life in a one-match situation. Devoid of fear on the big occasions, she won six Wimbledon singles titles and twelve majors altogether. A brilliant volleyer, she controlled contests with an intelligent attacking style, and a powerful personality. Had she not been driven by a multitude of interests, she might well have won more big tournaments.

9. MONICA SELES

Before she was stabbed in the back at a German tournament in the spring of 1993, she seemed certain to take the women's game into another realm. Her two-fisted strokes off both sides were devastatingly potent, and her intensity was unmatched. At nineteen, she had already won eight major titles. After the stabbing, she did not return for nearly twenty-eight months. Despite securing one more Grand Slam title in 1996, she was never the same player. Nonetheless her form from 1990 to 1993 made her one of the leading players of the century.

10. MARTINA HINGIS

As the century closed, this Swiss teenager displayed a match-playing prowess few could equal. She seized the last three Australian Opens of the century, won the Wimbledon and U.S. Open titles, and twice reached the final of the French Open. She became the youngest Grand Slam singles titlist of the century at the Australian Open and Wimbledon in 1997 when she was only sixteen. Her timing and ball control were exemplary.